CAMBRIDGE CLASSICAL TEXTS AND
COMMENTARIES

EDITORS
J. DIGGLE   SIR KENNETH DOVER   E. W. HANDLEY
H. D. JOCELYN   M. D. REEVE

28

CICERO:
CATO MAIOR DE SENECTUTE

CICERO
CATO MAIOR
DE SENECTUTE

EDITED WITH INTRODUCTION
AND COMMENTARY

BY

J. G. F. POWELL

University of Newcastle upon Tyne

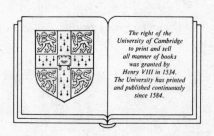

The right of the
University of Cambridge
to print and sell
all manner of books
was granted by
Henry VIII in 1534.
The University has printed
and published continuously
since 1584.

CAMBRIDGE UNIVERSITY PRESS

Cambridge

New York   New Rochelle   Melbourne   Sydney

Published by the Press Syndicate of the University of Cambridge
The Pitt Building, Trumpington Street, Cambridge CB2 1RP
32 East 57th Street, New York, NY 10022, USA
10 Stamford Road, Oakleigh, Melbourne 3166, Australia

First published 1988

Printed in Great Britain at
the University Press, Cambridge

British Library cataloguing in publication data

Cicero, Marcus Tullius
Cato Maior de senectute. – (Cambridge
classical texts and commentaries; 28).
1. Old age – Philosophy
I. Title   II. Powell, J. G. F.
305.2′6′01   HQ1061

Library of Congress cataloguing in publication data

Cicero, Marcus Tullius.
Cato maior de senectute.
(Cambridge classical texts and commentaries; 28)
Bibliography.
Includes index.
1. Old age – Early works to 1800. I. Powell, J. G. F.
II. Title. III. Series.
PA6296.C2   1987   305.2′6   87–11772

ISBN 0 521 33501 9

CONTENTS

PREFACE

Cicero's *Cato Maior de senectute* has been edited many times, but an edition and commentary on the present scale has not previously been attempted. In justification of the size of the present work, I say only that in the course of working on the *Cato* I have found it to raise a surprising number of particular problems, which have not been satisfactorily resolved by existing studies; and that, while I do not believe that a commentator has a duty to reproduce everything that has ever been written about the text under consideration, nevertheless some extra length was necessary in order to do justice to the volume of previous scholarship devoted to this work. Although it is a short and unassuming piece of writing, the *Cato* touches on a wide range of aspects of life and thought in the ancient world, which must be elucidated if the reader is to appreciate it fully.

This edition is a converted doctoral thesis, which has taken longer in the conversion than in the original writing. Begun in 1979 at Corpus Christi College, Oxford, under the guidance and at the suggestion of Professor R. G. M. Nisbet, it was submitted for the D.Phil. in October 1982. Since then, it has been substantially revised and rewritten. Between starting work on this edition and delivering it to Cambridge University Press in 1986, I have benefited from much help and advice from teachers, friends and colleagues. The thesis was supervised by Professor Nisbet, Mr (now Professor) D. A. F. M. Russell, and Mr L. D. Reynolds, the last especially concerned with the section on the manuscripts; my debt to them is very great. My examiners, Professor A. E. Douglas and Dr M. Winterbottom, made many helpful suggestions. A nearly final version of the work was read and criticised, after my move from Oxford to Newcastle, by

Professor D. A. West. For help on individual points at various times, I am grateful to Dr B. C. Barker-Benfield, Dr A. S. Gratwick, Dr D. Krömer, Miss H. K. Lomas, Mr P. J. Parsons, Mr J. J. Paterson, Miss E. D. Rawson, Professor M. D. Reeve, Dr D. R. Shanzer, Professor O. Skutsch, and Professor M. F. Smith.

I am grateful to the librarians of Lambeth Palace and Trinity College, Cambridge, and to the Bibliothèque Nationale, Paris, and the Bayerische Staatsbibliothek, Munich, for permission to consult manuscripts in person; to the following libraries for providing me with microfilms: Bibliothèque Nationale, Paris; Bibliothèque Royale Albert Ier, Brussels; Bibliotheek der Rijksuniversiteit, Leiden; Biblioteca Apostolica Vaticana; Biblioteca Medicea Laurenziana, Florence; Biblioteca Nazionale Marciana, Venice; Zentralbibliothek, Zürich; to Dr G. Poethke, Papyrus-Sammlung, Staatliche Museen zu Berlin, for providing me with photographs of P. Berol. 13407; to the staff of the *Thesaurus Linguae Latinae*, Munich, for their help during a two-week visit in September 1985, and to the staff of the Institut de Recherche et d'Histoire des Textes, Paris, who were similarly helpful when I visited them briefly in 1981; to the University of Newcastle upon Tyne for financial assistance for my visit to Munich; to Professor C. O. Brink, then an editor of the series, who made many useful comments on the draft typescript when I submitted it for publication; to Miss S. P. Moore, who undertook the sometimes provoking job of subediting the typescript, and to the rest of the staff of Cambridge University Press and to the typesetters; and to my mother, for help with the proofs and constant moral support.

I leave this book, not satisfied that the job has been done perfectly on my part, but with the reasonably certain assurance that further time and labour would not have made it much better than it is now. The help and criticism of those named above has contributed largely to whatever virtues it may have; I do not doubt that it still has many imperfections, for which nobody but myself must be held responsible. It is not easy to strike a balance that will please everyone between comment on text, language, interpretation and content; I have tried to give equal weight to all of these, and to cover all points that seemed to me to merit attention. My hope is that this edition will serve not only specialists, for whom it is naturally in the first place intended, but also readers of Cicero in general, and that it may perhaps encourage more sympathetic reading of Cicero's philosophical works than they have received in the past.

J. G. F .P.

Newcastle upon Tyne
July 1987

INTRODUCTION

I THE LITERARY CHARACTER OF THE *CATO*

(a) Circumstances of composition, and general character of the work

The *Cato Maior de senectute*[1] was written in the early part of 44 B.C. It is mentioned in a letter to Atticus, sent on 11 May in that year,[2] and, as a recent work, in the second book of the *De divinatione*[3] (which was completed in 44 at some time after the Ides of March). There is no certain evidence for a more precise dating, but probability seems to favour a date of composition before the Ides of March (see Appendix 1).

Chronologically, therefore, the *Cato* belongs to the main period of Cicero's philosophical writing, 45–44 B.C. It stands somewhat apart from the series of larger works that preceded it, since it is an essay on a single topic in practical ethics, rather than a technical exposition of a major area of philosophy. It is possible, however, to exaggerate the difference of literary character that this implies: even the more technical treatises often tend towards the popular and rhetorical (cf. below, pp. 11–15). The *Laelius de amicitia* was composed later in 44 in the same mould; Cicero regarded the two dialogues as companion-pieces,[4] and dedicated the pair to

---

[1] On the form of the title, see Commentary, p. 93–4. Although the title *De senectute* is usually preferred in English-speaking countries, I refer to the work throughout this edition as *Cato* or *Cato Maior* (cf. the convention of *TLL*): the original principal title of the work was *Cato Maior*, and *Cato* is convenient for brevity.

[2] *Att.* 14.21.3.

[3] *Div.* 2.3: on that passage, see also Appendix 1, and Commentary, p. 93n.

[4] *Lael.* 4; 11. For a list of parallels and similarities between the *Cato* and the *Laelius*, cf. P. R. Coleman-Norton, *CW* 41 (1947–8) 210ff.

Atticus, *senex* (in fact three years Cicero's senior) and *amicus*. The lost *De gloria* in two books, written in the early summer of 44 and similarly dedicated to Atticus,[5] was also a treatment of a particular moral theme which personally concerned Cicero; little, however, is known of its content.

Atticus was a suitable recipient for these three works. An example of cultured leisure and equanimity,[6] nominally an Epicurean, he had few pretensions to be considered a serious philosopher; but he was well equipped to appreciate this form of philosophically based moralising, cast in a polished literary form and seasoned with Greek and Roman historical allusions and anecdotes, and it appears from Cicero's replies to his letters[7] that he professed to find these works of some practical benefit, in addition to being a source of pleasure.

Cicero's decision to write on old age is explained partly by the existence of a tradition of philosophic writing on the subject (see below, pp. 15–16; 24–7), and partly by his personal circumstances at the time. In 44 B.C. he was sixty-two years old, already *senex* by Roman reckoning,[8] and he was experiencing difficulties both in private and in public life. Caesar's dictatorship had meant that he was effectively excluded from politics,[9] and on the personal side he was probably still affected by the death of his daughter Tullia in February 45 (for possible reflection of this in the *Cato*, see on

---

[5] *Att.* 15.27.2; 16.2.6; 16.6.4. Cf. Ruch, *Préambule* 300.

[6] Cf. *Cato* 1–2; Nep. *Atticus* 17.3. On Atticus' Epicureanism, cf. Shackleton Bailey, *Cicero's Letters to Atticus* 1 (Cambridge 1965) introd. 8; A. H. Byrne, *Titus Pomponius Atticus* (Bryn Mawr 1920) 34ff.

[7] *Att.* 16.11.3; cf. ibid. 15.2.4 on the *Tusculans*.

[8] Cf. *Cato* 2 and note; *Lael.* 5. A Roman of Cicero's time was reckoned to be *senex* at sixty, though the word could be used loosely of those considerably younger (in *De or.* 2.15, Crassus uses the word of himself at forty-eight). On the definitions of old age and of the other periods of life, see notes on §§4 (with literature there cited); 33–4; 60; 70; 76.

[9] Cf. *Cato* 1 and note; Appendix 1; on the biographical background, cf. T. Petersson, *Cicero: A Biography* (Berkeley 1920) 571ff.; E. Rawson, *Cicero* (London 1975, repr. Bristol 1983) 203ff., esp. 246; M. Gelzer, *Cicero* (Wiesbaden 1969) 322–4.

§12, etc.) and the subsequent divorce of his second wife Publilia. The approach of old age in these circumstances would not have been welcome. A letter to Atticus[10] in May 44 contains the wry comment that old age is making him irritable, and that he ought himself to read the *Cato* to counteract this. On a more serious level, the letters show fears for the Republic and for Cicero's own position:[11] he may well have thought that he would not live to see Rome restored to its proper condition, or regain the authority to which his age and experience entitled him. The consolations put forward in the *Cato* should be seen as real attempts to combat such feelings of desperation, in the same way as the *Consolatio* was meant as a real cure for grief after Tullia's death.[12]

It seems probable enough that Cicero felt the exact opposite of all the favourable sentiments about old age which he makes Cato utter in the dialogue. He was not so unrealistic as to think that he could really have the position of a Nestor, nor could he in reality be satisfied with the quiet country life of which he makes so much in §§51–8. No doubt, too, the afterlife of which he speaks in his peroration (§§77ff.) at times seemed as unreal to him as to any Epicurean.[13] But as a trained advocate he could apply his gifts to the task of self-persuasion, and he claims in the preface to the *Cato* (§2) that the treatment succeeded for a time. Without the evidence of the letters, we should have no explicit indication of Cicero's more personal feelings when he wrote this dialogue, and even with this evidence available, too many critics have mistaken his deliberately contrived optimism in the *Cato* for a bland and unthinking complacency. He stresses the attractive side of old age and plays down its unpleasant features, not because he was unaware of the evils

[10] *Att.* 14.21.
[11] *Att.* 12.21.5; 12.33.1; 12.28.2 (all from the spring of 45); for the period after the Ides of March, *Att.* 14.6; 14.13; etc.
[12] Cf. *Cato* 2. On the *Consolatio*, cf. *Att.* 12.14.3; R. Philippson, P.–W. 7A, 1123ff.
[13] Cf. perhaps *Tusc.* 1.24.

of old age, but because he was only too well aware of them and was trying to counteract them in his writing. One does not usually write consolations unless there is something about which one needs to be consoled.

The *Cato* was not written as a social document, and the reader who wishes to use it as one must be careful to allow for Cicero's rhetoric. Yet it does reflect one particular aspect of the reality of old age in the Roman world, in a way that should not be taken as mere rhetorical exaggeration. The Roman senatorial class did have a tradition of respect for the old, which must have made old age in some ways a pleasanter prospect than it is in some modern societies. The picture of the senior statesman with his *auctoritas*, his crowds of young followers (§§26; 28; 63) and his periods of relaxation on his country estates, is not an unrealistic invention of Cicero's, but a view of Roman life as it was or could be, given favourable circumstances. This element distinguishes the *Cato* from Greek moralistic treatments of old age, and makes it agreeably down-to-earth; indeed, some readers have found much to commend in it as a practical guide to coping with old age, even from the point of view of the modern gerontologist or psychologist.[14]

However this may be, the main claim of the *Cato* to be read in modern times is its charm as a literary work and its interest as a document of Roman humanism. The sections on agriculture (§§51ff.) and the immortality of the soul (§§77ff.) are particularly fine, but the whole work deserves notice for the literary portrait of Cato the Censor and the gallery of examples and anecdotes, both Roman and Greek; for the elegance of its style, which some have thought to exemplify Latin prose writing at its best; and for its commendation of a civilised, dignified and intelligent way of life.

[14] Cf. D. B. Bromley, *The Psychology of Human Ageing* (Harmondsworth 1966) 42; E. Hübener, *Das Altertum* 3 (1957) 46ff.; B. L. Ullman, *CJ* 29 (1933–4) 456–8; G. Twigg-Porter, *Classical Bulletin* (St Louis 1962) 1–4. On the other hand, M. Finley, *G. & R.* 28 (1981) 156ff. well typifies the social historian's disappointed reaction to the *Cato*.

(b) The dialogue form

All Cicero's extant philosophical works except the *De officiis* are cast in the form of a dialogue, and in all the dialogues except the *Tusculans* (where the characters are anonymous, though one apparently represents Cicero himself) the speakers are noble Romans. In the *Cato*, as previously in the *De republica* (and, among the rhetorical writings, *De oratore*), *Hortensius* and *Academica priora*, the dialogue is set in a past generation; the subsidiary characters of the *Cato*, Laelius and Scipio, are already familiar from the *De republica*, and Laelius appears again as the principal character in the dialogue named after him. In the *Laelius* (4–5), Cicero remarks on his use of historical characters as conferring greater *gravitas*, while in letters to Atticus he mentions the more prosaic motive of avoiding envy among the living.[15]

Most of the work consists of an uninterrupted speech by the principal character. In this respect it is similar to the *Laelius*, and to individual books of the *Academica*, *De finibus*, *De natura deorum* and *De divinatione*. The actual dialogue is confined to some polite conversation at the beginning, in which Cato is asked for his opinion by the other two participants; however, Cato is made to recognise the presence of Scipio and Laelius a number of times in the course of his speech.[16] It is a mistake to suppose that the dialogue form is here reduced to a mere convention: Cicero could have done without it had he wanted to (as he did in the *De officiis* or *Orator*), and it adds greatly to the charm of the work.

The antecedents and inspirations of the Ciceronian dialogue need only be briefly summarised here, in so far as they concern the *Cato* in particular. The influence of Plato, first of

[15] *Att.* 12.12.2; 13.19.4; cf. *Q. fr.* 3.5.1; Ruch, *Préambule*, 403–4.
[16] §§9; 19; 28; 34–5; 39; 49; 68; 77; 82; 85. A number of the *exempla* concern Scipio's family: see on 15; 29; 35; 50; 68; 77; 82. On characterisation in Cicero's dialogues in general, cf. W. Süss, *Hermes* 80 (1952) 419ff. For a less favourable view cf. D. Keiffer, *Rev. Inst. Publ. Belg.* N.S. 9 (1869) 73ff. On the characterisation of Cato in this work, see below, pp. 17–22.

all, should not be underestimated: Cicero clearly looked back to the founder of the genre, despite the differences between them. Cicero's preference for continuous speech over dialectical interchange has often been seen as an important point of contrast; but Plato is not all Socratic dialectic, and one should remember that the Platonic dialogues that were most read in Cicero's time, and by Cicero himself, were the more literary and expository ones.[17] Even in such a superficially un-Platonic dialogue as the *Cato*, Cicero adapts very closely one passage of conversation from Plato's *Republic* (*Cato* 6–8), and there is Platonic content in a number of other parts of the work.[18] The dialogues of Xenophon were also admired by Cicero, and by other Romans;[19] they perhaps provided a clearer precedent than Plato for the attribution of imaginary discourses to historical characters; and, with their practical ethical outlook and pleasant, uncomplicated style, they would have constituted a more accessible model than the heights of Platonic philosophy.

Scholars have tended to emphasise the influence on Cicero of the lost dialogues of Aristotle, and of various post-Aristotelian philosophers, particularly Heraclides Ponticus.[20] The ground for this in the case of the *Cato* is Cicero's own reference to these two philosophers as precedents for his method of writing dialogue (*Att.* 13.19.4; cf. *Q. fr.* 3.5.1): he

[17] *Rep.*, *Leg.*, *Phaedo*, *Phaedrus*, *Timaeus*, *Gorg.*, *Apol.*, *Menex.*: cf. P. Boyancé, *Assoc. G. Budé, Congrès de Tours et Poitiers: Actes du Congrès* (Paris 1953) 195–221.

[18] See on §§39ff.; 44; 46; 47; 77–8; etc.

[19] Cf. K. Münscher, *Philol.* Suppl. 13.2 (1920) 70ff.; for influence from Xenophon in the *Cato*, see notes on §§51ff.; 59; 79.

[20] Aristotle: Hirzel, *Dialog* I, 272ff.; Leeman-Pinkster on *De or.*, vol. I, 67–8; the Aristotelian features referred to at *De or.* 3.80 and *Fam.* 1.9.23 do not recur in the *Cato*. Heraclides: Hirzel, *Dialog* I, 321ff.; Wehrli on Heracl. fr. 24b. On the Ἡρακλείδειον of *Att.* 15.4.3 and 15.27.2, which is most certainly not the *Cato*, though erroneously connected with it by scholars, see Hirzel, *Dialog* I, 547n.; H. B. Gottschalk, *Heraclides of Pontus* (Oxford 1980) 8.

6

informs us that while Aristotle introduced himself as a major character in his dialogues (the practice followed by Cicero in e.g. *De finibus* and *De divinatione*), Heraclides used characters from the past and did not himself have a part, and thus produced dialogues which were more obviously fictitious. This should not be taken to mean more than it says; it may be that the use of historical characters was more constant in the works of Heraclides than elsewhere, and thus more characteristic of him than of other dialogue-writers, but this provides no reason to assume that a dialogue of Cicero's which (like the *Cato*) used historical characters was intended to be 'Heraclidean' in any other respect, whether in form, style or content.[21] In default of other evidence it is impossible to assess accurately what influence Aristotle or Heraclides may have had on Cicero's dialogue technique, in this work or elsewhere, in respects other than those which Cicero himself mentions.

Not much is known about the turns taken by dialogue-writing among other Hellenistic philosophers, though the surviving *testimonia* concerning some of their works show that they continued to write in this form.[22] It is quite possible that Cicero was influenced in the case of the *Cato* by lost Hellenistic works on old age,[23] notably the work of Aristo (of Ceos or Chios)[24] which he mentions in *Cato* 3; his reference to it implies that it was a dialogue of some sort, in which Tithonus was the principal speaker on the subject of old age. However,

[21] It appears to me that too much has been read into the mention of Heraclides in *Q. fr.* 3.5.1. Cicero could not very well have used the example of Plato, Aristotle or Xenophon in this disparaging context. In view of this, the double mention of Heraclides here and in *Att.* 13.19.4 becomes less striking.

[22] Cf. Hirzel, *Dialog* I, 308ff. for Hellenistic writers of dialogue in and after Aristotle's time; Ruch, *Préambule* 46; E. Martin, P.–W. 5, 546ff. (Dicaearchus). On the antecedents of Cicero's dialogue form in general, cf. Ruch, *Préambule* 31–71; Hirzel, *Dialog* I, 457ff.; 544ff. on *Cato* and *Laelius*.

[23] See below, pp. 15, 25–6.

[24] See note on §3 and Appendix 2.

this does not take us very far, and of the form of the other pre-Ciceronian Hellenistic writings περὶ γήρως we know nothing. Their loss probably does not leave much unexplained as regards the form of the *Cato*.

Another question, which there is not sufficient evidence to resolve, is whether Cicero was influenced by Latin predecessors. No Latin dialogues can be certainly dated before Cicero's *De oratore*, with one exception – a lost dialogue on civil law by M. Junius Brutus, the father of the conspirator, referred to in *De or.* 2.224. A connection has however been seen between Cicero and certain works of Varro, which may possibly have predated Cicero's philosophical writings. These are the so-called *Logistorici*,[25] some of whose individual titles are attested in later sources: *Catus de liberis educandis, Tubero de origine humana, Messalla de valetudine*, etc. There is clearly a parallel between these titles and Cicero's *Cato Maior de senectute, Laelius de amicitia*, implying perhaps a similarity of form (dialogues usually with Roman characters, of whom one is important enough to give his name to the whole work) and subject-matter (individual topics, suited to the chief character, treated in some cases from a clearly moralistic standpoint – as is evident from some of the available fragments). The dates of the *Logistorici* being unknown, it is impossible to say whether Cicero imitated Varro, or Varro Cicero, although it does seem reasonable to suppose a connection of some sort. Unfortunately it is not possible to be more specific, and it is to be observed that most work on this subject argues from the well-known features of the *Cato* and *Laelius* to some hypothesis about the character of the *Logisto-*

[25] Cf. F. Ritschl, *Opuscula* (Leipzig 1886) III, 403ff.; A. Riese, *Varronis Saturarum Menippearum Reliquiae* (Leipzig 1865) Prolegomena, 32ff.; R. Müller, *Varros Logistoricus über Kindererziehung*, Kl. Phil. Stud. 12 (Leipzig 1938); Hirzel, *Dialog* I, 546–7; H. Dahlmann, P.–W. Suppl. VI, 1261ff.; id., *ANRW* 1.3, 16–17; id. and R. Heisterhagen, *Varronische Studien* I, Abh. Akad. Mainz (1957) no. 4. Cf. Appendix 2 on 'Ariston' quoted in Varro's *logistoricus 'Catus de liberis educandis'*. On Varro's Menippean satire *Tithonus*, see p. 26–7.

rici; to use received opinion on the *Logistorici* as an explanation of the form of Cicero's dialogues is therefore an unsafe and circular proceeding.

(c) Rhetorical features

The speech of Cato, which makes up most of the work, is arranged according to a clear and simple rhetorical plan. There is an exordium, though a very informal one, setting out general principles and illustrating them with examples; there is a *partitio* in §15, and the main discussion is carried out under the four headings there specified, by the recognised rhetorical method of objection and refutation (see note ad loc.). The insertion of a digression (the section on agriculture, §§51ff.), between the third and fourth main divisions of the argument, contributes to an effect of informality, but this method of concealing art was itself well known to the rhetoricians (*egressio*).[26] The last part of the argument, in which discussion of death leads naturally to the topic of the immortality of the soul, forms an effective peroration.

The method of argument is often loose, proceeding by illustrations, examples and appeals to common sense, rather than strict logic. Philosophical arguments are alluded to or summarised, rather than expounded in detail (see e.g. §4 on self-sufficiency; §46 on moderation; §47 on the meaning of *carere*; §71 on the equation of 'good' with 'natural'; §78 on immortality, with arguments reproduced from Plato; see notes on all these passages). The many examples and anecdotes give the work a distinctive flavour:[27] again the technique derives from rhetorical practice. A number of them are

[26] Volkmann, *Rhetorik* 164–7.

[27] Volkmann, *Rhetorik* 233ff.; Nisbet–Hubbard on Horace, *Od.* 1.12.37 and literature there cited; M. Rambaud, *Cicéron et l'histoire romaine* (Collection d'études latines, série scientifique 28, Paris 1953). Cicero refers to his own use of *exempla* in *Cato* 26 and *Div.* 2.8. There seems no reason to suppose that the examples of old age, etc., were taken by Cicero from some rhetorical handbook, as argued by C. Bosch, *Die Quellen des Valerius*

simply Cicero's favourite *exempla* of old Roman virtue,[28] some without any special appropriateness to the context of old age, while others are used to illustrate specific points: long life, activity in old age, memory, physical strength, courage in mourning, and so on.

The final section of the *Cato*, on death and immortality, owes much to the philosophical and rhetorical tradition of consolatory literature. Cicero himself refers to the consolation as a recognised form of oratory (*Part. or.* 67); formal letters of consolation sent on occasions of bereavement, e.g. Cicero to Titius (*Fam.* 5.6) or Ser. Sulpicius to Cicero (*Fam.* 4.5), exhibit a standard repertoire of themes. The tradition of the philosophic consolation is supposed to derive from Crantor's Περὶ πένθους,[29] which Cicero imitated in his lost *Consolatio*. Particularly close to the subject of the *Cato* is the consolation on the approach of death in the pseudo-Platonic *Axiochus*, which contains a number of parallels in detail with

Maximus (Stuttgart 1929): the parallels with Valerius Maximus show no more than that V. Max. used Cicero, in common with other sources; V. Max. 8.13 ext. 1 on Masinissa cites the *Cato* explicitly, cf. on §34; a similar degree of paraphrase is evident in the items on Isocrates, Gorgias, Solon, Themistocles (8.7 ext. 15, with material from other sources), Duilius and Valerius Corvinus, and in the anecdote in V. Max. 4.5 ext. 2, probably derived directly from *Cato* 63. Cf. also A. Klotz, *Studien zu Valerius Maximus und den Exempla*, Sitzungsb. d. Bayer. Akad. d. Wiss., Phil.-hist. Abteilung (Munich 1942) Heft 5, pp. 1off. The other ancient collections of examples of long life may also be compared: Cicero shares material with Pliny, *NH* 7, Lucian (or pseudo-Lucian) in the short book entitled Μακρόβιοι or *Longaevi* (cf. F. Rühl, *RhM* 62 (1907) 422ff., and 64 (1909) 137ff.), and Censorinus, *De die natali*; the compilation περὶ μακροβίων of Phlegon of Tralles is mainly a list of names extracted from the census-records, but ends with the examples of Arganthonius (also in Cicero: see on §69) and the Sibyl, and may originally have contained more: cf. A. Giannini, *Paradoxographorum Graecorum Reliquiae* (Milan 1965).

On the use of anecdotes in the *Cato*, cf. also H. C. Gotoff, *Illinois Classical Studies* 6 (1981) 294–316.

[28] Fabricius, Curius, Coruncanius (15; 43; 55); the Decii and Scipiones; Atilius Calatinus, Cincinnatus, L. Brutus, Regulus, Marcellus.

[29] Diog. Laert. 4.27; Cic. *Acad. pr.* 2.135; cf. on §84 for an apparent parallel with Crantor.

the *Cato*[30] and more with the *Tusculans*; whether this is to be dated before or after Cicero is uncertain, but at all events it shows something of Cicero's debt to the Greek tradition. The *Cato* also contains numerous parallels with later consolatory works by Seneca, Plutarch, and other writers.[31]

The combination of philosophy and rhetoric seen in this and other works of Cicero was not new in his time, though the Ciceronian blend may be thought to have a special flavour on account of his unusual literary gifts and his background in Roman public life. We learn from Cicero's rhetorical works (*De inv.* 1.8; *De or.* 2.66ff.) that Hermagoras in the second century B.C. had gone so far as to prescribe, as subjects for rhetorical debate, such purely scientific questions as the shape of the earth or the size of the sun, or questions in general ethics such as whether virtue is the only good.[32] Cicero criticises this sort of topic as being unsuitable, but himself admits a variety of more practical, but no less philosophical questions for debate: *quibus officiis amicitia colenda sit* (*Part. or.* 62: the *Laelius* no doubt owes something to rhetorical *theses* of this sort), *quemadmodum sint colendi parentes* (ibid. 67), *sitne sapientis ad rem publicam accedere* (*Top.* 82), etc. An actual set of rhetorical treatments of philosophical questions, advertised as such in its preface, survives in Cicero's own *Paradoxa Stoicorum*, written in 46 B.C. before the main series of philosophical works: Cicero implies (*Parad.* 5) that he had previously debated on this sort of question in his

[30] See on §§4; 77–8; 80; 84. The *Axiochus* is conventionally dated to the first century B.C., but the arguments used seem insufficient to establish the date as precisely as this: the most that can be said is that it is probably later than the third century B.C. See the Budé edn. of J. Souilhé, esp. pp. 132ff.; J. Chevalier, *Étude critique du dialogue pseudo-platonicien l'Axiochos* (Paris 1915).

[31] See esp. on §§67ff.; Pohlenz's edn. of *Tusc.* I, p. 29; R. Kassel, *Untersuchungen zur griechischen und römischen Konsolationsliteratur*, Zetemata 18 (Munich 1958); R. Buresch, *Consolationum ... historia critica*, Leipziger Studien 9.1 (1886); T. Stork, *Nil igitur mors est ad nos* (Bonn 1970) 9ff.

[32] For Hermagoras see D. Matthes, *Lustrum* 3 (1958) 131–2. For philosophical θέσεις in the rhetorical schools, see S. F. Bonner, *Roman Declamation* (Liverpool 1969) 2ff.

rhetorical practice. In a well-known passage of the preface to the *Tusculans* (1.7) he explicitly discusses his application of rhetorical techniques to philosophical topics, stating his view that philosophy is improved by being expressed *copiose ornateque* – an opinion naturally not shared by all ancient, let alone modern philosophers. He contrasts the rhetorical practice of his younger days with the *maior et uberior ars* of philosophy, and calls his philosophical writing *senilis declamatio*: this is somewhat ironical, since on any view (one hopes) his philosophical works are more than rhetorical exercises, but their strong rhetorical colouring is evident, and these passages show that Cicero was well aware of the fact and cultivated it intentionally.

(d) The popular philosophical tradition

If Cicero was a rhetorician turned philosopher, there had also been philosophers who cultivated rhetoric in the attempt to impress their views on the public. The two arts, which Socrates and Plato had tried in theory to separate, were again united in such figures as Carneades,[33] while Cicero, in the *Tusculans* passage just referred to, traces his philosophical 'declamation' back to Aristotle and Isocrates. In the *De finibus*, when discussing methods of philosophical discourse, he distinguishes the 'rhetoric of the philosophers' from the forensic style,[34] and in the *Orator* (91ff.) he describes the 'middle' style of rhetorical composition as being particularly associated with the philosophical schools, and practised at its best by Demetrius of Phalerum. It was not unexpected that the philosophers should develop characteristic styles of exposition, or that Cicero when writing philosophy should follow them.

   In this connection, much has from time to time been made of the alleged influence on Cicero, with particular reference

---

[33] Cf. *De or.* 2.157ff.; Gell. 6.14.
[34] *Fin.* 2.17.

to the *Cato* and similar works, of what is called 'the diatribe'.[35] This term has been used by scholars to cover a
number of diverse aspects of Hellenistic philosophical writing. The word is sometimes used to mean a particular form
of writing, the direct philosophical 'sermon' as contrasted
with dialogues, letters, etc. The subject-matter of 'diatribe' is
characterised as moralising and concerned in particular with
ordinary life. 'Diatribe style' is alleged to be vivid and
abrupt, full of apostrophes, rhetorical questions and objections from imaginary opponents. 'Diatribe imagery' is the
repertoire of illustrations taken from areas of down-to-earth
experience like the theatre, ships, farming, etc. Finally, the
word 'diatribe' is often prefixed with the adjective
'Cynic–Stoic', implying that this type of philosophical literature was the prerogative of one particular group of philosophers. The resulting construct appears again and again in
discussions of ancient popular philosophical writing. It has
elements of truth, in so far as the various constituents of
'diatribe' all certainly exist individually, and sometimes exist
together (as in the work of Teles, the one clear pre-
Ciceronian example); but to define a genre of writing by
means of these features, in such a way that the presence of
one of them is held to imply the presence of the rest, has no
justification in the evidence. To suppose that when Cicero
talks about theatres he must have had a Cynic or Stoic
source is patently not sensible, yet some attempts to define
Cicero's sources have been based on no better logic than this.

The influence of 'diatribe' on Cicero has been seen particularly in his use of certain images and turns of thought, for
which parallels may be found in Greek popular philosoph-

---

[35] On the alleged influence of 'diatribe' in the *Cato*, see Wuilleumier's
editions; A. Oltramare, *Les Origines de la diatribe romaine* (Geneva 1926);
Kröger, *De Cic. in C. M. auctoribus*. On 'diatribe' in general, see *Reallexicon
für Antike und Christentum* (Stuttgart 1950) s.v. with bibliography; for recent
sceptical views, Brink on Horace, *Epist.* 2.2.60; H. D. Jocelyn, *LCM* 7
(1982) 3–7 and 8 (1983) 88–91.

ical writing.[36] Particular attention has been paid to a number of parallels with sayings of Bion of Borysthenes, sometimes (on no adequate evidence) identified as the originator of 'diatribe', and with Teles, already mentioned, who quotes Bion a number of times. However, these parallels are much more tenuous than has been supposed, and they certainly do not invite explanation in terms of direct or indirect influence: in every case there are other parallels elsewhere, some nearer than Bion. These ideas were simply floating about in the popular philosophic tradition and in non-philosophical literature as well: for some of them the nearest parallels are to be found not in Greek philosophy but in Roman comedy.

As for the style of exposition adopted by Cicero in the *Cato*, it must be remembered first that Cicero was an orator and naturally used rhetorical techniques; some of the alleged features of 'diatribe style' are nothing more than the application to philosophical subject-matter of techniques which are common to all ancient rhetoric. Secondly, any abruptness or forthrightness in the style of the *Cato* may easily be attributed to the character of the principal speaker: we do not expect Cato the Elder to beat about the bush. It is far-fetched to see stylistic influence from hypothetical Greek philosophical sources in Cicero, since we really have a very

[36] Theatre: 5; 48; 64; 70 and 85, and notes; plants, 5 and 71; ships, 17, 71 and 72; race-course, 83; etc. Parallels with Bion: 4 *quam ut adipiscantur omnes optant, eandem accusant adeptam* (fr. 63 Kindstrand), for which there are many other parallels; 5 *tamquam ab inerti poeta* (a not very striking similarity with fr. 16 K.); 20, the wisdom of old age contrasted with the rashness of youth (Bion, fr. 65 K., talks of the courage of youth, not rashness: the sentiment is among the most commonplace); 72 *breve vitae reliquum* (Bion fr. 64 K., λείψανον τοῦ βίου, but see note ad loc.); 84, cf. fr. 68 K. καθάπερ καὶ ἐξ οἰκίας ἐξοικιζόμεθα, but Cicero says *tamquam ex hospitio, non tamquam domo*; see note ad loc. on this very common form of imagery. Three passages of Teles have additionally been cited: pp. 8–9 H. on not blaming old age, etc., for one's troubles (cf. *Cato* 14); p. 16 H., the theatrical comparison, nearest to Cicero's in §64; p. 42, the quotation from Euripides (βαρύτερον Αἴτνας) alluded to by Cicero in §4; see notes on those passages. On the possibility of indirect influence from Bion via Aristo of Ceos, see Appendix 2, p. 271. On Bion in general, see J. F. Kindstrand, *Bion of Borysthenes* (Uppsala 1976).

inadequate idea of what such sources might have been like: too much has been deduced from the style of our text of Teles, which is an epitome and not in its original form.

It need not be doubted that Cicero owed certain of his ideas and arguments, together with the notion of applying rhetorical techniques to philosophy in the first place, to the tradition of Hellenistic popular philosophical exposition. However, attempts to be more specific about sources and influences must fail for lack of evidence.

Many Hellenistic philosophers wrote on particular topics in practical ethics, to judge from the titles preserved by Diogenes Laertius;[37] unfortunately we know hardly anything else about these works, though it is not unreasonable to guess that many of them were written in a popular style. Among these titles is a Περὶ γήρως by Theophrastus,[38] and another by Demetrius of Phalerum[39] of which one fragment survives. The work of Aristo[40] which Cicero mentions in *Cato* 3 has been assumed to be another popular philosophical work on old age. The topic was in any case clearly established in the tradition before Cicero's time, and continued to be discussed in later philosophical writing (see below, pp. 24–30).

How much Cicero owed to earlier writing Περὶ γήρως cannot be determined. This need not be regretted. Some of his debts are obvious (Plato, Xenophon);[41] some of the ideas in the *Cato* occur elsewhere in Cicero[42] and are not likely to reflect a specific Περὶ γήρως source; the many Roman

[37] E.g. Theophrastus, Περὶ φιλίας, Περὶ φιλοτιμίας, Περὶ εὐτυχίας, Περὶ πλούτου; Demetrius of Phalerum, Περὶ πίστεως, Περὶ χάριτος, Περὶ γάμου; Xenocrates, Περὶ πλούτου, Περὶ ἐγκρατείας, Περὶ φιλίας; etc.

[38] See below, pp. 25–6, n. 63.

[39] See below, p. 26, n. 64.

[40] See below, p. 26, and Appendix 2.

[41] See above, p. 6, notes 18 and 19.

[42] Compare especially the descriptions of the growth of plants in 51ff. with similar descriptions in *De nat. deor.* 2, and the peroration on immortality with passages in *Tusc.* 1, *Somnium Scipionis*, *Hortensius* fragments, and the speeches *Pro Scauro* and *Pro Rab. perd.* (see notes on 77ff.).

examples and references are without doubt Cicero's own. What remains after these have been set on one side? The rhetorical framework is probably Cicero's: the occurrence of the same individual headings in later authors[43] may be due to dependence on Cicero, though the germ of Cicero's *divisio* is already present in Plato. Some of the Greek examples and anecdotes may come from a Greek Περὶ γήρως source:[44] this is the only area in which such attribution is at all plausible, and even then it does not inform us about the Greek writings in any significant way. Finally one is left with some generalised philosophical moralising, which is never sufficiently doctrinaire to be pinned down to a particular school, let alone a particular philosopher. There may be unsuspected debts to lost works, but nothing is to be gained from guesswork, however complex and ingenious. Instead, it is advisable to concentrate on what Cicero actually says, and to appreciate the flavour of the completed dish, rather than worry because one cannot recover the origin of some of its ingredients.

(e) The Roman setting and historical background

The *Cato* is notably Roman in its atmosphere. The dialogue is set, presumably at Rome,[45] in the year 150 B.C. (cf. on

On the special problem of the Archytas speech in 39ff., which has close parallels with the *Hortensius*, see notes ad loc. Verbal echoes of other Ciceronian works will be found recorded in many places in the commentary.

[43] Especially in Musonius Rufus: see below, p. 28.

[44] Viz. Lysander's saying on old age (63) and the anecdote of Solon and Pisistratus (72), both shared only with Plutarch; the anecdote of Gorgias in §13, shared only with Valerius Maximus; and the old man in the theatre (63) found in both Valerius Maximus and Plutarch. It is probable that Valerius Maximus copied these items from Cicero (cf. above, pp. 9–10, n. 27); but Plutarch is unlikely to have used Cicero for Greek anecdotes, and Cic. must have had a Greek source of some sort. It is as likely as not that this source was one or other of the works on old age.

[45] See note on §3. On the Roman settings of Cicero's dialogues cf. Becker, *Technik u. Szenerie* 11ff.

§14). Cato the Elder was then in his eighty-fourth year (§32); the other characters, Scipio Aemilianus and Laelius, were in their middle thirties, Laelius somewhat older than Scipio. The conversation thus takes place in the year before Cato's death,[46] a feature which imparts a certain impressiveness, particularly since death itself is one of the subjects of discussion.

Cicero idealised the Romans of past generations, and none more than Cato, Scipio and Laelius.[47] The general suitability of Cato for the part of defender of old age is clear: *qui et diutissime senex fuisset, et in ipsa senectute praeter ceteros floruisset* (*Lael.* 4); Cato had remained politically active until his death at the age of eighty-five. Cicero admired him as a *novus homo* like himself, who had risen to the highest office with the help of native intelligence, oratorical gifts and hard work.[48] He had referred to Cato many times in his previous works.

[46] Cf. *Lael.* 11, *anno antequam est mortuus.* A. Cameron (CR 17 (1967) 258–9; *JRS* 56 (1966) 28–9; cf. Hirzel, *Dialog* 1, 467) has remarked on the occurrence of this feature in a number of dialogues, the inspiration presumably being Plato's *Phaedo* and the other dialogues set around the time of Socrates' death. Cicero's *De republica* was set just before Scipio's death in 129 B.C., the *Laelius* shortly afterwards.

[47] Scipio and Laelius: A. E. Astin, *Scipio Aemilianus* (Oxford 1967) 294. For other Ciceronian references to Cato the Elder, cf. *Brutus* 65 and *De or.* 3.135 (on Cato's speeches); *Arch.* 16; *De or.* 1.171. There is a considerable bibliography on Cicero's view of Cato, most of it stressing the various alleged distortions of the picture imported by Cicero's preoccupations. See Astin, *Cato*, esp. pp. 159ff. on this dialogue (and E. Rawson's review, *JRS* 70 (1980) 197ff.); Kammer, *Untersuchungen*; L. Alfonsi, *Parola del Passato* 9 (1954) 161ff.; André, *L'Otium* 41–58; F. della Corte, *Catone Censore* (Turin 1949, and 2nd edn 1969); R. Gnauk, *Die Bedeutung des Marius und Cato Maior für Cicero* (diss. Berlin 1936); R. E. Jones, *AJP* 60 (1939) 307ff.; Kienast, *Cato*; F. Padberg, *Cicero und M. Porcius Cato Censorius* (diss. Münster 1933); F. Leo, *Die griechisch-römische Biographie* (Leipzig 1901) pp. 168ff.; G. Panico in *Mélanges Lebel* (Quebec 1980) 257ff.; E. de St.-Denis, *L'Information Littéraire* 8 (1956) 93ff., cf. id., *Essais sur le rire et le sourire des Latins* (Paris 1965) 69–79; M. Rambaud, *Cicéron et l'histoire romaine* (Paris 1953) esp. p. 65; E. Pais, 'Questioni Catoniane', in *Mélanges Glotz* (Paris 1932) 681ff.; R. Helm, P.-W. 22, 108ff.; E. Rawson, *JRS* 62 (1972) 33ff.; see also Appendix 3.

[48] *Verr. II* 5.180: cf. Padberg (cited above) pp. 7–17, on Cato as an example in Cicero's speeches.

In *De inv.* 1.5 we already find the idea that Scipio Aemilianus was a 'disciple' of Cato's;[49] this reappears in the *De republica* (2.1) and is the basis of the *mise-en-scène* of the *Cato*. In that passage of the *De republica* Scipio praises him in terms which are obviously Ciceronian (*modus in dicendo et gravitate mixtus lepos*, etc.), but which reflect a judgement of Cato's character as moderate and humane. The same view of Cato is evident in *Pro Murena* 66, in which Cicero admonishes Cato the Younger that his Stoic severity does not compare well with the *comitas* and *humanitas* of his great-grandfather. Commentators on that passage have tended to suppose that Cicero is not serious, and that everyone really knew Cato the Elder as notably lacking in those qualities; granted, one must allow for Cicero's accustomed irony and urbanity, but if the description of the Elder Cato were not basically meant seriously, the passage would have no point at all, even as a joke at the Younger Cato's expense. Cato the implacable rustic is a schoolboy's caricature; in reality, as his own works as well as Cicero's descriptions show, he was a man of considerable intelligence, culture (after the manner of his time) and humour. He had strong views and made many political enemies; but Cicero talks of him from a different point of view, that of the young men who admired him and benefited from his friendship and wise direction. Livy (39.40) in his memorable summary of Cato's character talks of his *asper animus* and *acerba lingua*, but he was not concerned there with his private relations with his friends and juniors; while Plutarch, who is probably not independent of Cicero

---

[49] *Catonem neque Laelium neque eorum, ut vere dicam, discipulum Africanum:* '*Africanus*' there is of course Scipio Aemilianus Africanus Minor, not the elder Africanus, as taken by J. Martha, *Rev. Phil.* 31 (1907) 64–5; as for Scipio being Laelius' *discipulus* as well as Cato's, Laelius was the older and more intellectual of the pair, and *ut vere dicam* adds the necessary qualification. Cf. also *De rep.* 1.18; Kammer, *Untersuchungen* 21ff. Cato, Laelius and Scipio are linked also in *Top.* 78; *Fin.* 5.2; *Tusc.* 1.110; cf. Astin, *Latomus* 15 (1956) 159ff. Note also the family connection between Cato and Scipio Aemilianus: Cato's son married Scipio's sister Aemilia (§15).

but at least had access to other sources,[50] records Cato's abilities as a conversationalist (*Cato* 25). We must remember also that Cicero himself had a wide knowledge of Cato's works (cf. esp. *Brutus* 65), and was in a good position to assess his character, even though his view may sometimes seem a little distorted by his admiration for the man.

There remains, however, the question of whether Cicero pictures his hero in the *Cato* consistently with his usual view of him. This involves a number of separate points: (i) erudition and allusions to Greek literature; (ii) enthusiasm for Greek culture; (iii) general modesty and urbanity of manner; (iv) better relations with contemporaries than the historical evidence suggests; and (v) the expression of philosophical opinions that Cato himself may not have known, and of which he probably disapproved if he did know them.

Taking these in order, (i) Cicero himself apologises (*Cato* 3: see note) for making Cato talk with more erudition than the real Cato displayed in his books, as he had similarly needed to apologise for Crassus and Antonius in the *De oratore* and for Lucullus in the *Academica priora*. Nevertheless, Cicero does seem to have made some effort to make the Greek literary references fit the character of Cato. It was not unrealistic, for example, to make Cato quote Xenophon with approval (see on §59). On the other hand, it is not safe (in the absence of other evidence) to argue from the appearance in the dialogue of an allusion to a Greek author that the real Cato knew that author, or even that Cicero thought he did;[51] doubtless Cicero neglected ἠθοποιία when carried away by his own train of thought (as perhaps in the long list of Greeks in §23). (ii) Cicero seems to have known a tradition that Cato was converted to the enthusiastic study of Greek literature in his old age: the notion recurs in Nepos, Valerius

[50] On Plutarch's use of the *Cato*, see on §42 (the L. Flamininus story, where the reference is explicit); also §10 (Cato and Fabius), §§39–41 (Nearchus), §55 (M'. Curius), §46 (Cato's country dinner-parties), where influence from Cicero on Plutarch may be suspected.

[51] Cf. Astin, *Cato* 159ff.

Maximus and Quintilian (see on §3), although they may
have obtained it from Cicero. At any rate this is not a piece
of *ad hoc* tendentiousness on Cicero's part, thought up for the
specific purposes of this dialogue: he mentions the same
tradition in *Acad. pr.* 2.5, presumably before he thought of
writing the *Cato*, and both there and in the *Cato* preface he
speaks of it as being common knowledge. However, perhaps
Cicero goes a little too far in *Cato* 26, *quasi diuturnam sitim
explere cupiens* (see ad loc.). (iii) It is thought that the touches
of urbane modesty in the *Cato* (see on §§5 and 55) are
inconsistent with the character of the historical Cato; this
may be so, though there is really not enough evidence to
decide; and the important points to note are (a) that Cicero
himself believed Cato to have been notable for *comitas* and
humanitas (see above), and (b) that Cicero's dialogue-writing
doubtless reflected the manners of the author's own time
rather than Cato's. (iv) This point mainly concerns Cato's
relations with Scipio Africanus, whom he is made to mention
favourably (§19), whereas Nepos and Plutarch make it clear
that the two men were political enemies. However, the *Cato*
passage mentions nothing about Scipio apart from his gener-
alship, the virtues of which even Cato could not have denied;
and Cato is there talking to Scipio's own adoptive grandson,
years after Scipio's death – a fact which must have some
relevance. Editors also mention the references to Ennius
(*familiaris noster*, §10), and to Diogenes the Stoic (§23); but
Nepos confirms Cato's patronage of Ennius, despite Cato's
slighting remarks about Fulvius Nobilior's patronage of the
same poet (*Tusc.* 1.3) and about poets in general in the
Carmen de moribus (p. 83 Jordan); as for Diogenes, Plutarch
(*Cato* 22–3) certainly records that Cato was behind the
expulsion from Rome of the philosophical embassy in
155 B.C., of which Diogenes was a member, but nothing is
said in the *Cato* beyond the mention of his name as one of a
long list, the fact that he had visited Rome, and that he
carried on his philosophical activity to the end of his life. It

appears, therefore, that none of these points amounts to very much. (v) The real difference between the real Cato and the Cato of the dialogue is in the opinions which the latter is made to express, particularly the Platonic/Ciceronian views on immortality (see on §77). This should not cause surprise after Cicero's warning in *Cato* 3: *iam enim ipsius Catonis sermo explicabit nostram omnem de senectute sententiam.* As a matter of fact, the effect is less incongruous than it might have been. Cicero is careful to introduce intermediaries between Cato and the philosophers (§41, Nearchus of Tarentum; §43, the *maiores*; §78, *audiebam Pythagoram Pythagoreosque . . . numquam dubitasse; demonstrabantur mihi praeterea quae Socrates . . . disseruisset*).[52] The references to Pythagoreans are not necessarily unrealistic; Cicero may well have thought it more appropriate to make Cato derive his doctrines from Pythagoreans in Italy, rather than to depict him as having read Plato himself (cf. on §39).

Editors have often criticised Cicero's picture of Cato, but they have not always given due attention to those passages where he makes a positive attempt at characterisation. Most obvious of these are the large number of passages in which Cato reminisces, *more senum*, about his own career; in §§62 and 75 Cicero makes Cato quote from his own works, and one may suppose that some of the other references to Roman historical matters originate in Cato's writings,[53] although in one case, the degradation of L. Flamininus, Cicero seems not to follow Cato's account of events (for this see note on §42). Apart from these passages, there are some more or less clear reminiscences of Catonian opinions, sayings and interests: see on §§51 (the agricultural excursus), 27 (*quod est eo decet uti*), 36 and 69. For some elements in the language that may be intended to recall Cato's generation, see below (next section, p. 22–3). Slight though some of these touches may be, they contribute to an overall Catonian effect, and we

[52] Cf. G. Hendrickson, *AJP* 27 (1906) 185–6.
[53] Cf. E. Rawson, *JRS* 62 (1972) 40, and below, Appendix 3.

need not disagree too strongly with Cicero's statement in *Lael.* 4, *itaque ipse mea legens sic afficior interdum, ut Catonem, non me, loqui existimem.*

Finally one may note some more generally Roman elements: the quotations from Latin poetry,[54] the fiction of the oral tradition (§43), the etymologies of Latin words (*senatus, convivium, viator, occatio*), the reference to the institution of the augurate (§64) and the legal procedure of *interdictio bonorum* (§22).

(f)   Language and style

Generally the language and style is not very different from what is found in Cicero's other philosophical works. Only a few special features need be noted here.

Cicero does not attempt anything resembling a consistent imitation of Cato's language or style, but it seems difficult to deny that he used some words and forms with an archaic, or at least old-fashioned, flavour,[55] in order to suggest the style of Cato or his generation. Though it is often difficult to assess precisely the effect of an individual passage, the combined effect of a number of them seems significant: see on §§6 *quam ... ingrediundum sit*; 18 *male cogitanti*; 33 *ne requiras*; 42 *neutiquam*; 48 *propter* adverbial; 52 *requietem*: 56 *saturitate*; 71 *quasi = sicut*; 72 *audaciter*. Whether Cicero backed up this slightly old-fashioned impression by using archaic spellings, as has been alleged, is a question that is very difficult to determine; it belongs more properly to the subject of the constitution of the text, for which see below, pp. 49–50. In

[54] See on §§1; 10; 14; 16; 20; 24–5; 36; 61; 65; 73; cf. *Tusc.* 2.26; W. Zillinger, *Cicero und die altrömischen Dichter* (diss. Erlangen 1911).

[55] Cf. E. Bréguet (on the *De rep.*), in *Hommages J. Bayet*, Coll. Latomus 70 (1964) 122–31. On the language of the real Cato, see R. Till, *Die Sprache Catos*, Philol. Suppl. 28 (1935) 21ff. That there are different degrees of archaism or old-fashioned colouring in language is sometimes not made as clear as it should be, though the evidence is almost always insufficient to establish the precise effect of these archaic touches on a contemporary reader.

one place in the text I have ventured to introduce an archaic form by conjecture (§28 *sepse*: see notes on §§28 and 82).

Other rarities in the vocabulary are a number of agricultural terms, which occur naturally in a passage on that subject (see on §§51ff.). Under the heading of philosophical language come such words and phrases as *bene beateque vivere*, *naturalis modus (voluptatis)*, *secundum naturam* (§§4; 46; 71); and even such ordinary words as *sapientia, natura, virtus*, which acquired special philosophical connotations through association with their Greek equivalents, are sufficient to produce a particular atmosphere without necessarily being used to state a specific doctrine of the philosophical schools. The style of logical argument that occurs more often in technical philosophy is occasionally found (§§47; 78), but such passages are exceptional, and even when they occur they are too abbreviated and allusive to serve as philosophical arguments in any genuine way. The reader was doubtless expected to recognise the background of philosophical doctrine, as developed at length elsewhere in Cicero's works.

Stylistically, this work is notable for its exuberance of metaphor and comparison,[56] and for a quality of style in some passages (especially the section on agriculture) that may be called lyrical. When Cicero himself described, in *Orator* 91ff., the 'middle' style whose aim was *delectare*, he might have been providing a prescription for the style of his own philosophical writings, in their less technical and more rhetorical portions (cf. above, p. 1; 11–15): the chief qualities of this style are said to be *suavitas*, absence of *contentio*, richness of metaphor, and use of *sententiae* and *loci communes*. 'Sweetness' and 'relaxation' are vague terms, but it is not difficult to recognise them, along with the more definite features there mentioned, in the *Cato*. The genre of the dialogue called for a relaxed and informal style,[57] after the example of Plato, and Cicero incorporates into this his own

[56] See esp. §§7off.
[57] Cf. Demetr. Περὶ ἑρμηνείας 19ff.

representation of Roman politeness and urbanity.[58] Cicero's
characters compliment each other (§§4; 26; 39), and are
modest or deprecating about their own qualities and abilities
(§§5; 7; 55; 82); they do not tempt providence (§6, *speramus –
volumus quidem certe*); and they use polite formulae (see on §6)
as in actual conversation. When Cicero adapts the Cephalus–
Socrates conversation from Plato's *Republic* (§§7–8), he subtly
changes the tone so as to make the contributions of Laelius
conform to Roman dignity, where Socrates' questions had a
slightly mischievous tone (see notes ad loc.).

The *Cato* is written in Cicero's accustomed rhythmical
style, with the usual proportion of favoured clausulae;[59] in
this respect at least he makes no concessions to archaism or
Catonianism. Notes dealing with rhythmical matters will be
found on §§4, 7, 14, 26, 38, 43, and 77.

II OLD AGE IN THE PHILOSOPHIC TRADITION

(a) Philosophical writing on old age before Cicero

At the head of the tradition of reflective, moralising treatments of old age stands the conversation between Socrates
and Cephalus near the beginning of Plato's *Republic*, of
which Cicero adapted a substantial part in §§6–8 of the *Cato*,
and which he echoes three times elsewhere.[60] This Platonic
passage, which in the context of the *Republic* merely performs
the function of an introductory conversation and setting of
the scene, had a considerable influence on other writers on
old age as well as on Cicero. It is here that one first finds the
formulation and refutation of standard points of complaint
against old age (the absence of physical pleasures, and the
bad treatment of the old by their family and acquaintances),

[58] Cf. A. Haury, *L'Ironie et l'humour chez Cicéron* (Leiden 1955); Becker, *Technik und Szenerie* 11ff.
[59] Cf. A. Ausserer, diss. Innsbruck 1906.
[60] See notes on §§6–8; 46; 47; 77.

together with the general moralistic idea that how one fares in old age depends on one's character and behaviour more than on external circumstances (though it is conceded that poverty is likely to render old age disagreeable). Before Plato, philosophical and poetic comment on old age had tended to be pessimistic or realistic;[61] the observation of the bad effects of old age was not balanced by the exhortation to make the best of them. Even Socrates, as reported by Xenophon, had argued that death was preferable to the debility of extreme old age – an idea which had previously occurred in Mimnermus, and recurs in the later tradition, being particularly vividly developed in Juvenal's tenth satire.[62] On the other hand the proverbial wisdom of the old is frequently mentioned in Greek literature – often with the implication that not as much notice is taken of it as the old men would like.

Aristotle's *Parva naturalia* contain a Περὶ γήρως καὶ νεό-τητος which provides some physiological observations on old age, and a section of the *Rhetoric* (2.13.1389b) discusses the character of old men, together with that of the young and of men in the prime of life, in an objective and generalising fashion: clearly moralising was not in place in a treatise designed to set out a compendium of the characters of the different ages for rhetorical purposes. Aristotle's Peripatetic successor Theophrastus wrote a Περὶ γήρως,[63] of whose content nothing is known; it could have been scientific or

[61] On this subject see B. E. Richardson, *Old Age among the Ancient Greeks* (Baltimore 1933), rev. W. Schmid, *Gnomon* 10 (1934) 529ff.; W. Schade-waldt, *Die Antike* 9 (1933) 282ff., repr. in *Hellas und Hesperien* (Zürich & Stuttgart 1970) I, pp. 109ff.; F. Preisshofen, *Hermes* Einzelschriften 34 (1977); G. S. Kirk, *Eranos Jahrbücher* (1971) 123ff.; M. I. Finley, *G. & R.* 28 (1981) 156ff.; H. Herter, *Würzb. Jahrb.* N.F. 1 (1975) 83ff.; Stein, *Platons Charakteristik* 65ff.; J. P. V. D. Balsdon, *Life and Leisure in Ancient Rome* (London 1969) 169ff.; 392ff.

[62] Mimnermus fr. 6; Xen. *Apol.* 6 and 8; *Mem.* 4.8.1 and 8; [Plato], *Axiochus* 367b; Pliny, *NH* 7.168; Juv. 10.190ff.

[63] Diog. Laert. 5.42; P.–W. 7, 1354. It is possible to surmise some influence on Cicero from this work, in the light of Aulus Gellius' comment (1.3) on Cicero's use of Theophrastus' Περὶ φιλίας in the *Laelius*. For a very

ethical or a mixture of both. A work of the same title is recorded from the hand of Demetrius of Phalerum:[64] one fragment survives, preserved in two separate places in Diogenes Laertius, which says that Anaxagoras and Xenophanes buried their sons with their own hands (an instance of a theme also found in *Cato* 84, though there is no reason to assume direct influence: see ad loc.). This *exemplum* points to a moralistic treatment of old age, but no more is known of the work's content.

Next in chronological order comes the work of Aristo of Ceos (or Chios) mentioned by Cicero in *Cato* 3.[65] This seems to have been a dialogue in which the subject of old age was discussed by Tithonus, the standard mythological example of extended and uncomfortable senility. We know no more of this work than Cicero tells us, and the fact that Cicero mentions it (in connection with one specific point, i.e. the choice of characters for the dialogue) certainly does not imply that he borrowed extensively from it. The identity of Aristo – the Peripatetic from Ceos or the Stoic from Chios – is discussed below in Appendix 2, from which the reader may gather something of the ramifications of scholarly argument that have been devoted to this problem. The question is not of the first importance for the present purpose, since we know nothing of the nature or extent of Cicero's debt to this work.

Varro's Menippean satire, entitled *Tithonus* ἢ περὶ γήρως, should also be mentioned in this context. It seems reasonable, in default of other evidence, to suppose that it was written at the same time as the other Menippean satires, which are spoken of in Cicero's *Academica* (1.8–9) as 'old', and consequently that it predates the *Cato*. Five short

tentatively attributed fragment, see O. Hense, *Teletis Reliquiae*, edn 2 (Tübingen 1909) introd. p. 108.

[64] Title, Diog. Laert. 5.81; for the fragment, ibid. 1.13 and 9.20, =frr. 82–3 Wehrli.

[65] See note on §3, and Appendix 2.

fragments of this work survive;[66] they seem to indicate that the view of old age expressed in it was generally favourable (for comparison with themes in the *Cato*, see on §§71 and 83). It does not seem likely that there was any extensive influence from Varro on Cicero, in view of the difference of genre; however, the title of Varro's satire tempts one to speculate that it may have had some relationship to Aristo's work mentioned above (cf. Appendix 2, p. 270).

(b) The later tradition

A number of later writers treated the topic of old age in the same moralistic vein as Cicero. There is not sufficient space for detailed discussion of these works here; however, it is convenient that they should be listed, and that their relationship to Cicero in each case should be briefly outlined.

(i)   Seneca's letters concerning old age, i.e. nos. 12, 26, 30, 58 and 77.

(ii) Musonius Rufus, 17, Τί ἄριστον γήρως ἐφόδιον;

(iii) Plutarch, Εἰ πρεσβυτέρῳ πολιτευτέον (*An seni res publica gerenda sit* – hereafter referred to as *An seni*).

(iv) Favorinus, Περὶ γήρως.

(v)   Juncus, Περὶ γήρως.

(vi) Fragments of a work on old age in P. Berol. 13407 (P. Schubart 38).

(vii) Diogenes of Oenoanda, treatise on old age.

The letters of Seneca on old age show some striking parallels with Cicero,[67] and it seems very likely that these are due to direct reminiscence. It is possible that there is some

---

[66] Frr. 544–8 Bücheler; see H. Dahlmann, in *Studien zur Textgeschichte und Textkritik*, Festschrift Jachmann, ed. H. Dahlmann and R. Merkelbach (Cologne 1959) pp. 37–46. There is no evidence to suggest that this satire was a product of Varro's own old age.

[67] See notes on §§24; 34; 47; 49; 66; 67; 68; 69; 70; 72; 76.

Ciceronian influence to be found in Musonius,[68] but on the whole that author's doctrinaire Stoicism has little in common with Cicero's liberal and non-sectarian moralising. Plutarch's discussion of old men in public life tempts comparison with §§15ff. of the *Cato*, and it is certain that Plutarch knew Cicero's work (cf. §42, p. 188, and App. 3, p. 273) but the similarities between the two essays are rather difficult to interpret. Some have argued for Ciceronian influence on Plutarch,[69] while others favour common dependence on one or more of the lost Hellenistic works on old age: this has been a favourite area for attempts to reconstruct the content of the latter, but no certain results have been achieved. Some of the common material is so well known that it hardly proves any connection (the two anecdotes about Sophocles, *Cato* 22 and 47; Nestor, *Cato* 31; Appius Claudius, *Cato* 16). Other items may reflect a common source (Lysander, *Cato* 63; Solon and Pisistratus, *Cato* 72). The rest of the parallels are mostly general similarities of thought, which may simply have arisen by coincidence from the similar philosophic backgrounds of the two authors (see notes on *Cato* 9; 15; 20; 29; 35; 37; 49; 56; 62).

Favorinus's Περὶ γήρως survives only in a few fragments.[70] Again there are vague and general similarities with Cicero, but nothing that can be taken to prove a definite connection; Platonic influence on both authors is probably a sufficient explanation. Much the same is true of the quite substantial

[68] See notes on §§9; 15; 66. Cf. Hense's edition, 1905; C. E. Lutz, *Yale Class. Stud.* 10 (1947) 3ff.; A. C. van Geytenbeek, *Musonius Rufus and Greek Diatribe* (Assen 1963); A. Jagu, *Musonius Rufus, entretiens et fragments* (Hildesheim 1979).

[69] For dependence by Plutarch on Cicero, see C. O. Zuretti, *RFIC* 19 (1891) 362ff.; for a common source, C. Fornara, *Philologus* 110 (1966) 119ff., a speculative and not convincing attempt to identify the source as Demetrius; for Aristo of Ceos, M. Arullani, *Ricerche intorno all'opusculo plutarcheo* Εἰ πρεσβυτέρῳ πολιτευτέον (Rome 1928), and Wuilleumier's third edition.

[70] See A. Barigazzi, *Favorino di Arelate: Opere* (Florence 1966). For parallels with Cicero, see notes on §§9; 70; 77; 84.

extracts from Juncus' Περὶ γήρως preserved in Stobaeus.[71]
The identity of Juncus cannot be conclusively determined.
'Ιοῦνκος ὁ φιλόσοφος is mentioned by Photius (*Bibl.*
p. 144,17 Bekker) with no further information. The man's
name is Roman, though there is nothing Roman in the work;
he writes a virtually undatable Atticising Greek,[72] and his
allusions are as Attic and classical as his style; his philosophy
is Platonic. This combination suggests the Second Sophistic;
J. H. Oliver (*Hesperia* 16 (1967) 42ff.) has attempted to
identify Juncus as Aemilius Juncus, cos. suff. 127 (cf. Juv.
15.27, *consule Iunco* referring to that year), but the philosophic writer may be a less distinguished and otherwise
unknown bearer of the name. Juncus' work is notable for
containing not a mere enumeration of complaints against
old age, as in Cicero, but a full-scale rhetorical ψόγος (see
pp. 1049ff. W.–H.).

Fragments of a moralistic work on old age are to be found
in the Berlin papyrus no. 13407 (W. Schubart, *Griechische
Literarische Papyri* (Berlin 1950) no. 38), dated by Schubart to
the first/second centuries A.D.[73] The authorship cannot be
determined. There is one substantial parallel with Cicero
(see on §21). Of the other fragments, the longest concerns the
amorous activity of Socrates and Anacreon in old age; the

[71] 4, 50a, 27; 4, 50b, 85; 4, 50c, 95; 4, 53, 35 W.–H. See Hirzel, *Dialog* II,
252–3; Kroll, P.–W. 10, 953; J. A. A. Faltin, diss. Freiburg 1910; F.
Wilhelm, *Die Schrift des Iuncus* περὶ γήρως *und ihre Verhältnis zu Ciceronis Cato
Maior* (Breslau 1911); R. Philippson, *Berl. Phil. Woch.* 32 (1912) 872–4; A.
Dyroff, *RhM* 86 (1937) 241ff.; id., *Der Peripatos über das Greisenalter*, Studien
zur Geschichte und Kultur des Altertums, 21, Heft 3 (Paderborn 1939) (a
strange attempt to identify Juncus with Aristo of Ceos, which – stranger
still – found favour with F. Della Corte, *Catone Censore*[2], Turin 1969, 175ff.)

[72] Faltin, op. cit. (see n. 71).

[73] I have been able to check the transcription of the papyrus with a
photograph kindly supplied by Dr G. Poethke of Berlin. I do not believe in
Schubart's supplements [θ]εαταί in fr. D, [Στ]όαν in fr. E col. I, δὲ αὐτοῦ
κ[αὶ] in fr. F col. 2 line 10, or ὁ [βίος] in ibid. line 13. For F 2, 10, Mr P.
Parsons suggests δὲ αὖ τοῦ κ[αλοῦ], while for line 13 ὁ[δοῦσι] seems to fit
well (cf. Anacreon fr. 44). In G col. 3 (quoted in note on 21) ἄλ[λου
πράγματος] is my supplement. The last letter of fr. G may be ọ[...] or
ω[...].

others seem connected with the decline of strength and of the senses.

Finally, a number of fragments of the inscription of Diogenes of Oenoanda (second century A.D.) concern old age, and their epigraphical style suggests an independent treatise. This is apparently our only example of an Epicurean work on this subject; again, it contains familiar topics, but the text is too fragmentary to allow their connection and arrangement to be reconstructed. Full commentaries on the fragments are available elsewhere;[74] for possible parallels with Cicero, see on §§36 and 47.

III THE TEXT AND THE MANUSCRIPTS

(a) The manuscript tradition[75]

The text of this edition is based principally on eleven manuscripts;[76] some twenty others are occasionally quoted.

[74] See Chilton's translation and commentary (1971, with appendix containing new fragments); R. Philippson, P.–W. Suppl. 5 (1931) 166–7; for the new fragments, M. F. Smith, *Thirteen New Fragments of Diogenes of Oenoanda*, Denkschriften der österreichischen Akad. der Wissenschaften, phil.-hist. Klasse, 117 (Vienna 1974) 36ff.; 42ff.; id., *Prometheus* 8 (1982) 208ff. I am grateful to Professor M. F. Smith for drawing my attention to these articles. Cf. also J. Irigoin in *Studi De Falco* (Naples 1971) 475ff.

[75] The following discussion complements and amends in some points my account in L. D. Reynolds ed., *Texts and Transmission: A Survey of the Latin Classics* (Oxford 1983) (hereafter *T. & T.*) 116–20, to which the reader is referred for further information and bibliography on individual manuscripts.

[76] P: *T. & T.* pp. 117; 134; Munk Olsen p. 255. V: *T. & T.* pp. 49–50; 117; M.O. p. 204. B: *T. & T.* pp. 117–18; M.O. pp. 156–7; cf. also K. Simbeck, *De Ciceronis Catone Maiore* (Leipzig 1912). L: *T. & T.* pp. 118; 226ff.; M.O. p. 198. A: *T. & T.* pp. 118; 225–6; M.O. p. 280. D: *T. & T.* pp. 118; 226; 229; M.O. pp. 299–300. H: *T. & T.* pp. 62; 65–6; 7off.; 77; 90; 119; 123; 127; 141; 351; M.O. p. 211. M: *T. & T.* pp. 63; 66; 119; 351; M.O. p. 177. R: *T. & T.* pp. 63; 120; 124; M.O. pp. 319–20. S: T. & T. pp. 63; 120; M.O. p. 235. Z: M.O. p. 309. I have made fresh collations of all these MSS, from the original in the case of P, A, H and S, otherwise from microfilm. Z is here collated for the first time.

The principal manuscripts are as follows:

P   Paris, Bibl. Nat. lat. 6332, fols. 76v–88v, s. ix

V   Leiden, Bibl. der Rijksuniversiteit, Voss. Lat. O. 79, fols. 1v–27v, s. ix

B   (=b Simbeck, Wuilleumier, Br Moore) Brussels, Bibl. Royale 9591 (=9591–5, fols. 56v–65v), s. ix

L   Leiden, Voss. Lat. F. 12β (=F. 12, fols. 15r–24r), s. ix

A   Paris, nouv. acq. lat. 454, fols. 1r–15r, s. ix

D   Vatican, Reg. lat. 1587, fols. 66–80, s. ix

H   London, B. L. Harley 2682, fols. 64v–70v, s. xi

M   (=Ma Wuilleumier, m Simbeck) Florence, Laur. 50.45, fols. 97r–104v, s. x–xi

R   Zürich, Rheinau 127, fols. 1–50, s. xi or xii

S   Munich, Clm 15964 (Salisburgensis), fols. 2r–27v, s. xii

Z   Venice, Marc. lat. 14.222 (4007), fols. 50r–60r, s. xi or xii.

PVBLAD are of French origin; HMRSZ originate from the German-speaking area of Europe. A reasonably certain stemma can be drawn for PVBLADMH (see Fig. 1); there is

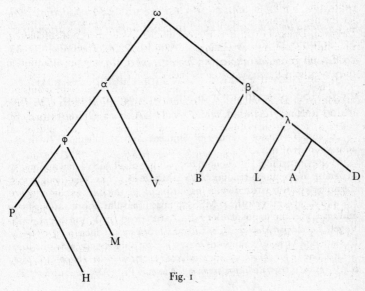

Fig. 1

a clear division between PVMH (designated α) and BLAD (designated β).[77] The characteristic errors of α are mostly shared by the majority of later MSS, but it is difficult to trace the precise relations of these within the stemma provided by the eight oldest MSS. R, S and Z are the oldest and best of this large class of more recent MSS, and they are fully represented in the apparatus, either individually (always so when they support a correct reading not otherwise well attested) or together with later MSS under the siglum ς.

The existence of a number of errors common to all these MSS implies a common archetype.[78] Of these, the following also occur in all other MSS known to me: 7 *usu evenirent* for *usu venirent* (corr. Otto), 13 *socratis* for *Isocratis*, 26 *ut ego feci* for *et ego feci* (corr. Madvig), 34 *habitus* for *avitus* (corr. Cujas), 52 *vitis radices* for *viviradices* (corr. Manutius), 61 *unicum* for *hunc unum* (corr. Madvig). Others are common to PVBLADMH, but are corrected in one or more MSS of the ςgroup (see below, p. 44).

In the following passages, the members of the α group agree in error, while the β group preserves the correct reading: 12 *nihil* β: *nihil est* α; 19 *simul* add. α; 20 *posteriore libro* α; 23 *num Homerum* misplaced in α; 24 *mirum est* β: *mirum sit* α; 27 *Aemilius* α for *Aelius*; 42 *exoratus* β: *ex(h)ortatus* α; 47 *desideratur* β: *desideratio* α; 55 *hanc vitam* α; 60 *illi* βς: *ille* α.

In the following considerably larger number of passages, the β MSS agree in error against α: 6 *quo* α: *quod* β; 10 *virtus* added before *gravitas* B, *virtus gravis* LAD; 11 *Q(uinte)* om. β;

---

[77] α and β=classes *x* and *y* of Simbeck and Wuilleumier (with the addition of HM to *x*).

[78] I use the symbol Ω to denote the reading of all MSS known to me; ω to denote the common reading of PVHMBLAD. It has been thought that the archetype was written in an insular hand, on the basis of confusions of *p*, *r* and *s*, especially in the β MSS, the use of insular abbreviations for *et* and *enim*, and the use of *finit* for *explicit* at the end (in V and L); cf. G. S. Vogel, *The Major Manuscripts of Cicero's De Senectute* (Chicago 1939) 6–14. Examples of 'insular' confusions are 39 *accirite* β for *accipite*, *ostimi* B, *ortimi* A¹D¹, *ortum* L¹ for *optimi*; 47 *carere: curase* L¹D¹; 70 *probetur: probohis* H¹, *probo is* PA² (*probo ir* B); 71 *ante partorum: ante pastorum* PL¹ (A¹?), *ante pastorem* D¹.

14 *facti sunt* om. β; 21 *meminerunt* α: *meminerint* β; 24 *ad se* α: *ase* β; 26 *dicit* α: *dicet* β(*dicet et* D[1]); 27 *desiderabam*: *-abant* β; 29 *et* (before *avi tui*) om. β; *effetum* α: *effectum* β; 30 *nostrae* α: *nostra* BL[1]A[1], *nostram* D[1]; 36 *utendum* ... *potionis* om. β; *sunt* ... *ignavae* om. β SgPa[1]; 37 *tantam* α: *tantas* β; 38 *agerem* β for *agere*; *non* ... *vita* om. β; 39 *accirite* β for *accipite*; *taureti* β for *Tarenti*; 41 *si* β for *ei*; 42 *neuti* β for *neutiquam*; *coniu(n)get* β for *coniungeret*; 44 *se* β for *classe*; 45 *computationem* β for *compot-*; 52 *nec* β for *ne* (before *silvescat*); 58 *exclusionibus* β for *ex lus-*; 61 *adulescente* β for *-entiae*; 65 *adelphisunt* β for *Adelphis sunt*; 69 *quicquid* β for *quidquam*; 73 *dolori* β for *-ore*; 78 *nondum* β for *non tum*; 81 *tuerentur* β for *tuentur*; 85 *atque* β for *ad quam*. In addition to these passages, the β manuscripts write varied gibberish in 27 *decet uti et*, 31 *Graeciae* ... *Aiacis*; 33 *Pythagorae tibi malis*; 36 *sic ista senilis*. It is clear already from this list that β has suffered more from superficial corruption than α; however, one may gather by the same token that it has been less subject to scholarly correction and editing, and in some passages it seems that β is nearer to preserving the truth for that reason (e.g. 33 *parti aetatis* Q Nonius: *parci etatis* β, where others have *parcitatis* or *parti*; cf. also my notes on 50 *atque haec* [*quidem studia doctrinae quae*] and 56 [*appetentem*] *occupantem*). Generally speaking the two families must be regarded as having equal authority, and it is not possible to trust either consistently in doubtful cases.

Within β, the three MSS LAD form a clear subgroup, which I have designated λ. This group is distinguished by the following errors: 1 *et hisdem* λ for *eisdem*; 2 *surgentis* λVi[1] for *urgentis*; 7 *Salinator*: *salintor* B, *intor* λ; *mihi non id*: *id* B, *mihi non* λ; 8 *gloriae* λ for *gloria*; *herculem quid* λ for *hercule inquit*; *esses* om. λ Sg; 10 *virtus gravis* λ (cf. above); 13 *cursum* λ for *quorsum* or *quorsus*; *maxime* λ for *Maximi*; *bella a se*: *a* om. λ; 15 *Q(uintus)*: *aut* λ, om. B; 16 *cum* ... *consulatum* om. λ; 18 *at*: *aut* λ; 19 *Scipio tibio reservent* λ; *aut comminus*: *ut c-* λ; 20 *qui*: *quia* λ; *p(ublicam)* om. λSg; *nonvis* λ for *novi*; 21 *qui Aristides esset*: *quiaristidiresset* B, *quia isti deesset* λ; 24 *committamus* λ for *omittamus*; 25 *quidem* λ for *equidem*; 29 *autuiduo* λ for *avi tui duo*; 31 *brevis* λ for *brevi*; 32 *quarto* λ for *quartum*; *possim* λ for *possem*; *enodem* λ for *eodem*; *Hispaniam* λ for *Hispania*; *enarravit* λ for *enervavit*; 33 *requiras: reliquias* λ(*reliquira* B); *pueritiam: pueri tam* λ(*pueri iam* L²A²D²); *praecipi* λ for *percipi*; 34 *cogemur* λ for *cogimur*; 35 *sunt* λ for *fuit*; 38 *aut* add. λ before *audierim*; *ex sene quaerem* λ for *exsequi nequirem*; 39 *libidine* λ for *libidines*; 40 *exercitari* λ for *excitari*; *hominisuiue* λ for *homini sive*; 42 *septem* (or *VII*): *VI* λ; *convivio: -ios* λ; *probari: prognari* λ; 44 *voluptates: -is* λ; 46 *quam maxime: quem m-* λ; 47 *adfecto: a(d)fectu* λ; 49 *animum: -am* λ; 50 *se* (after *senescere*) om. λ; 51 *fenero* λ for *fenore*; *sementem* λ for *semen*; 52 *stulta* λ for *fulta*; 55 *hominibus* λ for *omnibus*; *ergo* om. λ; *omnis* λ for *hominis*; 56 *quidem* λ for *quidam*; *operis . . . pratorum* om. λ; 58 (*h*)*asta* λ for *hastas*; 59 *scribitur* λ for *inscribitur*; 62 *oratione* (before *defenderet*): *-oni* λ; 65 *si veritatem* λ for *severitatem*; *acervitatem* λ for *acerb-*; 66 *restet: restat* λ; *eo: et* λ; *causa* om. λ; 68 *Scipio: suscipio* λPa (*o scipio* P²D²); 76 *quaedam studia: quidam st-* λ; *sic* (before *occidunt*): *si* λ; 80 *viverent* λ for *vivere*; 85 *quo: quod* λPa; *mortuus: -os* λ; *quae dicerem: quid d-* λ.

There is no passage in which the λ group has a clearly correct reading not shared by the other MSS, and it seems to me that one should be very cautious before backing λ against the consensus of the rest of the early witnesses. In my view the sole value of the first hands of LAD is as a guide to the reading of β. The precise relationships of the λ manuscripts to each other have not been conclusively determined. The view of previous editors, which I followed in my article in *T. & T.*, that A and D are virtual *gemelli* while L descends from λ independently of their common exemplar, is certainly too simple, though it is likely to be basically correct. There are many passages in which A and D agree in error, while L has either the correct reading or a different form of the corruption.[79] There is, however, a smaller but still substantial

---

[79] Common errors of AD: 2 *aequi* A¹D¹, *etsi te qui* BL¹ for *etsi te quidem*; 3 *id tribuitur* A¹D¹, *id tribuito* L¹, *id tribulato* B, for *attribuito*; 5 *incerti* (?) A¹D¹, *incesti* L¹ for *inerti*; 8 *suae* A¹D for *sua*, om. L¹; 25 *eque* A¹D¹ for *ea quae*; 27 *ex lateribus: et l-* A¹D; 30 *puerum* for *puer* AD; 31 *praedicet: -cit* AD¹; 34 *hospes*

number of passages in which L and A agree in error against
D, and in about half of these the error of LA is shared also by
B.[80] The most reasonable explanation of this would be that
these errors came from λ or β as the case may be, and that
they were corrected in the immediate exemplar of D –
whether by conjecture or from another manuscript, is difficult to say. Most of these corrections would probably not
have been beyond the power of an intelligent medieval
Latinist, and there are no signs in most of D that would
suggest contamination from an outside source. One passage,
however, is exceptional: D behaves oddly in §§80–1 of the
text, transferring its allegiance for a brief space to the α side
of the tradition; probably the best explanation for this is that
some lines were missing from D's exemplar, and that they

---

tuus: hospestus L[1], *hospastus* A[1]D[1]; 40 *voluptatis:* -*atibus* A[1]D[1]; 42 *commerentiam*
for *commercium* A[1]D[1]; 43 *con* A[1]D[1] for *C.* (*Gaium*); *si* added before *se* A[1]D[1];
46 *in* om. A[1]D[1] before *Symposio*; *compleo: completo* A[1]D[1], *completu* L[1] (*complector* A[2]D[2]); 47 *expletis: explens* L[1] *exemplens* A[1]D[1]; 59 *facitis: faciatis* A[1]D[1]
(*sciatis* A[2]D[2]); 66 *esse* om. A[1]D after *contemnendum*; 76 *maturum: naturum* A[1]D
(*naturam* LA[2]); 83 *vestros: nostros* A[1]D[1]. Cf. also the following omissions: 26
equidem . . . litt(eris) om. A[1]D[1]; 46 *(tempesti)vis . . . iam* om. A[1]D[1]; conversely 45 *epularem . . . coniunctionem* om. L; 53 *religatio et propagatio* om. L; etc.
BAD agree in error in 41 *iubebat: iubeat* BA[1]D[1] and 61 *Lepidum: lapidum*
BA[1]D; these two errors were easy enough for the writer of L to correct.

[80] 6 *multo: ut multo* L[1]A; 17 *multo: multa* BL[1]A[1]; 22 *quam multa: quamulta*
BL[1]A[1]; 26 *senem: se nec* BL[1]A[1]; 29 *quid: quis* BL[1]A[1]; 30 *esset: esse* L[1]A[1]; 35
imbecillus: -*illes* L[1]A[1]; *tenui: tenuit* BL[1]A; *ni ita: nita* L[1]A[1] *ita* B; *sed* inserted
after *exstitisset* L[1]A[1]; 38 *qui: quis* BL[1]A[1]; 43 *audisset* om. L[1]A[1]Sg; 44 *appellat:
appellatu* BL[1]A[1]; 45 *ad: a* L[1]A[1]; 51 *viriditatem:* -*ate* BL[1]A[1]; 52 *sarmentis:
armentis* L[1]A[1]; 59 *eo libro: e libro* BL[1]A[1]; 84 *existimem:* -*emus* LA[1]. Note also:
32 *mallem: mallim* L[1]A[1], *malum* D[1]; 50 *[maior] potest esse maior* BL[1]A[1]: *maior
potest esse* DR; 59 *ei tam: tam* LA[1] *ita* D[1]; 66 *quo viae: quo via* L[1]A[1] *covia* BD; 71
flammae vis: flammeus L[1]A[1]D[2], *flammeis* D[1]; 80 *quae* L[1]A[1] for *quaeque*. In 42 an
error of D's first hand (*libido* inserted before *consilium*) is found also in L[2]A[2].
According to B. C. Barker-Benfield (unpublished Oxford thesis), the texts
of Macrobius, *Comm. in Somn. Scip.* that accompany (or once accompanied)
the *Cato* in these three MSS show a closer affinity between L and A than
between either and D; but one could think of reasons why the two texts
suggest different *stemmata*. There is a further complication caused by the
provenances of the three MSS: L and D seem both to be products of
Fleury, and A of Corbie, and yet L and D are the furthest apart of any pair
out of the three.

were filled in from a MS of the α group.[81] Finally, there is a small collection of passages in which L and D agree in error against A:[82] these are probably not of much significance, but it is not in general improbable that LAD have a certain amount of mutual contamination in their ancestry.

Turning now to the α side of the tradition, one may notice that P, H and M agree against V in a number of passages, and that the β group tends on such occasions to side with V. I have designated PHM as a subgroup φ, which is character-ised by the following errors: 8 *sunt* om. φ; *ignobilis* add. φ (after *essem*); 17 *velocitatibus* φ for -*tate*; 34 *ne desint* φ (which cannot be right, whatever else is); 36 *exercitando* φ: *se exercendo* Vβ, probably preferable; 38 *nunc quam maxime* φ for *nunc cum maxime*; 44 *crebro* φ, *credo* Vβ (recte *cereo*); 65 *aetas naturae* φ for *natura*. However, in other passages the division is reversed: V and the β group agree in error, while φ gives a correct reading: 3 *C.* or *Gaio* φ: om. Vβ; 22 *quod propter* recte φ, *propter quod* Vβ; 25 *aitque* β and apparently V[1] for *atque*; 29 *prae* Vβ for *P.* (Publius); 32 *cum tribunus*: *cum* om. Vβ; 33 *ne ille* recte φ: *ne ille quidem* Vβ; 41 *regnum* Vβ for *regno*; *Ap.* (or *Appio*) φ: *P.* VBAD (*pre* L[1]); 44 *vicerat* Vβ: *devicerat* φ (no doubt better); 50 *usque ad adulescentiam*: *ad* om. Vβ; 51 *rationem cum* φ: *cum rationem* Vβ; *molito* Vβ for *mollito*; 69 *regnavit* V[1]β: *regnaverit* V[2]M, *regnaverat* PH; 72 *dicitur* (after *respondisse*) om. Vβ; 75 *ne* φ: *nec* Vβ cett. Note also 25 *cui serat*: *cuiuserat* V[1]BL[1]A[1]; 29 *et Gn(aeus) et P(ublius)*: *et neus et prae* V[1]BA[1]D[1], *et nieus prae* L[1]; 36 *levium*: *evium* V[1], *evum* B, *enium* λ; 38 *ius suum* φA[2]D[2]ς: *usum* V, *visum* BLA[1], *iussum* D[1].

This distribution of readings, cutting across the α/β divi-

[81] *exissent* DO[2]GQRE; (*quaeque* D cum cett.: *quae* L[1]A[1]); *discedant* DMH[2]O[2]PaGς; *discesserit* DSBe; (*atqui* D cum cett.: *atque* BL[1]A[1]); *sint*: *sunt* VD[1]Mς.

[82] 26 *uti*: *ut* L[1]D[1] (*utq* B); 27 *P.* (*Publius*): *prae* L[1]D[1] (*post* V); 35 *at*: *ad* BL[1]D[1]; 38 *quae iam*: *qui eam* BL[1]D[1]; 40 *impelleret*: *impleret* L[1]D[1]; 69 *centum viginti* (*CXX*): *XX* L[1]D[1]; 75 *non L.* (*non Lucium*): *M.* L[1]D[1] (*n̄r̄m Lucium* add. D[2]); cf. also 47 *carere*: *curare* BA[1] *curase* L[1]D[1]; 70 *suavitate*: -*atis* L[1]D[1] -*ati* A[1]P[2].

sion, seems to imply contamination of some sort. It may be that the contamination lies in V (though one might expect to see more obvious signs of it if that were so), or that something went into the making of φ that was not part of the ancestry of Vβ. It seems rather unlikely that all the correct readings peculiar to φ (among the earlier MSS) are due to medieval conjecture, though there do seem to be signs of conjectural interference in the φ MSS.[83] If contamination is present, it becomes impossible to decide on stemmatic grounds between φ and Vβ in cases of doubt: they must be treated as equal authorities.

Before saying more of the φ group, it is convenient to complete the history of the tradition between the ninth and eleventh centuries. In the first place, five out of the six ninth-century MSS (PVLAD) are heavily corrected; the second hands appear to be near-contemporary (L² is dated to the tenth century by Munk Olsen p. 198). P² is related to the β

---

[83] 25 *esse* φ for *eum se esse* Vβ, 41 *quam* φ for *tamquam* Vβ, 43 *ea a maioribus* φ for *ea maioribus* Vβ seem to be the result of conjectural emendation of a nonsensical text. In three passages, P (and in two of them also M) has a reading that may conceivably be the result of comparison with another text: 10 *unus homo*: the majority of MSS have *unus qui* (influenced by the Virgilian adaptation of the passage of Ennius) but P¹M insert *homo* before *qui*; *qui* is then deleted by P², while L²D², also related to P, give *homo* instead of *qui*. It appears that someone in the ancestry of P had access to the correct Ennian text. 11 *fugerat* P and MSS influenced by it: this may just be a mistake, but it seems an odd coincidence that Livy's account of M. Livius Macatus at Tarentum says that he had fled into the citadel, and it is possible that this accounts for the reading in P. 31 *vivebat* PM for *videbat*: it is generally much more likely that Cicero said that Nestor was now seeing the third generation of men, but Ovid says *nunc tertia vivitur aetas*, meaning that Nestor was now living through his third century (*aetas* in the sense of *saeculum* or maximum human lifespan), and this may have influenced writers of MSS. None of this is certain, of course, in the case of the last two passages, but the possibility should at least be noted. The general tendency among older editors to overvalue P (the first ninth-century MS to be used in editions, hence for a long time the oldest known) has given *fugerat* and *vivebat* a greater currency in editions than they deserve.

One instance of contamination going back beyond φ, and even beyond α, is clearly to be seen in §77 *equidem non enim.*

37

group; its non-β readings are usually easy conjectures, mostly wrong: e.g. 31 *at ut* P²L²D², etc.; 61 *est totum* (see note ad loc.); 68 *tum in* (correction of *tum*: recte *tu in*). L²D² are both very closely related to P, with the occasional agreement in non-β readings with P² (e.g. 31 *similem habeat ducem at ut* P²L²D²); there is not much of value in them. A² is very like L²D², but is distinguished by the addition of *et qua deprimeris* (1), shared with V² and later MSS, and the change in 69 *vita* for *natura*. A² deletes the intrusive *tantum* or *tanam* in 37 (found in all eight of the oldest MSS). V² is possibly the most useful of these second hands: like L²D²A², it is related to P, but provides the correct *regnaverit* in 69 (also in M) and the probably correct *sapienti* in 70 (shared with M and later MSS); it looks as if the exemplar of V² may have been a φ MS closer in some ways to M than to P.

There is one manuscript of the ninth century that has not so far been mentioned: this is K, containing the excerpts of Hadoard of Corbie. The *Cato* text in this MS derives from A in its corrected form, either directly or at one remove, and is of historical importance only.[84] K's only significant variation from A + A² is 4 *nihil mali potest*; this reappears in the later MSS OQE, thus casting some light on their ancestry.

O is a South German manuscript dated to the tenth or eleventh century.[85] The text of its first hand, like that of Hadoard's excerpts, is derived from A corrected, and is of no textual importance, although it provides some evidence for the history of the transmission (cf. below). The corrections of

---

[84] K: Vat. Reg. lat. 1762, fols 146ff. See *T. & T.* pp. 105; 118, 121ff.; 125; 134; 226; etc.; Munk Olsen pp. 300–1; the excerpts are given by P. Schwenke, *Philologus* Suppl. 5 (1889) 516ff. and 552ff. I have examined a microfilm in the Bodleian Library. For the derivation of K and of the first hand of O, note 10 *cum aetate* A²D²KOH; 15 *seniles: similes* P¹H¹A², *similes seniles* KO; 65 *vinum: vitium* A¹PaBe¹ *vinum vitium* A²K; 69 *natura: vita* A²KMO²Gς, *natura vel vita* O¹.

[85] O: Oxford, Bodleian Library, D'Orville 77, fols 34v–47v. See *T. & T.* pp. 65; 118–19; 122–3; 229; 351; Munk Olsen p. 246. I have collated the original MS.; the readings of O² have not previously been noted in editions.

O, by a near-contemporary hand,[86] are however of considerable interest. They contain a number of correct or plausible
readings shared with M and with later MSS, and also some
which occur here for the first time and are shared only with
various MSS of the ς group. Apart from these readings, O^2
shows varied affinities within the α group. It is clear that the
good readings of O^2 cannot be conjectural; they must derive
from a lost MS circulating in Germany contemporary with
O itself, and this MS must have been an ancestor of some of
the ς MSS, which contained traces of a tradition independent of either α or β as we have them. These readings are as
follows: 1 *non cognomen solum* O^2RE; 18 *cui* deleted after
Carthagini (see note); 29 *an ne has* O^2RE^2 (instead of *annales* of
the older MSS; the correct reading is probably Schiche's *an
ne tales*, which I have adopted); 37 *illa domo mos* O^2RE; 41
posset O^2RE; 48 *delectatur tamen etiam qui in ultima* O^2Pa^{2}RE
Nonius; 65 *morum vitia* O^2H^{2}Pa and later MSS; 67 *est tam*
O^2H^{2}GRE Nonius; *illud* (fort. recte) O^2GRE; 84 *habeat*
O^2H^{2}HbGQR. For correct readings shared with M, see
below.

The two Harleian fragments Ha and Hb[87] are of late
tenth-century date and originate from Germany. Ha is too
short to be definitely assigned to a particular group. Hb has
affinities with later German MSS, and shares the correct
reading *habeat* in 84 with O^2; it therefore probably derives
from the local German tradition, and it is a pity that we do
not have more of it. Significant variations in these fragments
are recorded in the apparatus.

In the eleventh century we find a close copy of P (made at
Fleury) in the Vatican manuscript Ra:[88] this would have

[86] This has been kindly confirmed for me by Dr B. C. Barker-Benfield.
[87] London, B. L. Harley 2716, fol. 74v (Hb) and fol. 77 (HA): *T. & T.*
pp. 63; 65; 119; 131; 351; Munk Olsen p. 213. In my article (p. 119) Hb is
mentioned first. Ha contains 43 *quod sua sponte* – 45 *metiebar*, Hb 84 *quid non
potius* – end. I have examined the original.
[88] Ra: Vat. Reg. lat. 1414. See C. E. Finch, *TAPA* 91 (1960) 76ff.; *T. &
T.* pp. 119–20; Munk Olsen p. 298. I follow Finch's collation.

been of very limited use were it not for the fact that the last few sections of the text are missing from P (from 78 *quin ex*). Ra is thus of considerable value as a guide to the readings of P in those sections, and is fully represented in the apparatus.

The two Paris manuscripts Pa and Vi[89] together form a complete text; it seems likely that Vi was written to complete the text of Pa after the loss of the latter's first leaf, and for practical purposes they may be treated as one copy. They are of French origin; Pa dates from the tenth or eleventh century, Vi from the eleventh. Their text appears to derive from a manuscript of the λ family, corrected from an α source. The non-λ readings are sometimes like P (11 *fugerat* Vi, 35 *possint* Pa, 38 *ultroque*, 48 *spectans*, 72 *dicitur*, etc.), sometimes nearer to V or M (3 *Aristoteles* Vi). The correct reading in 65, *morum vitia* Pa, is shared only with O²H² and later MSS, but could probably have been reached by conjecture (L¹A¹ read *morvitia*). Otherwise there is nothing of

[89] Pa (p Simb.): Paris lat. 5752 (not 5792 as given by Simbeck and Wuilleumier). Vi (k Simb.): Paris lat. 14699, from St.-Victor. Vi contains *Cato* 1–21 (last words *perceperat nomina*); Pa begins at 19 *num igitur si ad centesimum*, there being one leaf missing from the beginning. I have examined the original MSS. See Munk Olsen pp. 254 (Pa), 274 (Vi).

E. Pellegrin (*BEC* 103 (1942) 69ff.) identified Vi as having once been part of the composite St.-Victor MS KKK 25, of which the table of contents survives in Berne 327 fol. 1 (Pellegrin p. 73). According to this table, Vi was followed in KKK 25 (fols. 171–87) by a MS containing *Cato* (beginning at 21 *num igitur censetis eum*) and *Laelius*. This description fits Pa exactly, except for the *incipit*. Pa carries the folio numbers 171–87 (cf. Munk Olsen, p. 254); and the first words of Pa are similar enough to those given in the table of contents to make confusion likely, especially since the latter passage carries on immediately from the last word of Vi (*perceperat nomina: num igitur censetis eum*). Further, the script of Pa and Vi is very similar; and in the short passage where their texts overlap, both contain a characteristic error (*in nevii poetae libro*) found in no other MS. Vi itself breaks off before the foot of the page, and was therefore presumably never part of a complete MS. The natural deduction is that Vi was written, in the same place as Pa and from a similar source, to complete Pa's *Cato* text after the first leaf of Pa had been lost, and that the scribe of Vi went on two sections too far in the text, confusing the two similar passages 19 and 21. The same confusion accounts for the mistake in the table of contents as to the first words of Pa.

great interest in the text of Pa and Vi. The few corrections in Pa show affinities with O^2 and later MSS (cf. especially on §§48 and 68); they are probably derived from a text of this nature that was circulating in Northern France from the beginning of the twelfth century and possibly earlier. Vi has no corrections.

I return now to the φ group, which consists of P, M and H. P, which was for some time the oldest MS of the *Cato* known to editors, has always been treated with great respect; in contrast, M, which is hardly less good, has been neglected by editors. Munk Olsen has now dated it to the tenth century, and if that is right there is even less reason for neglecting it. The text of M is virtually a pure α text: its few agreements in error with β are probably fortuitous and non-significant. It also contains a number of correct readings not found in any of the MSS so far dealt with, apart from the second hands of O and H. These are as follows: 37 *et* before *disciplina* $MO^2H^2\varsigma$; 38 *nemini* $MO^2H^2RES^2Sg$ Nonius; 41 *tamque pestiferum quam* (which I believe to be correct) $MO^2H^2RSZBeEQ^2$ recc.; *longinquior* (similarly) $MO^2RSZBeE$ recc.; 55 *et* before *studio* $MO^2H^2RETSbLaLb$; 65 *alia* $MO^2RSZBeISgVa$; 68 *ad* after *exspectatis* $MO^2H^2Pa^2G\varsigma$; 75 *saepe profectas* $MO^2GQRTLaPb$. M also has for the first time the probably correct reading in 49 *mori videbamus in studio*, and the attractive *numeranda* in 77. M has few corrections, none of importance.

Within the φ group, P and H share a number of characteristic readings which are not found in M: 3 *ut* (before *Aristo*): *aut* PHL^2D^2; *suis libris*: *l- s-* PH; 4 *sapientiam*: *patientiam* $PHA^2\varsigma$; *difficilem* om. H^1, post *Laeli* P; 15 *seniles*: *similes* $P^1H^1A^2$ (*similes seniles* KO); 17 *multo* om. PH (*multa* BL^1A^1: *multo* L^2A^2); 47 *ergo hoc non desiderare*: *hoc* om. PH^1L^2; 57 *refrigerari*: *-are* PH; *nationes* P^1H for *venationes* (*natationes* VM etc.); 59 *quam* (before *studium*): *quamquam* P^1H^1; *e floribus*: *et fl-* PH^1L^2; *etiam*: *eam* PH^1; *intuentem*: *indu-* P^1H; *eius*: *metus* P^1H^1; 63 *ita* om. P^1H; 65 *ac morositas tamen*: replaced by *cum id ei* *videatis* from 67 in $P^1H^1L^2$ (*c- i- e- v-* inserted after *a- m- t-* in A^2D^2O); 69 *regnaverat* and *vixerat* PHL^2A^2; *tantum enim* PHL^2A^2 (recte *tantum*); *cumque* P^1H^1 for *cuique*; 71 *si sint* PHL^2A^2 for *si sunt*; 72 *minus* P^1H for *munus*; 73 *ni iussu* PHA^2D^2 for *iniussu*; 74 *isque*: *usque* $PHL^2A^2D^2M^2$; 78 *Pythagoram* om. P^1H^1. The following passages should be added, in which Ra and H agree in error: 80 *teneremus*: *tuerentur* $Ra^1H^1L^2A^2K^1$; 81 *plane*: *plene* $RaHA^2SBe$; *sin*: *si* $RaHL^2$ ($?D^2$); 82 *ipse*: *ipso* $RaHL^2D^2$; 84 *ad illum* RaH^1E; 85 *sum immortalis futurus* $RaHL^2E$ for *sumus immortales futuri*; *defetigationem*: *defectionem* $RaHPa^1A^3D^2Q$.

However, H sometimes diverges from the consensus of PM, and in these cases the readings show β influence: some at least of these readings derive from O or a manuscript very closely related to it, as is shown by 10 *cum etate condita gravitas cum aetate condita virtus gravis* OH and 36 *sed non proborum* misplaced after first occurrence of *adulescentium* OH.[90] H is corrected by a second hand which also contains β readings; but H^2 also shares some correct readings with O^2 and with M (cf. above). The contamination in H^1 is not so extensive as to obscure the manuscript's basic affinities with P and M; it is possible that some of the agreements with P may be attributed to the influence of A^2 and O, but a number of them do not occur in A^2 or O and must have been inherited independently from a common ancestor.

The remaining manuscripts used in this edition may conveniently be classed together;[91] as has been said, the

---

[90] Cf. G. S. Vogel, *The Major Manuscripts of Cicero's De Senectute* (Chicago 1939) 46ff. Other apparent β readings in H may be accidental (1 *mihi* om., 64 *facta* for *recta*, cf. *facere* in the same sentence).

[91] Cf. *T. & T.* p. 120: see list of sigla preceding the text of this edition. Note the following changes: Be = B of Simbeck, Wuilleumier and other edd. since Baiter–Halm; Va = v of Simbeck, Wuilleumier, Gemoll; Ad = a of Simb., Wuill., Petschenig (the correct shelfmark is Admont 363, not 383 as given by Petschenig and by editors); Pb = Paris lat. 18420 (not Pb of Dahl).

I have myself examined G Be I Pb Sb Sg T La Lb, Royal 15 a viii and Royal 15 a xx, and microfilms of Q and Et. For readings of E, I depend on three best of the class are R (s. xi or xii), S (s. xii in. according to Munk Olsen, though some editors refer to it as s. xi), and Z (s. xi acc. to Munk Olsen, s. xii in the Marciana catalogue). To these may be added the excerpt in G, here collated for the first time, which dates from the early twelfth century and contains a good text of *Cato* 66–end. There are between twenty and thirty other MSS dating from the twelfth century, which are all of a basically similar textual character. Geographically they divide into a south German group and an Anglo-Norman group, but they cannot be classified stemmatically; clearly sufficient progress had been made towards the establishment of a vulgate text, and sufficient mutual contamination had happened among the previously existing branches of the tradition, to make it virtually impossible to unravel the detailed relationships of these MSS. On the whole they share the characteristic errors of the α side of the tradition, and also a number which are previously found only in parts of α (P, V, M or H or some combination of these). A minority of the twelfth-century MSS show some β influence: this is most obvious in the French MSS Sg and Va (which however also have 'vulgate' features), but is found also in E, the Ciceronian collection of Wibald of Corvey, a hybrid whose origins are difficult to

Baiter–Halm; for Ad, on M. Petschenig, *Wiener Studien* 12 (1890) 321–3; for Mb and Mc, on F. Ramorino, *RFIC* 15 (1887) 247ff. (note that Mb dates from the twelfth century, not the fourteenth as Ramorino says; Mc is said by Munk Olsen to be either twelfth-century or a humanistic imitation; the text of Mc is very close to that of R; cf. Munk Olsen pp. 173 and 179); for Va I depend on W. Gemoll, *Hermes* 20 (1885) 331ff.; for Strozzi 36 on collations kindly made for me by Dr D. R. Shanzer. I have not had access to collations of the following twelfth-century MSS: Berlin, Deutsche Staatsbibliothek, Diez. C. oct. 11 and Diez. C. oct. 12 (Munk Olsen pp. 144–5); Ghent 395 (M. O. p. 186); Heiligenkreuz 228 (M.O. p. 188); Wolfenbüttel, Aug. 51.12 (M.O. p. 315: this MS is referred to by Baiter–Halm and quoted for one reading in §84); Trier 1081 (M.O. p. 288: this is presumably the Trevirensis used by Orelli, Madvig, Otto and other edd.: Otto gives a number of readings from it, which show affinity with E, but no full collation is available); Madrid, Bibl. Nac. 9448 (excerpts only: M.O. p. 221).

work out. Readings first noted in O² and M, which I have suggested may derive from a German tradition originally independent of α or β, reappear in a number of these MSS, but particularly often in R and E (and G for the part of the text it contains). The German, Swiss or Austrian MSS SZBe, together with Ad and I, show a considerable family resemblance within the larger group. Finally, some of these MSS provide us with corrections which occur here for the first time: note 3 *Aristo Ceus* RMc (supposing that this is right); 17 *non facit* Z; *meliora facit* STPbQ; 32 *cui fuerim* RQ²SbPb; 36 *comicos* Q²; 38 *augurium* RZT; 80 *quo diutius* GREQTLaLbAd²S². One correction occurs first in the thirteenth century, 44 *cereo* (see apparatus).

Corruption, contamination and propagation of the vulgate continued through the thirteenth, fourteenth and fifteenth centuries, and although the later medieval and Renaissance tradition has hardly been explored from a historical point of view, enough manuscripts of that period have been collated[92] to show that there is unlikely to be anything of textual value among the rest. The number of such copies extant is in the region of 450, and to collate them all is a task which any editor may happily leave to his successors.

(b) Testimonia to the text in ancient grammarians, etc.

The evidence of the manuscripts is supplemented by that provided by quotations in the ancient grammarians and other authors: more than fifty in Nonius, a dozen in Charisius, and one each in Lactantius, Priscian and the scholiast on Juvenal (this disregards the occasional more or less inaccurate quotation in other authors: such quotations,

---

[92] Examples may be found in Dahl, *Handschriftenkunde*; Ramorino, article cited in previous note; A. D. Michnay, *N. Jb. Kl. Phil.* Suppl. 2.1 (1883) 138ff.; G. R. Throop, *CPhil* 3 (1908) 285ff.; and in the older editions.

which throw no light on the text, are merely noted in the commentary). It is convenient to list all these testimonia here; their significant textual variations are recorded in the apparatus.[93]

Cato section	Nonius (pages of Mercier)	
2	347 (molle)	omnes absterserit – senectutem
4	315 (grave)	quod numquam – senserim
5	347 (molle)	quod ferundum – sapienti
10	301 (exultare)	et Hannibalem – molliebat
	347 (molle)	et Hannibalem – molliebat
25	363 (prodere)	non accipere – prodere
26	283 (ducere)	sic adulescentes – ducuntur
	346 (moliri)	iners non sit – moliens
28	383 (remittere)	sed tamen – remissus
	343 (mitis)	facitque persaepe ipsa [*sic*] – oratio
31	322 (insolens)	nec erat – loquax
33	371 (praestare)	ne vos – praestantior
	408 (tempestas [*sic*])	cursus est – data
	349 (maturum)	iam constantis – maturitas
34	246 (adduci)	nullo imbri – operto sit
	395 (siccum)	nullo imbri – corporis siccitatem [*sic*]
36	33 (ignavum)	quae vitia – somniculosae senectutis
37	329 (intendere)	intentum – succumbebat senectuti
38	105 (emancipatum)	ita enim – dominatur
	91 (commemorare)	Pythagoreorumque – vesperi
40	309 (facinus)	nullum denique – impelleret
42	34 (praestringere)	voluptas rationi – commercium
45	42 (convivium)	bene enim – nominaverunt
	193 (accubitionem)	bene enim – haberet
46	236 (aequales)	ego vero – vestra etiam aetate
	378 (restare)	nec cum – aetate
	372 (producere)	conviviumque – producimus

[93] On the Nonian citations, see principally S. S. Ingallina, *Studi Noniani* II (Genoa 1972) 67ff., on whom I depend for the readings of the MSS of Nonius; also N. Terzaghi, *Boll. Accad. Lincei*, N.S. Fasc. 7 (Rome 1959); P. Venini, *Rend. Ist. Lomb.* 93 (1959) 382ff.; S. Timpanaro, reviewing Ingallina, *Maia* 26 (1974) 343.

48	2	(bona aetas)	quod si – fruitur rebus
	417	(ultimum)	magis delectatur – ultima
	367	(propter)	sic adulescentia – senectus procul aspiciens [*sic*]
51	401	(subigere)	sed etiam – excepit
	42	(occatio)	sparsum – nominata est
	225	(spica)	culmoque – ordine structas [*sic*]
52	227	(satio)	quid – commemorem
	193	(acinus)	quae ex – vinaceo
54	270	(conserere) (in MSS misplaced under *constituere*)	nec consitiones (*constitiones* L², *constitions* L¹, *constitutiones* cett. codd. Nonii) – insitiones (*institutiones* codd.)
55	419	(vindicare)	et senectus – vindicare
56	488	(cultio)	num igitur – oblectabant
	170	(succidia)	iam hortum – vocant [*sic*]⁹⁴
57	482	(apricatio)	ubi enim – vel igni
	76	(adlectat)	ad quem – allectat senectus
	321	(invitare)	ad quem – allectat senectus
59	400	(subigere)	cum autem – atque puram
65	433	(morosa)	at sunt – senes
	436	(contemnere, despicere)	contemni – illudi
	30	(dirum)	intelligi potest – comitas
	100	(diritas)	in altero diritas [*sic*]
67	294	(explorare)	quis est tam – esse victurum
	315	(grave)	facilius – curantur
	409	(triste)	facilius – curantur
70	244	(accommodare)	ceterum et [*sic*] tempora – accommodata sunt
72	42	(coagmenta [*sic*])	vivendi est finis – dissolvit
78	41	(prudentia)	quid multa – prudentia
83	276	(cognoscere)	neque vero – conscripsi
	165	(repuerascere)	et si quis deus – vagiam
84	524	(turba)	cum in illum – discedam
	82	(conluvio)	cum ex hac – discedam

⁹⁴ Nonius quotes this as an example of *succidia* 'successio necessaria' (!), to be distinguished from *succidia* 'laridum': for the real explanation see note ad loc.

Cato section	Charisius (pages of Keil)	
2	206 (modice)	etsi te – certo scio
3	198 (eruditius)	qui si – libris
8	208 (nequaquam)	est istud quidem Laeli, sed nequaquam tibi concedendum fuit [*sic*]
11	224 (viritim)	Spurio Carvilio C. Flaminio tribuno – dividenti (omitting *collega quiescente*)
22	215 (proxime)	Sophocles – fecit: quem cum iudices a re familiari ut desipientem removissent, filiis eius arguentibus, cum senex Οἰδίπουν ἐπὶ Κολωνῷ quam proxime scripserat recitasset, liberatus est (so Keil: *tum senex ⟨dicitur⟩ . . . recitasse e⟨t⟩liberatus est* Barwick)
25	224 (vitiosius)	Caecilius vitiosius illud ait de senectute [*sic*]
34	215 (pedibus)	ingressus iter pedibus
39	198 (effrenate)	avidae libidines – incitarentur
42	208 (neutiquam)	mihi vero – libido
46	221 (tempestive C, -ius N)	tempestivis (-ive C, -ius N) quoque conviviis delector propter sermonis delectationem
51	215 (proxime)	et mihi – accedere
57	224 (vicissim)	vicissim – refrigerari

Cato section		
40	Lact. *Inst. Div.* 6.20.4–5	stupra vero – posse consistere[95]

[95] Cf. R. M. Ogilvie, *The Library of Lactantius* (Oxford 1978) 68. It is a curious fact that our earliest extant witness to any part of the text of the *Cato* is MS B of Lactantius (Bononiensis 701, s. vi–vii). Unfortunately, Lact. seems to have quoted the passage from memory, and his text is worse than that of the MS paradosis; nor does the passage in question contain any serious textual problems such as an independent witness would have helped to solve.

| 52 | Prisc., *Gramm. Ltd.*, ed. Keil, II, p. 242 (requietem) | ut meae – noscatis |
| 55 | Schol. Juv. 11.78 | Curio ad focum – imperare. |

There is no case in which the above testimonia preserve a correct reading unknown to our MSS. However, they support a minority of the MSS in a correct or highly plausible reading in a number of places: 2 *certo* Char.; 36 *ignavae* Non.; 38 *nemini emancipata* Non.; 51 *erecta* Non.; 52 *requietem* Prisc.; *e(x) fici* Non.; 59 *derectos* Non.; 67 *est tam* Non. On 28, where the manuscripts of both Cicero and Nonius vary between *compta* and *cocta*, see Commentary.

(c) The present text and apparatus

The construction of an apparatus from the considerable amount of evidence described above entails rigorous selectivity, if the result is not to prove overloaded and unusable. Following the usual practice, I have in the first place omitted *lectiones singulares*, on the calculation that anyone who might be interested in them will be in a position to get them from the MSS themselves. Orthographical variants have been similarly omitted, except in a few special instances which are discussed below. Readings that serve only to classify MSS, but which do not contribute significantly to the constitution of the text, are cited above in the discussion of the MSS, but not repeated in the apparatus.

The eleven primary manuscripts noted above, PVBLADMHRSZ, are cited in all cases: where some only are cited with variants, it may be assumed that the others preserve the correct reading. The collective sigla ω, α, β, φ and λ imply exact agreement, barring non-significant orthographical variations; however, the siglum ς denotes only a general consensus of RSZ and later MSS, and is not to be taken to imply exact agreement between MSS other than R, S and Z. Where there is a division between α and β, and the ς MSS are not cited, it may be assumed that they side with α. The second hands of PVLAD are only cited occasionally, their affinities being on the whole predictable, and the readings of hybrid MSS (K, O, Pa–Vi, E) are only cited where their reading seems to be of interest. Ra is cited in the absence of P in §78–end. On the whole, later and worse MSS tend to appear mostly when they preserve the truth or something like it: this should not on any account mislead the reader into thinking them better than they are. The abbreviation *recc.* denotes MSS later than the twelfth century.

It has been necessary also to restrict the number of editorial and scholarly conjectures recorded in the apparatus. I have on the whole included only those with some claim to be thought right. In cases where the MSS known to me do not offer a correct reading, I have noted the earliest occurrence (or occurrences) of the correction in printed editions that I have consulted. However, I have not done any extensive research on the early printed editions, any more than on the Renaissance MS tradition. The older editions that I have found most useful are those of C. Sweynheym and A. Pannartz (1469, the first complete edition of the philosophical works of Cicero), A. Moretus (1480), J. de Breda (*c.* 1490), A. Minutianus (1498, the *editio princeps* of Cicero's complete works), P. Victorius, A. and P. Manutius, D. Lambinus, J. Gruterus, and J. Graevius; also the notes of Erasmus, Langius and Gulielmius.

In the matter of orthography, I have aimed at consistency and ease of reading above all: I do not believe that any service is done to readers by departing from the generally accepted spelling of Latin, unless there is a special reason. There is such a reason in a small number of cases in the text. The MSS in various places present old-fashioned spellings, particularly of the gerundive (*ferundus* for *ferendus*, etc.), and these have been thought to represent a deliberate attempt to Cicero's part to recall the language of Cato's generation: this would fit in with the various mild archaisms in the language itself, discussed above (p. 22). This is not, indeed, absolutely certain, and other explanations are possible. Cicero may simply have used these spellings in some words as part of his normal usage, without any intention of archaising; there is not really enough evidence to decide precisely how old-fashioned, if at all, *ferundus* would have seemed to Cicero's readers. It is alternatively possible that the spellings are not Cicero's at all, but were inserted at a late stage in the transmission by medieval correctors with a taste for archaism: there certainly were such, and traces of their work can be seen in other texts.[96] Nevertheless, there is still a chance that the spellings were deliberate on Cicero's part and intended to recall old-fashioned usage. In view of this, I have retained these spellings in the text where the MSS seemed to warrant it: e.g. 5 *ferundum*, 6 *ingrediundum*, 9 *ecferunt*, 39 *ecfrenate*. It must however be realised that I make no consistent attempt to restore the actual spellings used by Cicero in general, with or without the assumption that he was archaising in this work. It is known from ancient evidence that Cicero, even when not archaising, wrote *caussa* and *maiior*, but only an eccentric editor would restore those spellings throughout; and if Cicero really was imitating the spelling of Cato's generation, he should have written not only *ferundum* etc. but *deicere* (for *dicere*), *vortere* and so on.

Similarly, I have dealt with abbreviations in the way that I hope will serve the reader's convenience, writing out *praenomina* in full where the abbreviated form conceals an ambiguity of case or a rhythmical clausula.[97] I have entirely

---

[96] Cf. M. Winterbottom, *Problems in Quintilian* (*BICS* Suppl. 25, 1970) 56.

[97] The MSS are very inconsistent over the use of abbreviations for *praenomina*, magistracies (cos., tr. pl.), numerals, and *sigla personarum* in the dialogue sections, §§4–8. Occasionally errors or variants in these matters are of use in classifying MSS, but more often they are not of any significance, and it seemed to me that they could well be omitted from the apparatus in most cases. On the *sigla personarum* (which I have replaced by the full names of Cato, Scipio and Laelius), see J. Andrieu, *Le Dialogue antique, structure et présentation*, Coll. d'études latines, série scientifique 29 (Paris 1954) 299 and 312–13.

reconsidered the punctuation of the text in the light of the sense and colometry of each passage, not in an attempt to reconstruct Cicero's punctuation, but in order to reflect as nearly as possible without confusion the actual divisions that should be made in reading aloud. Some compromise with modern conventions is inevitable, e.g. in the separation of vocatives by commas (a modern reader would not tolerate *aptissima omnino sunt Scipio et Laeli arma senectutis*, for example); but the 'syntactical' punctuation often used by modern editors simply does not fit Latin. We should not have to be confused by such things as *ego Q. Maximum, eum, qui Tarentum recepit, senem adulescens ita dilexi* (it does not mean 'the old man who recaptured Tarentum'), or *multa in vestro collegio praeclara, sed hoc, de quo agimus, in primis quod, ut quisque aetate antecedit* . . . (the articulation is *multa . . . praeclara, sed hoc de quo agimus in primis, quod ut quisque aetate antecedit* . . .).

In the division of the text into chapters and sections I have followed the edition of Orelli–Baiter–Halm, which seems mostly to be followed by later editors, though there are some minor divergences; the smaller divisions of the text, denoted by Arabic numerals and used for references, are in any case quite arbitrary, as in all of Cicero, but it is too late to think of changing them in favour of a system that reflects the sense more closely.

TEXT

SIGLA

P   Parisinus lat. 6332, s. ix 2/3
V   Leidensis Voss. Lat. O. 79, s. ix ex.
B   Bruxellensis 9591, s. ix
L   Leidensis Voss. Lat. F. 12β, s. ix med.
A   Parisinus n.a. lat. 454 (olim Ashburnhamensis), s. ix 2/3
D   Vaticanus Reg. lat. 1587, s. ix
K   Vaticanus Reg. lat. 1762, s. ix (Excerpta Hadoardi)
O   Oxoniensis, D'Orville 77, s. x vel xi in.
M   Laurentianus 50.45, s. x vel xi
Ha   Harleianus 2716 fol. 77 (fragmentum), s. x ex.
Hb   eiusdem fol. 74v (fragmentum)
Pa   Parisinus lat. 5752, s. x–xi
Vi   Parisinus lat. 14699 (Victorinus), s. xi
Ra   Vaticanus Reg. lat. 1414, s. xi
H   Harleianus 2682, s. xi
R   Turicensis Rhenaug. 127, s. xi vel xii
S   Monacensis 15964 (Salisburgensis), s. xii in.
G   Londiniensis Egertonianus 654 (excerptum), s. xii in.
Z   Marcianus Lat. xiv, 222 (4007), s. xi vel xii

Codd. saec. xii
Be   Monacensis 4611 (Benedictoburanus)

Q   Turicensis Rhenaug. 126
E   Berolinensis lat. fol. 252 (Erfurtensis)
Ad   Admontensis 363
Mb   Laurentianus 45.2
Mc   Laurentianus 76.31
Va   Leidensis Voss. Lat. F. 104
Sg   Parisinus lat. 13340 (Sangermanensis)
I   Monacensis 7809 (Indersdorfensis)
T   Cantabrigiensis, Coll. Trinitatis O. 8. 6 (1381)
Sb   Parisinus lat. 16588 (Sorbonnensis)

Recentiores
La   Londiniensis, Lambeth Palace 425, prima pars (s. xii–xiii)
Lb   eiusdem secunda pars (s. xii–xiii)
Et   Etonensis 90 (s. xii–xiii)
Pb   Parisinus lat. 18420 (s. xii–xiii)
St   Laurentianus Strozzianus 36 (s. xii vel xiii)

Ω   archetypus
ω   PVHMBLAD
α   PVHM et ç nisi aliter notatur
β   BLAD
φ   PHM
λ   LAD
ç   RSZ et codd. s. xii vel recc. nonnulli vel plurimi

M. TVLLI CICERONIS
CATO MAIOR DE SENECTVTE

1 1   'O Tite, si quid ego adiuero, curamve levasso
quae nunc te coquit et versat in pectore fixa,
ecquid erit praemi?' –

licet enim mihi versibus eisdem adfari te, Attice, quibus
adfatur Flamininum   5

   'ille vir haud magna cum re, sed plenus fidei';

quamquam certo scio non ut Flamininum

   'sollicitari te Tite sic noctesque diesque',

novi enim moderationem animi tui et aequitatem, teque non
cognomen solum Athenis deportasse, sed humanitatem et 10
prudentiam intellego. et tamen te suspicor eisdem rebus
quibus me ipsum interdum gravius commoveri, quarum
consolatio et maior est et in aliud tempus differenda; nunc
autem mihi est visum de senectute aliquid ad te conscribere.
2 hoc enim onere, quod mihi commune tecum est, aut iam
urgentis aut certe adventantis senectutis, et te et me etiam
ipsum levari volo, etsi te quidem id modice ac sapienter, sicut
omnia, et ferre et laturum esse certo scio; sed mihi cum de
senectute vellem aliquid scribere, tu occurrebas dignus eo 5
munere quo uterque nostrum communiter uteretur. mihi

De inscriptione v. adn.   **1** 1 ego: te *PD²*   adiuero: adiuro *P²*: adiuto
V¹M²ʂ codd. KR Donati ad Ter. Phorm. 34: adiuvo te *H*   levasso: levavero
BL: -asero *A¹D¹*: -abo *H*   2 *post* fixa *add.* et qua deprimeris
V²A²ViSZBeQ recc.   3 praemi: pretii *V¹HSZBeQ recc.*   4 mihi *om.*
β*H*   9–10 non cognomen *O²RQE edd. vett.*: c- n- ω   14 mihi est
visum: v- e- m- *P*: m- v- e- *MQ*   conscribere: scribere *BHViSZBe
recc.*   **2** 1 enim: autem *MZ*   2 et te et me etiam: et te et me
PHV²RSZBe: et temet *V¹*   4 certo *BLP²A²D²RZ Charis.*: certe *cett.*

quidem ita iucunda huius libri confectio fuit ut non modo
omnes absterserit senectutis molestias, sed effecerit mollem
etiam et iucundam senectutem. numquam igitur digne satis
laudari philosophia poterit, cui qui pareat omne tempus 10
3 aetatis sine molestia possit degere. sed de ceteris et diximus
multa et saepe dicemus: hunc librum ad te de senectute
misimus. omnem autem sermonem tribuimus non Tithono, ut
Aristo Ceus – parum enim esset auctoritatis in fabula – sed
Marco Catoni seni, quo maiorem auctoritatem haberet 5
oratio; apud quem Laelium et Scipionem facimus admirantes
quod is tam facile senectutem ferat, eisque eum responden-
tem. qui si eruditius videbitur disputare, quam consuevit ipse
in suis libris, attribuito litteris Graecis, quarum constat eum
perstudiosum fuisse in senectute. sed quid opus est plura? iam 10
enim ipsius Catonis sermo explicabit nostram omnem de
senectute sententiam.

II 4 SCIPIO. Saepenumero admirari soleo cum hoc Gaio Laelio,
cum ceterarum rerum tuam excellentem, Marce Cato,
perfectamque sapientiam, tum vel maxime quod numquam
tibi senectutem gravem esse senserim: quae plerisque senibus
sic odiosa est ut onus se Aetna gravius dicant sustinere. 5
CATO. Rem haud sane difficilem, Scipio et Laeli, admirari
videmini; quibus enim nihil est in ipsis opis ad bene beateque
vivendum, eis omnis aetas gravis est; qui autem omnia bona a
se ipsi petunt, eis nihil malum potest videri quod naturae
necessitas adferat. quo in genere est in primis senectus; quam 10
ut adipiscantur omnes optant, eandem accusant adeptam –
tanta est stultitiae inconstantia atque perversitas. obrepere

9–10 numquam . . . laudari: n- l- i- s- d- *P¹*: n- i- l- s- d- *P²*: n- i- s- l- d- ς: n-
etiam s- l- d- *M*   10 pareat: paret *B*: parat *L¹A¹* (*in D¹ deest*)   **3 4**
Aristo Ceus *RMc edd.* (Cius *Nauck, Reid*): A- Cheus *SbLaLbSt recc. alii*:
Aristoteus *recc. alii*: Aristoteles *VViSZAd* (-thot- *Va*): Aristotiles *BeIT*:
Aristoles *M*: Aristo *PHL²D²Q* (aut *pro* ut *PHL²D²Q¹*): Aristo Chius β*OE*:
v. adn. et App. 2   9 attribuito: id tribuito *L¹*: id tribulato *B*: id tribuitur
A¹D¹   **4** 1 C(aio) φς: *om. Vβ*   3 sapientiam: patientiam
PHL²A²SZBe   6 difficilem *om. H¹*: *post* Laeli *PRSZBe*   9 malum
potest: potest malum *PRSZBe*: mali potest *KOQE*   11 adeptam α:
adepti β*KOE*   12 stultitiae: stultitia *V¹O²RQ*

aiunt eam citius quam putavissent: primum quis coegit eos falsum putare? qui enim citius adulescentiae senectus quam pueritiae adulescentia obrepit? deinde qui minus gravis esset 15 eis senectus si octingentesimum annum agerent, quam si octogesimum? praeterita enim aetas quamvis longa, cum effluxisset, nulla consolatione permulcere posset stultam 5 senectutem. quocirca si sapientiam meam admirari soletis (quae utinam digna esset opinione vestra nostroque cognomine!), in hoc sumus sapientes, quod naturam, optimam ducem, tamquam deum sequimur eique paremus. a qua non veri simile est, cum ceterae partes aetatis bene 5 descriptae sint, extremum actum tamquam ab inerti poeta esse neglectum; sed tamen necesse fuit esse aliquid extremum, et tamquam in arborum bacis terraeque fructibus, maturitate tempestiva quasi vietum et caducum; quod ferundum est molliter sapienti. quid est enim aliud Gigantum modo bellare 10 cum dis, nisi naturae repugnare?

6 LAELIUS. Atqui, Cato, gratissimum nobis (ut etiam pro Scipione pollicear) feceris, si quoniam speramus – volumus quidem certe senes fieri, multo ante a te didicerimus quibus facillime rationibus ingravescentem aetatem ferre possimus. CATO. Faciam vero, Laeli, praesertim si utrique vestrum, ut 5 dicis, gratum futurum est.
LAELIUS. Volumus sane nisi molestum est, Cato, tamquam longam aliquam viam confeceris, quam nobis quoque ingrediundum sit, istuc quo pervenisti videre quale sit.

III 7 CATO. Faciam ut potero, Laeli; saepe enim interfui querelis aequalium meorum – pares autem vetere proverbio cum paribus facillime congregantur. quae Gaius Salinator, quae Spurius Albinus, homines consulares nostri fere aequales, deplorare solebant! – tum quod voluptatibus carerent, sine 5

---

16 quam si β (quasi L^1A^1): quam α   18 consolatione $HQ^1S^2EIMc^2$: consolatio *cett.*   **5** 6 descriptae φBL^2ς: discr- λV 8 fructibus: frugibus O^2RQ 9 vietum: vetum λ: vetiva B: vigetum VL^2SZBe *recc.* ferundum *sic scribunt* PVS, *codd.* LGen.G Non. *p. 347.3:* -andum B: -endum *cett., codd.* EB *Nonii: v. Introd. p. 50*   **6** 3 certe *om.* HMQ 8 quam: qua HSQ *edd. vett.*   9 ingrediundum *sic scribunt* P^1β$RSZBeI$

quibus vitam nullam putarent, tum quod spernerentur ab eis
a quibus essent coli soliti. qui mihi non id videbantur accusare
quod esset accusandum; nam si id culpa senectutis accideret,
eadem mihi usu venirent, reliquisque omnibus maioribus
natu; quorum ego multorum cognovi senectutem sine 10
querela, qui se et libidinum vinculis laxatos esse non moleste
ferrent, nec a suis despicerentur. sed omnium istiusmodi
querelarum in moribus est culpa, non in aetate; moderati
enim et nec difficiles nec inhumani senes tolerabilem
senectutem agunt, importunitas autem et inhumanitas omni 15
aetati molesta est.

8 LAELIUS. Est ut dicis, Cato; sed fortasse dixerit quispiam,
tibi propter opes et copias et dignitatem tuam tolerabiliorem
senectutem videri, id autem non posse multis contingere.
CATO. Est istuc quidem, Laeli, aliquid, sed nequaquam in
isto sunt omnia; ut Themistocles fertur Seriphio cuidam in 5
iurgio respondisse, cum ille dixisset non eum sua sed patriae
gloria splendorem adsecutum, 'nec hercule' inquit 'si ego
Seriphius essem, nec tu si Atheniensis esses clarus umquam
fuisses.' quod eodem modo de senectute dici potest: nec enim
in summa inopia levis esse senectus potest ne sapienti quidem, 10
nec insipienti etiam in summa copia non gravis.

9 Aptissima omnino sunt, Scipio et Laeli, arma senectutis
artes exercitationesque virtutum; quae in omni aetate cultae,
cum diu multumque vixeris mirificos ecferunt fructus; non
solum quia numquam deserunt ne extremo quidem tempore
aetatis (quamquam id quidem maximum est), verum etiam 5
quia conscientia bene actae vitae multorumque benefa-
IV 10 ctorum recordatio iucundissima est. ego Quintum Maximum, eum qui Tarentum recepit, senem adulescens ita dilexi
ut aequalem; erat enim in illo viro comitate condita gravitas,

---

7 9 usu venirent *Otto, recc. aliquot secutus, cf. eius Exc. II, pp. 224–30*: usu
evenirent Ω   16 aetati: aetate *RBe edd. vett., Wuilleumier*   **8** 2 tuam
om. V¹L¹   4 istuc *PMARSZBeI*: istud *BLDVHQ Charis.*   5 sunt *om.*
φϛ   8 *post* essem *add.* ignobilis φL²O²Viϛ   esses αBϛ: *om.* λSg
edd.   10 ne sapienti *PV²MRSZ¹BeI*: nec s- *cett.*   **9** 3 ecferunt *sic
scribunt A²M*: ecfecerunt *P¹*: hec ferunt *V*: efferunt *cett.*

nec senectus mores mutaverat; quamquam eum colere coepi
non admodum grandem natu, sed tamen iam aetate 5
provectum. anno enim post consul primum fuerat quam ego
natus sum; cumque eo quartum consule adulescentulus miles
ad Capuam profectus sum, quintoque anno post ad
Tarentum. quaestor deinde quadriennio post factus sum,
quem magistratum gessi consulibus Tuditano et Cethego, 10
cum quidem ille admodum senex suasor legis Cinciae de donis
et muneribus fuit. hic et bella gerebat ut adulescens cum plane
grandis esset, et Hannibalem iuveniliter exsultantem
patientia sua molliebat; de quo praeclare familiaris noster
Ennius: 15

> 'unus homo nobis cunctando restituit rem,
> non enim rumores ponebat ante salutem:
> ergo postque magisque viri nunc gloria claret.'

11 Tarentum vero qua vigilantia, quo consilio recepit! cum
quidem me audiente Salinatori (qui amisso oppido fuerat in
arce) glorianti atque ita dicenti, 'mea opera, Quinte Fabi,
Tarentum recepisti', 'certe,' inquit ridens, 'nam nisi tu
amisisses, numquam recepissem.' nec vero in armis 5
praestantior quam in toga; qui consul iterum, Spurio Carvilio
collega quiescente, Gaio Flaminio tribuno plebis quoad
potuit restitit, agrum Picentem et Gallicum viritim contra
senatus auctoritatem dividenti, augurque cum esset dicere
ausus est, optimis auspiciis ea geri quae pro rei publicae salute 10
gererentur, quae contra rem publicam ferrentur contra
12 auspicia ferri. multa in eo viro praeclara cognovi, sed nihil

---

10 7 eo *VHM*ς: ego *P*β   quartum *P¹R²*: quarto *cett.*   9 quaestor ...
quem *Pighius, edd.*: quaestor. deinde aedilis. quadriennio post factus sum
praetor. quem α*L²D²A³*: quaestor. quē *BA¹*: quaestor. quō *A²*: quaestor.
q̄m *L¹D¹*: quaestorque *Mommsen, Wuilleumier*   16 homo *P²D²L²S²I*:
homo qui *P¹MS¹Be*: qui *cett.* (*cf. Verg. Aen. 6.846*)   17 non enim Ω
(Ñenim *P*): noenum *Lachmann* (*Skutsch in textu Ennii, Ciceronem tamen
scripsisse* non enim *arbitratur*)   ponebat: -ant *P¹VM*   **11** 2 fuerat:
fugerat *PV²L²A²D²OVi*ς   3 arce: arcem *D²S²Va*   Q(uinte) *om.* β
4 tu: tu hic *L¹A¹*: tu hoc *D*: tu non *M*: *om. B*   **12** 1 nihil β: nihil est α

admirabilius quam quomodo ille mortem fili tulit, clari viri et
consularis; est in manibus laudatio, quam cum legimus, quem
philosophum non contemnimus? nec vero ille in luce modo
atque in oculis civium magnus, sed intus domique 5
praestantior: qui sermo, quae praecepta, quanta notitia
antiquitatis, scientia iuris augurii! multae etiam ut in homine
Romano litterae; omnia memoria tenebat, non domestica
solum sed etiam externa. cuius sermone ita cupide fruebar,
quasi iam divinarem, id quod evenit, illo exstincto fore unde 10
discerem neminem.

V 13   Quorsum igitur haec tam multa de Maximo? quia profecto
videtis, nefas esse dictu miseram fuisse talem senectutem. nec
tamen omnes possunt esse Scipiones aut Maximi, ut urbium
expugnationes, ut pedestres navalesque pugnas, ut bella a se
gesta, ut triumphos recordentur; est etiam quiete et pure 5
atque eleganter actae aetatis placida ac lenis senectus, qualem
accepimus Platonis, qui uno et octogesimo anno scribens
est mortuus; qualem Isocratis, qui eum librum qui
Panathenaicus inscribitur quarto et nonagesimo anno
scripsisse se dicit, vixitque quinquennium postea; cuius 10
magister Leontinus Gorgias centum et septem complevit
annos, neque umquam in suo studio atque opere cessavit. qui
cum ex eo quaereretur, cur tam diu vellet esse in vita, 'nihil
habeo' inquit 'quod accusem senectutem.' praeclarum
14   responsum et docto homine dignum! sua enim vitia insipientes
et suam culpam in senectutem conferunt. quod non faciebat is
cuius modo mentionem feci Ennius:

       'sicuti fortis equus, spatio qui saepe supremo
          vicit Olympia, nunc senio confectus quiescit' –   5

equi fortis et victoris senectuti comparat suam. quem quidem

---

2 fil(i)i *VH¹Q*: M(arci) filii *cett.*   9 externa *Meissner*: externa bella
Ω   fruebar: fruebar tunc *H²O²RSg* (t- f- *Q*): perfruebar *M*: perf- tunc
SZBe   **13** 1 quorsum *BL²ViS²Q* (cursum λ): quorsus α   4 navales-
que: navalesve φʂ   8 Isocratis *edd.* (*iam Sweynheym–Pannartz*): socratis Ω
(-es *LA¹*)   9 quarto et nonagesimo: quarto non- *PMʂ*: non- quarto
HQ   10 se dicit β*P²M*: se dicitur *P¹A²*: dicitur *VHOʂ*   **14** 3 feci
VD²Mʂ: fecit *PH*β (facit *L¹*)   Ennius *om. S¹ZBe*

probe meminisse potestis; anno enim undevicesimo post eius
mortem hi consules, T. Flamininus et M'. Acilius, facti sunt;
ille autem Caepione et Philippo iterum consulibus mortuus
est, cum ego quinque et sexaginta annos natus legem 10
Voconiam magna voce et bonis lateribus suasi. sed annos
septuaginta natus, tot enim vixit Ennius, ita ferebat duo quae
maxima putantur onera, paupertatem et senectutem, ut eis
paene delectari videretur.

15   Etenim cum complector animo, quattuor reperio causas
cur senectus misera videatur: unam quod avocet a rebus
gerendis, alteram quod corpus faciat infirmius, tertiam quod
privet fere omnibus voluptatibus, quartam quod haud procul
absit a morte. earum, si placet, causarum quanta quamque sit 5
iusta unaquaeque videamus.

VI   A rebus gerendis senectus abstrahit. quibus? an eis quae
iuventute geruntur et viribus? nullaene igitur res sunt seniles,
quae vel infirmis corporibus, animo tamen administrentur?
nihil ergo agebat Quintus Maximus, nihil Lucius Paulus 10
pater tuus, socer optimi viri fili mei? ceteri senes, Fabricii
Curii Coruncanii, cum rem publicam consilio et auctoritate
16 defendebant, nihil agebant? ad Appi Claudi senectutem
accedebat etiam ut caecus esset; tamen is cum sententia
senatus inclinaret ad pacem cum Pyrrho foedusque
faciendum, non dubitavit dicere illa quae versibus persecutus
est Ennius,   5

     'quo vobis mentes, rectae quae stare solebant
     antehac, dementes sese flexere viai? . . .'

7 anno enim undevicesimo *L²D²*: a- e- vigesimo *HEQ*: annum enim
undevicesimum *cett.* (annum enim ante vicesimum *SBe*)   8 M(anius)
om. VL¹D¹   9 consulibus *HQ*: consule *cett.*   11 suasi. Sed *Forchhammer*: suasisset *P¹H¹*: suassimsem *B*: suasissem *cett.* (-si- *altera manu V*):
suasissem. Sed *iam Manutius*   15 4 fere omnibus: o- f- *PMO²ViE*   8
iuventute: in iuv- *VHEQ*   10 Quintus: aut λ *om. B*   L(ucius)
PL²A²RSZBeI: *om. cett.*   16 7 dementes: dementi *O²RS²QE recc.*
sese flexere: se flexere *V²HS²BeQI recc.*: tendunt se flectere *recc. alii*   viai
Lambinus: via ω: ruina *Qrecc.*: vie *vel* vite *recc. alii*: vietae *Scaliger, probat
Skutsch*

ceteraque gravissime; notum enim vobis carmen est, et tamen
ipsius Appi exstat oratio. atque haec ille egit septimo decimo
anno post alterum consulatum, cum inter duos consulatus 10
anni decem interfuissent, censorque ante superiorem
consulatum fuisset; ex quo intellegitur, Pyrrhi bello eum
17 grandem sane fuisse; et tamen sic a patribus accepimus. nihil
igitur adferunt qui in re gerenda versari senectutem negant,
similesque sunt ut si qui gubernatorem in navigando nihil
agere dicant, cum alii malos scandant, alii per foros cursent,
alii sentinam exhauriant, ille autem clavum tenens quietus 5
sedeat in puppi. non facit ea quae iuvenes; at vero multo
maiora et meliora facit. non viribus aut velocitate aut
celeritate corporum res magnae geruntur, sed consilio
auctoritate sententia; quibus non modo non orbari, sed etiam
18 augeri senectus solet. nisi forte ego vobis, qui et miles et
tribunus et legatus et consul versatus sum in vario genere
bellorum, cessare nunc videor cum bella non gero: at senatui
quae sint gerenda praescribo et quomodo; Carthagini male
iam diu cogitanti bellum multo ante denuntio; de qua vereri 5
non ante desinam, quam illam exscissam esse cognovero.
19 quam palmam utinam di immortales, Scipio, tibi reservent,

---

9 App(i)i *om. BH¹Q*   9–10 septimo decimo anno *HQS²R² Ambros. D13*
(VII *et* X anno *St*): septem decim annos *vel* septem decem annos *cett.*:
septendecim annis *Erasmus*   12 bello eum *coni. Simbeck, in textum recepit
Wuilleumier*: bellum *PHL²A²Q*: bello *cett.*   13 grandem: grande *PHA²*
(?*M*)   **17** 3 similesque sunt *om. SZBeAdI*   ut si qui: ut his qui λ: in
his qui *B*   4 dicant β*RSQE*: dicunt α   6 non facit *Z* (*scr.* non fac̄),
Manutius: non faciat *cett.*   7 facit *SQTPb*: faciat *cett.*   velocitate:
velocitatibus φς   **18** 4 quomodo; Carthagini *distinxit Gruterus (post
Carthagini interpunctionem habent PMZ)*   4–5 quomodo ... denuntio *sic
habent O²SbEt*: quomodo ... cogitanti multum ante denuntio (*omisso
bellum) R*: quomodo ... bellum inferatur multo ante den- *HQS²E recc.,
Victorius, Manutius (rasuram unius litterae vel interpunctionis post* Carthagini
habet H: post multo *glossema* tpr *sc.* tempore *add. Q*): quomodo Carthagini
resistendum sit cui male ... denuntio *I recc.*: quomodo ... cogitanti
resistatur bellum ... denuntio *MbMc*: quomodo Carthagini cui male ...
denuntio *cett.*   *pro* cui *alii alia tentaverunt, ut cum Anz, quidem Schiche:
fort.* enim?   6 exscissam *Lambinus* (excissam *BVi*: exscisam *L¹*): excisam
cett.

ut avi reliquias persequare! cuius a morte tertius hic et
tricesimus annus est, sed memoriam illius viri omnes excipient
anni consequentes; anno ante me censorem mortuus est,
novem annis post meum consulatum cum consul iterum me 5
consule creatus esset; num igitur si ad centesimum annum
vixisset, senectutis eum suae paeniteret? nec enim excursione
nec saltu nec eminus hastis aut comminus gladiis uteretur, sed
consilio ratione sententia; quae nisi essent in senibus, non
summum consilium maiores nostri appellassent senatum. 10
20 apud Lacedaemonios quidem ei qui amplissimum
magistratum gerunt, ut sunt sic etiam nominantur senes.
quodsi legere aut audire voletis externa, maximas res publicas
ab adulescentibus labefactatas, a senibus sustentatas et
restitutas reperietis. 5

'cedo qui vestram rem publicam tantam amisistis tam cito?' –

sic enim percontantur, ut est in Naevi poetae Ludo:
respondentur et alia et hoc in primis,

    'proveniebant oratores novi, stulti adulescentuli.'

temeritas est videlicet florentis aetatis, prudentia senescentis. 10
II 21   At memoria minuitur. – credo, nisi eam exerceas, aut etiam
si sis natura tardior. Themistocles omnium civium perceperat
nomina: num igitur censetis eum, cum aetate processisset, qui
Aristides esset Lysimachum salutare solitum? equidem non
modo eos novi qui sunt, sed eorum patres etiam et avos; nec 5
sepulcra legens vereor quod aiunt ne memoriam perdam; eis
enim ipsis legendis in memoriam redeo mortuorum. nec vero

19 2 tertius: quartus *Pighius*: quintus *Ursinus (ex cod.; item cod. Contareni)*:
sextus *Manutius*: *v. App. 3*   5 consul βR: simul consul α   **20** 3 externa
$RS^2 \zeta TSb$: externas ω $S^1 BeQI$ 4 labefactatas: labefactas $HL^1 S^2 Q$ 7
percontantur Ω: -anti *iam Minutianus, Manutius*: -ibus *Mommsen*   ut est
φ$L^2 D^2$ς: ut *cett., del. Mommsen, Opitz, Schiche*   poetae Ludo βς: posteriore (*vel* -i) libro α (ludo P^2 *in marg.*): poetae libro *ViPa*: poetae Lupo
Ribbeck   9 proveniebant: proventebant L^1: proventabant $A^1 D^1$: pro-
venientur P^1 stulti: et stulti $PD^2 HQE$ **21** 6 ne *om.* $VBM^2 R$ eis
scripsi: is *B*: his *cett.*

quemquam senem audivi oblitum quo loco thesaurum
obruisset: omnia quae curant meminerunt, vadimonia
22 constituta, qui sibi, cui ipsi debeant. quid iurisconsulti, quid
pontifices, quid augures, quid philosophi senes, quam multa
meminerunt? manent ingenia senibus, modo permaneat
studium et industria; neque ea solum in claris et honoratis
viris, sed in vita etiam privata et quieta. Sophocles ad   5
summam senectutem tragoedias fecit; quod propter studium
cum rem neglegere familiarem videretur, a filiis in iudicium
vocatus est, ut quemadmodum nostro more male rem
gerentibus patribus bonis interdici solet, sic illum quasi
desipientem a re familiari removerent iudices; tum senex 10
dicitur eam fabulam quam in manibus habebat et proxime
scripserat, Oedipum Coloneum, recitasse iudicibus,
quaesisseque num illud carmen desipientis videretur; quo
23 recitato sententiis iudicum est liberatus. num igitur hunc,
num Homerum, num Hesiodum Simonidem Stesichorum,
num quos ante dixi Isocratem Gorgian, num philosophorum
principes Pythagoram Democritum, num Platonem, num
Xenocratem, num postea Zenonem Cleanthem aut eum   5
quem vos etiam vidistis Romae, Diogenem Stoicum coegit in
suis studiis obmutescere senectus? an in omnibus his
studiorum agitatio vitae aequalis fuit?
24   Age ut ista divina studia omittamus, possum nominare ex
agro Sabino rusticos Romanos, vicinos et familiares meos,
quibus absentibus numquam fere ulla in agro maiora opera
fiunt, non serendis, non percipiendis, non condendis
fructibus; quamquam in aliis minus hoc mirum est – nemo est 5
enim tam senex qui se annum non putet posse vivere – sed

10 qui: quis λ (*?V*[1])   **22** 6 quod propter φ*R*: p- q- *V*β*SZBeQI*   14
iudicum: iudicium *P*[1]*BL*[1]*A*[1]   **23** 2 num Homerum β*PaSg* (num *om.*
L[1]*?*): *transp. post* Gorgian (3) α   num Hesiodum α*LDPa*: num *om.*
BA   3 Isocratem *edd.* (*iam Sw.-P.*): Isocraten *L*[2] (*P*[2] *recenti manu*):
socratem *MPaQ*: socraten *cett.*   4–5 num Xenocratem: num *secl. Seyf-*
fert   7 omnibus his *VBHO*[2]ς: omnibus *PM*λ: omnibus iis *Victorius,*
Graevius, recc. aliquot ap. Otto   **24** 5 aliis: his *QE Manutius*   mirum est β:
mirum sit α   5–6 nemo est enim tam senex β*MSZEI* (est *om. L*[1]): nemo
enim est tam senex *PVHRQ*: nemo enim tam senex est *Be*

idem in eis elaborant quae sciunt nihil ad se omnino pertinere:

'serit arbores quae alteri saeculo prosient'

25 ut ait Statius noster in Synephebis; nec vero dubitat agricola, quamvis sit senex, quaerenti cui serat respondere, 'dis immortalibus, qui me non accipere modo haec a maioribus

VIII voluerunt, sed etiam posteris prodere.' et melius Caecilius de sene 'alteri saeculo' prospiciente, quam illud idem,   5

'edepol Senectus, si nil quicquam aliud viti
apportes tecum, cum advenis unum id sat est,
quod diu vivendo multa quae non vult videt' –

et multa fortasse quae vult; atque in ea quae non vult saepe etiam adulescentia incurrit. illud vero idem Caecilius 10 vitiosius,

'tum equidem in senecta hoc deputo miserrimum,
sentire ea aetate eumpse esse odiosum alteri.'

26 iucundum potius quam odiosum: ut enim adulescentibus bona indole praeditis sapientes senes delectantur, leviorque fit senectus eorum qui a iuventute coluntur et diliguntur, sic adulescentes senum praeceptis gaudent, quibus ad virtutum studia ducuntur; nec minus intellego me vobis quam mihi vos 5 esse iucundos.

Sed videtis ut senectus non modo languida atque iners non sit, verum etiam sit operosa et semper agens aliquid et moliens, tale scilicet quale cuiusque studium in superiore vita fuit. quid qui etiam addiscunt aliquid? ut et Solonem versibus 10 gloriantem videmus, qui se cotidie aliquid addiscentem dicit senem fieri, et ego feci, qui litteras Graecas senex didici? quas quidem sic avide adripui, quasi diuturnam sitim explere

---

8 saeculo Ω: saeclo *codd. RV¹G Cic. Tusc. 1.31* (*sed illic* saeculo *codd. K¹V²*)   prosient *P²*: prosint *cett.*   **25** 5 idem: ennii idem *BLP¹D²A²Sg*: enim idem *A¹D¹*   12 eumpse esse *Fleckeisen*: eum se esse *VβPa*: eum ipsum esse *Nonius (p.1 M.)*: esse φS¹ZBeQ *recc.*: se esse *H²L²E*: ei se esse *A²*: esse se *S²I* (esse odiosum se *R*)   **26** 10 quid qui: quicquid *V¹λ*: quid quod *D²*   12 et *Madvig*: ut Ω

cupiens, ut ea ipsa mihi nota essent quibus me nunc exemplis
uti videtis. quod cum fecisse Socratem in fidibus audirem, 15
vellem equidem etiam illud (discebant enim fidibus antiqui);
sed in litteris certe elaboravi.

IX 27   Nec nunc quidem vires desidero adulescentis (is enim erat
locus alter de vitiis senectutis), non plus quam adulescens
tauri aut elephanti desiderabam. quod est eo decet uti, et
quidquid agas agere pro viribus. quae enim vox potest esse
contemptior quam Milonis Crotoniatae? qui cum iam senex 5
esset, athletasque se exercentes in curriculo videret, aspexisse
lacertos suos dicitur, illacrimansque dixisse 'at hi quidem
mortui iam sunt' – non vero tam isti quam tu ipse nugator;
neque enim ex te umquam es nobilitatus, sed ex lateribus et
lacertis tuis. nihil Sextus Aelius tale, nihil multis annis ante 10
Tiberius Coruncanius, nihil modo Publius Crassus, a quibus
iura civibus praescribebantur; quorum usque ad extremum
28 spiritum est provecta prudentia. orator metuo ne languescat
senectute; est enim munus eius non ingeni solum, sed laterum
etiam et virium. omnino canorum illud in voce splendescit
etiam nescioquo pacto in senectute; quod equidem adhuc non
amisi, et videtis annos. sed tamen est decorus seni sermo 5
quietus et remissus, facitque per sepse sibi audientiam diserti
senis compta et mitis oratio. quam si ipse exsequi nequeas,
possis tamen Scipioni praecipere et Laelio: quid enim est
29 iucundius senectute stipata studiis iuventutis? an ne tales
quidem vires senectuti relinquimus, ut adulescentes doceat,

15 audirem: audire P^1VM **27** 1 nec: ne $VMSZBe$ 2 de vitiis:
divitias $PML^2A^2D^3$ (debitus D^2)   11 Ti(berius) *edd.*, *iam Moretus 1480*:
Titus Ω   **28** 5 est decorus seni *Madvig*: est decorus senis Ω: est senis *codd.*
Nonii p. 383.28   6 per sepse *scripsi*: pers(a)epe ipsa αB, *codd.* LEA^AG^2
Nonii p. 343.25 (saepe ipsa *cod.* G^1 *Nonii*): per se ipsa λ$PaSg$ 7 senis *omnes*
*praeter M, sic quoque cod. Gen.*² *Nonii* (*ibid.*): sermonis M *codd.* L^1E^1 *Nonii*:
sermonibus *codd.* $L^2E^2Gen.^1BHPG$ *Nonii*   compta α *codd.* $LGen.^2Cant.^2P$
Nonii (*ibid.*): cocta β (octa ?L^1) *cod.* E *Nonii*: coacta *cod.*
$Gen.^1BH^1Cant.^1Nonii$: om. *cod.* H^2G *Nonii*: composita Q *Lahmeyer, Reid*
29 1 an ne tales *Schiche*: an ne has O^2RE^2ITPb: an et has Q: an tales S^1:
nonne tales S^2 (*glossema?*): an has Sb: an eas Et: annales ω$PaZE^1BeSg$: an
ne eas *iam Sw.-P., Victorius, Manutius*: an ne illas *Halm*   2 senectuti: -tute
$P^1V^1A^2ZBe$: -tutis λ   relinquimus α: -emus β

instituat, ad omne offici munus instruat? quo quidem opere
quid potest esse praeclarius? mihi vero et Gnaeus et Publius
Scipiones et avi tui duo, Lucius Aemilius et Publius Africanus, 5
comitatu nobilium iuvenum fortunati videbantur; nec ulli
bonarum artium magistri non beati putandi, quamvis
consenuerint vires atque defecerint; etsi ipsa ista defectio
virium adulescentiae vitiis efficitur saepius quam senectutis:
libidinosa enim et intemperans adulescentia effetum corpus 10
tradit senectuti.

30   Cyrus quidem apud Xenophontem, eo sermone quem
moriens habuit, cum admodum senex esset, negat se umquam
sensisse senectutem suam imbecilliorem factam quam
adulescentia fuisset. ego Lucium Metellum memini puer, qui
cum quadriennio post alterum consulatum pontifex maximus 5
factus esset, viginti et duos annos ei sacerdotio praefuit, ita
bonis esse viribus extremo tempore aetatis, ut adulescentiam
non requireret. nihil necesse est mihi de me ipso dicere –
quamquam est id quidem senile aetatique nostrae conceditur.

X 31 videtisne ut apud Homerum saepissime Nestor de virtutibus
suis praedicet? iam enim tertiam aetatem hominum videbat;
nec erat ei verendum ne vera praedicans de se nimis videretur
aut insolens aut loquax. etenim ut ait Homerus, 'ex eius lingua
melle dulcior fluebat oratio'; quam ad suavitatem nullis 5
egebat corporis viribus; et tamen dux ille Graeciae nusquam
optat ut Aiacis similes habeat decem, sed ut Nestoris; quod si
32   sibi acciderit, non dubitat quin brevi sit Troia peritura. sed
redeo ad me: quartum ago annum et octogesimum. vellem
equidem idem possem gloriari quod Cyrus; sed tamen hoc
queo dicere, non me quidem eis esse viribus quibus aut miles
bello Punico aut quaestor eodem bello aut consul in Hispania 5
fuerim, aut quadriennio post cum tribunus militaris

5 L(ucius): b. *BL¹D¹*: *om. V*   8 ipsa ista: ista ipsa *VP²O²RSBe* (*fort.*
recte): ista *BMQ*: ipsa *H*   **31** 2 iam enim tertiam: t- i- e- *PR*: t- e- i-
Q   videbat: vivebat *PML²D²ς*   3 ne: nec βM   5 quam ad βς:
ad quam α   7 sed ut *Madvig*: sed VI *vel* sed sex ωPaς: at ut
P²L²D²H²O²RPb   **32** 3 possem *V¹BHMD²S¹ZBe*: possim λ: posse
PV²RS²QI   6 cum φO²L²A²ς: *om. V*β

depugnavi apud Thermopylas Manio Acilio Glabrione consule; sed tamen ut vos videtis, non plane me enervavit, non adflixit senectus; non curia vires meas desiderat, non rostra, non amici, non clientes, non hospites. nec enim umquam sum 10 adsensus veteri illi laudatoque proverbio, quod monet mature fieri senem si diu velis senex esse; ego vero me minus diu senem esse mallem, quam esse senem antequam essem. itaque nemo adhuc convenire me voluit cui fuerim 'occupatus.

33   At minus habeo virium quam vestrum utervis. – ne vos quidem Titi Ponti centurionis vires habetis; num idcirco est ille praestantior? moderatio modo virium adsit, et tantum quantum potest quisque nitatur, ne ille non magno desiderio tenebitur virium. Olympiae per stadium ingressus esse Milo 5 dicitur cum umeris sustineret bovem: utrum igitur has corporis an Pythagorae tibi malis vires ingeni dari? denique isto bono utare dum adsit, cum absit ne requiras – nisi forte adulescentes pueritiam, paulum aetate progressi adulescentiam debent requirere. cursus est certus aetatis, et 10 una via naturae eaque simplex; suaque cuique parti aetatis tempestivitas est data, ut et infirmitas puerorum, et ferocitas iuvenum, et gravitas iam constantis aetatis, et senectutis maturitas, naturale quiddam habeat quod suo tempore
34 percipi debeat. audire te arbitror, Scipio, hospes tuus avitus Masinissa quae faciat hodie nonaginta natus annos: cum ingressus iter pedibus sit, in equum omnino non ascendere, cum autem equo, ex equo non descendere; nullo imbri, nullo

7 Acilio: celio *V²: om. P¹V¹ML²Q*   14 cui *RQ²SbPb*: qui α: cum β*H² recc.*: quominus *V²SZBeI*   fuerim: fuerit λ*H²*   **33** 4 ne ille φ*O²RET* (nec ille *Pb*): ne ille quidem *cett.*   6 utrum *Manutius*: vivum α*PaQS*: virum β: vivum. utrum *D²H²O²RZBeEAdMbMc*: vires *A²O¹*   8 utare dum adsit: dum assit gaudeas *H¹*: cum a- g- *Q*   9 paulum: paululum λ*Q*   11 parti aetatis *Q, edd. hic et Non. p. 407.37*: parci etatis β: parcitatis *PVH¹Pa, codd. H²GE Nonii*: participitatis *MZI*: parti *H²O²S²BeR* (*in S sequitur rasura 5–6 litt.*): partis aetatis *codd. LFH¹ Par. 7666 Lugd. Nonii*: parcis etatis *cod. P Nonii*   12 ut et: ut enim *H²O²RE*   13 et senectutis: ita sen- *H²RE*: sic sen- *S²Q²*   14 habeat: habet *H²RS²E Reid* **34** 1 audire te: audis(s)etea λ: audisse *H²*   avitus *Cuiacius, Langius, A. Manutius in comm.*: habitus Ω   4 imbri: imbre *PL²ς*

frigore adduci ut capite operto sit; summam esse in eo 5
siccitatem corporis; itaque omnia exsequi regis officia et
munera. potest igitur exercitatio et temperantia etiam in
senectute conservare aliquid pristini roboris.

XI Non sunt in senectute vires? – ne postulantur quidem vires a
senectute: ergo et legibus et institutis vacat aetas nostra 10
muneribus eis quae non possunt sine viribus sustineri, itaque
non modo quod non possumus, sed ne quantum possumus
35 quidem cogimur. – at multi ita sunt imbecilli senes, ut nullum
offici aut omnino vitae munus exsequi possint. – at id quidem
non proprium senectutis vitium est, sed commune valetudinis:
quam fuit imbecillus Publius Africani filius, is qui te
adoptavit, quam tenui aut nulla potius valetudine! quod ni ita 5
fuisset, alterum illud exstitisset lumen civitatis; ad paternam
enim magnitudinem animi doctrina uberior accesserat. quid
mirum igitur in senibus, si infirmi sint aliquando, cum id ne
adulescentes quidem effugere possint? resistendum, Laeli et
Scipio, senectuti est, eiusque vitia diligentia compensanda 10
sunt; pugnandum, tamquam contra morbum, sic contra
36 senectutem; habenda ratio valetudinis; utendum exercitationibus modicis, tantum cibi et potionis adhibendum ut
reficiantur vires, non opprimantur. nec vero corpori solum
subveniendum est, sed menti atque animo multo magis.
nam haec quoque nisi tamquam lumini oleum instilles, 5
exstinguuntur senectute; et corpora quidem exercitationum
defetigatione ingravescunt, animi autem se exercendo
levantur. nam quos ait Caecilius 'comicos stultos senes', hos

---

6 siccitatem corporis: c- s- *PRE, Nonii codd. omnes p. 395.7*   7–8 in
senectute: senectute *PVMS¹ZBeI*: senectuti *HQ*   9 non sunt β*SZBeEI
recc.*: non desunt *V²* (non desinit *?V¹*): ne desint φ*L²A²D²*: ne sint
RTQ¹   11 q(uae) n(on) *AORE*: q(uonia)m φ*BDL²* (quō *SZBeI*): qn͞do
L¹: q͞m non *V*: quae *Q*   sustineri: -ere *VL*   **35** 2 possint *PL²D²PaO²ς*
(-int *in ras. H*): possunt *cett.*   4 Africani: -anus *PVM*   8 sint: sunt
A¹SZBeQI   11 morbum: morborum λ: morborum vim *L²D²*   **36** 7
se exercendo: exercitando φ*D²SZBeQI*   8 comicos *Q²edd.* (*cf. Lael. 99*):
comicus ω: comici *?Q¹* (*ante rasuram in qua est glossema* 'sunt qui in comediis
introducuntur')   hos β*H²RES²Sg*: hoc *PMV²PaS¹ZBeQI*: h. *H¹*: om. *V¹*

significat credulos obliviosos dissolutos; quae vitia sunt non
senectutis, sed inertis ignavae somniculosae senectutis. ut 10
petulantia, ut libido magis est adulescentium quam senum,
nec tamen omnium adulescentium sed non proborum, sic ista
senilis stultitia quae deliratio appellari solet, senum levium
est, non omnium.

37 Quattuor robustos filios, quinque filias, tantam domun,
tantas clientelas, Appius regebat et caecus et senex; intentum
enim animum tamquam arcum habebat, nec languescens
succumbebat senectuti. tenebat non modo auctoritatem, sed
etiam imperium in suos; metuebant servi, verebantur liberi, 5
carum omnes habebant; vigebat in illa domo mos patrius et
38 disciplina. ita enim senectus honesta est, si se ipsa defendit, si
ius suum retinet, si nemini emancipata est, si usque ad
ultimum spiritum dominatur in suos. ut enim adulescentem in
quo est senile aliquid, sic senem in quo est aliquid adulescentis
probo; quod qui sequitur corpore senex esse poterit, animo 5
numquam erit. septimus mihi liber Originum est in manibus;
omnia antiquitatis monumenta colligo, causarum illustrium
quascumque defendi nunc cum maxime conficio orationes,
ius augurium pontificium civile tracto; multumque etiam
Graecis litteris utor, Pythagoreorumque more, exercendae 10

10 ignavae H^2REIQ^1 TSbPb, Nonii codd. omnes p. 33.24 (cf. lemma): ignaviae
$PVML^2A^2D^2Pa^2SZBeQ^2$ (sed ... senectutis om. H^1: sunt ... ignavae om.
βPa^1Sg) **37** 1 filios, quinque A^2SREQ recc.: filios tantum quinque α:
filios tanam quinque β 6 vigebat: vivebat MO^2R: vigebant V^1 illa
domo mos O^2REMb recc.: illa domos B: illa domus L^1A^1: illa domu D^1: illo
domu A^2: illa domo PaVa: illo animus α: illa animus Sg: eo animus
Q patrius: patris D^1A^2Pa recc.: patria P^2D^2: patri A^1: patridomus
L^1 et $MO^2H^2\varsigma$: om. cett. **38** 2 si nemini emancipata Sg codd. LF
Nonii p. 105.16 (si nemeni em- cod. H^1 Nonii): si nemini mancipata
$MO^2H^2RES^2$ recc. (pro nemini rasuram habet S^1): si neminēmancipata λ:
mentesinemancipata B: simentipamantipata H^1: si menti mancipata (vel
manti-) $PVL^2A^2D^2PaZBeQ$; si menti emancipata codd. H^2PE Nonii: sin
menti em- cod. G Nonii: emancipata lemma Nonii 8 nunc cum β: nunc
quam $\varphi V^2L^2A^2D^2\varsigma$: nunquam V^1: nunc O^2E^1 9 augurium RZT:
augurum ω pontificium $\varphi V^2L^2A^2D^2RSZ$: pontifici V^1: pontificum
βH^2BeIQ

memoriae gratia, quid quoque die dixerim audierim egerim
commemoro vesperi. hae sunt exercitationes ingeni, haec
curricula mentis; in his desudans atque elaborans corporis
vires non magnopere desidero. adsum amicis, venio in
senatum frequens; utroque adfero res multum et diu cogitatas,   15 ·
easque tueor animi, non corporis viribus. quae si exsequi
nequirem, tamen me lectulus meus oblectaret, ea ipsa
cogitantem quae iam agere non possem. sed ut possim facit
acta vita: semper enim in his studiis laboribusque viventi, non
intellegitur quando obrepat senectus; ita sensim sine sensu   20
aetas senescit, nec subito frangitur, sed diuturnitate
exstinguitur.

XII 39   Sequitur tertia vituperatio senectutis, quod eam carere
dicunt voluptatibus. o praeclarum munus aetatis, siquidem id
aufert a nobis quod est in adulescentia vitiosissimum! accipite
enim, optimi adulescentes, veterem orationem Archytae
Tarentini, magni in primis et praeclari viri, quae mihi tradita   5
est cum essem adulescens Tarenti cum Quinto Maximo.
nullam capitaliorem pestem quam voluptatem corporis
hominibus dicebat a natura datam, cuius voluptatis avidae
40   libidines temere et ecfrenate ad potiundum incitarentur; hinc
patriae proditiones, hinc rerum publicarum eversiones, hinc
cum hostibus clandestina colloquia nasci; nullum denique
scelus, nullum malum facinus esse, ad quod suscipiendum non
libido voluptatis impelleret; stupra vero et adulteria et omne   5
tale flagitium nullis excitari aliis illecebris nisi voluptatis;
cumque homini sive natura sive quis deus nihil mente
praestabilius dedisset, huic divino muneri ac dono nihil tam
41   esse inimicum quam voluptatem; nec enim libidine
dominante temperantiae locum esse, neque omnino in
voluptatis regno virtutem posse consistere. quod quo magis

---

15 utroque $V\beta$: ultroque $\varphi L^2 A^2 Pa\varsigma$ 16 quae βRE: quas α   22
exstinguitur: *fort.* restinguitur?   **39** 3 a *om.* βRE 9 et ecfrenate *sic*
scribunt $P^1 V^2$: &frenate $BL^1 A^1 Be^1$: et effrenate *cett.*   **40** 5–6 omne tale:
omnia *vel* omne *codd. Lactantii Inst. 6.20.4*   9 esse *om. Lact.*   **41** 2
omnino *om. Lact.*   3 regno $\varphi V^2 L^2 A^2 D^2 PaRSBeIQ$ *Lact.*: regnum $V^1\beta$

intellegi posset, fingere animo iubebat tanta incitatum
aliquem voluptate corporis quanta percipi posset maxima: 5
nemini censebat fore dubium, quin tamdiu dum ita gauderet,
nihil agitare mente, nihil ratione, nihil cogitatione consequi
posset. quocirca nihil esse tam detestabile tamque pestiferum
quam voluptatem, siquidem ea cum maior esset atque
longinquior, omne animi lumen exstingueret. haec cum Gaio 10
Pontio Samnite, patre eius a quo Caudino proelio Sp.
Postumius T. Veturius consules superati sunt, locutum
Archytam, Nearchus Tarentinus hospes noster, qui in
amicitia populi Romani permanserat, se a maioribus natu
accepisse dicebat; cum quidem ei sermoni interfuisset Plato 15
Atheniensis, quem Tarentum venisse L. Camillo Ap. Claudio
consulibus reperio.

42   Quorsus hoc? ut intellegeretis, si voluptatem aspernari
ratione et sapientia non possumus, magnam habendam esse
senectuti gratiam, quae efficeret ut id non liberet quod non
oporteret. impedit enim consilium voluptas, rationi inimica
est, mentis ut ita dicam praestringit oculos, nec habet ullum 5
cum virtute commercium. invitus feci ut fortissimi viri Titi
Flaminini fratrem Lucium Flamininum e senatu eicerem,
septem annis postquam consul fuisset, sed notandam putavi
libidinem: ille enim cum esset consul in Gallia, exoratus in
convivio a scorto est, ut securi feriret aliquem eorum qui in 10
vinculis essent, damnati rei capitalis. hic Tito fratre suo
censore (qui proximus ante me fuerat) elapsus est, mihi vero et
Flacco neutiquam probari potuit tam flagitiosa et tam perdita
libido, quae cum probro privato coniungeret imperi dedecus.
XIII 43 saepe audivi a maioribus natu, qui se porro pueros a senibus

4 posset *O²RE recc.*: possit ω   8 tamque pestiferum quam
MH²O²RSZBeEQ² recc.: tamquam *V¹β*: quam *PH¹V²A²D²Q¹*   10
longinquior *MO²RSZBeE recc., Madvig, Lahmeyer*: longi *BL¹*: longior
cett.   16 Ap(pio): P. *VBADQ*: pre *L¹, del. L²*: ac P. *HRS²*   **42** 7
L(ucium): C(aium) *PMA²D²SZBeQI*   8–9 fuisset ... esset *om. S¹ZBe*
8 notandam: -um *VB Langius*   13 tam perdita *φϛ Charisius p. 208 K.*: tam
om. Vβ   14 probro: probo *V¹M¹A¹D¹Q*   **43** 1 a maioribus *MPa recc.*:
ea m- *V¹β*: ea a m- *PV²L²A²D²HSZBeQI*: e m- *O²RE fort. recte*   a
senibus: e s- *BA¹*: ac s- *L¹*: a senatibus *P¹*

audisse dicebant, mirari solitum Gaium Fabricium, quod
cum apud regem Pyrrhum legatus esset, audisset a Thessalo
Cinea esse quendam Athenis qui se sapientem profiteretur,
eumque dicere omnia quae faceremus ad voluptatem esse 5
referenda; quod ex eo audientes, Manium Curium et
Tiberium Coruncanium optare solitos ut id Samnitibus
ipsique Pyrrho persuaderetur, quod facilius vinci possent cum
se voluptatibus dedissent. vixerat Manius Curius cum Publio
Decio, qui quinquennio ante eum consulem se pro re publica 10
quarto consulatu devoverat; norat eundem Fabricius, norat
Coruncanius; qui cum ex sua vita, tum ex eius quem dico Deci
facto, iudicabant esse profecto aliquid natura pulchrum
atque praeclarum, quod sua sponte peteretur, quodque
spreta et contempta voluptate optimus quisque sequeretur. 15

44 Quorsus igitur tam multa de voluptate? quia non modo
vituperatio nulla sed etiam summa laus senectutis est, quod
ea voluptates nullas magnopere desiderat. caret epulis
exstructisque mensis et frequentibus poculis: caret ergo etiam
vinolentia et cruditate et insomniis. sed si aliquid dandum est 5
voluptati (quoniam eius blanditiis non facile resistimus –
divine enim Plato escam malorum appellat voluptatem, quod
ea videlicet homines capiantur ut pisces), quamquam
immoderatis epulis caret senectus, modicis tamen conviviis
delectari potest. Gaium Duilium Marci filium, qui Poenos 10
classe primus devicerat, redeuntem a cena senem saepe
videbam puer; delectabatur cereo funali et tibicine, quae sibi
nullo exemplo privatus sumpserat – tantum licentiae dabat

3 a Thessalo: e Th- *BA*[1]*R* (?*V*[1]): ae Th- *L*[1]: ue Th- *D*[1]   4 Cinea
Victorius, Manutius (Cynea *iam Moretus, Minutianus*): cive *vel* civi α: nice
β   7 Ti(berium) *edd., iam De Breda, Victorius, Manutius*: Titum Ω (T.
RBeQ)   8 quod: quo *PMV*[2]*A*[2]*D*[2]ς   9 dedissent: *fort.* dedidissent?
44 1 quorsus β: quorsum α*Ha*   3 caret (*post* immoderatis epulis)
PRSZBe: careat *cett.*   10 C(aium): O.β: Catonem *Ha*   Duilium *sic
scripsi*: duillium *A*[1]*D*[1]: duillum *B*: duellium *cett.*   11 devicerat
φ*HaL*[2]*A*[2]*Pa*[2]*RZBeQI*[2] (divicerat *S*: deficerat *Γ*): vicerat *V*β   12 cereo
St[2] *Royal* 15 A xx[2] *Ambr. E.15 inf., Manutius, Lipsius*: credo *V*[1]β*Ha*[2]*O*[2]*R*:
crebro φ*Ha*[1]*V*[2]*A*[2]*D*[2]*PaSZBeI*: crebro et *Q*   funali et tibicine α*Ha*: funali
etibicine β *fort.* funali, tibicine?

45 gloria. sed quid ego alios? ad me ipsum iam revertar. primum
habui semper sodales – sodalitates autem me quaestore
constitutae sunt sacris Idaeis Magnae Matris acceptis –
epulabar igitur cum sodalibus, omnino modice, sed erat
quidam fervor aetatis, qua progrediente omnia fiunt in dies 5
mitiora; neque enim ipsorum conviviorum delectationem
voluptatibus corporis magis quam coetu amicorum et
sermonibus metiebar. bene enim maiores accubitionem
epularem amicorum, quia vitae coniunctionem haberet,
convivium nominaverunt, melius quam Graeci, qui hoc idem 10
tum compotationem tum concenationem vocant, ut quod in

XIV 46 eo genere minimum est, id maxime probare videantur. ego
vero propter sermonis delectationem tempestivis quoque
conviviis delector, nec cum aequalibus solum, qui pauci iam
admodum restant, sed cum vestra etiam aetate atque
vobiscum; habeoque senectuti magnam gratiam, quae mihi 5
sermonis aviditatem auxit, potionis et cibi sustulit. quod si
quem etiam ista delectant (ne omnino bellum indixisse videar
voluptati, cuius est fortasse quidam naturalis modus), non
intellego ne in istis quidem ipsis voluptatibus carere sensu
senectutem. me vero et magisteria delectant a maioribus 10
instituta, et is sermo qui more maiorum a summo adhibetur in
poculo, et pocula sicut in Symposio Xenophontis est, minuta
atque rorantia, et refrigeratio aestate et vicissim aut sol aut
ignis hibernus. quae quidem etiam in Sabinis persequi soleo,
conviviumque vicinorum cotidie compleo, quod ad multam 15
noctem quam maxime possumus vario sermone producimus.

47   At non est voluptatum tanta quasi titillatio in senibus. –

45 2 semper *om. Ha: post* sodales *R*   9 quia *(sic codd. GE Nonii p. 42.9,
codd. H²G p. 193.29):* qui *BA¹, codd. H²P² Non. p. 42:* q̄ *D¹:* ꝗ *Q; quae codd.
LFH¹CᴬDᴬ Non. p. 42:* quo *cod. P¹ Non. ibid.:* quasi *codd. LFH¹ E Non.
p. 193*   **46** 3 nec cum: *sic codd. H²Cant.²G Bern. 347² Mont. Oxon. Nonii
p. 236.4, omnes Non. p. 378.29:* ne cum *(vel* necum) *V¹BL codd. L Gen. P Bern.
347¹ EH¹ Cant.¹Non. p. 236*   iam *om. PVMD²BeQ omnes codd. Non.
ambobus locis (qui pauci iam om. H¹)*   11 a summo *Lambinus, cod. Turnebi:*
a summo magistro Ω   15 compleo: completo *(vel* con-*) A¹D¹ codd. L Gen.
Cant. B H¹ Nonii p. 372.29:* completu *L¹:* complector *A²D²:* complecto *(vel
con-) codd. EH²G Nonii*   16 producimus: prodicimus *V¹:* dicimus λ

credo, sed ne desideratur quidem: nihil autem est molestum quod non desideres. bene Sophocles cum ex eo quidam iam adfecto aetate quaereret, utereturne rebus veneriis, 'di meliora!' inquit 'libenter vero istinc sicut ab domino agresti ac 5 furioso profugi.' cupidis enim rerum talium odiosum fortasse et molestum est carere, satiatis vero et expletis iucundius est carere quam frui – quamquam non caret is qui non desiderat,
48 ergo hoc non desiderare dico esse iucundius. quod si istis ipsis voluptatibus bona aetas fruitur libentius, primum parvulis fruitur rebus ut diximus, deinde eis quibus senectus etiamsi non abunde potitur, non omnino caret: ut Turpione Ambivio magis delectatur qui in prima cavea spectat, delectatur tamen 5 etiam qui in ultima, sic adulescentia voluptates propter intuens magis fortasse laetatur, sed delectatur etiam senectus procul eas spectans tantum quantum sat est.

49 At illi quanti est, animum tamquam emeritis stipendiis libidinis, ambitionis, contentionum, inimicitiarum, cupiditatum omnium, secum esse secumque ut dicitur vivere! si vero habet aliquod tamquam pabulum studi atque doctrinae, nihil est otiosa senectute iucundius. mori 5 videbamus in studio dimetiendi paene caeli atque terrae

---

47 2 ne: nec β*MQ*   desideratur β: desideratio α   4 veneriis (*vel* -eis): veneris *BL¹Q*   5 libenter vero: ego vero *PH¹L²A²Q*; ego vero libenter *H²*: l- e- v- *V²*   ab β: a α (*om. M*)   5–6 ac furioso: acurioso *V¹B*: accurioso *MS¹Be*: accuriose λ   9 ergo hoc non desiderare: ergo non des- *PH¹L²Q*; ergo hoc derare B: *om. A*   **48** 1 istis ipsis: istis *post ras.* V (? istis *Q*): ipsis *Non. p.2.9 codd. omnes*   5–6 delectatur qui in prima cavea spectat, delectatur tamen etiam qui in ultima *O²Pa²RE recc., codd. omnes Nonii p. 417.22 praeter G¹*: tamen etiam *transp. ante* qui in prima *B*: tamen *om. PMV²L²A²D²QSBeI*: qui in prima ... tamen *om. V¹*: qui in prima ... etiam *om.* λ: etiam *om. H²*: *totum locum om. H¹*: qui in prima ... delectatur *om. cod. G¹ Nonii*   6 voluptates: -em *VP²*   8 eas: eam *VPa*: *om. HQ*   spectans *PHD²PaRQ*: aspiciens *MSZBeI, codd. omnes Nonii p.367.28*: aspectans *cett.*   **49** 1 illi β: illa α (ille *Q*)   est *scripsi auctore Brink*: sunt Ω   5–6 mori videbamus in studio dimetiendi (*vel* dem-) *MRSZBeAdTSbSt* (m- v- in s- demenciendi *I*) (videbamur *BeAdSt*): mori videbamus (-ebam *D¹*) d- β: videamus in s- d- *PVH¹L²A²D²Pa²*: videamus studio in d- *O¹* (videbamus *O²*): videbamus mori in studio d- *H²*: videamus mori in studio d- (m- in s- *in ras.*) *E*: videamus demetiendi *Pa¹*: videbamus in studio d- mori *Q*: videbamus morari in s- d- *Va*: videbamus in s- d- *Madvig, alii alia*

Gaium Galum, familiarem patris tui Scipio – quotiens illum lux, noctu aliquid describere ingressum, quotiens nox oppressit cum mane coepisset! quam delectabat eum
50 defectiones solis et lunae multo ante nobis praedicere! quid in levioribus studiis, sed tamen acutis, quam gaudebat Bello suo Punico Naevius, quam Truculento Plautus, quam Pseudolo? vidi etiam senem Livium, qui cum sex annis antequam ego natus sum fabulam docuisset Centone Tuditanoque 5 consulibus, usque ad adulescentiam meam processit aetate. quid de Publi Licini Crassi et pontificii et civilis iuris studio loquar, aut de huius Publi Scipionis qui his paucis diebus pontifex maximus factus est? atque eos omnes quos commemoravi his studiis flagrantes senes vidimus; Marcum 10 vero Cethegum, quem recte 'Suadae medullam' dixit Ennius, quanto studio exerceri in dicendo videbamus etiam senem! quae sunt igitur epularum aut ludorum aut scortorum voluptates cum his voluptatibus comparandae? atque haec [quidem studia doctrinae quae] quidem prudentibus et bene 15 institutis pariter cum aetate crescunt, ut honestum illud Solonis sit, quod ait versiculo quodam ut ante dixi, senescere se multa in dies addiscentem: qua voluptate animi nulla certe potest esse maior.

XV 51   Venio nunc ad voluptates agricolarum, quibus ego incredibiliter delector; quae nec ulla impediuntur senectute, et mihi ad sapientis vitam proxime videntur accedere. habent enim rationem cum terra, quae numquam recusat impendium, nec umquam sine usura reddit quod accepit, sed 5 alias minore, plerumque maiore cum fenore. quamquam me

---

7 C(aium) Galum *edd.*: C. Gallum *iam Minutianus, Victorius, Gruterus ex codd.*: galum *P*[1]: gaium *H*: C. *Q*: gallum *cett.*   **50** 6 ad *om. VβQ*   8 P(ubli) Scipionis *RSZBe recc.*: Scipionis ω   9 atque β: atqui α   11 Suad(a)e: suadē *A*[1]*D*: suadā *VP*[2]*L*[2]*A*[2]: suadu *L*[1]: *fort.* Suadai?   14 atque β*RQ* (adque *B*): atqui α   15 [quidem studia doctrinae quae] *seclusi*: idē (=*id est?*) studia doctrinae quae β: quidem studia doctrinae quae α *edd. fere omnes*, quae quidem *omisit Manutius, Langius, Lambinus*   19 potest esse maior: maior potest esse maior *BL*[1]*A*[1]: maior potest esse *DR*   **51** 4 rationem cum terra: cum rationem terra *V*[1]β (terram *D*[1])   5 impendium *coni. Manutius*: imperium Ω

76

quidem non fructus modo sed etiam ipsius terrae vis ac natura
delectat; quae cum gremio mollito ac subacto sparsum semen
excepit, primum id occaecatum cohibet (ex quo occatio, quae
hoc efficit, nominata est), dein tepefactum vapore et 10
compressu suo diffundit, et elicit herbescentem ex eo
viriditatem; quae nixa fibris stirpium sensim adulescit,
culmoque erecta geniculato vaginis iam quasi pubescens
includitur; ex quibus cum emersit, fundit frugem spici ordine
exstructam, et contra avium minorum morsus munitur vallo 15
52 aristarum. quid ego vitium ortus satus incrementa
commemorem? satiari delectatione non possum – ut meae
senectutis requietem oblectamentumque noscatis – omitto
enim vim ipsam omnium quae generantur e terra, quae e fici
tantulo grano aut ex acini vinaceo aut ex ceterarum frugum 5
aut stirpium minutissimis seminibus tantos truncos ramosque
procreet; malleoli plantae sarmenta viviradices propagines,
nonne ea efficiunt ut quemvis cum admiratione delectent?
vitis quidem quae natura caduca est, et nisi fulta est fertur ad
terram, eadem ut se erigat claviculis suis quasi manibus 10
quidquid est nacta complectitur; quam serpentem multiplici
lapsu et erratico, ferro amputans coercet ars agricolarum, ne
53 silvescat sarmentis et in omnes partes nimia fundatur. itaque
ineunte vere in eis quae relicta sunt exsistit, tamquam ad
articulos sarmentorum, ea quae gemma dicitur; a qua oriens
uva se ostendit, quae et suco terrae et calore solis augescens,
primo est peracerba gustatu, dein maturata dulcescit, 5
vestitaque pampinis nec modico tepore caret et nimios solis
defendit ardores; qua quid potest esse cum fructu laetius, tum

8 mollito: molito $V^1\beta$ 9 occaecatum: occetatum λ: occatum
P^2HPaS^1ZBeQI: ccc. catum M 11 diffundit: diffindit *Gulielmius (ex cod.*
Celberdensi) fort. recte   elicit: eicit *coni. Lambinus, fort. recte*   13 erecta
$VPaO^2H^2RZBeE$ *recc., codd. omnes Nonii p. 225.30:* recta *cett.* (erecto Q)
14 emersit: mersit A^1D: emerserit $BH \, ?Q$ 15 ex(s)tructam BA^1D^1Pa:
structam $L^1HO^2REQ^1Sg$ *recc.:* structo $PVL^2A^2D^2Q^2$: exstructo $MSZBeI$
(fruges ... structas *codd. omnes Nonii ibid.*)   **52** 3 requietem
$PMA^2KPaRS^1ZBeQIT$ *Priscianus II, p. 242 K.:* quietem *recc.:* requiem *cett.*
4 e (*vel* ex) fici $P^2L^2M\varsigma$ *codd. omnes Nonii p. 193.15:* effici *cett.*   5 acini:
acino $L^1H^2O^2\varsigma$ 7 viviradices *Manutius:* vites (*vel* -is) radices Ω 8 ea
om. λ   **53** 6 tepore $P^2V^2A^2H^2PaSZBeITE^2$: tempore *cett.*

aspectu pulchrius? cuius quidem non utilitas me solum ut
ante dixi, sed etiam cultura et natura ipsa delectat –
adminiculorum ordines, capitum iugatio, religatio et 10
propagatio vitium, sarmentorum ea quam dixi aliorum
amputatio, aliorum immissio. quid ego irrigationes, quid
fossiones agri repastinationesque proferam, quibus fit multo
54 terra fecundior? quid de utilitate loquar stercorandi? dixi in
eo libro quam de rebus rusticis scripsi; de qua doctus Hesiodus
ne verbum quidem fecit, cum de cultura agri scriberet; at
Homerus, qui multis ut mihi videtur ante saeclis fuit, Laertam
lenientem desiderium quod capiebat e filio, colentem agrum 5
et eum stercorantem facit. nec vero segetibus solum et pratis et
vineis et arbustis res rusticae laetae sunt, sed hortis etiam et
pomariis; tum pecudum pastu, apium examinibus, florum
omnium varietate; nec consitiones modo delectant, sed etiam
insitiones, quibus nihil invenit agricultura sollertius. 10
XVI 55 Possum persequi permulta oblectamenta rerum
rusticarum, sed ea ipsa quae dixi sentio fuisse longiora;
ignoscetis autem, nam et studio rerum rusticarum provectus
sum, et senectus est natura loquacior – ne ab omnibus eam
vitiis videar vindicare. ergo in hac vita Manius Curius, cum 5
de Samnitibus, de Sabinis, de Pyrrho triumphavisset,
consumpsit extremum tempus aetatis; cuius quidem ego
villam contemplans – abest enim non longe a me – admirari
satis non possum vel hominis ipsius continentiam vel
56 temporum disciplinam. Curio ad focum sedenti magnum auri
pondus Samnites cum attulissent, repudiati sunt; non enim
aurum habere praeclarum sibi videri dixit, sed eis qui
haberent aurum imperare. poteratne tantus animus efficere
non iucundam senectutem? sed venio ad agricolas, ne a me 5
ipso recedam: in agris erant tum senatores, id est senes,
siquidem aranti Lucio Quinctio Cincinnato nuntiatum est

11 ea: eam *BA¹D*: eum *L¹*   **54** 4 ut: et *P¹H¹*   8 apium *L²RTSb*: et
apium *cett.* (et apum *HMS²Q*)   **55** 2 ea: haec λ   3 et
MH²O²RETSbLaLb: at *B*: ad λ: a *cett.*   4 natura *om. P¹VH¹Q (ante est
M)*   5 hac βϛ: hanc α   vita M(anius) ϛ: vita Marcus *I*: vitam
BD¹Pa¹: vita *L¹A¹*: vitam m. *(vel m̄)* α

78

eum dictatorem esse factum; cuius dictatoris iussu magister
equitum Gaius Servilius Ahala Spurium Maelium regnum
[appetentem] occupantem interemit. a villa in senatum 10
arcessebantur et Curius et ceteri senes, ex quo qui eos
arcessebant viatores nominati sunt. num igitur horum
senectus miserabilis fuit, qui se agri cultione oblectabant? mea
quidem sententia haud scio an nulla beatior possit esse; neque
solum officio, quod hominum generi universo cultura 15
agrorum est salutaris, sed et delectatione qua dixi, et
saturitate copiaque rerum omnium quae ad victum
hominum, ad cultum etiam deorum pertinent – ut quoniam
haec quidam desiderant, in gratiam iam cum voluptate
redeamus; semper enim boni assiduique domini referta cella 20
vinaria, olearia, etiam penaria est, villaque tota locuples est,
abundat porco haedo agno gallina lacte caseo melle. iam
hortum ipsi agricolae succidiam alteram appellant;
conditiora facit haec supervacaneis etiam operis aucupium
57 atque venatio. quid de pratorum viriditate aut arborum
ordinibus aut vinearum olivetorumve specie plura dicamus?
brevi praecidam: agro bene culto nihil potest esse nec usu
uberius nec specie ornatius; ad quem fruendum non modo
non retardat verum etiam invitat atque allectat senectus. ubi 5
enim potest illa aetas aut calescere vel apricatione melius vel
58 igne, aut vicissim umbris aquisve refrigerari salubrius? sibi
habeant igitur arma, sibi equos, sibi hastas, sibi clavam et
pilam, sibi venationes atque cursus; nobis senibus ex
lusionibus multis talos relinquant et tesseras – id ipsum utrum
libebit, quoniam sine eis beata esse senectus potest. 5
II 59 Multas ad res perutiles Xenophontis libri sunt, quos legite
quaeso studiose, ut facitis. quam copiose ab eo agricultura

56 10 [appetentem] occupantem *scripsi*: appetentem occupantem β: app-
occupatum α   11 arcessebantur β: -ebatur α   14 an nulla D^2 *edd.*:
nulla λ: ac nulla *Q*: an ulla *cett.*   16 qua: quam *PaVaBe recc.*   **57** 2
olivetorumve: olivetorumque BLA^1: olivarumque *D*   dicamus β: dicam
α   3 praecidam βRS^2: praedicam α (succidam *Q*)   **58** 1–2 sibi
habeant igitur: h- i- s- PA^2K: h- i- A^1: s- i- h- *HQ*   3 venationes *DT*:
(a)enationes BL^1A^1: nationes P^1H *recc.*: natationes $VMP^2L^2A^2RSZBe$
4 talos: tales $P^1H^1BD^2$ utrum β(?*M*)PaO^2ς: unum $PVHL^2D^2KO^1I$

laudatur in eo libro qui est de tuenda re familiari, qui
Oeconomicus inscribitur! atque ut intellegatis nihil ei tam
regale videri quam studium agri colendi, Socrates in eo libro 5
loquitur cum Critobulo, Cyrum minorem Persarum regem
praestantem ingenio atque imperi gloria, cum Lysander
Lacedaemonius, vir summae virtutis, venisset ad eum Sardis
eique dona a sociis attulisset, et ceteris in rebus comem erga
Lysandrum atque humanum fuisse, et ei quendam 10
consaeptum agrum diligenter consitum ostendisse; cum
autem admiraretur Lysander et proceritates arborum et
derectos in quincuncem ordines et humum subactam atque
puram et suavitatem odorum qui adflarentur e floribus, tum
eum dixisse mirari se non modo diligentiam sed etiam 15
sollertiam eius a quo essent illa dimensa atque descripta; et
Cyrum respondisse, 'atqui ego ista sum omnia dimensus, mei
sunt ordines, mea descriptio; multae etiam istarum arborum
mea manu sunt satae'; tum Lysandrum, intuentem purpuram
eius et nitorem corporis ornatumque Persicum multo auro 20
multisque gemmis, dixisse 'rite vero te Cyre beatum ferunt,
quoniam virtuti tuae fortuna coniuncta est.'

60 Hac igitur fortuna frui licet senibus, nec aetas impedit
quominus et ceterarum rerum et in primis agri colendi studia
teneamus usque ad ultimum tempus senectutis. Marcum
quidem Valerium Corvinum accepimus ad centesimum
annum perduxisse, cum esset acta iam aetate in agris eosque 5
coleret; cuius inter primum et sextum consulatum sex et
quadraginta anni interfuerunt – ita quantum spatium aetatis
maiores ad senectutis initium esse voluerunt, tantus illi cursus
honorum fuit. atque huius extrema aetas hoc beatior quam
media, quod auctoritatis habebat plus, laboris minus. apex est 10
61 autem senectutis auctoritas: quanta fuit in Lucio Caecilio

---

59 4 ut β*RZQE*: etiam ut α   6 loquitur $P^1 VHO^2$ς: quo loquitur β$P^2 Pa$
(quam . . . libro *om. M*): colloquitur *Mommsen*   9 comem β: communem
α   13 derectos *sic scr. B, omnes codd. Nonii p. 400.35*: directos *cett.*   16
descripta: discripta $P^1 L^1 Be$ 18 descriptio *VBHM*ς: discr- *P*λ   19
intuentem: induentem $P^1 H$: intuendum ! *A*   **60** 7 quadraginta (*vel*
XL): XXXL *B*: XXX λ   8 illi β*S*: ille α

Metello, quanta in Aulo Atilio Calatino! in quem illud
elogium:

> 'hunc unum plurimae consentiunt gentes
> populi primarium fuisse virum . . .' –   5

notum est enim totum carmen incisum in sepulcro; iure igitur
gravis, cuius de laudibus omnium esset fama consentiens.
quem virum nuper Publium Crassum pontificem maximum,
quem postea Marcum Lepidum eodem sacerdotio praeditum
vidimus! quid de Paulo aut Africano loquar, aut ut iam ante   10
de Maximo? quorum non in sententia solum sed etiam in nutu
residebat auctoritas. habet senectus honorata praesertim
tantam auctoritatem ut ea pluris sit quam omnes
III 62 adulescentiae voluptates; sed in omni oratione mementote
eam me senectutem laudare, quae fundamentis adulescentiae
constituta sit. ex quo efficitur id quod ego magno quondam
cum adsensu omnium dixi, miseram esse senectutem quae se
oratione defenderet; non cani nec rugae repente auctoritatem   5
adripere possunt, sed honeste acta superior aetas fructus capit
63 auctoritatis extremos. haec enim ipsa sunt honorabilia quae
videntur levia atque communia, salutari appeti decedi
adsurgi deduci reduci consuli; quae et apud nos et in aliis
civitatibus, ut quaeque optime morata est, ita diligentissime
observantur. Lysandrum Lacedaemonium (cuius modo feci   5
mentionem) dicere aiunt solitum, Lacedaemonem esse
honestissimum domicilium senectutis; nusquam enim tantum
tribuitur aetati, nusquam est senectus honoratior. quin etiam
memoriae proditum est, cum Athenis ludis quidam in
theatrum grandis natu venisset magno consessu, locum   10
nusquam ei datum a suis civibus; cum autem ad Lace-

---

61 2 A(ulo) *add. Fleckeisen*   4 hunc unum *Madvig*: unicum Ω (unum
hunc *iam Orelli, Klotz*)   5 virum: virium $P^1 V^1 A^2 D^2$ 6 est enim
totum *scripsi*: est totum $VP^2 L^2 A^2 D^2 H^2 Pa$ *recc.*: est itiotum $P^1 \beta$: estimotum
H^1: extimo Q: totum est $M\varsigma$: est id totum *Mommsen*   9 postea
M(arcum) $VMPaO^2\varsigma$: posteam BLD^1: postea $PAHD^2$ 10 aut ut iam
ante S^2(*ut vid.*), *Victorius, Gruterus*: aut iam ante ω (aut ante *Be*)   **63** 4
morata est: morata sunt $PHL^2 A^2$ 10 consessu: consensu $\varphi\lambda Q$

81

daemonios accessisset, qui legati cum essent certo in loco
consederant, consurrexisse omnes illi dicuntur et senem
64 sessum recepisse; quibus cum a cuncto consessu plausus esset
multiplex datus, dixisse ex eis quendam, Athenienses scire
quae recta essent, sed facere nolle. multa in vestro collegio
praeclara, sed hoc de quo agimus in primis, quod ut quisque
aetate antecedit, ita sententiae principatum tenet; neque 5
solum honore antecedentibus sed eis etiam qui cum imperio
sunt, maiores natu augures anteponuntur. quae sunt igitur
voluptates corporis cum auctoritatis praemiis comparandae?
quibus qui splendide usi sunt, ei mihi videntur fabulam aetatis
peregisse, nec tamquam inexercitati histriones in extremo 10
actu corruisse.

65 At sunt morosi et anxii et iracundi et difficiles senes: si
quaerimus, etiam avari. – sed haec morum vitia sunt, non
senectutis; ac morositas tamen et ea vitia quae dixi habent
aliquid excusationis, non illius quidem iustae sed quae
probari posse videatur: contemni se putant, despici, illudi; 5
praeterea in fragili corpore odiosa omnis offensio est. quae
tamen omnia dulciora fiunt et moribus bonis et artibus; idque
cum in vita, tum in scena intellegi potest ex eis fratribus qui in
Adelphis sunt – quanta in altero duritas, in altero comitas! sic
se res habet: ut enim non omne vinum, sic non omnis natura 10
vetustate coacescit. severitatem in senectute probo, sed eam
66 sicut alia modicam: acerbitatem nullo modo. avaritia vero
senilis quid sibi velit non intellego: potest enim quidquam esse
absurdius quam quo viae minus restet, eo plus viatici
quaerere?

XIX Quarta restat causa, quae maxime angere atque sollicitam 5
habere nostram aetatem videtur: appropinquatio mortis,

64 1 consessu: consensu P^1BA^1Q: cum sensu D^1 *om.* L^1 3 recta:
facta βH^1 vestro: nostro *SBe* **65** 2 morum vitia $H^2O^2Pa\varsigma$:
morosivitia *B*: morisvitia *D*: morvitia L^1A^1: morbi vitia α 9 duritas
$ML^2H^2PaRS^2ZQI$ *recc.*: duritias P^1: diritas *cett.*, *Nonius pp. 30.20 et
100.22 et in lemmate* 10 natura: aetas naturae φL^2A^2 12 alia
$MO^2RSZBeISgVaTLbPb$: aliam *cett.* **66** 3 minus: munus P^1V^1

quae certe a senectute non potest esse longe. o miserum senem
qui mortem contemnendam esse in tam longa aetate non
viderit! quae aut plane neglegenda est si omnino exstinguit
animum, aut etiam optanda si aliquo eum deducit ubi sit 10
futurus aeternus; atqui tertium certe nihil inveniri potest.
67 quid igitur timeam, si aut non miser post mortem aut beatus
etiam futurus sum? quamquam quis est tam stultus, quamvis
sit adulescens, cui sit exploratum se ad vesperum esse
victurum? quin etiam aetas illa multo plures quam nostra
mortis casus habet: facilius in morbos incidunt adulescentes, 5
gravius aegrotant, tristius curantur. itaque pauci veniunt ad
senectutem: quod ni ita accideret, melius et prudentius
viveretur; mens enim et ratio et consilium in senibus est, qui si
nulli fuissent, nullae omnino civitates fuissent. sed redeo ad
mortem impendentem: quod est istud crimen senectutis, cum 10
68 id ei videatis cum adulescentia esse commune? sensi ego in
optimo filio, tu in exspectatis ad amplissimam dignitatem
fratribus, Scipio, mortem omni aetati esse communem.

At sperat adulescens diu se esse victurum, quod sperare
idem senex non potest. – insipienter sperat: quid enim stultius 5
quam incerta pro certis habere, falsa pro veris? – at senex ne
quod speret quidem habet. – at est eo meliore condicione
quam adulescens, cum id quod ille sperat hic consecutus est:
69 ille vult diu vivere, hic diu vixit. quamquam o di boni! quid
est in hominis natura diu? da enim supremum tempus,
exspectemus Tartessiorum regis aetatem (fuit enim, ut

7 esse longe: longe abesse *VMO²ς* (abesse longe *Q*)   11 inveniri: -ire
P¹A¹D   **67** 2 est tam *O²H²GRETLaLbPb* omnes codd. *Nonii p. 294.13*: est
M: est etiam tam *SZBe*: etiam est tam *Q*: etiam *cett*.   3 sit (*post
quamvis*) *om. codd. Nonii*   4 nostra: -am *LA¹HM¹*   5 mortis casus
β*PaO²GREI²Q*: mortis *post ras. H*: casus mortis *cett*.   8 et ratio: ratio
PHA²   10 istud *Wesenberg*: illud *O²GREQ recc*.: istius ω (*del. H²*)
11 ei *om. VMH²Gς*   **68** 2 tu in exspectatis *Madvig*: tum in ex-
P²A²MH²OGς: tum inexspectati *D²*: tum exspectatis *cett*.   ad
MH²O²Pa²Gς: *om. cett*.   3 omni aetati: omni aetate *MRQ*: omnia etate
L¹A¹   4 se esse *D²*: esse se *A²KSg*: esse β*HP¹*: se *P²VML²PaGς*   **69** 2
natura: vita *A²KMO²Gς* (natura *vel* vita *O¹*)   supremum: summum *vel*
sommum *vel* somnum λ

scriptum video, Arganthonius quidam Gadibus, qui octo-
ginta regnaverit annos, centum viginti vixerit), sed mihi ne 5
diuturnum quidem quidquam videtur in quo est aliquid
extremum; cum enim id advenit, tum illud quod praeteriit
effluxit; tantum remanet quod virtute et recte factis
consecutus sis. horae quidem cedunt et dies et menses et anni;
nec praeteritum tempus umquam revertitur, nec quid 10
sequatur sciri potest; quod cuique temporis ad vivendum
70 datur, eo debet esse contentus. neque enim histrioni ut placeat
peragenda fabula est, modo in quocumque fuerit actu
probetur, neque sapienti usque ad 'plaudite' veniendum est;
breve enim tempus aetatis satis longum est ad bene
honesteque vivendum. sin processerit longius, non magis 5
dolendum est, quam agricolae dolent praeterita verni
temporis suavitate aestatem autumnumque venisse. ver enim
tamquam adulescentiam significat, ostenditque fructus
futuros; reliqua autem tempora demetendis fructibus et
71 percipiendis accommodata sunt; fructus autem senectutis est,
ut saepe dixi, ante partorum bonorum memoria et copia.

Omnia autem quae secundum naturam fiunt sunt habenda
in bonis; quid est autem tam secundum naturam quam
senibus emori? quod idem contingit adulescentibus 5
adversante et repugnante natura. itaque adulescentes mihi
mori sic videntur ut cum aquae multitudine flammae vis
opprimitur, senes autem sic ut cum sua sponte nulla adhibita
vi consumptus ignis exstinguitur; et quasi poma ex arboribus
cruda si sunt vi evelluntur, si matura et cocta decidunt, sic 10

---

4 Gadibus om. *VM*   5 regnaverit *V²MSZBeSb* (regnarit *RGPb*): regna-
verat *PHL²A²EIQ*: regnavit *V¹βPa Simbeck*: regnaret *T*   vixerit: -erat
PHL²A²Q: vixit *recc., Simbeck*   8 tantum: tantum enim *PHL²A²*   10
nec quid: ne quid *V¹A¹D*   11 cuique *P²L²A²KH²MGς*: cumque *P¹H¹*:
cuiquam *VβPaO*   70 3 sapienti *V²MGς*: sapientibus *cett.*   ad *om.*
MRQ recc.   est *om. BLDHGR*   4 est *om. P¹V¹H*   7 ver: vere
V¹λ   9 fructibus: frugibus *H codd. LEGen. G Nonii p 244.35* (frigibus *cod.*
B Nonii)   71 2 ante partorum *VMH²O²Gς*: ante pastorum *PL¹* (?*A¹*):
ante pratorum *Q*: ante pastorem *D¹*: ante peractorum *A²O¹*: peractorum
PH¹L²D²K   10 si sunt *VBMGς*: sunt *L¹*: *om. A¹D*: si sint
PHL²A²   vi *VMO²PaGς*: vix *cett.*   evelluntur: avell- *MPaς*

vitam adulescentibus vis aufert, senibus maturitas; quae
quidem mihi tam iucunda est, ut quo propius ad mortem
accedam, quasi terram videre videar aliquandoque in portum
72 ex longa navigatione esse venturus. senectutis autem nullus
est certus terminus, recteque in ea vivitur quoad munus offici
exsequi et tueri possis et tamen mortem contemnere; ex quo fit
ut animosior etiam senectus sit quam adulescentia et fortior.
hoc illud est quod Pisistrato tyranno a Solone responsum est, 5
cum illi quaerenti, qua tandem re fretus sibi tam audaciter
obsisteret, respondisse dicitur 'senectute'. sed vivendi est finis
optimus cum integra mente certisque sensibus opus ipsa suum
eadem quae coagmentavit natura dissolvit. ut navem, ut
aedificium idem destruit facillime qui construxit, sic hominem 10
eadem optime quae conglutinavit natura dissolvit; iam omnis
conglutinatio recens aegre, inveterata facile divellitur. ita fit
ut illud breve vitae reliquum nec avide appetendum senibus
73 nec sine causa deserundum sit; vetatque Pythagoras iniussu
imperatoris, id est dei, de praesidio et statione vitae decedere.

  Solonis quidem sapientis elogium est quo se negat velle
suam mortem dolore amicorum et lamentis vacare; vult,
credo, se esse carum suis; sed haud scio an melius Ennius 5

   'nemo me lacrimis decoret neque funera fletu
      faxit . . .' –

non censet lugendam esse mortem, quam immortalitas
74 consequatur. iam sensus moriendi aliquis esse potest, isque ad
exiguum tempus praesertim seni; post mortem quidem sensus aut optandus aut nullus est. sed hoc meditatum ab

72 3 possis et tamen mortem *VMPa²O²Gς*: possis et mortemque *H²*: possit
mortemque *PH¹O¹L²A²*: posset tamen mortem β: possit et tamen mortem
Pa¹   6 audaciter: audacter *V²RBe¹*   7 respondisse dicitur
φ*PaSZBeISg*: respondisse *V*β: respondit *GREQ*   10 destruit: distra(h)it
β: destruxit *Be*   12 divellitur: dev- *L¹A¹*   14 deserundum: adeseren-
dum *P¹*: adserendum *vel* -undum β*H¹* (-undum *scr.* *P²VBLASBeI*)   **73** 1
iniussu: ni iussu *PHA²D²S²*: in usu β   3 est *om. P¹HBLD*   5 credo:
credere *P²D²H*   se esse carum: carum se esse *SZBe*   scio
VMH²O²Pa²Gς: *om. cett.*   an melius: (h)(a)emilius *PL²A²D²O¹*:
omelius *H¹*: aut melius *M*

adulescentia debet esse, mortem ut neglegamus; sine qua
meditatione tranquillo esse animo nemo potest. moriendum 5
enim certe est, et incertum·an hoc ipso die: mortem igitur
omnibus horis impendentem timens, qui poterit animo
75 consistere? de qua non ita longa disputatione opus esse
videtur, cum recorder non Lucium Brutum qui in liberanda
patria est interfectus, non duos Decios qui ad voluntariam
mortem cursum equorum incitaverunt, non Marcum Atilium
qui ad supplicium est profectus ut fidem hosti datam 5
conservaret, non duos Scipiones qui iter Poenis vel corporibus
suis obstruere voluerunt, non avum tuum Lucium Paulum
qui morte luit collegae in Cannensi ignominia temeritatem,
non Marcum Marcellum cuius interitum ne crudelissimus
quidem hostis honore sepulturae carere passus est, sed 10
legiones nostras, quod scripsi in Originibus, in eum locum
saepe profectas alacri animo et erecto, unde se redituras
numquam arbitrarentur. quod igitur adulescentes, et ei
quidem non solum indocti sed etiam rustici contemnunt, id
docti senes extimescent?
15
76 Omnino ut mihi quidem videtur, studiorum omnium
satietas vitae facit satietatem. sunt pueritiae studia certa: num
igitur ea desiderant adulescentes? sunt ineuntis adulescentiae:
num ea constans iam requirit aetas quae media dicitur? sunt
etiam eius aetatis: ne ea quidem quaeruntur in senectute; sunt 5
extrema quaedam studia senectutis: ergo ut superiorum
aetatum studia occidunt, sic occidunt etiam senectutis; quod
cum evenit, satietas vitae tempus maturum mortis adfert.

74 5 esse animo nemo potest: a- e- p- n- *P¹*: a- e- n- p- *P²REQ*; a- n- e- p-
H²: animus esse potest *H¹*   6 et incertum: et id incertum *SZBe*   hoc
ipso *PHL²A²*: eo ipso *VMPaO²Gϛ*: ipso *B*: et ipso *L¹*: hac ipsa *A¹D*   7
qui (*ante* poterit) *P¹H¹BL¹A¹* (*?D*): quis *VMP²L²A²H²ϛ fort. recte*   **75** 9
ne φ: nec *cett.*   11–12 locum saepe profectas *O²MGQRTLaPb*: locum
profectas saepe *E*: locum saepe esse profectas *SZBe*: sepe locum esse
profectas *H²*: esse locum esse profectas *H¹*: locum esse profectas
PVL²A²O¹PaI: se profectas β   12 erecto *VPaRSZBeEI recc.*: erectos *M*:
erectas *GSb*: recto *cett.*   **76** 1 ut *om. P¹H¹βE*   studiorum: rerum
MO²GR recc. (rerum *post* omnium *Q*): s- r- *Z*   2 studia certa: certa
studia *V²MGREQ*: s- incerta *B*   6 quaedam studia: quidam studia λ:
studia quaedam *MH²GQRE*: studia quaedam studia *H¹*

XI 77 Non enim video cur quid ipse sentiam de morte non audeam vobis dicere, quod eo cernere mihi melius videor, quo ab ea propius absum. ego vestros patres, Publi Scipio tuque Gai Laeli, viros clarissimos mihique amicissimos, vivere arbitror, et eam quidem vitam quae est sola vita numeranda; nam dum sumus inclusi in his compagibus corporis, munere quodam necessitatis et gravi opere perfungimur. est enim animus caelestis, ex altissimo domicilio depressus et quasi demersus in terram, locum divinae naturae aeternitatique contrarium. sed credo deos immortales sparsisse animos in corpora humana, ut essent qui terras tuerentur, quique caelestium ordinem contemplantes, imitarentur eum vitae modo atque constantia. nec me solum ratio ac disputatio impulit ut ita crederem, sed nobilitas etiam summorum **78** philosophorum et auctoritas. audiebam Pythagoram Pythagoreosque, incolas paene nostros, qui essent Italici philosophi quondam nominati, numquam dubitasse quin ex universa mente divina delibatos animos haberemus; demonstrabantur mihi praeterea quae Socrates supremo vitae die de immortalitate animorum disseruisset, is qui esset omnium sapientissimus oraculo Apollinis iudicatus. quid multa? sic persuasi mihi, sic sentio: cum tanta celeritas animorum sit, tanta memoria praeteritorum futurorumque prudentia, tot artes, tantae scientiae, tot inventa, non posse eam naturam quae res eas contineat esse mortalem; cumque semper agitetur animus, nec principium motus habeat quia se ipse moveat, ne finem quidem habiturum esse motus quia numquam se ipse sit relicturus; et cum simplex animi natura esset, neque haberet in se quidquam admixtum dispar sui atque dissimile, non posse eum dividi: quod si non posset, non

---

77 1 non enim β: equidem non $H^2O^2G\varsigma$: equidem non enim $P^1VA^2O^1M$: non omni H^1 2 quo α: quod β   3 P(ubli) $VMO^2G\varsigma$: tu P. Pa^2: tu *cett.*   4 Gai (*vel* C.) *om.* DP^2R 5 numeranda MR^2Q: nominanda numeranda TMb: nominanda *cett.* (dominantem H^1)   **78** 3 quin ex *deficit P: substituitur Ra*   8 persuasi mihi: mihi persuasi H^2O^2GRQ *recc.*, codd. L^2FGPE *Nonii p. 41.31*   14 se ipse sit $MH^2G\varsigma$: se ipse esset *cett.*   16 posset: possit VH^1MRa

posse interire; magnoque esse argumento homines scire
pleraque antequam nati sint, quod iam pueri cum artes
difficiles discant, ita celeriter res innumerabiles adripiant, ut
eas non tum primum accipere videantur sed reminisci et 20
XXII 79 recordari. haec Platonis fere; apud Xenophontem autem
moriens Cyrus maior haec dicit: 'nolite arbitrari, o mihi
carissimi filii, me cum a vobis discessero nusquam aut nullum
fore. nec enim dum eram vobiscum animum meum videbatis,
sed eum esse in hoc corpore ex eis rebus quas gerebam 5
intellegebatis: eundem igitur esse creditote, etiamsi nullum
80 videbitis. nec vero clarorum virorum post mortem honores
permanerent, si nihil eorum ipsorum animi efficerent quo
diutius memoriam sui teneremus. mihi quidem numquam
persuaderi potuit, animos dum in corporibus essent
mortalibus vivere, cum excessissent ex eis emori; nec vero tunc 5
animum esse insipientem cum ex insipienti corpore evasisset,
sed cum omni admixtione corporis liberatus, purus et integer
esse coepisset, tum esse sapientem. atque etiam cum hominis
natura morte dissolvitur, ceterarum rerum perspicuum est
quo quaeque discedat, abeunt enim illuc omnia unde orta 10
sunt: animus autem solus nec cum adest nec cum discessit
apparet. iam vero videtis nihil esse morti tam simile quam
81 somnum; atqui dormientium animi maxime declarant
divinitatem suam; multa enim cum remissi et liberi sunt
futura prospiciunt: ex quo intellegitur quales futuri sint cum
se plane corporum vinculis relaxaverint. quare si haec ita
sunt, sic me colitote' inquit 'ut deum: sin una est interiturus 5
animus cum corpore, vos tamen deos verentes qui hanc

18 sint: sunt *HMREQ*   21 Platonis fere: Plato vester *VSZBeI*: Plato
dicit vester *M*   **79** 3 nusquam *VMRaL²D²H²O²Paς*: numquam *cett.*
7 videbitis: -batis *V¹L¹*   **80** 2–3 quo diutius *GREQTLaLbAd²S²*: quod
iustius β: quo iustius α   3 teneremus: tuerentur *Ra¹H¹L²A²K¹*   5
excessissent: exissent *DO²GRQE*: excessissent vel exissent M: exessissent
H¹: exossissent *BL¹*: exercissent *Z*   10 discedat: -ant *DMH²O²PaGς*
11 discessit: discesserit *DSZBe*: discedit *MPaGRI recc.*   **81** 1 atqui: atque
BL¹A¹Q   3 futuri sint: futuri sunt *VD¹MSZBeI recc.*   4 plane: plene
RaHA²S¹ZBeI   5 sin: si *RaHL²* (*?D²*)

omnem pulchritudinem tuentur et regunt, memoriam nostri
pie inviolateque servabitis.'

I 82 Cyrus quidem haec moriens; nos, si placet, nostra
videamus. nemo umquam mihi, Scipio, persuadebit aut
patrem tuum Paulum, aut duos avos Paulum et Africanum,
aut Africani patrem aut patruum, aut multos praestantes
viros quos enumerare non est necesse, tanta esse conatos quae 5
ad posteritatis memoriam pertinerent, nisi animo cernerent
posteritatem ad se ipsos pertinere. an censes (ut de me ipse
aliquid more senum glorier) me tantos labores diurnos
nocturnosque domi militiaeque suscepturum fuisse, si eisdem
finibus gloriam meam quibus vitam essem terminaturus? 10
nonne melius multo fuisset otiosam aetatem et quietam sine
ullo labore et contentione traducere? sed nescio quo modo
animus erigens se posteritatem ita semper prospiciebat, quasi
cum excessisset e vita, tum denique victurus esset. quod
quidem ni ita se haberet ut animi immortales essent, haud 15
optimi cuiusque animus maxime ad immortalitatem et
83 gloriam niteretur. quid quod sapientissimus quisque
aequissimo animo moritur, stultissimus iniquissimo? nonne
vobis videtur is animus qui plus cernat et longius videre se ad
meliora proficisci, ille autem cui obtusior sit acies non videre?

Equidem efferor studio patres vestros quos colui et dilexi 5
videndi, neque vero eos solos convenire aveo quos ipse
cognovi, sed illos etiam de quibus audivi et legi et ipse
conscripsi. quo quidem me proficiscentem haud sane quis

82 7 se ipsos *Opitz*: se *O²GREQTLaLb*: se posse *cett.*: sepse *tentavi*   an
censes *VO²Gς*: an cesses *M*: annecesses *B*: an necesse est *H*: anne censes
RaλO¹Pa   ipse: ipso *RaHL²D²RQ*   11 et quietam *VMHA²O²Pa²ς*:
om. *A¹DGPa¹ varie corrupta in BLRaO¹*   15 ni: nisi λ   16–17 immort-
alitatem et gloriam: immortalem gloriam *MPaQ recc.*: mortalem gloriam
RG: immortalitatis gloriam *SZBeI*   **83** 4 cui: cuius λ*GR*   6 vero
MGRSZBeEITSbLaLb, omnes codd. Nonii p. 270.42 et 276.1: enim *cett.* (*om.*
Q)   solos: solum *MGR recc., codd. Nonii omnes p. 270*   aveo *Victorius,*
Manutius: abeo *H¹L codd. EA^ACant. G Nonii p. 270*: habeo *cett., cod. H Nonii*:
ad eos *cod. L Nonii*

facile retraxerit, nec tamquam Peliam recoxerit; et si qui deus
mihi largiatur ut ex hac aetate repuerascam et in cunis 10
vagiam, valde recusem, nec vero velim quasi decurso spatio
84 ad carceres a calce revocari. quid habet enim vita commodi?
quid non potius laboris? sed habeat sane, habet certe tamen
aut satietatem aut modum. non libet enim mihi deplorare
vitam, quod multi et ei docti saepe fecerunt, neque me vixisse
paenitet, quoniam ita vixi ut non frustra me natum 5
existimem; et ex vita ita discedo tamquam ex hospitio, non
tamquam domo: commorandi enim natura deversorium
nobis, non habitandi dedit. o praeclarum diem, cum ad illud
divinum animorum concilium coetumque proficiscar,
cumque ex hac turba et colluvione discedam! proficiscar enim 10
non ad eos solum viros de quibus ante dixi, verum etiam ad
Catonem meum, quo nemo vir melior natus est, nemo pietate
praestantior; cuius a me corpus est crematum, quod contra
decuit ab illo meum; animus vero non me deserens sed
respectans, in ea profecto loca discessit quo mihi ipse cernebat 15
esse veniendum. quem ego meum casum fortiter ferre visus
sum, non quo aequo animo ferrem, sed me ipse consolabar
existimans non longinquum inter nos digressum et discessum
fore.
85 His mihi rebus, Scipio, id enim te cum Laelio admirari

9 nec tamquam Peliam recoxerit $V^1 I^2$: nec tamquam pilam recoxerit
$RaV^2 L^2 A^2 O^1 (?Pa^2) S^1 \zeta Be$: nec tamquam recoxerit pilam (*vel* pylam *vel*
philam) $MH^2 O^2 G^1 R$ *recc.*: nec tamquam retorserit pilam $G^2 E$ *recc. alii*: nec
tamquam pelam recoxerit Γ^1: nec tamquam pilam retorserit $S^2 I^3$: *om.*
$\beta HPa^1 QSg$ qui: quis $MH^2 O^2 G\zeta$, *omnes codd. Nonii p. 165.28*   10
repuerascam *sic scr.* H^1, *codd.* $LF^2 HEG$ *Nonii*: -escam *vel* -iscam *cett.*   **84**
2 habeat $HbH^2 O^2 GRS^2 Q$: habet ω   certe tamen: certe O: tamen certe
Hb 4 multi et ei docti (*vel* et ii) *edd., iam De Breda, Manutius*: multi
etiam docti V^2: multi et indocti $HbGRQITSg$: multi indocti $SBe\zeta$: multi et
docti *cett.*   me vixisse: vixisse me Hb *Bern. 104*   7 tamquam domo:
tamquam e(x) domo $VMHbH^2 O^2 G\zeta$ *fort. recte*   8 ad illud
$VMBH^2 A^2 PaS\zeta BeISg$: illud λ: in illud Hb *Aug. 51.12 recc.*: in illum GRT,
omnes codd. Nonii p. 524.30: ad illum $RaH^1 EQ$ 11 ad eos solum: ad eos
solos $RaA^2 D^2 Hb$: solum ad eos HQ 12 quo nemo vir melior natus est:
quo viro v- m- n- e- Ra: quo viro nemo vir m- n- e- L^2: quo viro vir melior
natus nemo est HQ: quo viro vir nemo melior natus est E: q̄m̄ nemo vir
melior natus est M 15 ipse: ipsi λ: ille M (*ante* cernebat)

solere dixisti, levis est senectus; nec solum non molesta, sed
etiam iucunda. quod si in hoc erro, qui animos hominum
immortales esse credam, libenter erro, nec mihi hunc errorem
quo delector, dum vivo, extorqueri volo; sin mortuus ut 5
quidam minuti philosophi censent nihil sentiam, non vereor
ne hunc errorem meum philosophi mortui irrideant. quod si
non sumus immortales futuri, tamen exstingui homini suo
tempore optabile est: nam habet natura, ut aliarum omnium
rerum, sic vivendi modum; senectus autem aetatis est peractio 10
tamquam fabulae, cuius defetigationem fugere debemus
praesertim adiuncta satietate.

Haec habui de senectute quae dicerem: ad quam utinam
perveniatis, ut ea quae ex me audistis re experti probare
possitis. 15

---

85 3 qui: quia *RaBDL²A²*   7 philosophi mortui: m- ph- *HbSZBe*:
mortui *G Reid*   8 sumus immortales futuri: sum -is -us *RaHL²EQ*
11 defetigationem (*vel* defat-): defectionem *RaHPa¹A³D²Q*   15 possitis:
possetis *A¹D²*: posistis *Ra.*

COMMENTARY

Cato Maior de senectute This form of the title is found as a heading in BLAD (hence presumably in their common exemplar) and in ViVaI; also as an *explicit* in B and Pa. The double title occurs in other MSS in variant forms: *Cato Maior vel de senectute* V, *Lib: Catonis de senectute* P, *de sententiis Catonis de senectute* O, etc. *Cato Maior* alone occurs as an *explicit* in S and Ad, *Cato* as the heading in S; while *De senectute* is found as a heading in M and later MSS, and as an *explicit* in L and V. However, M has the full double title for the *Laelius de amicitia*. H has no heading or *explicit*; nor have R, G and some later MSS. Medieval book-lists refer to *Tullius de senectute*.

The work is referred to by Cicero himself as *Cato Maior* three times (*Lael.* 4; *Off.* 1.151; *Att.* 14.21.3) and perhaps once as *Cato* (*Div.* 2.3)[1]; twice, in letters to Atticus (16.3.1; 16.11.3) and so informally, by the opening words *O Tite* or *O Tite si quid*; and C. employs the descriptive subtitle once in conjunction with the principal title (*Lael.* 4, *in Catone Maiore qui est scriptus ad te de senectute*), and also in *Div.* 2.3 (already mentioned: see footnote 1 on this page) where '*Cato*' in the same sentence may or may not refer to this work. Later Latin authors refer to *de senectute* (Val. Max. 8.13 ext. 1; Nonius, Charisius, Priscian), and *Cato Maior* (Lact. *Inst.* 6.20.4; schol. Juv. 11.78); Plutarch calls it Περὶ γήρως (*Cato* 17 and *Flamininus* 18: cf. note on §42).

There seems little doubt that *Cato Maior* is the original principal title and *de senectute* the subtitle; the manuscripts probably reflect Cicero's original *inscriptio*. C.'s formal style however tended to avoid using the

[1] *Interiectus est etiam nuper liber is quem ad nostrum Atticum de senectute misimus, in primisque quoniam philosophia vir bonus efficitur et fortis, Cato noster in horum librorum numero ponendus est.* '*Cato*' in this passage has often been taken to refer, not to the *Cato Maior*, but to the eulogy of Cato the Younger written by Cicero in 46 (cf. Pease ad loc.; Süss, *Cicero* 136 n.); but it is surely confusing to mention a different *Cato* in the second half of a sentence which began with a mention of the *Cato Maior*, without some very explicit indication. The *Cato Minor* is also out of place chronologically in this list, although this is not necessarily significant in view of the generally somewhat loose chronology in the passage. *Quoniam philosophia . . . fortis* may be seen as an excuse for including the *Cato Minor* in the list of philosophical works, since it must obviously have belonged to a different type of literature, although it may well have contained references to Cato's Stoicism. On the other hand, some excuse might also be thought to be necessary for the *Cato Maior*, which is not a work of academic philosophy, though its genre is that of a philosophic dialogue. I incline to think that the *Cato Maior* is meant.

prepositional phrase adjectivally, hence the circumlocutions *qui est scriptus ad te de senectute*, etc. Certainly both parts of the title are used by C., and there is no reason to conclude (as does K. A. Neuhausen in his introduction to the *Laelius* (Heidelberg 1981) 31ff.) that *de senectute* and *de amicitia* were not originally meant to be part of the titles of the *Cato* and *Laelius*. Later writers found the descriptive title *de senectute* convenient as a means of referring to the work (on the analogy of most of C.'s other philosophical titles), and it has tended to be known by that designation among English-speaking scholars in modern times.

The combination of the principal character's name with the subject-description occurs elsewhere among C.'s works only in the *Laelius de amicitia*. Not quite parallel, though similar, is the use of the names *Lucullus, Catulus, Torquatus* to refer to individual books of the *Academica* or *De finibus*. Proper names form the titles of the *Brutus* and *Hortensius*; there is no good evidence that subtitles were attached to these by Cicero, though the Renaissance knew the former as *de claris oratoribus*, and the latter could easily have been called *de philosophia*. Elsewhere in Latin, the double form of the title is found in the *Logistorici* of Varro, and also (with one or both elements in Greek) in the same author's Menippean satires. The *Logistorici* present a close parallel to Cicero's titles, e.g. *Catus de liberis educandis* (not *Cato*, however: H. Dahlmann in *Navicula Chiloniensis, Studia philologa Felici Jacoby ... oblata* (Leiden 1956) 114ff.), *Messalla de valetudine*, etc. Whether there is any substantial connection between Cicero's dialogues and the *Logistorici*, as some have thought to be shown by the similar form of title, is not known (cf. Introd. pp. 8–9).

Titles of this sort appear sporadically in Greek philosophic literature, and it is no doubt here that Cicero and Varro found their models. Plato's dialogues had subtitles attached to them, probably later than Plato's own time (H. Alline, *Histoire du Texte de Platon*, Bibl. École des hautes études, 218 (1915) p. 124), but some at least of these seem to have been current in Cicero's time: he calls the *Phaedo* 'de animo' in *Tusc.* 1.24. The catalogues of works in Diogenes Laertius attribute titles of this form to Aristotle, Theophrastus and Antisthenes; the same problem exists concerning these as with those of Plato. Later we find double titles among the works of Dio Chrysostom and Lucian. It is a possible speculation that the work of Aristo mentioned by Cicero in *Cato* 3 was called Τιθωνὸς ἢ περὶ γήρως (cf. Introd. p. 26). See Schanz–Hosius I, 561; Hirzel, *Dialog* I, 293; 329; 544ff.; L. Mercklin, *RhM* 12 (1857) 372ff.

1–3 Prologue dedicating the work to Atticus, and announcing the subject and characters of the dialogue The style of this prefatory section is dignified but not too formal, and tends to be allusive (we are not told the exact nature of the anxiety which is affecting Cicero and Atticus).

The troubles referred to are no doubt political, but the vagueness of the references precludes any precise deduction about the date and circumstances of writing (cf. Appendix 1). Cicero makes it clear that old age is a subject which personally interests both himself and Atticus; he compliments his friend on his well-known *humanitas*, and praises the general advantages of philosophy. See further Introd., pp. 1–3; Ruch, *Préambule* 173ff.; 300–1.

I 1 **'O Tite ...'** = Ennius, *Ann.* 10. 335ff. V², Skutsch. That the lines are Ennian was known or guessed by whoever glossed *ille vir* (below) with superscript *ennius* in A²V² (though the line is not about Ennius but by him), and by the glossator of R who wrote *versus enni* in the margin. As far as the context goes, the explanation of Madvig (*Opusc.* II, 290–6) has been generally accepted, and there are no serious competitors: the speaker of these lines, *ille vir* of the second quotation, is an Epirote shepherd offering help to T. Flamininus during the campaign against Philip V in 198 B.C. In Livy's account of these events (32.9–11, cf. Briscoe ad loc.) one shepherd was sent by the Epirote Charops to show Flamininus the way to Philip's camp; in Plutarch, *Flam.* 4, several shepherds come on their own initiative giving Charops as guarantee of their good faith (with which Skutsch compares *plenus fidei* in the second quotation). Cf. also Polyb. 27.15.2; Diod. 30.5; App. *Maced.* fr. 6; H. Nissen, *Kritische Untersuchungen über die Quellen der vierten und fünften Dekade des Livius* (Berlin 1863) 135ff.; N. G. L. Hammond, *JRS* 56 (1966) 52 n. 38.

This is the only extant instance in which Cicero begins a formal work with a quotation, though he sometimes so begins letters (e.g. *Fam.* 15.6.1). Cicero uses Ennius' lines to address *Titus* Pomponius Atticus: the effect of this play on the names is delicately urbane, not frivolous. By using the quotation Cicero calls Atticus by his *praenomen* – something he would not normally have done (though he does do so occasionally elsewhere): this, as it were, pulls Atticus into the poetic world. One may compare *Att.* 2.16.3 and 9.6.5 where the *praenomen* alone is used in conjunction with somewhat poetic or philosophical language: see my note in *CQ* 34 (1984) 238–9, and for the normal conventions, J. N. Adams, *CQ* 28 (1978) 145ff. It may be asked why Ennius' shepherd uses the *praenomen* to Flamininus. Poetical considerations are clear: *Flaminine* is excluded on metrical grounds, and *Quincti* alone would be odd, especially coming from a Greek: the Greeks tended to use the *praenomen* when referring to Romans (J. P. V. D. Balsdon, *Romans and Aliens* (London 1979) 158ff.). (Note that Enn. *Ann.* 109 V.², 104 Skutsch, the famous alliterative line, also begins *O Tite.*) In the case of Flamininus, in fact, there is particularly good attestation of the fact that the Greeks called him by his *praenomen*: Plutarch's life of Flamininus is entitled simply *Titus*, a paean addresses him as ὦ Τίτε σῶτερ (J. U.

Powell, *Collectanea Alexandrina* (Oxford 1925) 173), and there was a priest of Titus and dedications to 'Titus and Heracles' at Chalcis (Balsdon, ibid.).

ādiŭĕrō The normal and expected forms of the 1st sing. and 3rd pl. fut. perf. and 3rd pl. perf. subj. of *(ad)iuvare*, viz. *(ad)iūvero, -int*, are excluded by their form from dactylic verse, but Ennius, Catullus and Propertius (also Plautus and Terence in iambics) use forms with short *u*, conventionally written *(ad)iuero -int*. The spellings *(ad)iūro -int* are occasionally found in MSS and editions (P² here has *adiuro*), but *iŭĕrint* is guaranteed by the metre in Catull. 66.18 (at the end of a pentameter), while there is no instance in which the *-iŭĕr-* forms are metrically inadmissible. These forms are best explained by supposing that *iūvero* became *iŭero* as *audīvero* became *audĭero* or as *fŭvero* (attested in Ennius) became *fŭero* (Leumann, *Laut- u. Formenlehre* 596 n.4). Others explain *iuerint* as an aorist subjunctive form, derived from postulated *ioua-sint (parallel with *faxint*): Sommer, *Laut- u. Formenlehre* 562, 581, cf. 104; Leumann, ibid.; Fordyce on Catullus, loc. cit.; in that case *adiuero* and *levasso* here would be parallel in morphology, but one would have expected *iuvasso* from *iuvare*, and it is difficult to find a parallel instance of another first-conjugation verb with a form like *adiuero*.

V and later MSS read *adiuto*, a normalising variant, as does the text of Donatus *ad Ter. Phorm.* 34, p. 339. Such a coincidence requires explanation; in view of the fact that the quotation is present only in one branch of the tradition of Donatus (viz. the MSS K and R, the latter being in the relevant part of the text a copy of the former: M. D. Reeve, *CPhil* 74 (1979) 312, against O. Zwierlein, *Der Terenzkommentar des Donatus im Codex Chigianus H VII 240* (Berlin 1970) 99 n. 5, who thought the two MSS independent descendants of a common exemplar), and also of the fact that the reading *adiuto* is very common in late MSS of the *Cato*, it seems to me that by far the easiest explanation is to suppose that the quotation was interpolated in cod. K of Donatus, or its ancestor, from a contemporary copy of the *Cato* (cf. also P. Wessner, *RhM* 52 (1897) 80, before the discovery of K). Skutsch on the Ennius passage thinks the quotation was originally in Donatus, 'although it involves the difficult assumption that the quotation was dropped independently in two different branches of the Donatus transmission'. Difficult assumption indeed; and it is also difficult (though not impossible) to suppose that *adiuto* in the Cicero transmission is an ancient variant that survived only in V among the older MSS, or that *adiuero* was corrupted to *adiuto* independently in the text of Cicero and in the Ennius text used by Donatus. Nor am I convinced by Skutsch's further arguments that Donatus 'generally illustrates his comment with an example' (sometimes he does not), and that other Ennian fragments, otherwise unattested, occur in the *Phormio* commentary (this one is

COMMENTARY: I 1

exceptional since it would have been well known from Cicero).

levasso The archaic forms of the first conjugation in *-asso* (future) and *-assim* (subjunctive) correspond to forms like *faxo, faxim*, and are morphologically parallel to the Greek sigmatic future and aorist: see Leumann, *Laut- u. Formenlehre* 621–4; Sommer, *Laut- u. Formenlehre* 585; A Ernout, *Morphologie historique du latin* (Paris 1974) 163; E. Benveniste, *Bull. Soc. Ling.* 23 no. 70 (1922) 32ff. Benveniste distinguishes the meaning of these forms from that of the ordinary future and subjunctive, arguing that they tend to imply a successful result rather than simple futurity. Historically they have no relation to the future perfect and perfect subjunctive, whose meaning they often approach, and which they superficially resemble in verbs with a sigmatic perfect stem. Here the meaning is something like 'if I succeed in lightening your worry'.

coquit et versat in pectore fixa *coquit, versat* and *fixa* are probably to be taken together as parts of a single image, that of turning on a spit (Wuilleumier ad loc.; D. West, *Reading Horace* (Edinburgh 1967) 68). Skutsch ad loc. compares Homer, *Od.* 20.24ff. which has the similar though not identical image of a pudding being turned over in the fire. *versare* is well attested in the literal meaning of turning on a spit (or otherwise turning in culinary contexts): cf. esp. Hor. *Sat.* 1.5.72 *dum turdos versat in igni*; Plaut. *Asin.* 180; Lucr. 2.882; note also Cato, *Agr.* 79 *coquito versatoque*, and the etymology of *veru* as if from *versare* given by Varro, *LL* 5.128. *coquere* alone occurs with similar metaphorical meanings, Plaut. *Trin.* 225; Virg. *Aen.* 7.345 *curaeque iraeque coquebant*; Quint. *Inst.* 12.10.77; also ὀπτᾶν in Greek: Ar. *Lys.* 839; Callim. *epig.* 43; Theocr. 7.55. *figere* is used metaphorically of ideas, images or emotions fixed in the mind, though not apparently elsewhere of *curae* (*TLL* 6,1,718); here the image of the spit (if that interpretation is right) gives it a particular concreteness, 'piercing the breast'. Ennius uses the archaic scansion *versāt*, as usually in endings of this type: see Skutsch, *Ennius*, introd. 58–9; Lindsay, *ELV* 137; Leumann, *Laut- u. Formenlehre* 111; Sommer, *Laut- u. Formenlehre* 126; 146–7; 511.

adfari A word belonging to the high style, absent from Cicero's speeches or letters, which here has a similarly urbane effect to the use of the poetic quotation to address Atticus. Cf. *TLL* 1,1245–6.

ille vir The shepherd: see above on *O Tite . . .*

plenus On the dropping of final *s*, making this word trochaic, see Skutsch, introd. 56; E. Hamp, *CPhil* 54 (1959) 165ff.

fideī On the scansion see Skutsch ad loc.

noctesque diesque A poetic phrase (*noctes diesque, noctes et dies* are common prose equivalents). Double *-que* in general is characteristic of poetic style, but it is not clear that it was originally foreign to Latin (as Fraenkel thought, *Plautinisches im Plautus* (Berlin 1922) 211); such phrases

97

as *susque deque* (Plaut. *Amph.* 886, etc.) can hardly be imitations of Greek epic, though no doubt the Homeric precedents (and metrical convenience) gave impetus to the poetic use of double *-que*. Cf. H.-Sz. 515; K.-S. II, 35; Brink on Horace *AP* pp. 92–3 and index p. 544; id. on *Epist.* II, p. 580; D. O. Ross, *Style and Tradition in Catullus* (Harvard 1969) 63–5; G. Dunkel, *Glotta* 58 (1980) 99; W. John, *Glotta* 33 (1954) 296. It seems to be generally accepted that the isolated use of *noctesque diesque* in Ciceronian prose, *Fin.* 1.51 *easque ipsas sollicitudines quibus eorum animi noctesque diesque exeduntur*, is likely to be an Ennian reminiscence (K.-S. ibid.; Landgraf on *Rosc. Am.* 6; Vahlen and Skutsch on the Ennius passage; Madvig however disagreed, cf. his note ad loc.).

moderationem Not moderation, but being well controlled (*moderari*): cf. §33 below. On Atticus' *moderatio*, cf. *Att.* 1.20.1; for *moderatio* as a Latin equivalent of σωφροσύνη, cf. *Tusc.* 3.16; *TLL* 8,1206.

The word order is characteristically elegant: by the device called *coniunctio* (*Ad Her.* 4.37), *animi tui*, which goes with both *moderationem* and *aequitatem*, is placed after the first of the pair: cf. English 'good men and true'. *aequitas animi* is the Ciceronian phrase for what would be called *aequanimitas* by a later writer: *TLL* 1,1014,11ff. *aequanimitas* in Ter. *Phorm.* 34 and *Ad.* 24 means 'fair-mindedness', which would be simply *aequitas* in classical prose; conversely *aequitas* alone is occasionally used to mean 'equanimity' in Seneca, Tacitus and later.

non cognomen solum O²RE: *cognomen non solum* ω. The reading of the older MSS has been defended by taking *solum* as an adjective agreeing with *cognomen*, rather than as an adverb: there would clearly be nothing wrong with e.g. *teque cognomen non ineptum deportasse*, and cf. below, §83, *eos solos*, *Lael.* 102, *Fin.* 1.44 and Madvig's note; Dahl, *Handschriftenkunde* I, 11; Krebs–Schmalz, *Antibarbarus* II⁷, 587. However, this ignores the presence of *sed humanitatem et prudentiam*: one can say *Gaius non solus venit sed cum uxore*, but not *Gaius non solus venit sed uxor*. *non* must precede *cognomen*; I therefore accept the reading of O²RE, as in a number of other places (cf. Introd. p. 39). Cf. also A. C. Clark's review of Simbeck's edn., *CR* 28 (1914) 205.

Cicero also comments on Atticus' *cognomen* in *Fin.* 5.4; cf. *Att.* 2.1.3; D. R. Shackleton Bailey, *Cicero's Letters to Atticus*, introd. 3–4.

deportasse For compounds with *de* used of movement from a province to Rome, cf. *decedere de provincia*, Greek κατελθεῖν; and for this figurative use of *deportare*, cf. *Att.* 6.1.7 *benevolentiam deportassem*. (The meaning 'deport', 'banish', is not found until after Cicero's time.)

humanitatem 'that untranslatably Roman amalgam of kindness and culture, width of mind and tact of manner' (Shackleton Bailey, cited above). Here the culture, and particularly philosophy, is more in view than the kindness. Untranslatable the abstract noun may be; our word 'civilised', in some contexts, comes near to being an equivalent of the adjective. One supposes that a truly 'civilised' man would not give way to desperation at the approach of old age: in the same way, Atticus' *humanitas* and *prudentia* mean that he will take such things calmly. Despite the fact that Athens is here supposed to be the source of Atticus' *humanitas*, there does not seem to be a proper Greek equivalent of the term: the nearest is φιλανθρωπία, but that is only a partial equivalent, covering the kindness but not the culture. For Atticus' *humanitas*, see *Leg.* 3.1; Nep. *Att.* 4.1; 16.1; also below on §26.

prudentiam Athens was naturally famous for 'wisdom' and culture: cf. Plato, *Apol.* 29d; Cic. *Rosc. Am.* 70 and Landgraf's note; *Flacc.* 62; Nep. *Att.* 3.3; Pliny, *Ep.* 8.24.2; E. Wölfflin, *ALL* 7, 144–5.

et tamen The sense of the passage here requires the translation 'and yet', καίτοι. However, the logical connection here is slightly different from most Ciceronian occurrences of this combination of particles, which may be classified into two more or less distinct types, (a) when two co-ordinated statements are both affirmed as true, despite the expectation that the former excludes the latter: the appropriate translation here is 'and still' or 'and at the same time' (cf. §72 below; *Fam.* 9.22.3; *Verr. II* 4.124; *De rep.* 1.55; *Div.* 2.106; etc.); and (b) where a second statement is made proving the same point as the first, and is affirmed irrespective of the truth of the first (cf. on §16 below; Madvig on *Fin.* 2.84); in such cases the English equivalent is 'and anyway'. The same range of uses is found with *ac tamen*. The meaning 'and yet' for *et tamen* and *ac tamen* seems to occur more often in later authors, e.g. Juv. 4.69; Tac. *Ann.* 6.30, etc. I have wondered whether *sed tamen* or *at tamen* (for the latter cf. Housman, *Papers* III, 1053, but not quite the usage described by Madvig on *Fin.* 2.85) might fit the context, and Ciceronian usage, better in this passage, as the connection seems to be more adversative than additive; however, the *et* of *et tamen*, like our 'and' in 'and yet', seems on occasion to lose some of its additive force, even in Cicero: if this passage were changed, one would also have to change at least *Verr. II* 5.9 *et tamen coeptum esse in Sicilia moveri aliquot locis servitium suspicor* (note *suspicor* there as in the present passage). There is probably no advantage to be gained from such 'tidying up' of the usage of particles in Cicero: the context makes the connection clear in each case.

quibus me ipsum This passage is more or less a standard example of 'attraction' (K.–S. I, 719: see the other examples there quoted). The term is misleading: such sentences are best explained as elliptical, and in most cases it is easy enough to complete the sense by repeating words from the main clause. However, in others (as here; *Att.* 13.45.1; *Leg.* 1.52; etc.) such a completion of the sense results in illogicality: *te suspicor eisdem rebus quibus me ipsum suspicor commoveri* is not sensible; *quis enim suspicatur de se ipso?* (Erasmus ad loc.). The construction must simply be noted as an idiom. Cf. Madvig on *Fin.* 2.88; for another instance of 'attraction' cf. below on §56.

consolatio 'the task of consoling': *TLL* 4,476. The abstract noun in *-tio*, as often in earlier Latin, refers to the activity or process, rather than to the completed action as in later writers and in the derived languages; cf. *confectio* below in this section, and the words denoting agricultural processes in §§51–4.

maior A greater, i.e. more difficult (not 'more important') task than writing about old age. The sentence contrasts proleptically with *nunc autem. . .*

conscribere = *scribere* with the added idea of composition: cf. *Brut.* 132; *Att.* 13.5.1; etc.

2 onere . . . levari For old age as a burden, cf. §§4 and 14; Anaxandrides fr. 53 Kock τῶν φορτίων μέγιστον; Sen. *Ep.* 30.1.

adventantis Cic. speaks rather euphemistically, as both he and Atticus were over sixty, the age at which *senectus* was usually reckoned to begin: Cicero was sixty-two, Atticus three years older. Cf. Introd. p. 2 n. 8.

modice . . . ferre For this phrase cf. *De or.* 1.132; *Tusc.* 1.111; 4.40; *Fin.* 1.46; *Planc.* 11; Livy 24.4.1; *TLL* 8,1236; *OLD* s.v. *modice*, 1a.

certo scio This should be read, even though the consensus of the MSS is in favour of *certe*. *certo scio* is the regular form in Cicero and earlier (K.–S. 1, 800); Cic. would be unlikely to follow *certo* above with *certe* at so short a distance. It is not surprising that *certe*, the later form, occasionally intrudes itself into MSS of earlier authors. There are only a couple of places in Cicero where the MSS are uniformly in favour of *certe* (*Phil.* 12.29; *Att.* 12.41.3): it is more probable that the MSS are in error than that Cicero altered his usage. There seems to be no observable difference in meaning between the two forms.

It is not correct to suppose that *certo* is used only with *scire*: see e.g. *Tusc.* 5.81 *certo futurum*; *Att.* 10.14.3; Plaut. *Poen.* 787; etc.

occurrebas dignus The use of a predicative adjective with this verb is unusual, and I know of no exact parallel; it may be a Graecism (παρίστασό μοι ἄξιος ὤν). K.–S. (1, 16) list this passage among instances of 'kopulaartige Verben'. Livy 25.24.12 *Atheniensium classes demersae et exercitus deleti occurrebant* is sometimes quoted as a parallel, but the participles there are in the *ab urbe condita* construction and present no problem. For *occurrere* in the sense of 'occur to one's mind', with personal subject, cf. *TLL* 9,2, 397, 23ff.

confectio A Ciceronian word, rare elsewhere, like many abstracts in *-tio*: *TLL* 4,170. For the meaning, cf. on *consolatio* above.

absterserit Cf. *Tusc.* 3.43 *luctum omnem absterseris*; *Top.* 86, *oratio . . . aegritudinem abstergens*; *Fam.* 9.16.9; *Q. fr.* 2.8.4; *TLL* 1, 189, 66ff.

pareat The subjunctive is best explained as due to attraction to the mood of *possit*, which has a causal sense: 'insofar as anyone who obeys philosophy is able to ...' There are many instances of this type of attraction in Cicero: see K.–S. II, 202 and 204 n. 4; Madvig on *Fin.* 2.86. Reid takes *possit* as potential subjunctive, 'would be able', with *qui pareat = si quis pareat* 'if anyone were to obey'; this seems less characteristically Ciceronian, though such things do occur, e.g. *Lael.* 53; *Leg.* 2.2; Nepos, *Att.* 16.3.

omne tempus aetatis For the idea that philosophy is advantageous in all ages of life, cf. Epicurus, *Menoec.* 122 (a protreptic context), referred to below on §38.

sine molestia Cf. Musonius Rufus 17, p. 91 H. (cf. Introd. p. 28), where it is said that one with correct education will be able to bear old age ἀλύπως.

3 ceteris I.e. other matters in philosophy: this anticipates and contrasts with *hunc librum ... de senectute.* Cf. *Tusc.* 4.4 *sed de ceteris studiis alio loco et dicemus, si usus fuerit, et saepe diximus.*

diximus Cicero has shifted to the first person plural: the man has become the author. On the 'plural of authorship', see H.–Sz. 19; R. S. Conway, *T. Camb. Phil. Soc.* 5. 1 (1899) 12; 18; 33; E. Hancock, *CQ* 19 (1925) 45ff.; W. Maguinness, *CQ* 35 (1941) 127ff.

multa ... saepe On pleonastic phrases of this sort, cf. Löfstedt, *Synt.* II, 177–8.

Tithono The story of Tithonus, the husband of Eos, who obtained for him immortality but not eternal youth, is first narrated in *Hom. Hymn Ven.* 218–38; for other passages mentioning the myth see P.–W. 6A, 1518–19. Tithonus would clearly have been excellently qualified to speak on the subject of old age, although one would not have thought that he would have much to say in its favour: on the question of the contents of Aristo's work here referred to, see Introd. p. 26. For Tithonus elsewhere as an example of old age, cf. Plaut. *Men.* 854; Hor. *Od.* 2.16; Plut. *An seni* 792e; Headlam on Herodas 10; Otto, *Sprichwörter* p. 349.

Aristo Ceus On the identity of Aristo, the Cean or the Chian, see Appendix 2, and cf. Introd. pp. 7; 15; 26. With the majority of scholars I believe that the Aristo concerned is the Cean, and hence read *Ceus*: this Aristo succeeded Lycon as head of the Lyceum around 225 B.C.; for a collection of the fragments of his works with commentary, see F. Wehrli, *Die Schule des Aristoteles*, IV, *Lykon und Ariston von Keos* (Basle 1952).

The MSS give a number of variants, including the two possible ones *Aristo Ceus* (RMc) and *Aristo Chius* (BLADOE). It is impossible to decide on purely stemmatic grounds what the archetype read. The agreement of BLAD shows that their common exemplar read *Aristo Chius*; what α read is not at all clear, but it is just possible that the readings of the α MSS could be corruptions of *Aristo Ceus* (*Aristoteles* via *Aristoteus*). In any case, the occurrence of *Aristo Ceus* in one relatively late branch of the tradition is difficult to explain, whether or not it is the correct reading. *Lectio difficilior* arguments are worthless, and the spelling *Cius* for the ethnic from Ceos merely provides a convenient mechanism for corruption (Nauck, Reid, etc.); the spelling *Cius* would not have been the classical one (Housman, *Papers* II, 887) and there is no warrant for introducing it into the text. The MSS provide no good ground for choosing one or other Aristo, and the choice must be made on other grounds.

parum enim esset auctoritatis Aristo of Ceos is criticised by Cicero for lack of *auctoritas* in *Fin.* 5.13 (there the identification of Aristo is not open to doubt). For the bearing of this on the Ceos/Chios question here, see Appendix 2.

Marco Catoni seni On the use of historical characters in Cicero's dialogues, and the choice of Cato in particular, see Introd. pp. 5–7; 17. The dramatic date of the dialogue is 150 B.C. (§14), when Cato was 83 (cf. §32 *quartum ago annum et octogesimum*), one or two years before his death.

Laelium et Scipionem It was not unreasonable to make Laelius and Scipio the interlocutors in this dialogue with Cato, as Cicero seems to have known a tradition that Scipio Aemilianus admired Cato (*De rep.* 2.1; Introd. p. 18). From a historical point of view, Cic. was careful enough to choose a dramatic date when Scipio was in Rome (H. Nissen, *RhM* 28 (1871) 271; F. Padberg, *Cicero und M. Porcius Cato Censorius* (diss. Münster 1933) 46ff.), though the exact place of the dialogue is not specified (as it is not in *Lael.* or *Part. or.*): cf. Becker, *Technik und Szenerie* 26–7.

facimus admirantes Cf. §54 below, *Homerus ... Laertam lenientem desiderium ... facit*; *Orat.* 85; *Tusc.* 1.40; *Att.* 13.19.3; etc.; cf. Greek ποιεῖν; for the use of the participle in these phrases, see Laughton, *Participle* 51 and 127.

eruditius ... disputare This refers both to learning (Greek allusions, etc.) and to fineness of argument and style. Cicero does not mean here that he is making Cato talk beyond his intelligence or education (Cato was clearly intelligent enough to understand philosophy, even if he did not approve of it); merely that the Cato of the dialogue displays his learning more than the real Cato did in his books (cf. below on *litteris Graecis*). Nevertheless, this sentence is a slightly ironical apology for making Cato retail Ciceronian opinions with a certain amount of Ciceronian urbanity (cf. Introd. p. 21). Cicero goes to much greater lengths to apologise for making Lucullus talk philosophy in the *Academica priora*, and cf. also the treatment of Crassus and Antonius in the *De oratore* (cf. Ruch, *Préambule* 189 and 263–7). It is clear enough from this that the *Cato* should not be used as evidence for the real Cato's literary knowledge or tastes (Astin, *Cato* 159), although Cicero does include some touches of authentic characterisation (cf. Introd. pp. 21–2).

attribuito The second person imperative in -*to* is slightly archaic, slightly formal and less peremptory than the ordinary imperative. It is traditionally called the 'future imperative', and is often used, as here, when there is a dependent clause in the future tense (K.–S. 1, 196ff.), though it clearly has nothing to do with the future in form. It is common in legal and didactic language; in ordinary Latin it becomes rarer from Cicero's time onwards, tending to be replaced in polite commands by the future indicative (compare with the present passage *De or.* 2.14 *si cupidius factum existimas, Caesari attribues*). Here the slight formality is in keeping with the urbane style.

litteris Graecis The idea that Cato was converted in old age to the study of Greek literature occurs first in Cic. *Acad. pr.* 2.5, then here (cf. §§26 and 38 below); Nepos, *Cato* 3.2; Val. Max. 8.7.1; Quint. *Inst.* 12.11.23. Even if all these later mentions of the matter derive from Cicero, there is no reason why we should not believe Cicero (cf. Introd. pp. 19–20). There is no evidence to the contrary except the late and abbreviated testimony of [Victor], *De vir. ill.* 47, which says that Cato was taught *litterae Graecae* by Ennius (presumably earlier in his life): some have tried to reconcile this with the other evidence by taking it to mean that Ennius taught him the Greek language. (Valerius Maximus, in contrast, says that Cato came late even to *Latinae litterae*.) There is no implication in Cicero, etc., that Cato was ignorant of Greek before he turned to the study of Greek literature; Plutarch, *Cato* 12 and Val. Max. loc. cit. attest that he knew the language, though his Roman pride did not allow him to speak it in public. Nor is the idea of a conversion to the study of Greek literature inconsistent with Cato's opposition to many aspects of Greek culture; it is clear from Cato's writings that he was familiar with Greek historians and other writers, and Plutarch (*Cato* 2) and Pliny (*NH* 29.14) note his use of unacknowledged quotations from Greek authors (cf. Astin, *Cato* 162ff.). Cato himself in the advice given to his son, preserved in Pliny, tells him *quod bonum sit illorum litteras inspicere, non perdiscere*; this implies that he saw nothing wrong with a certain amount of Greek learning. An interest in Greek literature need not imply that one agrees with everything one reads there; no doubt the philosophers still seemed *mera mortualia* to him even if he read their works. See further Introd. pp. 19ff.; Kienast, *Cato* 101ff.; Kammer, *Untersuchungen* 118ff.

perstudiosum This word occurs nowhere outside Cicero (this passage, *Tusc.* 5.63, *Att.* 5.20.10; the adverb in *Brut.* 206). These compounds with *per-*, in general colloquial, are characteristic of the polite, urbane language of Cicero's dialogues and letters. In general see J. André, *REL* 29 (1951) 121; Axelson, *Unpoetische Wörter* 37; Hofmann, *Umgangssprache* 76; Brink on Horace, *AP* 349; H.–Sz. 164. There is no suggestion of irony in *perstudiosum* here.

iam enim ipsius ... Cf. *Lael.* 5 *tu velim a me animum parumper avertas, Laelium loqui ipsum putes.* On characterisation in this dialogue, cf. Introd. pp. 21–2.

4–5 Introductory conversation To Scipio's enquiry and expression of wonder at Cato's bearing in old age, Cato replies with some general philosophic precepts. The enquiry by a subsidiary character is a convenient way of opening the dialogue: cf. *Lael.* 16; *De or.* 1.98; 1.205; *Part. or.* 1; Becker, *Technik und Szenerie* 17.

II 4 Saepenumero admirari soleo 'I have often been amazed' is a convenient rhetorical opening: cf. Isocr. *Paneg.* 1; Xen. *Mem.* 1.1; the spurious preface to Theophr. *Characters*; also *cogitanti mihi saepenumero, De or.* 1.1, and similar openings; for the word *saepenumero*, often used in such contexts, see Landgraf on *Rosc. Am.* 67; Sall. *Cat.* 52.7; Tac. *Ann.* 14.43; G. Bernardi Perini, *Ž. Ant.* 22 (1972) 131.

sapientiam On Cato's *sapientia* – naturally to be taken as practical wisdom and common sense, rather than proficiency in academic philosophy – cf. on §5 below; *Lael.* 7 and 9. There seem to be no obvious Ciceronian parallels for *sapientia* with a dependent genitive (*ceterarum rerum*), though *prudentia* with gen. is frequent enough.

quod ... senserim For this slightly illogical idiom (the object of wonder is Cato's bearing in old age, not Scipio's perception of it), fairly common in various forms, see K.–S. II, 200.

Aetna gravius The allusion is to Euripides, *HF* 637, ἁ νεότας μοι φίλον αἰεί, τὸ δὲ γῆρας ἄχθος | βαρύτερον Αἴτνας σκοπέλων ἐπὶ κρατὶ κεῖται (so Fritzsche: for variant readings see Bond ad loc.). The Euripides passage is recalled by Callimachus, *Aetia* fr. 1, 35ff. (cf. Apollod. *Bibl.* 1.6.2; R. Pfeiffer, *Hermes* 63 (1928) 328ff.) and twice by Teles (pp. 42 and 51 H.); the parallel with Teles had led to speculation about lost philosophical sources (cf. Hense's introduction, pp. 121–2), but presumably Cicero was quite able to recall Euripides directly. The reference to the captivity of the rebellious giants under Etna is picked up below, §5, *Gigantum modo bellare.* (Note the position of *se* in second place, a good example of 'Wackernagel's Law': J. Wackernagel, *IF* 1 (1892) 333–436 = *Kleine Schriften* (Göttingen 1953) I, 1ff.).

Scipio et Laeli Laelius, having no *cognomen*, is addressed by his *nomen gentilicium*. Note that Cato uses the more familiar *cognomen* or *nomen* alone in talking to his juniors, except in the climactic passage §77 below, where see note. Scipio on the first occasion uses the more respectful *praenomen* + *cognomen*, *Marce Cato.* Cf. Adams, cited above on §1.

bene beateque vivendum A common phrase of Ciceronian philosophy: cf. *Lael.* 45; *Fin.* 1.5; 1.14; 2.20; etc. etc. (see Merguet, *Lexikon* s.v. *bene, beate*, I, 325 and 327); it is used presumably as an equivalent of Greek phrases like εὖ ζῆν, μακαρίως ζῆν, εὐδαιμονεῖν. On alliterative pairs of this sort in Latin, see E. Wölfflin, *Ausgewählte Schriften* (Leipzig 1933) 255ff. This type of phrase is not exclusively philosophical: cf. Catull. 14.10; 23.15 *bene ac beate.*

qui autem ... adferat Cf. *Lael.* 7, *hanc esse in te sapientiam existimant, ut omnia tua in te posita esse ducas, humanosque casus virtute inferiores putes*; *Tusc.* 5.36 *cui viro ... ex se ipso apta sunt omnia quae ad beate vivendum ferunt*, which occurs in an adaptation of Plato, *Menexenus* 247e ὅτῳ γὰρ ἀνδρὶ εἰς ἑαυτὸν ἀνήρτηται πάντα τὰ πρὸς εὐδαιμονίαν φέροντα ἢ ἐγγὺς τούτου..., τούτῳ ἄριστα παρεσκεύασται ζῆν. The present passage is also near to Plato's words and it is possible that Cicero had them in mind here, or at least was unconsciously recalling his own version of them in the *Tusculans*. It is therefore wrong to see, as some have done, specifically Stoic content in this passage. The second half of this sentence does indeed bear a tenuous similarity to a fragment of Aristo of Chios (on which see Appendix 2), but it is such a commonplace sentiment that Cicero needed no specific source for it.

a se ipsi petunt *ipsi* agrees with the subject of *petunt*; this is regular in Cicero, cf. K.–S. 1, 632.

nihil ... adferat Cf. §71 below and note; *Fam.* 4.9.2; and above on *qui autem ... adferat.*

quam ut adipiscantur ... adeptam A common idea; first in Euripides, fr. 1080 N.² (Stob. 4.50b.40) ὦ γῆρας... πᾶς τις εἰς σὲ βούλετ' ἀνθρώπων μολεῖν · | λαβὼν δὲ πεῖραν, μεταμέλειαν λαμβάνει | ὡς οὐδέν ἐστι χεῖρον ἐν θνητῷ γένει; Menander fr. 644 Koerte (555 Kock, Stob. 4.50b.41) ὦ γῆρας βαρύ, | ὡς οὐδὲν ἀγαθόν, δυσχερῆ δὲ πόλλ' ἔχεις | τοῖς ζῶσι καὶ λυπηρά · πάντες εἰς σὲ δὲ | ἐλθεῖν ὅμως εὐχόμεθα καὶ σπουδάζομεν; Antiphanes fr. 238 K. (Stob. 4.50a.8, under the lemma Κράτητος ἐξ Ἀντιφάνους; = Crates, fr. 19b K.; cf. Hense, *Teletis Reliquiae* pref. p. cxix n.) ὠνείδισάς μοι γῆρας ὡς κακὸν μέγα | ... οὗ πάντες ἐπιθυμοῦμεν, ἂν δ' ἔλθη ποτέ, | ἀνιώμεθ' · οὕτως ἐσμὲν ἀχάριστοι φύσει; id. frr. 94 and 256 K.; Menecrates ap. Stob. 4.50b.62 γῆρας ἐπὰν μὲν ἀπῇ, πᾶς εὔχεται, ἢν δέ ποτ' ἔλθη, | μέμφεται · ἔστι δ' ἀεὶ κρεῖσσον ὀφειλόμενον; Bion fr. 63 Kindstrand (ap. Diog. Laert. 4.51) μὴ δεῖν ἔφασκεν ὀνειδίζειν τὸ γῆρας, ἐς ὃ πάντες εὐχόμεθα ἐλθεῖν; Democritus fr. 206 D.–K.; Theodectes, Meineke, *Fragmenta Comicorum Graecorum* IV, 690; [Hippocrates], *Ep.* 17.40–1; Sen. *Const. sap.* 17.2; Aug. *In Evang. Ioann.* 32.9; Apostolius 5.41 (Leutsch–Schneidewin, *Paroem.* II, 344); and lastly a medieval imitation of our passage, Marbod of Rennes, *Liber decem capitulorum* 5 (*de senectute*) 63–4, *cumque senectutem cupiunt omnes adipisci,* | *accusant omnes et detestantur adeptam.*

With so many parallels it is impossible to single out one as a source, or to decide in what relationship they stand to one another: the idea is simply a piece of popular wisdom of the sort that is repeated over and over again in popular philosophy, comedy and other genres. There is some possibility that Bion of Borysthenes was a nearer source than some of the others (cf. Introd. p. 14 and Appendix 3); alternatively Cicero may have found the sentiment in a lost Roman comedy (though there is no need, as Scaliger did, to attempt to make iambics out of Cicero's words here). See further Otto, *Sprichwörter* 316; Schröter, *De Cic. C. M.* 46.

omnes optant The ancients prayed for old age itself, not just for long life. Cf. εὐχόμεθα in the Menander and Bion quotations above, πᾶς εὔχεται in Menecrates. See Euripides fr. 369.2 N.² μετὰ δ' ἡσυχίας πολιῷ γήρᾳ συνοικοίην; Hor. *Od.* 1.31.19 and Nisbet–Hubbard ad loc.; Leonidas of Tarentum, *Anth. Pal.* 7.163.7, cf. Antipater of Sidon, ibid. 7.164.9.

adeptam α: *adepti* β. It is impossible on MS grounds, and extremely difficult on others, to decide between these two forms; but one has to print something. I prefer *adeptam* on two very marginal grounds: (a) it may be slightly old-fashioned, in keeping with the characterisation of Cato (Introd. p. 22): cf. its use in this sense in Sall. *Jug.* 101.9 *adeptam victoriam*, *Catil.* 7, and in Silver Latin (cf. Neue–Wagener III, 23; *TLL* 1,690, 21ff.); (b) it seems slightly awkward that *adepti* should share an object (*eandem*) with *accusant*, at any rate for normal Ciceronian style. On deponent past participles with passive meaning, see K.–S. I, 111; they occur in Cicero more often than is sometimes supposed: cf. in this work §59 *dimensa*, §74 *meditatum*. There is a similar textual problem at Ov. *Trist.* 4.8.19.

stultitiae inconstantia The stupid man is *inconstans*, as the wise man is supposed to be *constans* (*Acad. pr.* 2.23; *Lael.* 8; 64; *Off.* 1.69; Sen. *De constantia sapientis*; etc.). *constantia* is a Roman virtue, and is referred to in Latin philosophical and other literature more often than its equivalents καρτερία and βεβαιότης are in Greek philosophy. The denunciation of *stultitia* is reminiscent of Stoicism, but this could be due to Cicero and does not cast any light on his sources: cf. above on *qui autem omnia . . . adferat*.

atque This is used here for the sake of the clausula, according to Cic.'s usual practice, which is to use it before a consonant only in circumstances where it helps the rhythm (contrast §66 below). See J. Wolff, *N. Jahrb. Kl. Phil.* Suppl. 26 (1901) 637ff.; Axelson, *Unpoetische Wörter* 83–4; Nisbet on Cic. *Pis.* 85.

obrepere Cf. §38 below and note; [Plato], *Axiochus* 367b λαθὸν ὑπῆλθε τὸ γῆρας; Herodas 1.63; Cic. *Tusc.* 1.94; Sen. *Brev. Vit.* 9.4; *Ep.* 108.28; Juv. 9.129.

qui enim citius Adverbial *qui* in Cicero occurs most commonly in the following circumstances: (a) with verbs: (i) with the verb *posse* (very common throughout Cicero), (ii) with *convenire, constare* in contexts of logical argument (common in the philosophical works, cf. also *Pro Caec.* 7; *Mil.* 54), (iii) with *fieri, evenire* (*Fin.* 2.12; *Div.* 2.37; *Phil.* 3.17, etc.), (iv) with *licet, decet* (*Leg. Agr.* 2.21; *Pis.* 49; *Acad.* 2.90), (v) with verbs of perceiving, judging or understanding (*distinguere*, *Acad.* 2.22, etc.; *discernere*, *De or.* 1.50; *iudicare*, *De rep.* 1.50; *intellegere*, *ND* 3.14; etc.); (b) with comparatives, as here: cf. *De rep.* 1.11; 3.45; *Tusc.* 3.55; *ND* 2.5; *Att.* 8.2.2; etc. Cf. also Landgraf on *Rosc. Am.* 116, p. 219.

citius The word here means 'sooner' rather than 'quicker': the latter meaning would not fit so well with *obrepere*. *TLL* 3,1211. Cf. Plato, *Symp.* 195b (Agathon's speech), playing on the similar double connotation of ταχύς.

putavissent For the historic verb after the generalising (primary) *aiunt*, see E. C. Woodcock, *A New Latin Syntax* (London 1959) 233.

adulescentiae senectus ... obrepit The human lifespan is here divided into three periods: *pueritia*, *adulescentia* and *senectus*. The Romans did not always count middle age as a separate period, though they sometimes did, cf. §§33 and 76. Aristotle's division of life into three (*Rhet.* 1389b) corresponds to *adulescentia*, *aetas media*, *senectus* rather than to that found in this passage. On the divisions of human life in general, cf. on §33 below; F. Boll, *N. Jahrb. Kl. Alt.* 31 (1913) 93ff. = *Kleine Schriften* (Leipzig 1950) 171ff.; Brink on Horace, *AP* 153ff.; C. Harcum, 'The Ages of Man', *CW* 7 (1914) 114ff.; E. Eyben, *RhM* 116 (1973) 150ff.; D. Sluşanski, *Revue Roumaine de Linguistique* 19 (1974) 103ff.

nulla consolatione HQ¹EI gives better sense than *nulla consolatio*, the reading of the older MSS: the subject of *permulcere posset* ought to be *praeterita aetas*, the meaning being that one's past life cannot console one now that it has passed away, however long it may have been. The reading *consolatio* weakens both the flow and the logic.

5 utinam digna esset 'would that it were' (as it is not): Cato is made by Cic. to be becomingly modest (cf. Introd. p. 24). One may note the variation between *sapientiam meam* (more personal: *nostram* there would be inappropriate) and *nostroque cognomine* (more public). On the difference between singular and plural in the first person referring to the speaker alone, see articles cited above on §3.

cognomine It is not clear whether this refers to the *cognomen* Cato (as one would naturally take it) or to supposed appellation *sapiens* which Cicero elsewhere attributes to Cato: *Lael.* 6, *quasi cognomen iam habebat in senectute sapientis*; *Div. in Caec.* 66, *M. Cato sapiens*; *Verr. II* 2.5; *Leg.* 2.5; *Off.* 3.16. There is no evidence outside Cicero that Cato was ever regularly called *sapiens*, and Cicero's evidence does not justify writing *Sapiens* with a capital as though it were an actual name. The name 'Cato' itself was popularly linked with *catus* 'clever' (for which cf. Varro, *LL* 7.44 *non ut aiunt sapiens, sed acutus*; Nonius p. 92 M. *catus pro sapiente*); Plutarch, *Cato* 1, says that Cato was originally named M. Porcius Priscus (cf. Hor. *Od.* 3.21.11 *prisci Catonis*) but that the name was changed on account of his cleverness; whether this is true or not, it confirms the existence of the popular etymology. The true etymology of *Cato* is not known; it may not be Latin: R. Syme, *Tacitus* (Oxford 1958) 617 says that it is Illyrian (why?), whereas *Der Kleine Pauly* s.v. *Cato* says 'vielleicht kelt. Herkunft' (it could be related to Irish *cath*, Welsh *cad*, 'battle', and Gaulish or British names beginning *Cat-*). It is difficult to parallel the formation of a name in *-o* from an adjective, though there are plenty of examples from nouns (Cicero, Naso, etc.), and the adjective *Catus* itself was used as a name without alteration (Sex. Aelius Paetus Catus). Cf. Helm, P.–W. 22.108; Della Corte, *Catone Censore*[2] 250; E. V. Marmorale, *Cato Maior* (Catania 1944) 26–7; P. Fraccaro, *Att. Acad. Mant.* (1910) 11 n. 3; Kammer, *Untersuchungen* 99.

sumus sapientes A dactylic rhythm, but not avoided by Cic. since it would be inadmissible at the end of an epic hexameter. Other such rhythms in the *Cato* are (*molli̅*)*te̅r sa̅pie̅nti̅* (in this section), *de̅spĭce̅re̅ntu̅r* (§7), *i̅n Sy̆ne̅phe̅bi̅s* (§24), *re̅i̅ ca̅pĭta̅li̅s* (§42). There are three genuine *clausulae heroicae*, (*de̅plo̅*)*ra̅re̅ so̅le̅ba̅nt* (§7), (*pro̅*)*bĕ mĕmĭ*)*ni̅ssĕ pŏte̅sti̅s* (§14), and (*ŏpŭs*)*e̅ssĕ vĭde̅tu̅r* (§75). Cf. F. W. Shipley, *CPhil.* 6 (1911) 410ff.; E. Fraenkel, *Leseproben aus Reden Ciceros und Catos* (Rome 1968) Anhang 6, pp. 198–200.

naturam, optimam ducem Cf. *Lael.* 19 *hos viros bonos ... appellandos putemus, quia sequantur naturam optimam bene vivendi ducem*; *Fin.* 5.69 *utentes tamquam duce natura*; ibid. 1.71; *Off.* 1.22; 1.129; *Tusc.* 1.30; 3.2; *Orat.* 58; Merguet, *Lexikon* s.v. *dux*, I, 783; comparable also is the remark put into the mouth of Cato the Younger in *Fin.* 3.11, concerning the old Roman heroes, *sine ulla doctrina naturam ipsam secuti*. The point of the present passage is that Cato is contrasting his 'natural' wisdom with the so-phisticated *sapientia* of the philosophers; but Cicero makes him do so in a way which itself recalls Greek philosophy (ζῆν κατὰ φύσιν, etc.). See also Sen. *Vit. beat.* 8.1.2; id. *Phaedra* 481; Pliny, *NH* 10.155; Quint. *Inst.* 4.5.3; Stat. *Theb.* 12.645; etc.; *TLL* 5,1,2326, 6off. (s.v. *dux*); A. O. Lovejoy and G. Boas, *Primitivism and Related Ideas in Antiquity* (Baltimore 1935) 252–3.

tamquam deum Cf. *Fin.* 5.43 *eam* (sc. *rationem*) *quasi deum ducem subsequens*. In *Fin.* 3.73 the precept *sequi deum* is referred to: in Greek, ἕπου θεῷ is attributed to Pythagoras (Stob. vol. II, p. 29 W.); cf. Plato, *Laws* 716b; *Phaedrus* 248a; Plut. *De ser. num. vind.* 550d; also the Stoic formula ἀκολούθως τῇ φύσει ζῆν (Diog. Laert. 7.88).

partes aetatis E. Fraenkel, *Mus. Helv.* 23 (1966) 194, proposed deletion of *aetatis*, but the qualification is necessary to avoid confusion with the other possible meaning of *partes*, 'parts', i.e. dramatis personae. Cf. §2 above, *tempus aetatis*; §33 below, *parti aetatis*: *aetas* here means the whole human lifespan, as contrasted with the use in §4 *omnis aetas*, §§7 and 9.

descriptae 'written out', 'delineated' (contrasted with *neglectum*): not *discriptae*, which means 'divided' or 'apportioned', though some edd. (after

Gulielmius) have favoured this reading (cf. also F. Bücheler, *RhM* 13 (1858) 601ff.): the two prefixes are constantly confused, cf. §59 below; Housman, *Papers* II, 476–7. The passage is imitated by Marbod, *Lib. dec. cap.* 9 (*de bono mortis*) 86ff. *cum velut a docto bene sit descripta poeta ... fabula vitae.*

extremum actum The theatrical image recurs in various forms in §§48, 64, 70 and 85 (see notes on those passages). Cic. has it also in *Q. fr.* 1.1.46 (cf. on §64 below) and *Fin.* 1.49. Versions of the image are common throughout Hellenistic and Roman popular philosophy, occurring in Bion and Teles, Seneca, Epictetus, Marcus Aurelius and many other authors: its presence here does not help to determine Cicero's sources in this work: cf. Introd. p. 13. In this version, Nature is the poet, and men like actors have to comply with her wishes: similarly elsewhere, the poet is said to represent ὁ θεός or τύχη, as in Bion fr. 16 K. (= Teles, p. 5 H.); Maximus of Tyre 1.1; etc. See in general M. Kokolakis, *The Dramatic Simile of Life* (Athens 1960) esp. p. 29; R. Helm, *Lucian und Menipp* (Leipzig 1906) 44ff.; E. R. Dodds, *Pagan and Christian in an Age of Anxiety* (Cambridge 1965) 8ff.; E. Curtius, *European Literature and the Latin Middle Ages* 138ff. in English edn (London 1953); Pöschl, *Bibl. Bildersprache* 545–6; 569.

inerti *iners* here has its ordinary meaning 'lazy' (cf. *esse neglectum*), though this shades into the original and archaic meaning 'artless', *in-* + *ars*, ἄτεχνος; cf. *TLL* s.v. *iners*, 7,1,1308ff. With this passage cf. Sulpicius Severus, *Vita S. Martini* 26.1 *ut inertes poetae extremo in opere neglegentes.*

aliquid extremum Cf. §69 below; *Pro Marc.* 27.

arborum bacis For the phrase cf. *Div.* 1.116 *fruges terrae bacasve arborum*; for the image, M. Aur. 4.48; §71 below and note. It is not clear whether Cic. intended the use of agricultural imagery to fit in with Cato's character and interests.

maturitate Cf. §§33; 71; 76.

vietum Past participle of *viescere* 'wilt, bend over'; cf. *viere* 'bend, weave'; *vimen*; etc.; Ernout–Meillet 1107. Cf. the comic use of this word of an old man in Ter. *Eun.* 688 *hic est vietus vetus veternosus senex.* It seems that the image in *vietum* is more appropriate to *terrae fructibus* (corn and other crops), while *caducum* fits *arborum bacis* better: the order would then be chiastic.

molliter 'compliantly', cf. Val. Max. 8.13. ext. 1 *mollius senectutem ageret*; Tac. *Ann.* 1.12.1; Nonius p. 347 M. (quoting this passage); otherwise *molliter ferre* usually means to bear something in a cowardly manner; *TLL* 8,1381–2.

quid est ... repugnare? The Latin idiom *quid est aliud X nisi Y?* gives rise to some confusion, since in many cases a verbatim English translation gives the wrong sense. The meaning depends on whether *X* is the subject and *Y* the predicate, or vice versa. If the former, the phrase is equivalent to

English 'What is X if not Y?'. But if, as is more common, X is the predicate and Y the subject, the unidiomatic 'What (subj.) is X (pred.) if Y (subj.) is not X (pred.)?' must be rendered as 'If Y isn't X, what is?'; a sentence like *Quid est aliud furere si hoc non est?* should be translated 'If this isn't madness, what is?' (Sometimes the *sic hoc non est* or similar is left out, e.g. *Pis.* 47 *quid est aliud furere?*: the translation is the same.) This latter form of the construction occurs often in Cicero (*Off.* 2.83; 3.55; *Tusc.* 1.64; 1.75; *Rosc. Am.* 54; *Verr. I* 28; etc.); however, there are one or two Ciceronian examples of the other type: *Phil.* 2.70 'What else is Antony but . . .?'; ibid. 2.5; 3.21; *Part. Or.* 79. Some have taken the present passage in this way, 'What else is fighting the Gods as the Giants did, but resistance to nature?', which would be a straightforward statement of an allegorical and moralistic interpretation of the myth; but the logic of the passage is better served by the other possibility, 'If resistance to nature (as opposed to compliance) is not fighting the Gods as the Giants did, what is?' This makes the sentence grow logically out of what precedes, rather than suddenly jumping back to the words of the previous speaker (*Aetna gravius*, §4 above) without preparation. (Cf. K. Meissner, *N. Jb. Kl. Phil.* 103 (1871) 57; F. G. Moore, *AJP* 23 (1902) 436ff.)

Gigantum modo bellare This picks up Scipio's words *onus Aetna gravius* (§4); the Giants were punished by confinement under Etna for their rebellion against the gods; similarly if one finds old age as troublesome as the Giants' imprisonment, it is one's own fault for rebelling against nature: the image alluded to by Scipio is turned round to suit Cato's argument. The Gigantomachy myth is similarly used as an image for resisting natural forces (in that case Venus and Cupid) by Plautus, *Persa* 26–7 *disne advorser quasi Titani?*; for other allegorical uses of the myth cf. Cic. *Har. resp.* 20; Hor. *Od.* 3.4; Plut. *De facie* 926d–e; F. Vian, *REG* 65 (1952) 1–39; Cicero in another context dismisses it as an invention (*ND* 2.70–1).

naturae repugnare Cf. *Off.* 1.110.

6–8 Laelius invites Cato to expand on his remarks concerning old age, and he agrees. Then follows an adaptation of part of the conversation between Socrates and Cephalus at the beginning of Plato's *Republic*, 328d–330a; the part of Socrates is transferred to Laelius, that of Cephalus to Cato.

6 gratissimum nobis … feceris A common formula of polite request: cf. *Lael.* 16; *Att.* 10.3; Hofmann, *Umgangssprache* 134.

quoniam speramus – volumus quidem certe Laelius corrects himself, and the construction carries on regularly after *volumus*; *speramus* is forgotten (otherwise we should have had a future infinitive). *speramus* means 'we expect' rather than 'we hope', and *senes fieri* should be translated 'to live to be old', not 'to become old'. For *quidem certe* so used,

COMMENTARY: II 6

cf. *Off.* 1.138, *Att.* 1.1.4; M. Haupt, *Opuscula philologica* (Leipzig 1875–6) II, 359.

futurum est 'is going to be': on the difference between the periphrastic form and the simple future, see H.–Sz. 312.

Volumus sane The adaptation of Plato begins here and ends at the end of §8. Here is Cicero's version side by side with the original:

"καὶ μήν," ἦν δ' ἐγώ, "ὦ Κέφαλε, χαίρω διαλεγόμενος τοῖς σφόδρα πρεσβύταις· δοκεῖ γάρ μοι χρῆναι παρ' αὐτῶν πυνθάνεσθαι ὥσπερ τινὰ ὁδὸν προεληλυθότων, ἣν καὶ ἡμᾶς ἴσως δεήσει πορεύεσθαι, ποία τίς ἐστιν, τραχεῖα καὶ χαλεπή, ἢ ῥᾳδία καὶ εὔπορος· καὶ δὴ καὶ σοῦ ἡδέως ἂν πυθοίμην, ὅ τί σοι φαίνεται τοῦτο, ἐπειδὴ ἐνταῦθα εἶ τῆς ἡλικίας, ὃ δὴ 'ἐπὶ γήραος οὐδῷ' φασὶν εἶναι οἱ ποιηταί, πότερον χαλεπὸν τοῦ βίου ἢ πῶς σὺ αὐτὸ ἐξαγγέλλεις."	*Volumus sane nisi molestum est, Cato,* tamquam longam aliquam viam confeceris, quam nobis quoque ingrediundum sit, istuc quo pervenisti videre quale sit.
"ἐγώ σοι," ἔφη, "νὴ τὸν Δία ἐρῶ, ὦ Σώκρατες, οἷόν γέ μοι φαίνεται. πολλάκις γάρ συνερχόμεθά τινες εἰς ταὐτὸν παραπλησίαν ἡλικίαν ἔχοντες, διασώζοντες τὴν παλαιὰν παροιμίαν.	Faciam ut potero, Laeli; saepe enim interfui querelis aequalium meorum – pares autem vetere proverbio cum paribus facillime congregantur. *Quae C. Salinator, quae Sp. Albinus, homines consulares, nostri fere aequales, deplorare solebant!*
οἱ οὖν πλεῖστοι ἡμῶν ὀλοφύρονται συνιόντες, τὰς ἐν τῇ νεότητι ἡδονὰς ποθοῦντες καὶ ἀναμιμνησκόμενοι περί τε τἀφροδίσια καὶ περὶ πότους τε καὶ εὐωχίας καὶ ἄλλ' ἄττα ἃ τῶν τοιούτων ἔχεται, καὶ ἀγανακτοῦσιν ὡς μεγάλων τινῶν ἀπεστερημένοι καὶ τότε μὲν εὖ ζῶντες, νῦν δὲ οὐδὲ ζῶντες. ἔνιοι δὲ καὶ τὰς τῶν οἰκείων προπηλακίσεις τοῦ γήρως ὀδύρονται, καὶ ἐπὶ τούτῳ δὴ τὸ γῆρας ὑμνοῦσιν ὅσων κακῶν σφίσιν αἴτιον. ἐμοὶ δὲ	tum quod voluptatibus carerent, sine quibus vitam nullam putarent, tum quod spernerentur ab eis a quibus essent coli soliti. qui mihi non id videbantur

111

δοκοῦσιν, ὦ Σώκρατες, οὗτοι οὐ τὸ
αἴτιον αἰτιᾶσθαι.

εἰ γὰρ ἦν τοῦτ' αἴτιον, κἂν ἐγὼ τὰ
αὐτὰ ταῦτα ἐπεπόνθη, ἕνεκά γε
γήρως, καὶ οἱ ἄλλοι πάντες ὅσοι
ἐνταῦθα ἦλθον ἡλικίας. νῦν δὲ
ἔγωγε ἤδη ἐντετύχηκα οὐχ οὕτως
ἔχουσιν καὶ ἄλλοις, καὶ δὴ καὶ
Σοφοκλεῖ ποτὲ τῷ ποιητῇ
παρεγενόμην ἐρωτωμένῳ ὑπό
τινος, 'πῶς', ἔφη, 'ὦ Σόφοκλεις,
ἔχεις πρὸς τἀφροδίσια; ἔτι οἷός τε
εἶ γυναικὶ συγγίγνεσθαι;' καὶ ὅς,
'εὐφήμει,' ἔφη,' ὦ ἄνθρωπε,
ἀσμενέστατα μέντοι αὐτὸ
ἀπέφυγον, ὥσπερ λυττῶντά τινα
καὶ ἄγριον δεσπότην ἀποφυγών.'
εὖ οὖν μοι καὶ τότε ἔδοξεν ἐκεῖνος
εἰπεῖν, καὶ νῦν οὐχ ἧττον.
παντάπασι γὰρ τῶν γε τοιούτων
ἐν τῷ γήρᾳ πολλὴ εἰρήνη γίγνεται
καὶ ἐλευθερία· ἐπειδὰν αἱ ἐπιθυμίαι
παύσωνται κατατείνουσαι καὶ
χαλάσωσιν, παντάπασιν τὸ τοῦ
Σοφοκλέους γίγνεται, δεσποτῶν
πάνυ πολλῶν ἔστι καὶ μαινομένων
ἀπηλλάχθαι. ἀλλὰ καὶ τούτων
πέρι καὶ τῶν γε πρὸς τοὺς οἰκείους
μία τις αἰτία ἐστίν, οὐ τὸ γῆρας, ὦ
Σώκρατες, ἀλλ' ὁ τρόπος τῶν
ἀνθρώπων. ἂν μὲν γὰρ κόσμιοι καὶ
εὔκολοι ὦσιν, καὶ τὸ γῆρας μετρίως
ἐστὶν ἐπίπονον· εἰ δὲ μή, καὶ
γῆρας, ὦ Σώκρατες, καὶ νεότης
χαλεπὴ τῷ τοιούτῳ συμβαίνει."

Καὶ ἐγὼ ἀγασθεὶς αὐτοῦ
εἰπόντος ταῦτα, βουλόμενος ἔτι
λέγειν αὐτὸν ἐκίνουν καὶ εἶπον, "ὦ
Κέφαλε, οἶμαί σου τοὺς πολλούς,
ὅταν ταῦτα λέγῃς, οὐχ
ἀποδέχεσθαι ἀλλ' ἡγεῖσθαί σε
ῥαδίως τὸ γῆρας φέρειν οὐ διὰ τὸν
τρόπον ἀλλὰ διὰ τὸ πολλὴν

accusare quod essent accusandum;

nam si id culpa senectutis
accideret, eadem mihi usu
venirent,
reliquisque omnibus maioribus
natu;
quorum ego multorum cognovi
senectutem sine querela,

qui se et libidinum vinculis laxatos
esse *non moleste ferrent*,

nec a suis despicerentur. Sed
omnium istiusmodi querelarum in
moribus est culpa, non in aetate;

moderati enim et nec difficiles nec
inhumani senes tolerabilem
senectutem agunt,
importunitas autem et
inhumanitas omni aetati molesta
est.

Est ut dicis, Cato; sed fortasse
dixerit quispiam, tibi propter opes
et copias et dignitatem tuam
tolerabiliorem senectutem videri,
id autem non posse multis contingere.

οὐσίαν κεκτῆσθαι· τοῖς γὰρ
πλουσίοις πολλὰ παραμύθιά φασιν
εἶναι."

"'Αληθῆ," ἔφη, "λέγεις· οὐ γὰρ
ἀποδέχονται. καὶ λέγουσι μέν τι,
οὐ μέντοι γε ὅσον οἴονται· ἀλλὰ τὸ
τοῦ Θεμιστοκλέους εὖ ἔχει, ὃς τῷ
Σεριφίῳ λοιδορουμένῳ καὶ λέγοντι
ὅτι οὐ δι' αὑτὸν ἀλλὰ διὰ τὴν
πόλιν εὐδοκιμοῖ, ἀπεκρίνατο ὅτι
οὔτ' ἂν αὐτὸς Σερίφιος ὢν
ὀνομαστὸς ἐγένετο οὔτ' ἐκεῖνος
'Αθηναῖος.

καὶ τοῖς δὴ μὴ πλουσίοις, χαλεπῶς
δὲ τὸ γῆρας φέρουσιν, εὖ ἔχει ὁ
αὐτὸς λόγος, ὅτι οὔτ' ἂν ὁ ἐπιεικὴς
πάνυ τι ῥᾳδίως γῆρας μετὰ πενίας
ἐνέγκοι, οὔθ' ὁ μὴ ἐπιεικὴς
πλουτήσας εὔκολός ποτ' ἂν ἑαυτῷ
γένοιτο."

Est istuc quidem, Laeli, aliquid,
sed nequaquam in isto sunt
omnia; ut Themistocles fertur
Seriphio cuidam in iurgio
respondisse, cum ille dixisset non
eum sua sed patriae gloria
splendorem adsecutum, 'nec
hercule' inquit 'si ego Seriphius
essem, nec tu si Atheniensis esses
clarus umquam fuisses.'
quod eodem modo de senectute
dici potest: nec enim in summa
inopia levis esse senectus potest ne
sapienti quidem, nec insipienti
etiam in summa copia non gravis.

This passage is a free adaptation of Plato to Cicero's own purposes, not a
literal translation: its source is not acknowledged, although no doubt
Cicero's readers would have recognised the *imitatio*. The passage fulfils
excellently the function of leading into the main discussion of old age, it
reads well as Latin, and no more need be expected of it. It is quite
misguided to criticise Cicero's translation on grounds of inaccuracy, as
does R. Poncelet, *Cicéron traducteur de Platon* (Paris 1957) 258–60: Cicero
was not aiming at an accurate translation, and even so keeps closer to the
substance of Plato's meaning than Poncelet acknowledges. The differences
are due mostly to stylistic considerations: Plato tends to garrulity, which
would come over in Latin as ponderous verbosity, and Cicero's version is
substantially abbreviated. Roman dignity is also a consideration: see
below on *nisi molestum est, quod voluptatibus carerent* and §8 *Est ut dicis*.

On Platonic translations in Cicero, see in general, apart from Poncelet
(a difficult and one-sided account), D. M. Jones, *BICS* 6 (1959) 22ff.; M.
Puelma, 'Cicero als Platonübersetzer', *Mus. Helv.* 37 (1980) 137ff., with
bibliography. On this passage in particular, see the discussion by F. de
Caria, *Vichiana* 3 (1974) 219ff.; also Kammer, *Untersuchungen* 127ff. On the
Platonic passage itself, in addition to the commentators, see Stein, *Platons
Charakteristik* 68ff.

nisi molestum est A common locution in polite requests: cf. Plaut.

Trin. 932; Catull. 55.1; Cic. *Att.* 1.5.7; *Fam.* 13.23.3; *Fin.* 1.28; *Tusc.* 1.26; etc.; Reid on *Acad.* 1.14; Becker, *Technik und Szenerie* 20; Hofmann, *Umgangssprache* 134. Cf. also Platonic phrases like εἰ μή τί σοι χαλεπόν (*Tim.* 17b). Cicero changes Plato's sentence καὶ μήν, ἦν δ' ἐγώ..., partly to make it carry on more smoothly from what precedes, and partly because Socrates' remark 'I like talking to very old men' contains a hint of mischief that would be unsuitable in the present context. Cf. also Juncus p. 1049 W.-H. (on Juncus' Περὶ γήρως see Introd. p. 29).

longam aliquam viam *longam* is an addition of Cicero's; it compensates for the omission of τοῖς σφόδρα πρεσβύταις, and adds weight to the sentence.

quam ... ingrediundum sit The construction of the impersonal gerund + a part of *esse* with an accusative object is archaic; it occurs in Plaut. *Trin.* 869; Afranius, *com.* 99; Lucr. 1.111; 2.492; 5.43; Catull. 39.9 (by conjecture); and often in Varro, who deliberately archaises; later it is revived by Silius Italicus (11.562), and it is used by the jurists, who no doubt inherited it as part of legal language. (Cf. K.-S. I, 734; H.-Sz. 372.) This occurrence of the construction is probably unique in Cicero. *Scaur.* 13 used to be quoted as a parallel; but editors now punctuate that passage so as to remove the construction, and this seems necessary. Here a more regular Ciceronian construction could be obtained by reading *qua* with HS[2], some older editions and Brieger, progr. Posen 1873; but *quam* may be retained, since the old-fashioned construction suits the characterisation of Cato (cf. Introd. p. 22); and the accusative reflects Plato's Greek, ἦν καὶ ἡμᾶς ἴσως δεήσει πορεύεσθαι.

istuc Presumably neuter pronoun (Plato's αὐτό), not adverb. For the 'I know thee who thou art' construction in Latin, see K.-S. II, 579. Cicero here abbreviates the original: he conflates into one Socrates' two questions, (a) ὁδόν... ποία τίς ἐστιν, τραχεῖα καὶ χαλεπή, ἢ ῥᾳδία καὶ εὔπορος, and (b) ἐπειδὴ ἐνταῦθα εἶ τῆς ἡλικίας... πότερον χαλεπὸν τοῦ βίου ἢ πῶς σὺ αὐτὸ ἐξαγγέλλεις, i.e. (a) what is the way to old age like? and (b) what is old age itself like? To have retained the original alternative 'difficult or easy' might in any case have seemed inconsistent with Scipio's admiration of Cato's bearing in old age: it has already been said that Cato does not find it difficult.

III 7 aequalium meorum Poncelet objects to this as inexact compared with Plato's παραπλησίαν ἡλικίαν ἔχοντες, and to Cicero's omission of τινες and οἱ πλεῖστοι; but these expressions are more characteristic of Platonic style than essential for the meaning.

vetere proverbio διασώζοντες τὴν παλαιὰν παροιμίαν. Cicero specifies the proverb where Plato does not, perhaps because it was in the first instance a Greek proverb, not a Latin one. It has a variety of forms: see especially Arist. *Rhet.* 1.1371b 15: ὅθεν καὶ αἱ παροιμίαι εἴρηνται, ὡς "ἧλιξ ἥλικα τέρπει" καὶ "ὡς αἰεὶ τὸν ὁμοῖον" καὶ "ἔγνω δὲ θὴρ θῆρα" καὶ "καὶ γὰρ κολοιὸς παρὰ κολοιόν" καὶ ὅσα ἄλλα τοιαῦτα. For ἧλιξ ἥλικα τέρπει, cf. Plato, *Phaedrus* 240c; Diogenianus 5.16 (Leutsch–Schneidewin, *Paroem.* 1, 61) quotes a fuller version, particularly appropriate to the present context: ἧλιξ ἥλικα τέρπε, γέρων δέ τε τέρπε γέροντα. This form of the proverb is most probably the one of which Plato and Cicero were thinking, as it is the only one specifically concerned with contemporaries in age, rather than those who are similar in other respects. ὡς αἰεὶ τὸν ὁμοῖον ἄγει θεὸς ὡς τὸν ὁμοῖον is a Homeric line, *Od.* 17.218; cf. Plato, *Symp.* 195b; *Gorg.* 510b; *Lysis* 214a. For κολοιός etc. see also Arist. *NE* 1155a34 (in the Doric form κολοιὸς ποτὶ κολοιόν), *EE* 1235a8, [Arist.] *Magna Moralia* 1208b9 καὶ γὰρ κολοιὸς παρὰ κολοιὸν ἱζάνει. Cf. also Plato, *Protagoras* 337d; [Plut.] *Prov.* 1.66; Theocr. 9.31–2; Democr. fr. 372 D.–K. (1, p. 359); Schol. Hom. *Od.* 3.36; Schol. Plat. 314; Leutsch–Schneidewin, *Paroem.* 1, 253; 11, 33; etc. For the Latin use of the proverb, cf. Hor. *Epist.* 1.5.25 *ut coeat par | iungaturque pari*; Quint. *Inst.* 5.11.41 (quoting Cicero somewhat inaccurately); Amm. Marc. 28.1.53; Macrob. *Sat.* 8.7.12; Lupus of Ferrières, *Epist.* 62; Otto, *Sprichwörter* 264; D'Arcy W. Thompson, *A Glossary of Greek Birds* (London 1936, repr. Hildesheim 1966) s.v. κολοιός, p. 157.

quae C. Salinator ... Editors have taken this to be a relative clause following on from the last sentence, and have had difficulty in finding an antecedent for *quae*. *Lael.* 14 and *Fam.* 2.8.2 are quoted as parallels, but are both easier than this passage: in *Lael.* 14, *cuius disputationis fuit extremum fere de immortalitate animorum, quae se in quiete per visum ex Africano audisse dicebat*, the relative clause is in apposition to *extremum*; in the latter passage, *nullis in aliis nisi de republica sermonibus versatus sum, quae nec possunt scribi nec scribenda sunt, quae* ('things which') is in apposition to and explanatory of *sermonibus*. Here editors have said that *quae* picks up *querelis*, but it was not their own complaints that Cato's contemporaries were lamenting; and to say that *quae* is a Greek-style internal accusative (as if equivalent to ἃ ὀλοφύρεσθαι ἐφίλουν) is merely to replace one difficulty with another. The solution is simple: the sentence is an exclamation. This was noticed by M. Grant, who in his translation (in *Cicero: Selected Works* (Harmondsworth 1960)) renders these words as 'how they used to grumble!'. This is not quite right, however, since *quae* is the direct object of *deplorare*: Cato is affecting surprise at the nature of the complaints, not at their volume, and the sentence should run 'what things they used to grumble about! – sometimes that they had lost their physical pleasures ...', etc. (For what it is worth, one of the best MSS, D, also has an exclamation or question mark after *solebant*.) The fact that there is no such exclamation in Plato need not weigh very heavily against this interpretation: Cicero does not always reproduce

exactly the constructions of his model. The passage is effective as Latin
and suitable for the character of Cato.

Gaius Salinator He was consul in 188, died in 170 (P.–W. 13, 888ff.,
s.v. *Livius* 29): the usual calculation of date of birth from consulate minus
40 makes him fifty-eight at his death, and five or six years younger than
Cato; it would however be more consistent with this passage if he were a
few years older than this (though Cicero may well have employed a loose
definition both of old age and of *aequales*: note *fere*).

Spurius Albinus Cos. 186, died 180 (P.–W. 22, 1, 921ff., s.v. *Postumius*
44): probably younger than Salinator, but not necessarily very much
younger; even so, as a contemporary of Cato he would only have been in
his early fifties when he died, and it is odd to find him here as an example
of one who complained about old age. The two names give the passage
some Roman colouring, being inserted without scruple into an otherwise
Platonic context. It is not clear why Cicero picked on these relatively
obscure consulars: one might guess that he found them mentioned in
Cato's speeches. (It seems wrong to make a distinction, as some translators
have done, between *aequalium meorum* previously mentioned and these two
men who are only *fere aequales*: *fere* can hardly have this sort of emphasis,
and the two consulars are evidently meant to be examples of Cato's
contemporaries.)

deplorare 'lament' rather than just 'complain': it is equivalent to
Plato's ὀλοφύρεσθαι. *deplorare solebant* forms a genuine heroic clausula, one
of three in this work (cf. §§14 and 75): cf. above, note on §5.

voluptatibus carerent Cicero abbreviates Plato, again probably with
concern for Roman dignity. It would be unsuitable to have Roman
consulars (especially as reported by Cato) complaining that they had been
deprived of τἀφροδίσια καὶ πότους τε καὶ εὐωχίας.

For this complaint against old age, see (in addition to the Plato passage)
§§15 and 39ff. below, and notes; Musonius 17, p. 91 H. (Stob. 4.50c.94: cf.
Introd. pp. 27–8) τὴν στέρησιν τῶν ἡδονῶν τῶν ἐπὶ νεότητος; Juncus, Περὶ
γήρως, Stob. 4.50b.85, p. 1049 W.–H., Ἐπειδὴ γὰρ ὁρῶ σε τὰς μὲν ἐπὶ τῆς
νεότητος καὶ ἀκμῆς ἡδονὰς καὶ ἀπολαύσεις αἳ πᾶσιν ἔργοις ἕπονται,
συνελόντι δὲ εἰπεῖν τὴν ἀνθρώπειον εὐδαιμονίαν ἀπολιπόντα; ibid., ἐμοὶ
γὰρ δύσκολος ὁ ἐν αὐτῷ βίος καταφαίνεται διὰ τὴν τῶν αἰσθήσεων
στέρησιν κατ’ ὀλίγον ἀποσβεννυμένων. διόπερ ἡδὺ μὲν οὐδὲν ἔτι παρ-
ακολουθεῖν φασι τοῖς γεγηρακόσιν . . .; Hor. *Epist.* 2.2.55–6 *singula de nobis
anni praedantur euntes:* | *eripuere iocos, Venerem, convivia, ludum;* ibid. 214; Plut.
An seni 786a; Juv. 10.203ff.; Maximian 1.121.

vitam nullam putarent (For the phrase, cf. *Lael.* 86; *De or.* 2.20; *Fam.*
7.1.4.) Cf. Simonides fr. 71 B. (Athen. 12.512c); Soph. *Ant.* 1165–7;
Moschion fr. 7 N.², Philemon fr. 71 K.; Mimnermus fr. 1 τίς δὲ βίος, τί δὲ
τερπνὸν ἄτερ χρυσῆς Ἀφροδίτης;

quod spernerentur τὰς τῶν οἰκείων προπηλακίσεις. *spernere* is a strong word and appropriate for προπηλακίζειν; but it is not clear why Cicero chooses to paraphrase rather than translate οἰκεῖοι, unless for extra weight in the second half of the sentence.

For this complaint, see below on §25; Hes. *W. & D.* 185; Thgn. 271ff.; Soph. *OC* 1237 γῆρας ἄφιλον; Musonius p. 91 H. καταφρονούμενος ὑπὸ τῶν πλησίον . . . ἀμελούμενος ὑπὸ τῶν οἰκείων καὶ φίλων; Juncus p. 1051 W.–H.; Juv. 10.201 *gravis uxori natisque sibique*.

eadem mihi usu venirent κἂν ἐγὼ τὰ αὐτὰ ταῦτα ἐπεπόνθη: πάσχειν is best translated in Latin as in English by the use of a word meaning 'happen to'. The word is *usu venire*, not (as the MSS here and in *Rosc. Com.* 30 read) *usu evenire*: cf. F. W. Otto's edition, 1830, Excursus II, 224. For the 'variety' of *accideret . . . usu venirent*, cf. Nep. *Hannibal* 12.3 *ne usu veniret quod accidit*.

maioribus natu Rather euphemistic for *senibus*: Plato has a different but still euphemistic phrase, ὅσοι ἐνταῦθα ἦλθον ἡλικίας.

senectutem sine querela Plato has ἐντετύχηκα οὐχ οὕτως ἔχουσιν καὶ ἄλλοις, which is difficult to translate into Latin both because of the participle and because of the phrase οὕτως ἔχειν; Cicero's Latin is characteristically more explicit. *sine querela* is used adjectivally and qualifies *senectutem*; for prepositional phrases used in this way, particularly those with *cum* and *sine*, see K.–S. I, 215; they are more common than is often thought.

The example of Sophocles is left out here, but reappears later in §47 below (see note ad loc.). The omission was necessary: Cato is being made to recall his own acquaintances, as Cephalus recalled his, and the intrusion of a Greek example into Cato's speech at this point would be inappropriate. However, the absence of the anecdote makes it a little difficult to see immediately the point of the image in *libidinum vinculis*, which is introduced by Plato as an explanation of Sophocles' reply (ἐπειδὰν αἱ ἐπιθυμίαι παύσωνται κατατείνουσαι καὶ χαλάσωσιν, etc.).

qui se et libidinum vinculis Note the order: *se* really only goes with the first clause, *libidinum . . . ferrent*, but is placed before *et*: Wackernagel's Law here takes precedence over strict logic (cf. above on §4).

libidinum vinculis For the idea that the desire for pleasure is an evil from which old age releases one, cf. below, §§39, *o praeclarum munus aetatis, siquidem id aufert a nobis quod est in adulescentia vitiosissimum!*; 42; 44; 46; 47; 49. See also Sen. *Ep.* 12.5 (cf. Introd. p. 27), *aut hoc ipsum succedit in locum voluptatum, nullis egere*; ibid. 26.3 (also ibid. 78.11, in a different context); Favorinus, Περὶ γήρως, fr. 14 Barigazzi (cf. Introd. pp. 27–8), ἡδονῆς γὰρ ὁ μὲν ἑκὼν εἰργόμενος σοφός, ὁ δὲ μὴ δεόμενος μακάριος. τὸ δὲ γῆρας πρὸς ἀμφότερα ἐπιτήδειον· καὶ γὰρ φρονιμωτέρους τοὺς ἀνθρώπους ἀπεργάζεται καὶ τῶν ἡδέων ἀμελεστέρους (= Stob. 4.50a.23); Juncus pp.

1026–7 W.–H., τὸ μέντοι τῶν ἐπιθυμιῶν ἐστερῆσθαι τοὺς γέροντας μηδὲν ὑπ' αὐτῶν ἔτι παρενοχλουμένους, μέγιστον τοῦτο καὶ πρεπωδέστατον ἡγοῦμαι δεδόσθαι τοῖς ἀνθρώποις δῶρον ὑπὸ τῶν θεῶν ; cf. also notes on §47 below; Plut. *An seni* 788e; John Chrysostom, *In Ep. ad Hebr.* IV, 7 (Migne 63, cols. 65–6).

in moribus est culpa, non in aetate μία τις αἰτία ἐστίν, οὐ τὸ γῆρας ἀλλ' ὁ τρόπος τῶν ἀνθρώπων: one of the most important themes of Cicero's argument, cf. §§10; 14; 65. The fact that this occurrence of the idea is in a translation from Plato ought to have discouraged scholars from citing the other instances of it as evidence for Cynic or Stoic influence. Juncus ap. Stob. p. 1061 W.–H. develops the idea, presumably directly from Plato rather than from Cicero (cf. Introd. p. 29); cf. also Anaxandrides fr. 53 K. (Stob. 4.50c.88), οὗτοι τὸ γῆράς ἐστιν, ὡς οἴει, πάτερ, | τῶν φορτίων μέγιστον, ἀλλ' ὃς ἂν φέρῃ | ἀγνωμόνως αὔθ', οὗτός ἐστιν αἴτιος; Teles pp. 8–9 H.; Marbod, *Lib. dec. cap.* 5.100–1.

moderati enim et nec difficiles nec inhumani A slightly ponderous but effective equivalent for κόσμιοι καὶ εὔκολοι. *Moderati* means 'orderly', 'self-controlled', not 'moderate' in our sense: cf. §1 above. For *difficiles* cf. §65 below, and note; Hor. *AP* 173 *difficilis, querulus* (echoed by Sen. *De ira* 2.19.4); Ter. *Heaut.* 535; *TLL* 5,1,1087. Cicero may have intended his phrasing here to be read as a compliment to Atticus, to whose *moderatio animi* and *humanitas* he referred in §1 above.

importunitas ... et inhumanitas This does not correspond to anything in the Greek, and seems to have been inserted by Cicero purely to balance the sentence; for *importunitas* cf. *TLL* 7, 1, 622, 51ff.

omni aetati 'for every age'. Wuilleumier reads *aetate* with RBe and some older editions, without any notable advantage in sense and with a considerable disadvantage to the rhythm (heroic clausula at the end of a paragraph). For the dative, cf. Plato's τῷ τοιούτῳ.

8 est ut dicis Laelius is here very much more polite than Socrates, who says in the original ὦ Κέφαλε, οἶμαί σου τοὺς πολλούς, ὅταν ταῦτα λέγῃς, οὐκ ἀποδέχεσθαι ...', etc. Cato was notoriously frugal in his mode of life, and Socrates' comment in its original form would perhaps be less appropriate if addressed to him; while to suggest to a senior Roman consular that 'most people do not accept' what he says would doubtless not be in order. So Laelius is made to say *fortasse dixerit quispiam*; οὐ διὰ τὸν τρόπον is omitted; and *dignitatem* is added to *opes et copias*.

fortasse dixerit quispiam Cf. such Greek phrases as ἴσως ἂν τις εἴποι. There is a slight break after *quispiam*; *tibi* begins its clause and is emphatic, being contrasted with *multis* in the next clause.

id autem non posse multis contingere Added by Cicero, again for balance and contrast. The original has the proverbial-sounding phrase τοῖς γὰρ πλουσίοις πολλά παραμύθιά φασιν εἶναι, which Cicero does not reproduce.

est istuc quidem, Laeli, aliquid λέγουσι μέν τι; cf. *Tusc.* 3.52 *est id quidem magnum, sed non sunt in hoc omnia*. Both Greek and Latin used *est, est istuc, sunt ista* (*Lael.* 6, etc.), ἔστι ταῦτα as forms of assent: cf. App. Verg. *De Est et Non*. With *aliquid*, cf. the phrase *esse aliquid* in *Tusc.* 5.104; *Att.* 4.2.2; Catull. 1.4; with *sunt omnia*, *De or.* 2.215; *Leg.* 2.24; *Fam.* 15.14.5.

ut Themistocles fertur The original anecdote is in Hdt. 8.125: Τιμόδημος Ἀφιδναῖος ... ἐνείκεε τὸν Θεμιστοκλέα ... ὡς διὰ τὰς Ἀθήνας ἔχοι τὰ γέρεα τὰ παρὰ Λακεδαιμονίων, ἀλλ' οὐ δι' ἑωυτόν. ὁ δὲ ἐπείτε οὐκ ἐπαύετο λέγων ταῦτα ὁ Τιμόδημος, εἶπε "οὕτω ἔχει τοι· οὔτ' ἂν ἐγὼ ἐὼν Βελβινίτης ἐτιμήθην οὕτω πρὸς Σπαρτιητέων, οὔτ' ἂν σὺ ὤνθρωπε ἐὼν Ἀθηναῖος." There the man who argued with Themistocles is an Athenian himself (of the deme Aphidna); Themistocles refers to Belbina merely as a place of proverbial insignificance, and the last part of his reply means 'nor would you, even though you are an Athenian'. Plato's version is presumably the less historically accurate of the two, but it has more symmetry and point, and it was this version that was repeated by Plutarch (*Them.* 18.3; *Apophth.* 185c) as well as by Cicero here; cf. also Orig. *Cels.* 1.29.347e. The version that we have here need not have been invented by Plato; Adam ad loc. suggests that Plato's use of the definite article, τῷ Σεριφίῳ, implies that the story was well known already in that form. For the insignificance of Seriphos, cf. Ar. *Ach.* 542; Cic. *ND* 1.88; Juv. 10.170; Ov. *Met.* 5.242.

iurgio *iurgium* is not so much a quarrel as an argument or altercation: it is usually verbal, temporary and not serious. Cf. esp. Cic. *De rep.* 4.8 (Nonius p. 430) *benivolorum concertatio, non lis inimicorum, iurgium dicitur*; TLL 7, 2, 665.

non eum sua For other examples of 'Wackernagelian' pronouns in second place coming between *non* and the word it negates, cf. Caes. *BG* 1.39.6; Cic. *Fam.* 5.2.9; 6.1.5; *De or.* 2.285; etc. (See above on §4 for Wackernagel's Law.)

si Atheniensis esses *esses* is the transmitted reading, and there is no reason to prefer the reading of LADSg which omit it.

nec enim ... potest For the combination of old age and poverty cf. §14; Aeschin. *Timarchus* 88 γῆρας καὶ πενία, τὰ μέγιστα τῶν ἐν ἀνθρώποις κακῶν; Men. *Sic.* 375–6; fr. 648 Koerte (592 Kock), ὅταν ᾖ γέρων τις ἐνδεής τε τὸν βίον, | οὐδὲν τὸ θνῄσκειν δεινόν...; *monost.* 656 J.,πενίαν φέρειν καὶ γῆράς ἐστι δύσκολον; Diog. Laert. 6.51 (an anecdote of Diogenes the Cynic), ἐρωτηθεὶς τί ἄθλιον ἐν βίῳ, ἔφη "γέρων ἄπορος"; Juncus p. 1051 W.–H., εἰ δὲ καὶ πενία πως ἀνδρὶ γεγηρακότι συμπέσοι, αὐτὸς ἂν ἐκεῖνος εὔξαιτο ἀπαλλαγῆναι τέλεον τοῦ βίου διὰ τὸ ἄπορον ἐπὶ πᾶσιν; *Anth. Pal.* 7.336; Enn. *Hecuba* fr. 92 (cf. Eur. *Hec.* 497–8), *senex sum: utinam mortem oppetam priusquam evenat* [sic] | *quod in pauperie mea senex graviter* *gemam*; Apostolius 5.41b (Leutsch–Schneidewin, *Paroem.* II, 344), Ἡρώδου· γῆρας καὶ πενία δύο τραύματα δυσθεράπευτα; cf. Arsenius 14.83; 16.85; Maximus Confessor, *Loci communes* 41 fin. Here Plato and Cicero follow the common-sense line that old age is unpleasant if one is poor; there is no moralising about the wise man being independent of external circumstances, as one finds in e.g. Teles p. 14 H. Cicero seems at first sight to come nearer to the latter view in §14 below, where he talks about Ennius' frugal old age; but there is a great difference between ordinary *paupertas* and *summa inopia* (see on that passage).

sapienti For Plato's ἐπιεικής, 'sensible' or 'reasonable' rather than 'wise'.

non gravis The end of the adaptation from Plato.

9–14 Cato now returns to the question originally asked by Laelius, *quibus facillime rationibus ingravescentem aetatem ferre possimus*; a new paragraph should start here.

9 arma senectutis The closest parallel to this idea in the context of old age seems to be the saying of Caesar quoted by Amm. Marc. 29.2.18 *miserum esse instrumentum senectuti recordationem crudelitatis* (*instrumentum* = 'equipment', especially for a journey or campaign): Cicero here makes the converse point. The image of armour or weapons, referring to moral qualities etc., is common in various contexts: cf. *Tusc.* 2.33 *tectus volcaniis armis, id est fortitudine*; ibid. 2.51; *De or.* 1.172 (*prudentia*); ibid. 1.32 (eloquence, cf. Quint. *Inst.* 2.16.10; 5.12.21); *Brut.* 7; *Har. resp.* 7; *Sull.* 79; Soph. *El.* 995–6 τοιοῦτον θράσος ... ὁπλίζῃ; Hor. *Sat.* 2.3.297 (philosophical or moral precepts); perhaps the best-known occurrence of the image is St Paul's πανοπλία θεοῦ (Eph. 6.13, etc.), which has a close antecedent in *Wisdom of Solomon* 5.18ff. Cf. *TLL* 2, 601–2 s.v. *arma*.

Elsewhere the image of the *viaticum*, ἐφόδιον (cf. Caesar's *instrumentum*) is used to make more or less the same point: Arist. ap. Diog. Laert. 5.21 κάλλιστον ἐφόδιον τῷ γήρᾳ τὴν παιδείαν ἔλεγε; [Bias], ibid. 1.88, ἐφόδιον ἀπὸ νεότητος εἰς γῆρας ἀνελάμβανε σοφίαν; Plut. *De lib. educ.* 8c ἐν νεότητι τὴν εὐταξίαν καὶ τὴν σωφροσύνην ἐφόδιον εἰς τὸ γῆρας ἀποτίθεσθαι; [Pittacus] ap. Stob. 2.31.100, p. 219 W.–H.; and the title and first paragraph of Musonius 17, Τί ἄριστον γήρως ἐφόδιον (see Introd. pp. 27–8). The image occurs in Latin in Persius 5.63–4 (concerning philosophy) *petite hinc puerique senesque | finem animo certum miserisque viatica canis.*

artes exercitationesque virtutum There seems little doubt that *artes* should be taken with *virtutum* and parallel with *exercitationes*: the idea of *artes virtutum* seems to combine the old Latin use of *artes* to mean 'qualities' (of character, as in *bonae artes* and similar phrases) with the Platonic or Socratic analogy of the virtues with τέχναι (cf. T. Irwin, *Plato's Moral Theory* (Oxford 1977) 71ff.). *artes* refers to the qualities themselves, *exercitationes* to the practice of them. For *ars* in similar senses in Cicero, cf.

Leg. Manil. 36; *Fin.* 2.115. (The alternative interpretation of *artes* here as 'the (liberal) arts' does not fit the context well.) It is not impossible that Cicero here had in mind the ancient etymologists' connection of *ars* with ἀρετή (Diomedes, *Gramm. Lat.* ed. Keil, I, p. 421; [Prob.] ibid. IV, p. 47; Aug. *Civ. Dei* 4.21; etc.), and perhaps also the connection, which modern philologists accept, of *ars* and *arma* (cf. *arma senectutis* above: Ernout–Meillet 73–4; 76). Cf. *TLL* 2, 656 s.v. *ars*. (If one accepts that there is a word-play here, one may then compare Musonius 17 init., which plays on ἐφόδιον / ζῆν ὁδῷ.)

in omni aetate One must prepare for old age by living virtuously in youth and middle age. For similar ideas cf. §§29; 38; 62; Pind. *Nem.* 9.44 ἐκ πόνων δ' οἳ σὺν νεότατι γένωνται | σύν τε δίκα, τελέθει πρὸς γῆρας αἰὼν ἀμέρα; Men. *monost.* 536 J. νέος ἂν πονήσῃς, γῆρας ἕξεις εὐθαλές; see also the passages quoted above on *arma senectutis*, and note on §62 below.

diu multumque Here pleonastic: for the phrase, cf. §38 below *multum et diu cogitatas*; *Orat.* 1; *Off.* 1.118; *De or.* 1.152; etc.; Löfstedt, *Synt.* II, 177–8 (cf. *multa ... saepe* above).

ecferunt This spelling, or obvious corruptions of it, occurs often in MSS, and seems likely to be classical: it may have been felt as slightly old-fashioned in Cicero's time, cf. Introd. p. 22; §39 below *ecfrenate*; *TLL* 5, 2, 143; Leumann, *Laut- u. Formenlehre* 558–9; Housman, *Papers* I, 179; Brink, *Horace on Poetry* III, 583 and 600.

efferre/ecferre is common with *fructus* in agricultural contexts, and enriches the metaphor here; cf. *De rep.* 2.9; *Brut.* 16; *ND* 2.86; Virg. *Georg.* 2.169; etc. For *fructus* in the context of old age, cf. §§62 and 71 below; *Cael.* 76; Sen. *Ep.* 104.4; Plut. *An seni* 789f.

numquam deserunt One cannot lose the virtues once one has them. This idea, implicit in Aristotelian and particularly Stoic views of virtue, is developed at length by Cicero in *Tusc.* 5.40ff.

conscientia bene actae vitae Cf. §§69 and 71 below; *Tusc.* 1.109; 3.61 *acta aetas honeste ac splendide tantam adfert consolationem*; *Fin.* 1.57; 2.104ff.; *De rep.* 6.8 (fragment introducing *Somn. Scip.*); *Att.* 10.4.5; Cato, *or.* fr. 17 Malcovati (quoted on §69 below); Martial 10.23; Favorinus, Περὶ γήρως fr. 14 Barigazzi (Stob. 4.50a.24) περιγίνεται δὲ [pleasure] ἐκ τῶν καλῶν μαθημάτων καὶ τῶν ἐνδόξων κατορθωμάτων ... ὑπάρχει τῷ γέροντι πρὸς ἑαυτὸν ἀναμιμνήσκεσθαι καὶ καθάπερ κτήμασι τέρπεσθαι; Xen. *Mem.* 2.1.33 (Choice of Hercules) οἱ δὲ γεραίτεροι ... ἡδέως μὲν τῶν παλαιῶν πράξεων μέμνηνται, εὖ δὲ τὰς παρούσας ἥδονται πράττοντες; Arist. *NE* 1166a25 τῶν γὰρ πεπραγμένων ἐπιτέρπεις αἱ μνῆμαι; in *Rhet.* 1390a Aristotle refers to the same phenomenon seen objectively – old men ζῶσι τῇ μνήμῃ μᾶλλον ἢ τῇ ἐλπίδι; cf. also Diog. Laert. 10.22 (letter of Epicurus shortly before his death). (Contrast Maximian, *Elegy* 1.291, *dura satis miseris memoratio prisca bonorum*.)

benefactorum recordatio This recalls Catull. 76.1 *Si qua recordanti benefacta priora voluptas*; commentators there do not admit that the similarity is more than accidental, and certainly specific reminiscence (of Catullus by Cicero) is highly unlikely; yet the Catullus poem gains point if it is seen as alluding to a currently popular moralistic idea (for parallels see previous note).

IV 10 Quintum Maximum (see P.–W. 6, 1829ff. s.v. Fabius 116): Quintus Fabius Maximus is introduced as an example of a man whose virtuous life led to a pleasant old age; the anecdotal style, however, somewhat obscures the point, and Cicero has to remind his readers of it below in §13.

There is no reason to doubt the truth of Cicero's idea that Cato as a young man attached himself to Fabius Maximus. It appears also in Plutarch (*Cato* 3.4; cf. *An seni* 791a), but he may have got the information from Cicero (cf. Introd. p. 19 n.50). Cicero seems to have been particularly keen on the idea that young men at the start of their careers should learn from the constant presence of some respected senior figure, both by instruction and by example: cf. in general §§25–6 and 29 below; *Lael.* 101; and on Cicero's own career in particular, *Lael.* 1. On this element in Roman education, cf. H. Marrou, *Histoire de l'éducation dans l'antiquité* (Paris 1948) 345–6 (233–4 in English edn, London 1956); S. F. Bonner, *Education in Ancient Rome* (London 1977) 84; Marquardt, *Privatleben* 124ff.; Blümner, *Privataltertümer* 335ff.; Warde Fowler, *Social Life at Rome in the Age of Cicero* (London 1908) 191ff. The modern designation for this period in a young Roman's life, *tirocinium fori*, derives from passages like Quint. *Inst.* 2.10.9 *tirones in foro*; Suet. *Aug.* 26; *Nero* 7; it is not Ciceronian; cf. P.–W. s.v. *tirocinium fori*; Tac. *Dial.* 34 with Gudeman[2] 449.

eum qui Tarentum recepit 'the man who recaptured Tarentum': the comma should be before *eum*, not between *eum* and *qui*; cf. §35 below; *Off.* 3.1; etc.; G. Lahmeyer, *Philol.* 20 (1864) 284ff. For other mentions of Fabius Maximus in Cicero cf. *Off.* 1.108; 1.84; *Tusc.* 3.70; *ND* 3.80; *Brut.* 57; 77; *Verr. II* 5.25; *Fam.* 4.6.1.

comitate condita gravitas A characteristically Ciceronian commendation of Fabius' personality. It has some support from the historical tradition, since Fabius was allegedly nicknamed 'Ovicula' on account of his gentle character; but more importantly, it is very similar to the terms used of Cato himself by Cicero in *Mur.* 66 (speaking to Cato the Younger), *sed si illius comitatem et facilitatem tuae gravitati severitatique asperseris, non ista quidem erunt meliora quae nunc sunt optima, sed certe condita iucundius*; and in *De rep.* 2.1 Scipio talks of Cato's *gravitate mixtus lepos*, much as Cato here talks of Fabius. Cf. Kammer, *Untersuchungen* 51. For *condītus*, 'seasoned', in this metaphorical sense, see *TLL* 4,143.

nec senectus mores mutaverat In *Lael.* 33 it is said that *mores* may change in old age, or for other reasons, and have an adverse effect on friendship.

non admodum grandem natu *admodum*, a word characteristic of conversational style, is particularly common with words denoting age: *TLL* 1, 757. *grandis natu* is a standard prose locution for 'old', and does not share the colloquial flavour of *grandis* in other meanings (cf. Löfstedt, *Synt.* II, 340); it occurs in comedy, Cicero, Seneca, once in Horace (*Epist.* 1.7.49) and later. More poetic equivalents are *grandis aevo* and *grandaevus* (the latter Virgilian). *grandis* without *natu* is used in this sense by Cicero below in this section and in §16, where there could be no ambiguity; for a similar instance cf. Plaut. *Capt.* 1019. Otherwise that usage is rare (Ter. *Phorm.* 362, Lucr. 2.1164 and in late Latin), no doubt because of the possibility of confusion with other meanings of *grandis*. See *TLL* 6, 2180.

anno enim post ... natus sum Cato was born in the (consular) year 234; Fabius was consul for the first time in 233 (Broughton, *MRR* 1,224). *anno post* simply means 'in the year after', not necessarily 'a full year after'; cf. *Lael.* 11 *anno antequam est mortuus*, and below on *quintoque anno post* for similar expressions. On the chronology and events of Cato's career narrated in this passage, see Appendix 3. There is no ground for supposing that Cicero's information is seriously incorrect, though naturally he does not give a full account of Cato's early life: he merely recalls occasions on which Cato and Fabius were associated.

cumque eo quartum consule In 214 (Broughton, *MRR* 1,258). *quartum consul* is regular, rather than *quarto*: cf. Gell. 10.1; *TLL* 4, 569, 67; 5, 1, 1001, 18–19; H.–Sz. 214; G. Viré in *Grec et Latin en 1980, Études et documents dédiés à E. Liénard* (Brussels 1980) 129ff.

adulescentulus Cato refers to himself as a young man, using a 'modest' diminutive; this is not evidence against Nepos' statement that Cato was military tribune in 214. (Cf. *paene miles* used of Scipio as military tribune in *De rep.* 6.11.) On the adjectival use of *adulescentulus* cf. Landgraf on *Rosc. Am.* 64.

ad Capuam For *ad* with names of towns as fields of campaign, see Hand, *Tursellinus* 1, 74ff.

quintoque anno post I.e. 209 (for the recovery of Tarentum in that year, cf. below, §11). In expressions of time of this sort, *post* may be an adverb or a preposition, and either the cardinal or the ordinal numeral may be used: hence there are four possible locutions, *quinto anno post* (as here; *Att.* 5.20.1; *De or.* 2.21; *Verr. II* 1.149); *quinque annis post* (cf. §19; *Lael.* 3; 42; *Brut.* 61; 161; 316); *post quintum annum* (*Att.* 9.10.4; *Mil.* 44); and *post quinque annos* (not in Cicero: Vell. 1.8.4; Suet. *Nero* 6.1): K.–S. 1, 403.

quaestor deinde quadriennio post factus sum, quem magistratum gessi Pighius' correction, the simplest and only satisfactory one.

The trouble in the MSS arose from the mistaken attachment of *quaestor* to the previous sentence, and the resulting nonsensical text is 'corrected' in α by the successive glosses *aedilis* and *praetor*, while β by accident or design omitted *deinde . . . factus sum*. Cato was quaestor in 204 (Broughton, *MRR* I, 307 and 310 n. 4; Livy 29.25.10; on Nepos' account, see Appendix 3), and was therefore clearly elected to the office in 205 (*quadriennio post*, four years after 209). It may seem otiose to specify both dates, but the conversational style excuses it, and there is certainly nothing wrong with the Latin. If, as some have maintained, *deinde . . . factus sum* were an interpolation, one would expect the text to be easily corrected once it had been removed; but the readings of the β MSS do not make sense, and Mommsen's correction *quaestorque magistratum gessi* cannot be accepted in default of parallel instances of *consul/praetor/quaestor magistratum gessi* for 'I held office as . . .' (Wuilleumier is quite wrong in saying that Mommsen is supported by the Benedictoburanus: I have ascertained for myself that this MS has the α reading.)

Tuditano et Cethego The consuls of 204: cf. *Brut.* 60. This was one year before Fabius' death in 203 (cf. Appendix 3).

suasor In technical language, one who publicly supported a bill (cf. *lator*, the proposer, and *auctor*, vaguer and non-technical, an influential person behind a legal proposal): cf. Vell. 2.44.4; Suet. *Tib.* 27; for *suasor* in non-technical usage cf. *Off.* 3.109; *Att.* 6.7.2; 6.16b.2 (= 16.16.9); *Phil.* 2.29; etc.

legis Cinciae Passed by the tribune M. Cincius Alimentus, forbidding advocates to receive fees or gifts, and forbidding gifts of any sort above a certain amount, except between relatives and some other classes of persons. Cato is made to mention the law with approval by Livy, 34.4.9; cf. ibid. 29.20.11; 29.37.1; Cic. *Att.* 1.20.7; *De or.* 2.286; Tac. *Ann.* 11.5; 13.42; 15.20; P.–W. 5, 1535ff. (s.v. *donatio*); Watson, *Roman Private Law*, 73–4.

et . . . et The two statements are contrasted: Fabius conducted the war with the same energy as a younger man, and at the same time his added *patientia* was an extra advantage; it is nowhere else suggested that Fabius' delaying tactics were connected with old age.

iuveniliter exsultantem Hannibal was 29 when he entered Italy in 218, Fabius probably in his late sixties (cf. Appendix 3). *exsultantem*, literally 'jumping about', throwing his weight around (not 'exulting' in the English sense): cf. *Off.* 1.90; *De rep.* 2.25; *Div.* 1.60; etc.

molliebat 'softened' by attrition: cf. Flor. 1.22 *sic maceravit Hannibalem ut qui frangi virtute non poterat, mora comminueretur*. The more usual metaphorical meaning of *mollire* is 'enervate' (with luxury, etc.). *TLL* 8, 1368–9.

familiaris noster Ennius That there was an association between Cato and Ennius is supported by Nepos, *Cato* 1.4, where it is said that Cato brought Ennius to Rome from Sardinia; this seems therefore to reflect genuine tradition; cf. Introd. p. 20; J. K. Newman, *G. & R.* 10 (1963) 132ff. On Ennius and Ennian quotations in the *Cato*, see §§1; 14; 16; 50; 73. Cicero similarly evokes Laelius' patronage of Pacuvius in *Lael.* 24.

'unus homo nobis ... claret' The well-known lines from *Annales* 12, fr. 370ff. V.², 363 Skutsch; for the context of the lines, and for other quotations of the first of them in ancient literature, see Skutsch ad loc. The majority of MSS here transmit the text *unus qui nobis* (from Virg. *Aen.* 6.846); a conflation of this with the true Ennian reading occurs in P¹MS¹Be, while the correct *unus homo* is found only as a correction in PDLS and in the (generally inferior) twelfth-century MS I (cf. Introd. p. 37 n. 83).

non enim This reading is also preserved in the other extant citation of this line, *Off.* 1.84; Skutsch thinks Cicero wrote it, while approving Lachmann's *noenum* (proposed on Lucr. 3.199) for Ennius himself. That Ennius wrote *noenum* is quite likely, though not proved. It has been argued that *non enim* would have been metrically possible for Ennius: there are, it seems, parallels for the necessary form of *brevis brevians* in Plautus and in Ennius' *Hedyphagetica* (see Skutsch's note ad loc.). Skutsch considers the absence of metrical parallels from the extant fragments of the *Annales*, and the absence from there of the word *enim* itself, as conclusive against *non enim*: I find it difficult to share his certainty, since the evidence is negative and from a limited sample, although undoubtedly these factors weaken the defence of *non enim*. There is probably nothing to choose on grounds of sense: a causal *enim* could be thought desirable, in comparison with the rather abrupt *noenum*, but that sense of *enim* is unlikely for Ennius' time.

If Ennius wrote *noenum*, the question remains when it was 'modernised' to *non enim*. The latter reading is of course unmetrical by the standards of Cicero's time and later, and Cicero knew enough about metre and about Latin not to substitute it for *noenum*, if that had been what he found in his text of Ennius. I therefore assume that, if Cicero wrote *non enim*, he found it already in the text; so it must have been due either to Ennius or to a pre-Ciceronian copyist. If, on the other hand, both Ennius and Cicero wrote *noenum*, it is necessary to assume independent corruption here and in *Off.* 1.84: this would not be very surprising, particularly if there was editorial interference with the text of Cicero in either or both places.

In view of all this, it is possibly over-cautious to retain *non enim*, but there remains a residue of doubt; I am not convinced that *non enim* could not have been written by either Cicero or Ennius, and have thought it best to display the MS evidence for what it is worth.

rumores Murmurings of the people: cf. Livy 22.39.18 (Fabius' speech); 44.22.10.

ponebāt Cf. *versāt* in the quotation in §1, though long *-āt, -ēt, -īt* in a syllable without ictus occurs only here and in frr. 78 Skutsch (*essēt*) and 385 (*infīt*): cf. Skutsch's introd., p. 59.

postque magisque A singular phrase: no emendation has improved it, nor has any explanation proved really satisfactory: cf. Skutsch, p. 532; the text (like that of the first line) is supported by the quotation of the same passage in *Off.* 1.84. It is usually explained as meaning something like 'the longer afterwards, the more his glory increases', with reference to the *topos* of continuously increasing posthumous fame found in Catull. 68.48; Hor. *Od.* 3.30.7; 1.12.45–6 with Nisbet–Hubbard; Pind. *Pyth.* 4.74; Lucr. 6.7; [Cic.] *Ad Her.* 4.44.57; the inscription quoted in Pliny, *NH* 35.115 is of disputable relevance (Vahlen, *Ges. Phil. Schr.* II (1923) 229–30n.; Bergk, *Kl. Schr.* I, 605n.); cf. also W. John, *Glotta* 33 (1954) 296. The parallels are not close to Ennius' words, and the fact that this sort of thing is often said does not show that Ennius meant to say it here. The thought seems to me to be rather that now (*nunc*) after the event, Fabius' glory is greater than it was when he was actually operating his delaying tactics, which were unpopular (cf. *rumores*); there is a sort of contrast between *post* and *magis*, and possibly the phrase is to be explained as an imitation of such Homeric phrases as ὀλίγη τε φίλη τε, 'both small and welcome', i.e. 'though small, nevertheless welcome': hence *postque magisque* might mean 'though afterwards, nevertheless more'. *post* cannot mean 'in future' (which would contradict *nunc*, despite John, art. cit.). However, certainty as to the meaning is impossible, particularly in view of the doubt about the context of the lines in Ennius (Skutsch, p. 530). On double -*que* in Ennius, see above on §1 *noctesque diesque*.

claret *clarere* is an archaic and poetic equivalent of *clarescere*: Enn. *scaen.* 326; Cic. *Arat.* 6; Turpilius, *com. fr.* 152; Lucr. 6.937; and in late Latin.

11 Tarentum Tarentum was lost by the Romans to Hannibal in 213 and recovered by Fabius in 209. For the historical context, see Polyb. 8.25ff.; Livy 26.39; 27.25; Wuilleumier, *Tarente* 150ff.

cum quidem me audiente ... recepissem This anecdote is repeated by Cicero from the collection in *De or.* 2.273: *ut Salinatori Maximus, cum Tarento amisso arcem tamen Livius retinuisset multaque ex ea proelia praeclara fecisset, cum aliquot post annis Maximus id oppidum recepisset rogaretque eum Salinator ut meminisset opera sua se Tarentum recepisse, Quidni, inquit, meminerim? numquam enim recepissem nisi tu perdidisses.* The anecdote recurs in Livy 27.25.5 and Plut. *Fabius* 23 and *Apophth. Rom.* 195f–196a (Fabius 6), where the name of the man concerned is given as M. Livius without *cognomen*: elsewhere the man who held the citadel of Tarentum is called M. Livius Macatus (Livy 27.34.7), while according to Livy Macatus' relative Salinator took no part in the war (ibid.); Polybius talks of Gaius Livius (8.25, with Walbank ad loc.). It is generally accepted that Macatus is the correct name, and that Cicero confused the two Livii, an easy mistake since his source probably gave no *cognomen*; further explanation seems unnecessary (e.g. K. Allen, *AJP* 19 (1898) 437).

Cicero gives no precise setting for the anecdote, except that *me audiente* implies that Cato was present. Both Plutarch and Livy say that the exchange took place in the Senate, and possibly the formal mode of address in Cicero's version, *Quinte Fabi*, supports this. Though Livy places it among the events of 208, immediately after the recapture of Tarentum, one presumes that Cato cannot have heard it in the Senate until his quaestorship in 204. (Cicero's *cum quidem* no doubt has an elastic temporal significance.) Cicero may be wrong in supposing that Cato actually heard the exchange: this supposition might have arisen from Cicero's having found the anecdote in Cato's writings (which is not proved, though quite likely in view of the fact that Cato's collection of anecdotes is mentioned in *De or.* 2.271, shortly before the passage quoted above). Livy attributes the boastful remark not to Macatus himself but to his friends in the Senate, and says that Salinator was among these: this might be an attempt to reconcile Cicero's mention of Salinator with the other evidence.

fuerat The alternative reading *fugerat* is only in P and MSS probably derived from it; it is not supported by the fact that all MSS have *in arce* except D²S²Va, where the change to *arcem* was presumably made because of *fugerat*. Livy indeed says that Macatus had 'fled' into the citadel (25.10.3), but this idea would not fit well with Cicero's *glorianti* or with *multa ex ea proelia praeclara fecisset* in the *De or.* version, and it is best to retain *fuerat* here. (Whether someone in the ancestry of P had read Livy is another question: cf. Introd. p. 37 n. 83).

inquit ridens For *inquit* followed by a nominative participle cf. *Brut.* 253; *Fin.* 2.119; 5.96; *TLL* 7, 1, 1778. This sort of phrase is not common, and may be modelled on such Greek phrases as ἔφη γελάσας.

consul iterum In 228 with Sp. Carvilius Maximus Ruga cos. II (P.–W. 3, 1360). On the historical problem raised by this passage, see Appendix 3, pp. 276–7. For Flaminius, see P.–W. 6, 2496; Cic. *Inv.* 2.52; *Brut.* 57; 77; *Acad. pr.* 2.13; Livy 21.63.2; Val. Max. 5.4.5; Z. Yavetz, *Athenaeum* 40 (1962) 325ff.

collega quiescente For *quies* and *quiescere* used of political inactivity, see *Att.* 2.3.3; 7.9.2; 8.11.5; 9.10.10; Nep. *Att.* 7.3 (on Atticus' *quies* during the Civil War).

agrum Picentem et Gallicum The land taken from the Senones in northern Italy: cf. Cato, *Orig.* 2, fr. 43 Peter, *ager Gallicus Romanus vocatur qui viritim cis Ariminum datus est, ultra agrum Picentium.*

augurque cum esset The anecdote presumably belongs to the occasion just described (cf. Appendix 3). *cum* has concessive force: such a statement would be surprising from an augur, even in Cicero's time, though by then political manipulation of the auspices was commonplace. There is little evidence for earlier periods, and perhaps we should not assume that Fabius' generation was much more pious about such things than Cicero's. The similarity of thought with Hector's famous words in *Iliad* 12.243 (noted by commentators since Erasmus) need not have any bearing on the authenticity of the saying here attributed to Fabius; nor the similarity to Cicero's own words in *Phil.* 11.28 *ut omnia quae rei publicae salutaria essent, legitima et iusta haberentur*, which were written later than the *Cato*. On Cicero's own views on augury, cf. C. W. Tucker, 'Cicero augur', *CW* 70 (1976) 171ff. Fabius Maximus was supposed to have been augur for 62 years (cf. App. 3).

12 quomodo ille mortem fili tulit Not *M. fili*: Fabius' son, like himself, was Quintus: P.–W. 6, 1789. Cato is made here to admire qualities in Fabius for which he himself was admired by Cicero (as above, *comitate condita gravitas*): *Lael.* 9 (Laelius talking about Cato) *quomodo ut alia omittam mortem fili tulit!* There were a number of standard *exempla* of men who had borne the death of their sons bravely: in addition to Fabius and Cato, Sulpicius Galus, Aemilius Paulus (for both these see *Lael.* ibid., for the latter, §68 below), and among the Greeks, Pericles, Xenophon and Anaxagoras. Cicero collected examples in his *Consolatio* (referred to in *Tusc.* 3.70); *Fam.* 4.6.1 (reply to Ser. Sulpicius); Valerius Maximus has a section devoted to this topic (5.10); cf. also Sen. *Contr.* 4, praef. 4ff., with further examples; Sen. *Marc.* 12.6; *Polyb.* 14.4; etc. On Fabius' son, cf. *Fam.* 4.6.1 *Q. Maximus, qui filium consularem, clarum virum et magnis rebus gestis, amisit*; *ND* 3.80; Plut. *Fabius* 24.

  consularis Cos. 213.

  laudatio Mentioned also by Plutarch, *Fab.* 24, as having been published: cf. Malcovati, *ORF* p. 5. On funeral laudations in general, cf. W. Kierdorf, *Laudatio Funebris*, Beitr. zur Klass. Phil. Heft 106 (Meisenheim am Glan 1980); Cicero refers to them (and to their historical inaccuracy) in *Brutus* 61ff. For *in manibus*, cf. *Lael.* 96, *sed adfuistis et est in manibus oratio*: the phrase seems to mean *in manibus omnium*, published and available, though in other contexts it usually means either 'in my possession' (a possible meaning here?) or, in the context of an author working on a piece of writing, 'in hand' (cf. §§22 and 38 below); *TLL* 8, 363, 47.

  quem philosophum non contemnimus? This remark is naturally suitable for Cato, who distrusted philosophers (cf. Plut. *Cato* 23; Gell. 18.7.3), but would not perhaps have been made in quite this way by Cicero *in propria persona*.

  in luce ... atque in oculis Cf. *Q. fr.* 1.1.7 *in luce Asiae, in oculis provinciae*; *Mur.* 21; *Verr. II* 1.129; *Att.* 4.3.1; etc.   *in oculis*+gen. is equivalent to 'in the sight of', not 'in the eyes of'.

multae ... litterae Cf. *ND* 1.91 *ut mihi quidem admirari liberet, in homine esse Romano tantam scientiam.* For the use of *ut* here ('for a Roman'), cf. *Brut.* 102 *scriptor ut temporibus illis luculentus*, ibid. 41; *De or.* 3.66; Nep. *Epam.* 5.2; Livy 4.13.1; etc.

sed etiam externa Meissner's deletion (*N. Jb. Kl. Phil.* 103 (1871) 59) of *bella*, which all MSS read after *externa*, is generally accepted by recent editors (e.g. Simbeck, Wuilleumier). The usual meaning of *domestica bella* is 'civil wars' (Cic. *Catil.* 2.11; 2.28; *Leg. agr.* 2.90; *Har. resp.* 49; Caes. *BG* 5.9; P. Jal, *La Guerre Civile à Rome* (Paris 1963) 23 n.3) of which there were none until after Fabius' time. A. Manutius explained the transmitted reading as *Domestica, gesta a Romanis; externa, exterarum nationum*, but such meanings are difficult to parallel. In any case, it is undesirable to limit Fabius' powers of memory to wars, whether domestic or foreign. *non domestica solum sed etiam externa*, 'not only domestic but also foreign affairs', gives much more appropriate sense; cf. §20 below *si legere aut audire voletis externa*; *Off.* 2.26, *externa libentius in tali re quam domestica recordor.* The context (*litterae* before, *sermone* after) is general throughout. The change cannot be objected to on rhythmical grounds, and the intrusion of *bella* is easily explained as a gloss by someone unfamiliar with the use of *domestica* and *externa* in this sense.

ita ... quasi Cf. Sall. *Jug.* 85.19 *ita aetatem agunt quasi vestros honores contemnunt*; also on §26 below.

unde For this personal use cf. *De or.* 1.67; 2.285; Horace, *Od.* 1.12.17 with Nisbet–Hubbard (who characterise the usage as 'grandiose'); Löfstedt, *Synt.* II, 149ff.; H.–Sz. 208ff.

V 13 quorsum There is no way of deciding whether Cicero wrote this (as in B, cf. *cursum* λ) or *quorsus* (α). The same problem exists in §44, where, conversely, the α MSS read *quorsum*, the β MSS *quorsus*.

quia profecto videtis *quorsus/quorsum* is answered indifferently by a causal or final clause: for the former, in addition to this passage cf. §44 below; *Brut.* 292; for the latter, §42 below; *Red. Quir.* 5. For *profecto* = 'of course' (not 'certainly' or 'truly'), see Landgraf on *Rosc. Am.* 30.

Scipiones aut Maximi This use of the plural of proper names is quite common, and does not seem to have the colloquial flavour of the English plural ('we can't all be Einsteins'): translate 'Not everybody can be a Scipio or Maximus'. Cf. §15 below *Fabricii Curii Coruncanii*; *Or.* 2.290; *Brut.* 67; *Verr. II* 3.209; *Cael.* 39; and often elsewhere in Cicero; Val. Max. 4.4.11; Quint. *Inst.* 12.2.30; Gudeman on Tac. *Dial.* 21.12; K.–S. I, 72; and for Greek, see [Longinus], *De subl.* 23: the plural has a more grandiose effect in Greek than it seems to have in Latin.

pedestres navalesque pugnas Neither Scipio nor Maximus was involved in any sea battles; the expression is conventional and 'polar' (E. Kemmer, *Die polare Ausdrucksweise* (Würzburg 1903)); cf. Greek πεζομαχίαι καὶ ναυμαχίαι, Hdt. 8.15; Thuc. 1.112; etc.; A. Momigliano, 'Terra Marique', *JRS* 32 (1942) 62.

est etiam ... senectus The quiet or contemplative life is for Cicero a rather inferior alternative to the active life: see *De rep.* 3.6; *Off.* 1.71; etc. On the distinction in general, cf. R. Joly, *Le Thème philosophique des genres de vie dans l'antiquité classique*, Mém. Acad. Royale de Belgique 51 (1956). It is not altogether accidental here that Cicero's examples of the quiet life are all Greek, while the examples of the active life are Roman.

quiete et pure atque eleganter For *et ... atque* see *TLL* 5, 2, 879, 71ff.; there is no difference in force between the *et* and the *atque*.

pure In the moral sense, like our 'clean living': cf. Catull. 76.19; *Cons. Liviae* 41 *quid tibi nunc mores prosunt et puriter actum | omne aevum?*; Varro, *Men.* 488 Bücheler (*Sexagesis* fr. 4); Apul. *Plat.* 2.20. (*OLD* also gives for *purus* a meaning 'refined' or 'cultivated', which would fit well here if it could be proved to exist, but it is not clear that *purus* has that meaning in either of the two passages quoted, Prop. 2.13.12 and Gellius 19.8.1). The Greek philosophers use καθαρός in a similar way in the context of the quiet life and abstention from politics: see Plato, *Rep.* 496d–e and Epicurus fr. 99 Usener.

eleganter 'with discrimination' (cf. *eligere*): cf. Livy 35.31.14 *ob eleganter actam vitam*; Cic. *Sull.* 79 *cum summa elegantia atque integritate vixistis.* However, for the real Cato *elegantia* was a vice: *Carmen de moribus* ap. Gell. 11.2 (p. 83 Jordan). Atticus was noted for *elegantia* (Nep. *Att.* 19.2) and Cicero may have had him in mind here (cf. Introd. p. 2 on the dedication of the *Cato* to Atticus).

Platonis Plato is traditionally supposed to have died at the age of 81 (Diog. Laert. 3.2, quoting Hermippus; Val. Max. 8.7, ext. 3; Lucian, *Macr.* 21; Sen. *Ep.* 58.30–1; Cens. *Nat.* 15.1; Aug. *Civ. Dei* 8.11; Jerome, *Ep.* 52.3.5 (clearly imitating Cicero: cf. below, §23); Anon. *Proleg. Plat. Phil.* 6.1–7; F. Jacoby, *Apollodors Chronik* (Berlin 1902) 304ff.; Riginos, *Platonica* 174–5); though Cicero's phrase here strictly means that he was 80. Neanthes reported by Diog. Laert. loc. cit. said that he died at 84. It is commonly reported that he was engaged in literary work until the end: the *Laws* were supposed to have been left unfinished (Diog. Laert. 3.37; Anon. *Proleg.* 24.10–15; 25.2–7), and there is a (comparatively late) tradition that the mimes of Sophron were found by his bed when he died: Val. Max. loc. cit. *altero etiam et octogesimo anno decedens sub capite Sophronis mimos habuisse fertur: sic ne extrema quidem eius hora agitatione studii vacua fuit*; Quint. *Inst.* 1.10.17; *Suda* s.v. Πλάτων, Σόφρων; cf. also Dion. Hal. *Comp. verb.* 25; Riginos ibid. Cicero's *scribens est mortuus* invites some such translation as 'died in the act of writing', 'pen in hand', but this is not paralleled in other accounts of his death; probably it should be translated 'died while still engaged in writing' (viz. the *Laws*). On the various incompatible and more or less apocryphal anecdotes about the circumstances of Plato's death, see Riginos, op. cit. 194ff.

Isocratis (The genitive of this declension is in -*is* or -ī in Republican Latin, the latter more commonly: cf. *Orat.* 190; *Att.* 2.1.1; Madvig on *Fin.* 1.14; Neue–Wagener, *Formenlehre* I³, 509ff.) Isocrates died by his own hand at the age of 99. Cf. Val. Max. 8.7 ext. 9, apparently based on this passage of Cicero; Lucian, *Macr.* 23; Plut. *Vit. dec. or.* 837e–f (says Isocr. died at 98 or 100); Cens. *Nat.* 15.3; Dion. Hal. *Isocr.* 1; Philostr. *Vit. soph.* 1.17.4; Jerome, *Ep.* 52.3.5; Paus. 1.18.8.

Panathenaicus See *Panath.* 3 τοῖς ἔτεσι τοῖς ἐνενήκοντα καὶ τετταρσὶν ἃ ἐγὼ τυγχάνω γεγονώς (confirming the reading *se dicit* in this passage); however, the speech was not finished (ibid. 270) until Isocrates was 97, having been interrupted by illness.

inscribitur For the present tense, cf. §59 below; *Acad. post.* 1.12; etc.; the perfect is rather less common, cf. *De or.* 2.61; *Div.* 2.1; *TLL* 7, 1, 1847.

cuius magister For Gorgias as the teacher of Isocrates, cf. Arist. ap. Quint. *Inst.* 3.1.13.

Leontinus Gorgias (Cicero often places the ethnic before the name of a Greek: cf. §43 *Thessalo Cinea*; *Tusc.* 1.111; *Leg.* 1.55; *Lael.* 88 and Seyffert–Müller; contrast §39 *Archytae Tarentini*.) A crop of anecdotes grew up concerning the aged Gorgias; this one is reproduced by Valerius Maximus (8.13 ext. 2) in virtually the same words, but does not occur elsewhere; others are recounted in Lucian, *Macr.* 23; Clearchus ap. Athen. 12.548d; Aristotle ap. Stob. 4.51.28; Ael. *VH* 2.35 (cf. D.–K. II, 275). His age is given variously as 105, 107, 108, 109 or 110. Cf. also Pliny, *NH* 7.156; Quint. *Inst.* 3.1.8; Paus. 6.17.9; Philostr. *Vit. Soph.* 1.9.6; Apollod. *Chron.* fr. 33 Jacoby; Diog. Laert. 8.58; Suda s.v. Γοργίας.

qui cum ex eo quaereretur A less common alternative for *a quo cum quaereretur*: K.–S. II, 316. The point of the anecdote, such as it is, seems to be explained in the next sentence, *sua enim vitia. . .*: Gorgias did not blame old age for whatever troubles he may have had.

praeclarum responsum Cf. *Off.* 3.1 *Magnifica vero vox et magno viro ac sapiente digna.*

14 sua enim vitia Cf. Sall. *Jug.* 1.4 *suam quisque culpam auctores ad negotia transferunt*; Sen. *Ep.* 50.1 *intellegas tua vitia esse, quae putas rerum*; Teles p. 9 H. πολλοὶ οὐχ ἑαυτοῖς ἀλλὰ τοῖς πράγμασι τὴν αἰτίαν ἐπάγουσιν; cf. also §7 above.

Ennius Cf. §10 above.

'sicuti ... quiescit' *Annales* fr. 374–5 V., 522 Sk. *sicuti* is dactylic by *brevis brevians*: cf. Ann. 536 V. = 549 Sk. (see Skutsch ad loc., p. 697); Lucil. fr. 198; 1029; 1298 M.; Lucr. 2.536 and 3.816; Lindsay, *ELV* 186; 220–1. Emendation is unnecessary (cf. Skutsch p. 673). On the Ennian context of

COMMENTARY: V 14

the lines, see Skutsch ad loc.; the image of the aged horse occurs a number of times, from Ibycus (7.5ff. Diehl) onwards; possibly the nearest to Ennius is Tibullus 1.4.31–2; also well known is Horace, *Epist.* 1.1.8 (though not notably similar to this passage); cf. Wilamowitz on Eur. *Heracl.*, edn 2 (Berlin 1909) pp. 242–3; there is not much to commend W.'s idea that Cic. substituted the Ennian quotation for a reference to ἵππου γῆρας in a Greek philosophical source; see also Brink on Hor. *AP* 84.

spatio … supremo *spatium* here is a lap of the race-course: cf. Virg. *Aen.* 5.327 *extremo spatio*; Sen. *Ep.* 30.13 *septimo spatio*; Ov. *Hal.* 68; *OLD* s.v. 1b; in Cic. *Arch.* 30 *usque ad extremum spatium* and Juv. 10.358 *spatium vitae extremum* the meaning may be either 'the last lap', as here, or 'the end of the course' (envisaging only a single circuit of the track). Ennius here means that the horse has won many races on the last lap, that being naturally the most exciting way to finish.

vicit Olympia A Graecism: cf. Hor. *Epist.* 1.1.50 *coronari … Olympia*; according to Skutsch the usage occurs also in Vitruvius and Pliny.

senio confectus It is usually assumed that *senium* here is equivalent to *senectus*, and there may indeed be an etymological connection between the two words. However, in earlier Latin up to the time of Cicero, *senium* seems to be used either simply to mean 'weariness' in contexts where old age is not in question (esp. in the phrase *senio confectus*: *Mil.* 20; *Tusc.* 3.27; cf. Val. Max. 5.1 ext. 1), or at any rate to have strong connotations of weariness and decline. It is only in Silver Latin that the literal meaning of 'old age' becomes common (see Sen. *Med.* 258; *Oed.* 167; Pliny, *NH* 11.221; Tac. *Hist.* 1.5; etc.).

equi … victoris Cf. Virg. *Georg.* 3.499; *Aen.* 7.656; it is possible that the phrase is itself an Ennian reminiscence; though the adjectival use of *victor* here would not be against Ciceronian usage (cf. e.g. *Leg. Manil.* 25 *victor exercitus*), it has a somewhat poetic flavour. For nouns in -*tor* thus used adjectivally see H.-Sz. 157.

probe meminisse potestis A remarkable dactylic rhythm (see above on §7 *deplorare solebant* and §5 *sumus sapientes*). *probe* is often used by Cicero with the verbs *nosse, meminisse, scire*; the adverb in general belongs to colloquial language.

anno enim undevicesimo (Cf. on §10 *quintoque anno post*.) The consuls are those of 150 (cf. Introd. pp. 16–17). This passage and *Brut.* 78 imply that Ennius died in 169; Jerome says 168; cf. also Gell. 17.21; see Skutsch, *Ennius* introd. 1–2 and *BICS* 27 (1980) 103–4; Schanz–Hosius I, 88.

legem Voconiam The *Lex Voconia de mulierum hereditatibus* prohibited under certain circumstances the appointment of women as heirs, and contained various other provisions concerning inheritances. Cf. *Verr. II* 1.106; *Balb.* 21; *De rep.* 3.17; *Fin.* 2.55; [Livy], *Periocha* 41; P.–W. 12, 2418; H. Sauppe in Orelli–Baiter, *Onomasticon Tullianum* (Zürich 1836) III,

294–305. For Cato's *suasio*, see Malcovati, *ORF* pp. 60–1, frr. 156–60. The *Periocha* dates the law to 174, not 169 as here, but the Ciceronian dating is usually preferred: cf. Malcovati ad loc.

suasi. sed Forchhammer's correction, reported by Madvig (*Adversaria Critica* (Copenhagen 1873) II, 244). In fact it is hardly changed from the reading *suasisset* found in P¹ (clearly the reading of the first hand: the '&' ligature can be seen despite the erasure made by the corrector in order to substitute a final *m*) and H¹ (which looks as though it may originally have read *suasis.et*). *sed* had previously been inserted by Manutius: the connection is obviously desirable. As for the tense of the verb, it is clear that the meaning ought to be 'he died in the year when I spoke in favour of the Voconian law', and that requires a perfect indicative in normal Latin (cf. Hale, *The Cum Constructions* 189: Hale finds *suasissem* 'difficult', but apparently did not know of Forchhammer's conjecture). The correction also brings a mild improvement to the clausula.

annos septuaginta natus Cf. above on *anno enim undevicesimo*: Jerome says that Ennius died *septuagenario maior*.

paupertatem et senectutem See on §8 above. *paupertas* implies frugality rather than indigence: cf. Hor. *Epist.* 2.2.99, and Porphyrio ad loc. *paupertas etiam honestae parsimoniae nomen est, et usurpatur in fortuna mediocri*; Nisbet–Hubbard on Hor. *Od.* 1.12.43; Tibull. 1.1.5. It is not clear how much independent value is to be attached to the notice in Jerome's *Chronicle* (an. 1777, = 240 B.C., on the birth of Ennius; p. 133 H.), generally supposed to be derived from Suetonius, *De poetis* (see Rostagni's edition of the fragments, p. 23): *Ennius ... habitavit in monte Aventino, parco admodum sumptu contentus et unius ancillae ministerio.* The information concerning the maidservant may be a mistaken extrapolation from the anecdote in Cic. *De or.* 2.276 (*illud Nasicae, qui cum ad poetam Ennium venisset eique ab ostio quaerenti Ennium ancilla dixisset domi non esse ...,* etc.); cf. Vahlen, *Ennianae poesis reliquiae*, p. xii. Nevertheless, there is no reason to doubt the tradition of Ennius' frugality. Cf. Schanz–Hosius I, 88; Leo, *Plautinische Forschungen*² (Berlin 1912) 76.

15 Enumeration of complaints against old age Cato's speech so far may be considered as a very informal *exordium*. Cicero now follows rhetorical convention in introducing the main part of the discussion with a *partitio* or formal enunciation of divisions of the subject, which are to be considered in order in what follows. The division into four, exemplified here, was particularly favoured by the rhetoricians (cf. Volkmann, *Rhetorik* 167ff.). Each part of the argument begins with the statement of a point to be refuted, a procedure well recognised in Greek rhetorical theory: the initial statement of the point (sometimes represented as an objection from an imaginary opponent) was called ἀντίθεσις; the refutation itself, λύσις (Volkmann, pp. 239ff.). This method of organising an argument is found also in *Paradoxa* 3, and there are examples of *theses* constructed in this way among later Greek writings (e.g. Apthonius in Spengel, *Rhetores Graeci* II, 50ff.). On this and other forms of rhetorical influence in the *Cato*, see Introd. pp. 9–12.

A similar division to Cicero's occurs in Musonius 17, p. 91 H. (cf. Introd. p. 16; 28), with substitution of Plato's complaint (cf. §7 above) that old men are badly treated by friends and family, instead of Cicero's about public life. It is quite likely, though not certain, that Musonius was there influenced by Cicero; the omission of the point about public life may have something to do with the nature of Musonius' audience or with changed conditions under the Principate. Musonius does not offer a discursive refutation of the various points but simply (in traditional Stoic fashion) recommends correct training as the remedy for all of them. For other occurrences of the particular complaints, see notes on the respective passages.

unam ... alteram ... tertiam In simple enumeration, Latin says 'one ... a second ... a third' (cf. e.g. *Fin.* 5.9; *Off.* 1.152); the ordinals *primam ... secundam ...* might tend to imply an order of importance.

privet fere omnibus voluptatibus *omnes fere* + noun is much commoner in Cicero than *fere omnes* + noun (*TLL* 6, 1, 494; Merguet, *Lexikon* s.v. *fere*; Krebs–Schmalz, *Antibarbarus* I⁶, 533), and a minority of MSS (PMO²ViE) here actually read *omnibus fere voluptatibus*; I have, however, retained the better attested reading, which could be defended (if defence were needed) by arguing that *fere* here qualifies *privet* as much as *omnibus*. *fere* should certainly not be deleted, as Wuilleumier does for no better reason than that the MSS differ as to its position.

si placet A common polite formula in Cicero. It does not mean 'please', as in later Latin, but 'if you wish', 'if you will', 'if you don't mind', either acceding to a request (cf. e.g. *Part. or.* 2) or asking for approval before proceeding (as here; *De or.* 3.51; etc.). Cf. Becker, *Technik und Szenerie* 20 (with list of examples); Hofmann, *Umgangssprache* 134.

15fin.-20   First complaint: old age makes it impossible to take part in public life

VI   A rebus gerendis senectus abstrahit Cf. Plut. *An seni* 793a τὸν ἀποσπῶντα τῆς πολιτείας λόγον (a striking coincidence of phraseology: for the very uncertain relation between Plutarch and Cicero, see Introd. p. 28); the whole of Plutarch's work deals at length with this aspect of old age. The complaint also occurs in Juncus p. 1051 W.–H.

It is hardly possible not to imagine that Cicero was thinking, when he wrote this passage, of the state of Rome in his own time, and reflecting bitterly on his own exclusion from public life during Caesar's dictatorship.

The contrast between the rashness of young men and the wisdom of the old is conventional (see note on §20), but Cicero would doubtless have been thinking of particular individuals – Catiline, Clodius, Curio – who had had in his estimation a bad influence in Roman politics. No doubt Cicero saw himself as potentially a wise counsellor of the sort that he describes here, and it is possible that he intended this passage as a gentle reminder of his presence to his fellow-senators. However, it is going too far to suppose that this was the main reason why he wrote the *Cato* (E. Stettner, *Z. Oest. Gymn.* 61 (1910) 684ff.; 865ff.), since this passage is only a relatively small part of the work; nor is it legitimate to draw conclusions about the dating, since there are no definite references to Cicero's own situation (cf. Appendix 1).

quae iuventute geruntur The word *iuventus* does not mean 'youth', the period of life, until later antiquity; in classical Latin that meaning is expressed by *adulescentia, iuventas, iuventa*. Here and in Sall. *Cat.* 5.2 it means 'youthful vigour'; elsewhere it has the concrete collective meaning of 'young men' (as in *princeps iuventutis*, etc.); *TLL* 7, 2, 743.

infirmis corporibus, animo tamen On the physical weakness of old age, cf. on §§27ff. below; on the existence of tasks appropriate to old men and their physical and mental condition, cf. §33; *Off.* 1.123; Plut. *An seni* 789d; 792d; 797e.

nihil ergo agebat ... nihil agebant The repetition, at the end of a passage, of its first words is called κύκλος in Greek rhetorical terminology: Volkmann, *Rhetorik* 471.

Quintus Maximus See §§10–12 above.

Lucius Paulus The victor of Pydna, Scipio Aemilianus' natural father; his daughter Aemilia married Cato's son. He was already in his sixties at the time of the Macedonian war; he was censor in 164, four years after Pydna, and died in 160. Cf. *Att.* 4.13.2; Livy 44.41.1; Plut. *Aemilius* 10; Diod. 30.20; P.–W. 1, 576. Paulus is one of Cicero's favourite Roman heroes, and is particularly appropriate here, both as an example of activity in old age and because of his family relationship with Cato and Scipio.

pater tuus I.e. Scipio's. Cf. §§49; 77; 82; also 61.

optimi viri fili mei Cf. §68 and 84.

Fabricii Curii Coruncanii (For the plural, see note on §13 *Scipiones aut Maximi.*) C. Fabricius Luscinus (P.–W. 6, 1931), M'. Curius Dentatus (4, 1841) and Tib. Coruncanius (4, 1663), three contemporaries from the first half of the third century, are standard Ciceronian examples of old Roman virtue. The three appear together again in §43; Coruncanius (as a jurist) in §27; and Curius in §§55–6, where an anecdote of his old age is told. Less seems to be known, however, about the activities of the others in old age; the proverbial sound of the names, and the natural veneration for men of past generations (among Romans of Cicero's cast of mind, at least) was enough to compensate for the lack of specific factual information. Cf. *Cael.* 39; *Parad.* 1.12; *Sest.* 143; *Tusc.* 1.110, and many other places in Cicero; Val. Max. 4.4.11, etc.; Otto, *Sprichwörter* 102, 129; Introd. pp. 9–10 nn. 27 and 28.

16 Appi Claudi Another almost proverbial figure. Cf. §37 below; *Tusc.* 5.112, *Appium quidem veterem illum, qui caecus annos multos fuit, et ex magistratibus et ex rebus gestis intellegimus in illo suo casu nec privato nec publico muneri defuisse*, together with other examples of blindness. His dissuasion of the Senate from making peace with Pyrrhus, one of the best-known episodes in his life, is mentioned frequently: Cic. *Phil.* 1.11; *Brut.* 61; Plut. *Pyrrhus* 19; *An seni* 794e; Val. Max. 8.13.5; Sen. *Ep.* 114.13; Tac. *Dial.* 18.4; 21.7; [Livy], *Periocha* 13, and the historians of the Livian tradition; App. *Samn.* 10.4; Justin–Trogus 18.2.10; Ov. *Fasti* 6.203–4; Quint. *Inst.* 2.16.7; Suet. *Tib.* 2.1; cf. Lévêque, *Pyrrhos* 351n. The present passage contains only an abbreviated version of the incident, though we are indebted to Cicero for the reference to Ennius, which does not occur elsewhere (cf. below).

accedebat ... ut For the difference between *accedit ut* and *accedit quod*, see K.–S. II, 240 and 273; the former implies a matter of additional importance, as we might say 'In addition to his old age *it was his misfortune that he should be* blind.'

non dubitavit dicere Cicero regularly uses *non dubito* + inf., 'I do not hesitate to do', but not *dubito* + inf. without an expressed or implied negative (this is a certain reading only in *ND* 1.113); cf. *TLL* 5, 1, 2094ff.

illa The pronoun is properly demonstrative, not equivalent to *ea*: the meaning is 'those well-known words'.

persecutus est 'related' or 'described': cf. §55 below, etc.

'quo vobis mentes...' Enn. *Ann.* 6, 202–3 V.², 199–200 Skutsch. This passage is the only source for the lines. The relationship between the speech put in Appius' mouth by Ennius, the speech attributed to him by the historical tradition (Plut. *Pyrrhus* 19; App. *Samn.* 10.5), the speech which circulated under Appius' name in Cicero's time (*Brut.* 61) and later, and Appius' actual words, is discussed by Skutsch ad loc. (pp. 360–1). The beginning of the Ennian version, quoted here by Cicero, is different from the beginning of Appius' speech as given in the historians, and appears to be based on Hom. *Il.* 24. 201, ὤμοι πῇ δή τοι φρένες οἴχονθ', ᾗς τὸ πάρος περ|ἔκλε' ἐπ' ἀνθρώπους ξείνους ἠδ' οἷσιν ἀνάσσεις; It seems most likely that Ennius recast the opening of the speech along Homeric lines, though there is no guarantee that the version of the historians is any nearer to what Appius actually said. Cf. also B. Niese, *Hermes* 31 (1896) 493; Malcovati, *ORF* p. 1.

mentes ... dementes An oxymoron reminiscent of Greek poetic phrases like γάμος ἄγαμος, hardly attributable to the native Latin taste for alliteration and word-play (as by Palmer, *Latin Language* 104): for discussion of the figure see Skutsch ad loc.; M. Puelma, *Mus. Helv.* 34 (1977) 184. Cf. also August. *Civ. Dei* 1.33.1 *o mentes amentes* (Augustine is fond of the figure elsewhere, as e.g. *Conf.* 3.2.3; 3.3.6; so this need not be a reminiscence of this passage of Ennius).

viai I retain Lambinus' *viai* for the transmitted *via* (unmetrical), despite the strictures of Skutsch ad loc., taking it as partitive genitive after *quo* (cf. H.–Sz. 53). Admittedly the existence of phrases like *quo loci* (*OLD* s.v. *locus* 25) does not constitute proof that *quo viai* is admissible, but it surely serves as a parallel to some extent. I do not see what force there may be in the general and theoretical argument that '*via* hardly lends itself to partition': why less so than the singular *locus*? Nor, in the face of such quite ordinary Ciceronian passages as *Fam.* 5.16.4 *quid est enim iam non modo pudori probitati virtuti, rectis studiis, bonis artibus, sed omnino libertati ac saluti loci?*, does it seem that it would be beyond the power of a Roman listener to connect *quo* with *viai* (Skutsch implies that such a separation would only be permissible with an established phrase such as *ubi gentium*: but in the example just quoted, is *quid loci* an 'established phrase' rather than just an instance of a partitive genitive?). While accepting that the credentials of *viai* are not established beyond suspicion, I cannot see that Skutsch is justified in calling it 'senseless and ungrammatical'; in my view it is still the best conjecture available. Skutsch favours Scaliger's *vietae* (cf. Fleckeisen, *N. Jb. Kl. Phil.* 93 (1866) 47; Dahl, *Handschriftenkunde* I, 13): he explains it as contrasting with *rectae*, as *mentes* with *dementes* and *sese flexere* with *stare*, and quotes Varro, *LL* (exc. ex Aug.) p. 241, 15 for an old use of *flexum* as equivalent to *incurvum* or *vietum*. (The 'similar corruption of *vietum*' in §5 above – not actually very similar – seems hardly relevant.) The objection to *vietae* consists in (a) the awkwardness of the two predicative adjectives *dementes* and *vietae* coming together in the same clause, and (b) the difficulty of translating *quo*: 'where have your minds wilted to?' is a strange question, even allowing for poetic rhetoric. Supporters of *vietae* might have argued that *quo* here is not local, but means 'why' or 'to what purpose': Skutsch quotes Vahlen, *Ges. Phil. Schr.* II, 179n. for this view, though he himself rejects it, and it is disputable whether it would improve the sense very much. Skutsch argues that the contrast with *rectae stare* must be 'stooping' rather than 'taking the wrong road': certainly, taking the wrong road can only be contrasted with taking the right road, but nothing is said about taking the wrong road; the sense with the reading *viai* is 'where have your minds wandered off to, that used to stand firmly upright?'. S.'s argument works better against the alternative way of taking *viai* (C. Knapp, *AJP* 35

(1914) 281; R. A. Anderson, *CPhil* 11 (1916) 98–9) as an ablative-equivalent with *flexere* ('wandered off the way'); but that is in any case hardly Latin (cf. Skutsch p. 362 n. 10).

The MS variants recorded in the apparatus are probably not significant, and do not help to determine the correct reading. Q's *ruina* simply shows that someone in the twelfth century knew how to write hexameters, and is consequent on the change from *dementes* to *dementi* made in O²RQES², originally (one presumes) in order to agree with *via*. The readings *vie* or *vite* found in Oxford, Bodl. Rawl. G 38 (s. xiii) and Leiden, Voss. Lat. F. 14 (s. xv: cf. Dahl, cited above) respectively, are curious in that they are nearer to either of the proposed conjectures than is the reading of the majority of MSS; but where they came from, and what they were supposed to mean, cannot be determined.

ceteraque Cicero adds the enclitics *-que, -ve, -ne* to short open final syllables more often than is commonly believed: addition to short *-e* is less common than to short *-a*, but is not unexampled: §22 *quaesisseque*; *Off.* 1.124 *debereque*; *Tusc.* 1.98; *ND* 1.26; *Phil.* 14.26; *Acad. pr.* 2.29 *dissimileque* is a rare instance in which the penultimate (and in fact also the antepenultimate) is also short. See Lebreton, *Études* 416; Landgraf on *Rosc. Am.* p. 216.

et tamen For this combination of particles, cf. §1 above: here the meaning is clearly 'and anyway'. Cf. §31 below; *Fin.* 1.15; 2.15; 2.84 with Madvig's note; *Att.* 7.3.10; 1.14.4; *Q. fr.* 1.2.3; Lucr. 1.1050; 5.1125; 5.1177 with Munro; also *ac tamen, atque tamen* (with a word intervening), in §65 below, Cato *Pro Rhod.* 2, etc. The meaning of the whole passage is 'you know the poem, and anyway Appius' own speech is extant'; similarly a few lines below, 'from which we may understand that he was well advanced in age at the time of the war with Pyrrhus; and anyway, that is the tradition we have heard from our fathers'. (*et tamen* here has been much misunderstood and unnecessarily emended; e.g. by Halm to *etiam*, cf. J. P. Binsfeld, *RhM* 26 (1871) 304.)

exstat oratio Cf. above on the Ennius quotation. In *Brutus* 61 Cicero notes that the speech was in circulation in his time, having been preserved in family records. The authenticity of the version referred to there (and presumably here) by Cicero has been doubted, but there is no compelling indication that it was a forgery, and as regards its reflection of the exact words of Appius, the same problem exists with many ancient speeches, including Cicero's own. If what Appius said was at all memorable, the likelihood is that the tradition preserved at least some features of the speech that he made, whoever was responsible for the written version. The accounts in Plutarch and other historians are generally supposed to derive from the version referred to by Cicero (though they may do so at several removes); we may suspect poetic licence in the Ennian version, though the context of Cicero here may perhaps be taken to imply that it did not diverge too far from the traditional version of the speech.

septimo decimo anno 'in the seventeenth year after', i.e. after an interval of not less than sixteen and not more than seventeen years. Appius' second consulate was in 296; Cicero therefore places the events here described in 279 (strictly, at any time between March 279 and March 278, as the consular year at this time began in March). Cicero has unnecessarily been thought to be wrong in this dating: in fact it does not conflict with the consensus of the other evidence, as is explained in Appendix 3. Nor is it necessary to invoke the common but groundless supposition that the seventeenth year is reckoned 'inclusively'. The year of Appius' consulate was not the first year after his consulate, either to us or to the Romans.

duos consulatus 307 and 296: there is a clear interval of ten years between the end of the former and the beginning of the later: again no 'inclusive reckoning'.

censorque Appius Claudius (censor in 312: Broughton, *MRR* I, 160; E. S. Staveley, *Historia* 6 (1959) 410 n. 1) was one of eighteen recorded non-consular censors (out of a total of 188 holders of the office): most of these belong to the fourth century B.C., and in later periods it was clearly exceptional to hold the censorship before the consulate, but it was not so in Appius' time. See J. Suolahti, *The Roman Censors* (Helsinki 1963) 543ff., esp. 549.

bello eum An excellent emendation by Simbeck (for *bellum* or *bello* codd.), recorded tentatively in the apparatus of his 1912 edition, and adopted in the text by Wuilleumier. The addition of *eum* not only provides a subject for the infinitive clause, which it badly needs, but also places it correctly in second place (*Pyrrhi bello* being treated naturally as one unit).

grandem On the use of *grandis* for *grandis natu*, see on §10 above. Appius' exact age at the time is not known, nor apparently was it to Cicero.

et tamen See above on this section (p. 138).

17 **adferunt** *adferre* is used often of reasons or proofs: *Inv.* 1.53; *ND* 3.23; *Cluent.* 71; etc.; *TLL* I, 1203.

similesque sunt ut si qui There seems little doubt that this is the right reading (the alternative would be *eis* instead of *ut si*, from *ut his* or *in his* of BLAD): this and similar locutions seem well enough attested, cf. *Div.* 2.131; *Off.* 1.42; 1.87; *Tusc.* 4.41; Meissner, *N. Jb. Kl. Phil.* 103 (1871) 57ff. Cf. old-fashioned English 'like as if'.

gubernatorem ... dicant The comparison of the state to a ship is commonplace: cf. Plato, *Rep.* 488a ff.; Hor. *Od.* 1.14 and Nisbet–Hubbard; Pöschl, *Bibl. Bildersprache* 561–2. This passage also has an affinity with the fable of the Belly and Members (Livy 2.32).

foros The deck (not 'gangways', as seems sometimes to be thought; the plural form may perhaps reflect the discontinuous construction of some ancient decks). See C. Torr, *Ancient Ships* (Cambridge 1894) 57–8; L. Casson, *Ships and Seamanship in the Ancient World* (Princeton 1971) 179 n. 54.

clavum tenens Cicero uses this image of his own political activity in *Fam.* 9.15.3; *Att.* 2.7.4. Cf. also Plut. *An seni* 790d.

non facit All MSS known to me except for Z read *sedeat in puppi, non faciat ea quae iuvenes*, and all except STPb continue *at vero multo maiora et meliora faciat.* It is clear enough that *at vero* must introduce a new main clause, and that *facit* should be read there. The preceding *non faciat* has also been changed to *non facit* by editors since Manutius, and that reading is now found in the manuscript Z (s. xi or xii). The flow of the passage is much improved if the previous sentence ends at *sedeat in puppi* (which has, incidentally, a good clausula rhythm). The next sentence then forms a neat antithesis, conceding that the helmsman (symbolising the elder statesman) does not do the same things as the young men, but asserting that the things which he does are more important. (Alternatively, *non facit ea quae iuvenes* could be taken as an imagined objection, to be countered by *at vero . . .*, but although such objections are common enough in this work, the introduction of one here would be surprisingly abrupt. Moore's reading *ne faciat*, not in itself implausible, fails to take account of the full force of *at vero*, which could hardly be used apodotically like simple *at* after a concessive clause. For a textual problem in some ways similar, see below on §34 *non sunt in senectute vires.*)

iuvenes Cicero usually prefers *adulescens* to *iuvenis*, but uses the latter word in the plural (apparently with the sense of 'young men collectively', whereas *adulescentes* would be used to refer to a number of individuals). Cf. *iuvenes* in §§29 and 33 below; *adulescentes* in §39. On the difference, mainly stylistic, between the two words, see B. Axelson in *Mélanges Marouzeau* (Paris 1948) 7ff.; *TLL* 7, 2, 734; J. J. Delgado in *Atti del I Congresso Internazionale di Studi Ciceroniani* (Rome 1961) II, 433ff.

velocitate aut celeritate *celeritas* is more general than *velocitas*: the latter applies only to physical motion from one place to another, while the former can be used of any action (not necessarily physical); one runs *velociter*, but does a mathematical problem or sweeps the deck of a ship *celeriter*. See *Tusc.* 4.31 *velocitas autem corporis celeritas appellatur* (i.e. *celeritas* of body is called *velocitas*); *TLL* 3, 755, 1ff.

consilio auctoritate sententia Cf. *Phil.* 2.11 (the same phrase); below, §19; §67; *Off.* 1.123; a similar expression in Plut. *An seni* 789d, οὐ ποδῶν ἔργα καὶ χειρῶν ἀπαιτοῦμεν ἀλλὰ βουλῆς καὶ προνοίας καὶ λόγου; ibid. 792d; 797e; also §38 below, *animi non corporis viribus*. The words *consilium, auctoritas, sententia*, though their import here is general, strongly suggest the Roman senate, which is mentioned in the next section.

quibus Has to be taken in slightly different senses with *orbari* (abl. of separation) and *augeri* (abl. of respect).

18 et miles et tribunus Cato is also made to mention his own military career in §§10 and 32; on the chronology, see Appendix 3.

legatus Cf. Cato, *orat*. 73 (on the occasion of his praetorship in Sardinia in 198), *cum essem in provincia legatus*.

et quomodo; Carthagini male iam diu cogitanti In most of the older MSS, this passage appears as follows: *et quomodo Cart(h)agini (K-) cui male iam diu cogitanti bellum multum ante denuntio*; PMZ punctuate after *Carthagini*. This is nonsensical: it is clear that there must be punctuation after *quomodo* (*quae sint gerenda et quomodo*); *cui* is omitted by O² and some later MSS (cf. Introd. p. 39); also by R which omits *bellum*, and HQS²E which add *inferatur* after *bellum* (as if it were *et quomodo Carth. bellum inferatur*). The omission of *cui* gives perfect sense, the example of Carthage being introduced with asyndeton, as particular examples to prove a general point often are in Cicero (cf. e.g. §§21 and 22 below, Themistocles and Sophocles). It is not difficult to suppose that *cui* is a mistaken insertion made to restore sense after the punctuation had been misplaced. Among emendations seeking to take account of *cui*, the best is probably *Carthagini quidem male* (Schiche, Kayser); *cum* Anz followed by Simbeck, *qui* Rinn both introduce an awkward word order (there being no special emphasis on *Carthagini* of a sort that would justify postponement of the conjunction or relative pronoun); I have wondered about *enim* (enī corrupted to *cui*); but the omission of *cui* is simplest.

This passage is our earliest source for Cato's persistent hostility to Carthage; cf. *Off*. 1.79; Vell. 1.13.1; [Livy], *Periocha* 48–9; Diod. 34/35.33.3; App. *Pun*. 69; Plut. *Cato* 26–7; Flor. 2.15.4; [Victor], *De vir. ill*. 47.8. Something of a tradition concerning what Cato himself said may perhaps be extracted from comparison of the following sentence of Cicero here with Vell. 1.12.7 *neque se Roma iam ... securam speravit fore, si nomen usquam stantis maneret Carthaginis, ... neque ante invisum esse desinit quam esse desiit* (this is however given as a comment of the author, not a quotation from Cato), and App. *Pun*. 69, καὶ ὁ Κάτων μάλιστα ἔλεγεν οὔ ποτε Ῥωμαίοις βέβαιον οὐδὲ τὴν ἐλευθερίαν ἔσεσθαι πρὶν ἐξελεῖν Καρχηδόνα. The tradition that he added a pronouncement concerning Carthage to the end of every speech he made in the Senate appears in Diodorus, Appian and Plutarch; all three give his words as (δοκεῖ δέ μοι καὶ) Καρχηδόνα μὴ εἶναι (cf. Velleius' *esse desiit*). This is usually taken to represent the proverbial *Carthago delenda est*, but it is not the obvious Greek translation of that phrase; the word *delere* occurs in Vell. 1.13.1 *ante triennium quam Carthago deleretur, M. Cato, perpetuus diruendae eius auctor . . . mortem obiit* (not evidence for Cato's words), in the Livian *Periocha, Catone suadente bellum et ut tolleretur delereturque Carthago*, in Val. Max. 8.15.2 *cuius . . . consilio . . . deleta Carthago est*, in Pliny, *NH* 15.74, and in Florus and the *De vir. ill.*, both of which give the well-known words in indirect speech. In these circumstances the exact words of Cato cannot be recovered with certainty; cf. C. E. Little, *CJ* 29 (1933–4) 429ff.; S. Thurlemann, *Gymn.* 81 (1974) 465–75 shows that the common formulation *ceterum censeo Carthaginem esse delendam* dates only from the nineteenth century.

male . . . cogitanti This phrase is usually thought to be a Catonian echo, and may indeed be so, since it is not used elsewhere by Cicero: Cato, *Agr.* 1.4 is quoted, *minimeque male cogitantes sunt qui in eo studio occupati sunt*. However, it is not uncommon outside Cicero: see Caelius ap. Cic. *Fam.* 8.12.1; Brutus ap. Cic. *Ad Brut.* 1.4a.2 (4); Publil. *Mim.* 27; Sen. *Ep.* 104.6; *Benef.* 2.23.1; Pliny, *NH* 18.26; *TLL* 3, 1468–9.

bellum multo ante denuntio This must be a non-technical use of *denuntio*, although of course *bellum denuntiare* very often has the technical sense of 'to declare war'. Cf. *Div.* 1.97 *quibus portentis magna populo Romano bella perniciosaeque seditiones denuntiabantur*; for the combination *ante denuntio* cf. *Verr. I* 36 *moneo, praedico, ante denuntio*.

de qua vereri An unusual instance of this phrase: elsewhere *vereri de aliquo* means 'to fear for' (*Rab. Post.* 10; *Att.* 10.4.6; Virg. *Aen.* 9.207). But it is clear that 'to fear concerning Carthage', coming from Cato, can only mean 'to fear what Carthage may do'; no ambiguity is possible.

exscissam *exscissam* from *exscindere*, or *excisam* from *excidere*? The spellings in L (*excisam*) and in B (*excissam*) may perhaps imply the former; but MS evidence is virtually negligible in this sort of case, particularly since Cicero probably wrote *excissam* for the participle of *excidere* (cf. Quint. *Inst.* 1.7.20; Leumann, *Laut- u. Formenlehre* 181). In tenses where MSS can be trusted to distinguish (i.e. those from the present stem), *exscindere* seems to be much commoner than *excidere* in contexts of destroying cities etc. (cf. *De rep.* 6.11 *Numantiam exscindes, Off.* 1.76, *Mil.* 90, Virg. *Aen.* 12.643, etc.), though the use of the latter verb in such contexts is proved by its occurrence in *Res Gestae Div. Aug.* 1.14. In the tenses of the perfect stem and the past participle, it is hardly possible to decide which verb is intended in any particular case: rhythmical considerations may sometimes help, as in *Sest.* 95 where the clausula favours *excīdit*. Some have tried to replace forms of *exscindere* in every instance (cf. G. Lahmeyer, *Philol.* 38 (1879) 150–9; Neue–Wagener III, 568; Lambinus and other edd. on *Sest.*

35 and 95; I. Müller, *Bursian* 14 (1878) 227); but it does not seem that this procedure can be certainly justified. Cf. *TLL* 5, 2, 1240, 23ff.

19 avi reliquias 'what your grandfather left behind': cf. *Fam.* 12.4.1 (to Cassius after the Ides of March) *nunc me reliquiae vestrae exercent*; Virg. *Aen.* 1.30 *reliquias Danaum*. War was actually declared on Carthage in 149, the year of Cato's death and the year after the dramatic date of this dialogue: the reference is therefore particularly appropriate here. Plutarch, *Cato* 27 records Cato as having commented favourably on Scipio's conduct of the preliminary stages of the war, and takes his comment as a dying man's prophecy of its successful conclusion. In *De rep.* (*Somn. scip.*) 6.11 Cicero makes the spirit of Africanus prophesy the destruction of Carthage – this also in 149. Cf. also *Off.* 1.116, where this is used as an example of the principle that one should follow one's ancestors, an idea characteristic of the Roman aristocracy.

tertius hic et tricesimus annus est The chronology here is confused, unless *tertius* is corrupt: for discussion, see Appendix 3.

paeniteret 'would he have been dissatisfied?': on this meaning of *paenitet*, the earlier and original one, see E. Fraenkel, *Horace* (Oxford 1957) 5–6n., and cf. below, §84.

nec enim excursione *excursio* is well documented as a military term ('excursion' or 'sortie': *TLL* 5, 2, 1294, 51ff.), though *TLL* records the present passage (ibid. 39–40) as an instance of the simple sense of 'running'. *saltus* does not seem to have a precise technical meaning of this sort, though as an exercise in preparation for battle it is mentioned by Veg. 1.9 *ad saltum etiam ... exercendus est miles*. *saltus* meaning 'jumping' occurs only here in Cicero.

consilio ratione sententia Cf. on §17 above.

summum consilium ... senatum The etymology of the word 'senate' is referred to again below in §56, *senatores id est senes*, and previously by Cicero (also with a reference to the Spartan Gerousia) in *De rep.* 2.50: *ex quo nostri idem illud secuti* [sc. the Spartan institution], *quos senes ille* [sc. Lycurgus] *appellavit, nominaverunt senatum, ut etiam Romulum patribus lectis fecisse diximus*; also *Div.* 1.95; Ov. *Fasti* 5.57 and Bömer ad loc.; Dion. Hal. *Ant. Rom.* 2.12.3 Mommsen, *Staatsrecht* III³, 835; P.–W. Suppl. 6, 660 (O'Brien Moore); W. Porzig, *Gymn.* 63 (1956) 318ff., thinks *senatus* is a calque of *gerousia*. Both the Spartan and the Roman councils are also referred to by Plutarch, *An seni* 789e, διὸ τὴν μὲν ἐν Λακεδαίμονι παραζευχθεῖσαν ἀριστοκρατίαν τοῖς βασιλεῦσιν ὁ Πύθιος πρεσβυγενέας, ὁ δὲ Λυκοῦργος ἄντικρυς γέροντας ὠνόμασεν· ἡ δὲ Ῥωμαίων σύγκλητος ἄχρι νῦν γερουσία καλεῖται. Many other Greek (Doric) states had γερουσίαι as well as Sparta, and other Italian (not only Latin) towns had 'senates'.

20 amplissimum The most honourable, but not the most powerful: the ephors had for a long time held more practical power than the γέροντες.

ut sunt sic etiam nominantur Cf. Plutarch, quoted above, ἄντικρυς γέροντας; Xen. *Cyr.* 1.13 (on the Persian age-groups) τοὺς γεραιτέρους ὄντας τε καὶ καλουμένους.

maximas res publicas Cf. *Inv.* 1.1 *nam cum et nostrae rei publicae detrimenta considero et maximarum civitatum veteres animo calamitates colligo*; this seems more to be a conventional general statement than to refer to any concrete instances; the Naevius quotation which follows seems intended to illustrate it, but there is no indication in the text of which state it refers to (a glossator in A says Troy, but presumably this is merely a guess).

labefactatas ... sustentatas In both these verbs Cicero prefers the more substantial-sounding frequentative form of the past participle to the simple *labefactus* and *sustentus*. According to *TLL* 7, 2, 764ff. (which however discounts MS variants) Cicero has *labefactatus* eight times, *labefactus* twice. *sustentus* apparently does not occur in Cicero at all, and is rare elsewhere; *sustentatus* is treated as a past participle of *sustinere* in the sense of 'maintain', 'preserve'; cf. *Mur.* 3 *sustinenda ... sustentata*.

a senibus It is doubtless a commonplace that old men are better as leaders than young men, though again the choice of examples is left to the imagination of the reader. Plutarch, *An seni* 788e, gives the example of Timotheus at Athens (not as clear an example of the principle as Plutarch seems to think; opinions concerning him vary considerably). For the general idea, cf. Thrasym. Περὶ πολιτείας fr. 1 D.–K. τῶν πρεσβυτέρων ὀρθῶς τὴν πόλιν ἐπιτροπευόντων; Plut. *An seni* 789e, quoting Pind. fr. 199 (213) Bgk.–Schr., καὶ μάλιστα σῴζεται πόλις "ἔνθα βουλαὶ μὲν γερόντων, καὶ νέων ἀνδρῶν ἀριστεύοισιν αἰχμαί"; ibid. 790d.

restitutas Historians concerned with Augustus' 'restoration of the Republic' should take note of this passage as an example, not obscured by special circumstances, of the phrase *restituere rem publicam*. (Another is Livy 3.20.1.) Plainly all that is meant here is 'states ... put back on their feet', 'restored to stability'. Cf. F. Millar, *JRS* 63 (1973) 61ff.; *CR* 18 (1968) 265–6; E. A. Judge in *Polis and Imperium, Studies in honour of E. T. Salmon*, ed. J. A. S. Evans (Toronto 1974) 279–311.

cedo qui vestram ... adulescentuli Naev. *praetext.* 7–8 (Ribbeck, *Trag. Frr.* p. 278). These two lines are iambic octonarii, scanned as follows: *Cedo qui | vestram | rem publicam | tantam amisistis tam | cito? – Proveni- ebant orātores | novi, | stulti adulescentuli.* For the context of the lines (much disputed), see below. (Cf. E. H. Warmington, *Remains of Old Latin* (Loeb), II, 110; E. V. Marmorale, *Naevius Poeta*, edn 2 (Florence 1950) 155ff.; 216; W. Sellar, *The Roman Poets of the Republic*, e . 3 (Edinburgh 1889) I, 56; Schanz–Hosius I, 52.)

sic enim percontantur, ut est 'that is the question they ask, as is written in . . .', 'as we read in . . .': for this use of *ut est* cf. §46 below, *sicut in Symposio Xenophontis est, Phil.* 2.65 *ut est apud poetam nescioquem; Div.* 1.88; *Off.* 1.32; 1.64; 1.118; etc.; T. Birt, *Philologus* 83 (1928) 37. The passage has seemed unacceptably loose, but there is nothing wrong with the Latin or with the sense. The absence of a subject of *percontantur* is not surprising; this is an indefinite use of the third person plural in a context where the identity of the speakers does not matter; cf. also the use of the singular in *Tusc.* 1.31 *ut ait in Synephebis* (where later manuscripts unnecessarily insert *Statius* or *ille*). The only MS variation in these words is between *ut est* and *ut*: the parallels cited above (and others) argue for the former, and *ut* alone might give the wrong sense: it is not very sensible to say 'that is what they ask, as in the play of Naevius' unless 'they' are different from the characters in the play who are quoted. Attempts at emendation have not improved the passage greatly. Schiche, Opitz, and others delete *ut est*: *sic enim percontantur in Naevi poetae Ludo* is simple and sensible, but there is no compelling reason for the change. *percontanti* for *percontantur*, plus deletion of punctuation after *Ludo*, is an old conjecture, mentioned by Erasmus and Gruterus and revived (apparently independently) by H. Deiter (*Philologus* 46 (1886–7) 174; supported also by Anz, *Prog.* Quedlinburg 1890, p. 14: this produces a somewhat unwieldy sentence, if read together with the two quotations. Mommsen proposed *percontantibus*, omitting *ut est*. The prize for ingenuity goes to Moore, who on the basis of a somewhat fanciful theory about the content of the Naevius play (for which see *AJP* 23 (1902) 437ff., and his edition) changed *ut est* into *Veientes*.

Naevi poetae Naevius seems, alone of his compatriots, to have been distinguished by the semi-permanent title *poeta*: cf. *dabunt malum Metelli Naevio poetae* (quoted in Ps.-Ascon. on Cic. *Verr. I* 29), *flerent divae Camenae Naevium poetam* (Gellius 1.24.2); Plaut. *Mil.* 211 *poetae barbaro* (cf. Festus p. 36 M.); Varro ap. Gell. 17.21.45; W. Suerbaum, *Unters. zur Selbstdarstellung älterer römischer Dichter*, Spudasmata 19 (Hildesheim 1968) 13; Beare, *Roman Stage* 23ff., on Naevius in general. Usually the point is made that *poeta* is the Greek word, and that Naevius' adoption of it suggested emulation of the Greeks.

Ludo The text is given as in the β group of MSS; α has *posteriore libro* instead of *poetae Ludo* (a fairly clear corruption: *poete – poste – posteriore*; Baehrens' *ludorum posteriore libro* (*N. Jb. Kl. Phil.* 133 (1886) 405) carries little conviction). *Ludus* may be either the Latin *ludus*, or a transcription of the Greek Λυδός (cf. Plaut. *Bacch.* 129, where a pun is made on *ludus* and *Ludus* = *Lydus*), or a corruption of some other name. The first would be an odd name for a play, though perhaps not an impossible one: if this is the true explanation, nothing more is known of the play or its content. Ribbeck emended *Ludo* to *Lupo*: it is fairly clear that there was a play of

Naevius called *Lupus*[1], a *fabula praetexta* concerning Romulus and Remus (if the slender evidence is to be trusted). This has the advantage that it links Cicero's citation with a known play of Naevius, but it suffers from two difficulties: Cicero's quotation has no obvious place in the story of Romulus and Remus; and a Romulus and Remus play is the last thing one would expect after the preceding sentence, *quodsi legere aut audire voletis externa*. The second of these problems may be surmounted by supposing that the quotation is not meant as an example to support the preceding general statement (so Fraenkel, P.–W. Suppl. 6, 627); but if this is so, the logic of the passage becomes very loose indeed. As to the content of the lines, Ribbeck takes it to show that they are from a *fabula praetexta* of some sort, but this is not necessary; it could equally well be argued that *oratores* suggests a Greek background (cf. Ar. *Ach.* 680, ὑπὸ νεανίσκων ἐᾶτε καταγελᾶσθαι ῥητόρων). A minor point in favour of Ribbeck's emendation is that *Naevi poetae Lupo* gives a favoured Ciceronian clausula rhythm, but this does not weigh very much against the difficulties just mentioned. The most likely explanation is that *Ludus* is equivalent to *Lydus*, and refers to a play adapted from a Greek original – possibly the *Lydus* of Antiphanes (Kock II, 70): cf. Fraenkel, cited above; E. Norden, *Sitzungsberichte der Preussischen Akademie* (1924) 229; M. Lenchantin de Gubernatis, *RFIC* 40 (1912) 44ff. This would fit in well with *externa* above; probability is not strained by supposing that Naevius wrote both a *Ludus* and a *Lupus*. Again there is no indication as to the content of the play. (We need not be detained by the idea that *Ludus/Lydus* might mean Etruscan, because of the supposed Lydian origin of that race: this, and much more, is hypothesised by Moore, cited above, p. 145.)

proveniebant 'came forward'; *provenire* is used comparably of actors in Plaut. *Pseud.* 568; but there is probably a derogatory nuance deriving from the common use of *provenire* for a crop or growth (of plants, etc.): cf. Pollio, *hist.* 5 ap. Sen. *Suas.* 6.24 *maxima noxiorum multitudo provenit*; Quint. *Inst.* 12.10.11 *oratorum ingens proventus*; Pliny, *Ep.* 1.13. *provenire* is not a Ciceronian word.

[1] The evidence for the *Lupus* is as follows: (a) a very corrupt citation in Festus p. 334, 9–12 L. (Naevius, *praet.* 5 Klotz): *Redhostire: referre gratiam. Naevius (Navius* cod.: *Novius* L. Müller) *in Lupo. Vel Veiens regem sal⟨u⟩ta[n]t Vibae Albanum ⟨A⟩mulium|comiter (-em* cod.) *senem sapientem contra redhostit (-is* cod.) †*menalus:* for restorations of these lines see Ribbeck, *Trag. Frr.* p. 278; F. Leo, *Geschichte der römischen Literatur* (Berlin 1913) 90–1 n. 1; V. Tandoi in *Gli storiografi latini tramandati in frammenti*, ed. S. Boldrini and others, Studi Urbinati, serie B, no. 1 (1976); (b) a notice in Donatus on Ter. *Ad.* 537, denying the story that a wolf appeared during the performance of Naevius' play on Romulus and Remus, thus originating the proverbial saying *lupus in fabula*: Donatus does not say that the play itself was called *Lupus*, but it might well have been, and the occurrence in the Festus quotation of (apparently) Amulius of Alba makes it likely enough that the play from which it came concerned Romulus and Remus (cf. Livy 1.4ff.).

oratores … adulescentuli Cf. Ar. *Ach.* 680, quoted above, p. 146.

temeritas est … florentis aetatis The rashness of the young is often contrasted with the wisdom of the old, from Homer downwards: cf. Hom. *Il.* 3.108–10 αἰεὶ δ᾽ ὁπλοτέρων ἀνδρῶν φρένες ἠερέθονται · | οἷς δ᾽ ὁ γέρων μετέῃσιν, ἅμα πρόσσω καὶ ὀπίσσω | λεύσσει, ὅπως ὄχ᾽ ἄριστα μετ᾽ ἀμφοτέροισι γένηται; Eur. *Phoen.* 528ff. ὦ τέκνον, οὐχ ἅπαντα τῷ γήρᾳ κακά, | Ἐτεόκλεες, πρόσεστιν, ἀλλ᾽ ἡμπειρία | ἔχει τι λέξαι τῶν νέων σοφώτερον; *Peleus* fr. 619 N.²; Aeschin. *Timarchus* 24 (50) οἱ πρεσβύτεροι τῷ μὲν εὖ φρονεῖν ἀκμάζουσιν, ἡ δὲ τόλμα ἤδη αὐτοὺς ἄρχεται ἐπιλείπειν διὰ τὴν ἐμπειρίαν τῶν πραγμάτων; Pherecr. fr. 146 K.; [Archytas], Περὶ ἀνδρὸς ἀγαθοῦ καὶ εὐδαίμονος ap. Stob. 4.50b.28, D.–K. I, 47B, 9, 7. Other passages contrast the wisdom of the old with the advantages of youth (physical strength, etc.): Eur. *Bellerophon* fr. 291 N.²; *Melanippe* fr. 508 N.² (cf. Hes. fr. 321 M.–W.); Pind. fr. 199 (213) Bgk.–Schr.; Bias, D.–K. I, 65, 10; Arist. *Pol.* 1329a15; Bion ap. Diog. Laert. 4.50, fr. 65 Kindstrand; also Democritus fr. 294 D.–K. Or the wisdom of the old is seen as a compensation for the other disadvantages of old age, as in Cic. *Tusc.* 1.94 *prudentia … quam, ut cetera auferat, adfert certe senectus*; Hom. *Il.* 4.310ff.; Eur. *Phoen.* 528–30; Men. fr. 676 K.; Sall. *Cat.* 6.6.

VII 21 At memoria minuitur The next part of the argument, concerning the decline of memory in old age, is not one of the four main divisions announced in §15 (see ad loc.), but is a subsidiary point arising from the topic of old men in public life. The immediate train of thought seems to be that the decline of memory may detract from the *prudentia* mentioned just before. Cicero may have been thinking of the importance of memory for the orator, though he does not mention it explicitly: oratory is mentioned in a rather different context below (§28). The question of remembering people's names may strike a modern reader as a somewhat trivial point; yet it was a point of honour with Romans, more perhaps than with us, not to appear to forget names (hence the institution of the *nomenclator*: cf. Marquardt, *Privatleben* p. 148). Cicero moves rapidly from the topic of memory to that of intellectual activities in general, where he is, and perhaps felt himself to be, on firmer ground: one presumes that he knew as well as anyone that the decline of memory is not in practice fully within one's control (though he could have had no idea of the physical explanation of this), but his appeal to the continued intellectual powers of lawyers, philosophers and poets is certainly justified. For this complaint against old age in general, cf. *Att.* 12.1.2 γεροντικώτερον *est memoriola vacillare*; Plato, *Phaedr.* 276d; *Lach.* 189c (Stein, *Platons Charakteristik* 71); Xen. *Mem.* 4.8; *Apol.* 6; Arist. *Mem.* 450b6, 453b4; Ar. *Nub.* 129; 854; Sen. *Contr.* 1, praef. 2–5 and 18; Juv. 10.233–6; Maximian 1.123; Lact. *Inst.* 7.12.13; Iambl. *VP* 21.

credo 'no doubt': cf. §47 below.

nisi eam exerceas Cf. §§36 and 38 below; Pliny, *Ep.* 8.14.3 *difficile est tenere quae acceperis nisi exerceas. exerceas* is subjunctive because of the generalised 2nd person singular: cf. on §27.

aut etiam, 'or again', not 'or even'.

Themistocles (For the example introduced asyndetically cf. §22 below, *Sophocles*, also above on §18 *Carthagini*.) This item of information about Themistocles occurs elsewhere only in Val. Max. 8.7 ext. 15, probably based on this passage. Otherwise Themistocles' learning of Persian in a short time (though Thuc. 1.138 says only that he learnt as much Persian as he could) is cited as evidence for his good memory (Val. Max. ibid.; Plut. *Them.* 29; Quint. *Inst.* 11.2.50), and an anecdote repeated by Cicero in *De or.* 2.299, ibid. 2.351, *Fin.* 2.104 and *Acad. pr.* 2.2 relates that he said that he would rather learn the art of forgetting than that of remembering. (For Themistocles as an example elsewhere in Cicero, see A. J. Podlecki, *Life of Themistocles* (Montreal and London 1975) 115–17.) Feats of memory similar to that attributed here to Themistocles are recorded of Cyrus the Elder, who is said to have known all his soldiers by name (Val. Max. 8.7 ext. 16; Quint. *Inst.* ibid.; Pliny, *NH* 7.88; Solinus 1.109), although what is presumably the source of this idea, Xen. *Cyrop.* 5.3.47, says only that he knew the names of all his officers (cf. also Lucian, *Macr.* 14). Cineas, Pyrrhus' ambassador, is supposed to have learnt the names of all the Roman senators and knights in one day (Sen. *Contr.* 1, praef. 9; Pliny and Solinus locc. citt.; cf. Cic. *Tusc.* 1.59), and one L. Scipio to have known the names of all Roman citizens (Pliny and Solinus locc. citt.).

qui Aristides esset The relative clause neatly avoids the ugly and ambiguous double accusative. The predicative accusative is usual with *salutare*, as with *vocare*: most commonly with titles (*regem, imperatorem salutare*, etc.): for use with names, cf. *Att.* 14.12.2 *quem quidem* [sc. *Octavium*] *sui Caesarem salutabant, Philippus non*; Tac. *Ann.* 12.41.15 *obvii inter se Nero Britannicum nomine, ille Domitium salutavere.* (The subjunctive *esset* is due to indirect speech: not 'concessive', as Reid explains.)

Lysimachus was the name both of Aristides' father and of his son: either could be meant. Confusion of generations is doubtless a common manifestation of the failure of memory among the elderly; but this passage implies the existence of a story to the effect that Themistocles did actually call Aristides Lysimachus, though no such thing appears to be recorded elsewhere, and it would be somewhat surprising in any case: Themistocles was not very old when he was ostracised from Athens (*c.* 471: in his middle to late fifties?) and presumably had no opportunity thereafter of greeting Aristides. One may suspect that, if the anecdote is genuine, it had some point not concerned with failure of memory, which is now beyond recall.

eos ... qui sunt 'present citizens'. Cato would no doubt have known a large number of Roman citizens, through his censorial duties and otherwise.

sepulcra legens Presumably in the course of his historical researches: cf. §38 below, *omnia antiquitatis monumenta colligo.*

quod aiunt, ne memoriam perdam *Vulgo putabatur officere memoriae, si quis legeret inscriptiones sepulcrorum* (Erasmus ad loc.). This superstitious belief is apparently not recorded elsewhere in classical antiquity, but it is referred to in the Talmud (Babylonian Talmud, *Horayoth* 13b) where it is said that some believe that reading tombstones is 'bad for memorising study': this may be a remnant of a more widespread ancient superstition. The belief has also been recorded in Germany in modern times: E. Hoffmann-Krayer and H. Bächtold-Stäubli, *Handwörterbuch des deutschen Aberglaubens* III (Berlin 1930–1) col. 1108. Cf. E. Arens, *N. Jahrb. Kl. Alt.* 49 (1922) 457; Otto, *Sprichwörter* 218; L. Friedländer, *Sittengeschichte Roms*, edn 10 (Leipzig 1921) IV, 99. (I see no connection at all with the proverbial phrase *vivorum meminisse*, quoted by Wuilleumier following Madvig on *Fin.* 5.3.)

eis enim ipsis MSS cannot be trusted to distinguish between *his* and *eis*, and the latter seems preferable here: 'it is by reading those very inscriptions that I remind myself of men who are now dead'. For *in memoriam redeo* cf. *Verr. II* 1.120; *Inv.* 1.98; Plaut. *Capt.* 1022; Sen. *Benef.* 5.23.2; etc.

nec vero ... oblitum. Cf. the anonymous work on old age in P. Berol. 13407 fr. G, col. 3, οὐδ' ἄλ[λου πράγματος] οὐδενὸς τῷ[ν ὑπ' αὐ]τοῦ διεσπο[υδασμέ]νων· ἢ δ⟨ε⟩ιξάτ[ω τις] ἡμῖν γέροντ[α ἐπι]λελησμένον ο[... (on this papyrus and its text see Introd. p. 29 n. 73). This is the only substantial similarity between the papyrus and the *Cato*, and is not enough to inform us positively about this Greek discussion of old age. One is tempted to wonder, in view of the parallel with this passage, whether the papyrus continued, e.g., ὅπου τὸν θησαυρὸν ἀπέθηκεν.

22 Quid ... meminerunt? On this form of sentence cf. §50 *quid in levioribus studiis ... quam gaudebat Bello suo Punico Naevius...?*; Val. Max. 6.1.4 *quid P. Maenius quam severum pudicitiae custodem egit?* Whether there should be a question mark or an exclamation mark at the end is disputable, but in my view the interrogative force of *quid* 'what about ...?' extends to the end of the sentence. It seems wrong to punctuate *quid? iurisconsulti ... quid? philosophi senes quam multa meminerunt!* (Simbeck); the meaning is 'What about the amount that old lawyers ... remember?' Cf. H.–Sz. 425; C. W. Nauck, *N. Jb. Kl. Phil.* Suppl. 12 (1846) 558ff.

iurisconsulti Cf. *Leg.* 1.10 for Cicero's view of the law as a suitable occupation for an elder statesman.

studium et industria Valerius Maximus' section 8.7 is entitled *De studio et industria*, and includes many of Cicero's examples: cf. Introd. pp. 9–10 n. 27.

neque ea solum ... (*ea* refers back to *ingenia*.) Again the active life and the quiet life are contrasted: cf. on §13 above. Plutarch (*An seni* 785a–c) also uses the contrast, with the example of Sophocles as here, but in a slightly different way, arguing that if poets and philosophers do not retire, neither should statesmen.

in claris et honoratis viris For *in* = 'in the case of' cf. §26 *in fidibus*: many examples in Seyffert–Müller on *Lael.* 9. Sophocles, a Greek and a poet, does not count as *clarus et honoratus*: the latter adjective in particular conveys the idea of *honores* in the semi-technical sense of Roman magistracies.

Sophocles On Sophocles' activity in old age in general, cf. Val. Max. 8.7 ext. 12 (who does not mention the courtroom anecdote). His age at his death (in 406 B.C.) is generally given as ninety; Lucian, *Macr.* 24 says 95, Val. Max. *prope centesimum annum*; cf. Schmid–Stählin I, 2, p. 321 and literature there cited; F. Jacoby, *Apollodors Chronik* 253.

a filiis in iudicium vocatus est This notorious anecdote is found in a number of places, none in their present form earlier than this passage, though Anon. *Vit. Soph.* quotes from Satyrus (3rd cent. B.C.): Anon. *Vit. Soph.* 13; Plut. *An seni* 785a; Lucian, *Macr.* 24; Apul. *Apol.* 37; Athen. 12.510b; Jerome, *Ep.* 52.3.6 (clearly copying Cicero). The common form of the anecdote is as given here; Cicero and Plutarch (with the correction παίδων for πολλῶν codd.) talk of 'sons' in the plural, without naming them, while the other versions name Iophon specifically; Plutarch specifies that Sophocles read the famous chorus Εὐίππου ξένε, while the other versions, including Cicero's, say 'read the *Oedipus Coloneus*' or some such phrase, implying (less than plausibly, one may think) that he gave a preview of the whole play in court. The version in the *Vita*, however, has some peculiar features. At the beginning it appears to refer to a real lawsuit (ἡ πρὸς τὸν υἱὸν Ἰοφῶντα γενομένη αὐτῷ δίκη ποτέ): then, having explained that Sophocles had more affection for his grandson Sophocles the younger (son of Iophon's half-brother Ariston) than for Iophon, the *Vita* continues as follows: καί ποτε ἐν δράματι εἰσήγαγε τὸν Ἰοφῶντα αὐτῷ φθονοῦντα καὶ πρὸς τοὺς φράτορας ἐγκαλοῦντα τῷ πατρὶ ὡς ὑπὸ γήρως παραφρονοῦντι· οἱ δὲ τῷ Ἰοφῶντι ἐπετίμησαν. Σάτυρος δέ φησιν αὐτὸν εἰπεῖν, "εἰ μέν εἰμι Σοφοκλῆς, οὐ παραφρονῶ, εἰ δὲ παραφρονῶ, οὐκ εἰμὶ Σοφοκλῆς", καὶ τότε τὸν Οἰδίποδα παραναγνῶναι. The obvious meaning of this is that the courtroom scene took place in a play, and as the text stands, one written by Sophocles himself: that is highly implausible, and attempts have been made to supply the name of a comic playwright in the text (see literature cited by O. Hense, *Studien zu Sophocles* (Leipzig 1880)

289ff.). It appears to me that, if it is true that the scene occurred in a comedy, then we need look no further for the origin of the anecdote: the inclusion in a comedy of such a scene need have no more warrant in historical fact than a vague rumour that Iophon had some cause of discontent against his father, and the rest of the details could without difficulty have been invented by a comic playwright. (Note that Satyrus in his life of Euripides treats the plot of Ar. *Thesm.* as fact, fr. 39 col. x, cf. *Vit. Eur.* 6: K. J. Dover, *Proceedings of the Classical Association* 82 (1985) 21.) If this is not so, (1) the part of the *Vita* which refers to a play must be thoroughly garbled, and there is in that case little reason to trust it for other details like the reference to the *phratores* (which has loomed large in attempts to make historical sense of the story); (2) the whole story bristles with implausibilities anyway. There was indeed, it appears, a recognised action in Athenian law called δίκη παρανοίας (Xen. *Mem.* 1.2.49; Arist. *Ath. pol.* 56.6; Isaeus 6.9; A. R. W. Harrison, *The Law of Athens* (Oxford 1968) 1, 80–1 and 151; W. Lacey, *The Family in Classical Greece* (London 1968) 116ff.), in which the head of a family could be accused of mismanaging his affairs owing to senility or insanity; this, however, had nothing to do with the *phratores*, coming rather within the province of the archons. It may not be possible to rule out some quarrel between Iophon and his father on the ground either that more or less friendly collaboration seems implied in Ar. *Ran.* 73, or that Phrynichus fr. 31 K. implies that the end of Sophocles' life was unmarred by anything unpleasant (such as a family quarrel might have been); yet one presumes that sons called their fathers into court less often in real life than in comic imagination, even in Athens; and it seems hardly fruitful to speculate on the plausibility or otherwise of Sophocles' alleged manner of defence. Anecdotal material of this sort is in general a highly uncertain basis for historical reconstruction. Cf. further M. Lefkowitz, *Lives of the Greek Poets* (London 1981) 55 and 84–5; T. B. L. Webster, *Introduction to Sophocles* (Oxford 1936) 14–15; Hense, op. cit.; P. Mazon, *REA* 47 (1945) 82ff.

nostro more ... bonis interdici solet (For *solet* with impersonal passive infin. cf. *De or.* 2.208 *invideri solet*.) Roman law had a procedure of *interdictio bonorum* which was applied in cases where the head of a family was negligent in administering his family property: Paul. *Sent.* 3.4a.7 quotes the formula pronounced by the praetor, *Quando tibi tua bona paterna avitaque nequitia tua disperdis liberosque tuos ad egestatem perducis, ob eam rem tibi ea re commercioque interdico.* This procedure did not involve an action in law, and was thus different from the Greek procedure alleged to have been invoked against Sophocles. A similar procedure was involved in providing for management of the affairs of an insane person (*cura furiosi*: cf. F. Schulz, *Classical Roman Law* (Oxford 1951) 197; A. Watson, *Roman Private Law* 41). However, the *actio dementiae* referred to by the declaimers (S. F. Bonner,

Roman Declamation 93ff.) has no reference to actual Roman practice, as far as can be seen, being a mere imitation of the Greek action for παράνοια.

quam in manibus habebat et proxime scripserat Implausible though the anecdote may be, it did not cause Cicero to write nonsense: those who think this sentence is self-contradictory forget that a play is still 'in preparation' (*in manibus*) until it has been performed. For *in manibus* in this sense cf. §38 below; *Acad.* 1.2; *Tusc.* 5.18. Nor does it mean that Sophocles just happened to be holding the manuscript (Mazon).

quaesisseque For addition of enclitics to short final vowels see on §16 above.

23 num Homerum Hesiodum Simonidem Stesichorum There is naturally as little evidence about Homer's activity in old age as about other aspects of his life; portraits usually depict him as fairly old, and [Longinus] (9.11–15) mentions and approves a view that he wrote the *Odyssey* in old age. However, it is probably the venerable associations of his name and antiquity that chiefly led to his inclusion in this list (note *OLD* s.v. *senex* 1c for the word itself used in such circumstances). Much the same may be true of the mention of Hesiod; cf. Virg. *Ecl.* 6.70 *Ascraeo ... seni*, Marc. Arg. *Anth. Pal.* 9.161 ὦ γέρον Ἡσίοδε; the proverbial phrase Ἡσιόδειον γῆρας does not reflect any knowledge about Hesiod's age, but refers to a story about his having been exhumed and reburied, and was thence applied to those in the last stages of old age: Arist. fr. 565 Rose and material cited by Rose ad loc.; M. Lefkowitz, *Lives of the Greek Poets* 3. For Simonides there is much firmer evidence: he describes himself as eighty years old in fr. 147 (203) Bergk (III p. 496) ap. Plut. *An seni* 785a – an epigram celebrating a poetic victory; the *Suda* and the *Marmor Parium* give his age at death as 89, while Lucian, *Macr.* 26 makes him live to be over 90; cf. also Val. Max. 8.7 ext. 13. See Lefkowitz pp. 54ff. Stesichorus is said by Lucian ibid. to have died at the age of 85.

These four poets seem also to be mentioned together (though the text is lacunose) in *De rep.* 2.18–20 (reconstructed by Mommsen, *RhM* 15 (1860) 167, partly on the basis of the parallel with this passage). This whole list of *exempla senectutis* (minus Diogenes the Stoic) is reproduced by Jerome, *Ep.* 52.3.5.

quos ante dixi In §13 above.

Isocratem Gorgian Housman, *Papers* II, 817ff, demonstrated that the Augustan poets (whose usage can, naturally, be checked by metre) form the accusative of Greek third-declension names in -*es* with the Latin ending -*em*, while they preserve the Greek accusative endings -*an* and -*en* for first-declension names. In the case of the former, it is most unlikely that Cicero's practice was any different, since a form like *Isocraten* is neither Latin nor Greek. It seems safe, therefore, to write -*em* in such cases irrespective of the MSS. On the other hand, the question is not so clear with regard to first-declension names, since Cicero may have followed (at least in part) the earlier practice (abundantly exemplified in Roman tragedy and comedy) of assimilating them to the Latin first declension. Here the MSS read *Gorgian* but *Pythagoram*: cf. §41 *Archytam*, and *Pythagoram* again in §78: the MSS of Cicero only once give Pythagoras an -*n*, in *Tusc.* 4.44; see also §54 below on *Laertam*; Neue–Wagener I³, 58–60 record many other Ciceronian occurrences of -*am*. Naturally the evidence of MSS is hardly to be trusted on this sort of point, but there is no other way of telling what Cicero's practice was, and in this passage and others I simply reproduce the MS readings for names in -*as*. (Cf. also M. Winterbottom, *BICS* Suppl. 25 (1970) 48ff.)

philosophorum principes Referring to priority in date or to eminence? For the latter, cf. §§77–8 and note (there *summi philosophi* = Pythagoras, Socrates and Plato). Pythagoras, Democritus and Plato are mentioned together in *Fin.* 5.50; 5.87; *Tusc.* 4.44; Val. Max. 8.7 ext. 2–4. Pythagoras' age at death is given as 80 or 90 by Diog. Laert. 7.44; that of Democritus as 104 by Lucian, *Macr.* 18, as 109 by Hipparchus ap. Diog. Laert. 9.43, and as 90 by Diod. 14.11.5; cf. also Cens. *Nat.* 15.3. For Plato see §13 above.

num Xenocratem For Xenocrates to have a *num* to himself seems to over-emphasise his importance, and he would pair well with Plato; hence Seyffert (*Zeitschr. f.d. Gymnasialwesen* 15 (1861) 67) and others may be right to delete *num* here. On the other hand, there is no reason why Cicero should have listed all these names in pairs (indeed, to have done so might be thought monotonous); and the eminence of Plato might account for his isolation, the isolation of Xenocrates being merely a consequence of this. In view of the equal arguments on both sides I have left the text as it is in the MSS.

Xenocratem Xenocrates lived to be 84 according to Lucian, *Macr.* 20; 82 according to Diog. Laert. 4.14, and 81 according to Cens. *Nat.* 15.2.

Zenonem Lucian, *Macr.* 19, says that Zeno lived to be 98, Diog. Laert. 7.28 gives his age as 72: the discrepancy may possibly be due to confusion of homonymous philosophers.

Cleanthem Lucian, *Macr.* 19, Val. Max. 8.7 ext. 11 and Cens. *Nat.* 15.3 agree on a figure of 99 for Cleanthes' age; Diog. Laert. 7.176 records one of 80. Cf. *Ind. Stoic. Herc.* col. 28, 9–29, 1.

Diogenem Stoicum Diogenes of Babylon was one of the three philosophers who came as ambassadors to Rome in 155 B.C. (cf. *De or.* 2.155–60; *Acad. pr.* 2.137; *Tusc.* 4.5; *De rep.* 3.9; *Att.* 12.23.2); cf. Introd. p. 20; Cato's attitude to Diogenes can hardly be said to be misrepresented in this passage, as it is not specified here what it was. It is implied that Diogenes had died before the dramatic date of the dialogue (150): cf. J.

Glucker, *Antiochus and the Late Academy*, Hypomnemata 56 (Göttingen 1978) 19 n. 18. Lucian, *Macr.* 20 gives Diogenes' age at death as 88.

omnibus his *his* has relatively good support from the MSS; its independent omission in PM and in λ is no problem, as it could easily have occurred by haplography after *omnibus*, and independent insertion in V, H and B would be more difficult to explain. Baiter–Halm read *his*, but comment: 'his om. P, in quo videtur iis, quod haud scio an praeferendum sit, post us intercidisse.' *iis* is read also in older editions (Victorius, Graevius) and in some late MSS cited by Otto. For the sense there is nothing to choose between *his* and *iis/eis*, but it is desirable that one or other should be read.

agitatio Cf. *De or.* 3.88; Val. Max. 8.7 ext. 3 (on Plato) *ne extrema quidem eius hora agitatione studii vacua fuit*; *TLL* 1, 1329.

24 divina studia Cf. *De rep.* 6.19; *TLL* (5, 1, 1623) gives no other parallel for this phrase before Tertullian.

possum nominare 'I could name', cf. §55 below; K.–S. 1, 171 for the indicative in such contexts.

ex agro Sabino The prepositional phrase is used virtually as an adjective qualifying *rusticos Romanos*; cf. §7; K.–S. 1, 215.

percipiendis Harvesting (§70 below; *ND* 2.156; etc.).

condendis Storing (*TLL* 4, 148). The theme of agriculture as an occupation for old men is developed at length in §§51ff. below.

in aliis *id est in iis quae sciunt ad se pertinere* (Lambinus ad loc.), making a proleptic contrast with *eis . . . quae sciunt nihil omnino ad se pertinere*. The sense is that most farming operations bring some sort of profit within the year, so it is not surprising that old men still carry them out with enthusiasm, since nobody is so old that he does not think he will live another year. If *his* (QE and Manutius) were read, it would refer directly to the activities just mentioned, sowing, harvesting and storing; but *aliis* makes a better contrast with the second half of the sentence. There seems to be no advantage in *illis*, proposed by A. Weidner, Progr. Dortmund 1885 (cf. P. Schwenke, *Bursian* 47 (1887) 291ff.), and printed by Wuilleumier without explanation and without noting any variant.

nemo est enim This seems to be the more normal order (W. S. Watt, 'Enim Tullianum', *CQ* 30 (1980) 120), but cf. §28 *quid enim est*. For the sense cf. Sen. *Ep.* 12.6 *nemo tam senex est ut improbe unum diem speret*; Seneca may be influenced by Cicero, cf. Introd. p. 27 n. 67.

serit . . . prosient Caec. Stat. *com.* 210 Ribbeck (*Com. Frr.* p. 70); also quoted in *Tusc.* 1.31 (in an argument about the immortality of the soul; cf. note on §82 below). The MSS favour *saeclo* in the *Tusc.* passage, *saeculo* here: on purely linguistic grounds the former seems more likely, being the earlier form; on the other hand *saeculo* makes the scansion marginally easier (see below: *saeculum* apparently also occurs in a cretic *canticum* in

Plaut. *Trin.* 283). *prosient* (which occurs only in P² among the MSS) is more likely for Caecilius than *prosint*. Much effort has been expended on attempts to scan this quotation, including further changes to the text (which should have been discouraged by the double attestation). The rhythm seems to be cretic: *árbŏrēs| qu(ae) áltĕrī*, possibly *saécŭlō*, probably *prŏsĭent*. *saeclo* could be admitted without disturbing this scansion too much, on the parallel of two Plautine lines (*Most.* 108 and *Truc.* 589) in which a cretic is apparently replaced by a spondee (see the metrical appendix to Lindsay's Oxford text). This only leaves *serit*, which could be a resolved long syllable, or (as G. Hermann scanned it, cf. Ribbeck's note; Anz, Progr. Quedlinburg 1890, p. 5) the last word of the previous line with *brevis in longo, sērīt||*. Clearly enough, there is no way of telling from Cicero's text whether the quotation is a complete single line, or if not, where any line-division comes; in any case, line-divisions in *cantica* can only be established (if at all) by reference to a regular pattern, which a fragment as short as this cannot provide. Any further attempt to determine the metrical scheme is therefore mere guesswork. (Ribbeck, assuming that the quotation was a single complete line, scanned it as a bacchiac tetrameter, but this involved an impossible lengthening *sĕrīt*; L. Havet, *CRAI* 44 (1900) 148, retained this scansion by changing to *sēret* with original long *e* in the last syllable, but the double corruption in the MSS would be hard to explain. The same objection holds good for Kühner's scansion as an iambic senarius, changing the order of the words to *saeclo prosint alteri* (note on the *Tusc.* passage), and for that of Anz (*saeclo alteri quae prosient*). Hermann's scansion seems the most natural and least implausible.)

The idea of planting trees for posterity is commonplace in ancient literature: Virg. *Ecl.* 9.50 *carpent tua poma nepotes*; *Georg.* 2.58; 2.294; Hor. *Od.* 2.14.22 with Nisbet–Hubbard ad loc.; Philodemus, *De morte* 4.38.34ff. (Gigante, *Ricerche filodemee* 182 and 220: Philodemus says that old men are foolish to plant trees from which they will not benefit); Sen. *Ep.* 86 *hoc nobis senibus discere necessarium est, quorum nemo non olivetum alteri ponit*; Hesiod, *Theog.* 599; Leutsch–Schneidewin, *Paroem.* 1, 205; and the reversal of the theme in Hor. *Od.* 2.13.3 *in nepotum perniciem* (see Nisbet–Hubbard ad loc.). The idea also occurs a number of times in Jewish and Arabic literature: *Midrash Rabbah* on Leviticus 25.5 (an anecdote in which the Emperor Hadrian is surprised at a centenarian planting trees); *Midrash Tanchuma*, *Kedoshim* 8; Babylonian Talmud, *Taanith* 23a; H. Jacobson, *Mnem.* 4.30 (1977) 291; Arabic parallels quoted in Stith Thompson, *Motif-index of Folk-literature* (Copenhagen 1955) J 701.1. Cf. also the 'New England story' in O. W. Holmes, *Autocrat of the Breakfast-Table* ch. 7 (discussing this passage in the context of a highly whimsical account of the whole of the *Cato*).

Statius noster Caecilius Statius was a near-contemporary of Ennius, and would have been known to Cato (cf. Suet. *De poetis* 25 Rostagni; Schanz–Hosius I, 102; P.–W. 3, 1189ff.) He is quoted again in §§25 and 36. Cato's *noster* here probably does not imply any such personal connection as in the case of Ennius (§10 above), but simply recognises Caecilius as a Roman poet.

Synephebis The *Synephebi* was adapted from a play of the same title by Menander: see *Fin.* 1.4; Ribbeck, *Com. Frr.* p. 69. The play is quoted by Cicero also in *ND* 1.13, in addition to the *Tusc.* passage quoted above.

25 nec vero ... prodere The most plausible view of this passage is that *agricola* is a character in the Caecilius play just mentioned, that someone in the play asks him for whose benefit he is sowing, and that his reply is paraphrased in the following words, *dis immortalibus ... prodere*. It is not however possible to reconstruct the exact words of Caecilius from this paraphrase with any certainty, still less to emend the text so as to produce verses (as was attempted by H. Anz, Progr. Quedlinburg 1890, p. 5, who tried to rewrite the passage in senarii, and by L. Havet, *CRAI* 44 (1900) 148 and *Ann. École Pratique des Hautes Études* (1901) 5ff., who attempted to turn it into a continuation of the cretic *canticum* from which he supposed the line *serit arbores ...* to come). The vocabulary and construction of the sentence is thoroughly Ciceronian, and Nonius p. 363 M. quotes the passage as from Cicero, not Caecilius (contrast p. 247 M. where the Caecilius quotation is correctly attributed); it should not be necessary to add that the double-cretic clausula also is Ciceronian, and adds nothing to the likelihood of the passage having originally been in verse. It would be quite possible to maintain that the passage had nothing to do with Caecilius, being merely a general statement about the sort of thing a farmer might say, although this would detach it from the surrounding context in a rather unsatisfactory way.

VIII alteri saeculo This clearly refers back to the quotation, and it seems justified therefore to enclose it in inverted commas.

idem I.e. Caecilius again (subject of an implied verb of saying).

edepol Senectus Caec. Stat. *com.* 173ff. (Ribbeck, *Com. Frr.* p. 65); Nonius p. 247 M. quotes the first two lines and ascribes them to the *Plocium* of Caecilius (without mention of Cicero). The *Plocium* was translated from Menander (cf. Gomme–Sandbach 704ff.).

quod diu vivendo multa quae non vult videt This recalls Solon's speech to Croesus in Hdt. 1.32.1: ἐν γὰρ τῷ μακρῷ χρόνῳ πολλὰ μὲν ἐστὶ ἰδεῖν τὰ μή τις ἐθέλει. The idea in general is commonplace: Eur. *Oenomaus* fr. 575 N.² μακρὸς γὰρ αἰὼν μυρίους τίκτει πόνους (another similar line is attributed to Euripides in Stob. 4.50b.35); Men. fr. 555 K., ὀχληρὸς ὁ χρόνος ὁ πολύς; Publil. *sent.* 212, *heu quam multa paenitenda incurrunt vivendo* *diu*; Plaut. *Men.* 759–60 (of old age) *nam res plurimas pessimas, cum advenit, adfert*; Favorinus, Περὶ γήρως fr. 9 Barigazzi πολύς τοι μόχθος ἐν μακρῷ χρόνῳ; Hor. *AP* 169; Xen. *Apol.* 8; Antiphanes frr. 240b and 255 K.; Bion fr. 62 K.; [Plato], *Axiochus* 367b; Soph. fr. 863 N.².

tum equidem ... alteri Caec. *com.* 28–9. (Ribbeck. *Com. Frr.* p. 40): again preserved in Nonius (p. 1 M.) and attributed there to a play called *Ephesio*: this was possibly adapted from Menander's *Ephesius*, hence some have emended Nonius' *Ephesione* to *Ephesio* (abl.).

senecta This archaic and poetic alternative to *senectus* appears originally to have been an adjective agreeing with an implied *aetas* (J. N. Adams, *CQ* 22 (1972) 352 n. 4): it is found, apart from this passage, in Plaut. *Mil.* 623, *Most.* 217, Ter. *Ad.* 954, Nep. fr. 2 Winstedt (epist. Corneliae), Varro, *LL* 5.5 (all in the phrase *in senecta*, as here); Lucil. 743 M.; Varro ap. Serv. *Aen.* 5.295 (listing the five ages *infantia pueritia adulescentia iuventa senecta*); then in the Augustan poets, Livy, Seneca's tragedies, Pliny the Elder and Tacitus.

deputo 'consider': *deputare* with double accusative in this sense occurs in comedy, then in later prose: cf. Plaut. *Trin.* 748; *Amph.* 158; Ter. *Heaut.* 135; *TLL* 5, 1, 621.

sentire ... alteri *ea aetate* qualifies *sentire*, and there is a slight break after it; the meaning is 'to feel at that age that one is oneself annoying to others', not 'to feel that it is at that age that one is annoying to others' (which would be the effect of having *ea aetate* first in its clause): cf. Nauck, *N. Jahrb. Kl. Phil.* Suppl. 12 (1846) 558.

eumpse (Archaic accusative of *ipse*.) This is Fleckeisen's correction, clearly right, for *eum se* of the major manuscripts (*eum ipsum* Nonius): *N. Jahrb. Kl. Phil.* 91 (1865) 566; cf. Bergk, ibid. 101 (1870) 833; Housman, *Papers* II, 873.

odiosum alteri Cf. Ter. *Hec.* 619, *odiosa haec est aetas adulescentulis*.

26 potius quam odiosum This appears to have a dactylic rhythm, but it seems possible that *quam* could have been left unelided, thus giving one of Cicero's favourite clausulae, -ūs quăm ŏdĭōsŭm. The poets sometimes give final -*m* consonantal force, up to the Augustan period: Enn. fr. 336 V., *milia militum octo*, etc.; Lucr. 2.681; 3.394; 3.1082; 3.1095; 6.276; Gallus fr. (see *JRS* 69 (1979) 125ff.) *tum erunt;* Hor. *Sat.* 2.2.28 (the only instance in Horace); cf. F. Leo, *Plaut. Forsch.* edn 2 (Berlin 1912) 331. Wolff, *N. Jahrb. Kl. Phil.* Suppl. 26 (1901) p. 655, objects to this method of improving clausulae, quoting *Tusc.* 1.93 *mori miserum esse* as the only instance in Cicero where it might work; but the present passage is surely another, and instances occur occasionally in other writers.

ut enim adulescentibus ... delectantur The mutual friendship of young and old men is also commended in *Lael.* 101; cf. also §29 below, and

COMMENTARY: VIII 26

§10 above on Cato and Fabius Maximus; Plut. *An seni* 791a and 795c–d. Nepos, *Atticus* 16, says that one of the ingredients of Atticus' *humanitas* was his ability to form friendships equally well with his seniors, juniors and contemporaries. Cf. K. Büchner, *Gymn.* 62 (1955) 299ff. (repr. in Büchner, *Cicerobild* 417ff.)

leviorque ... diliguntur Cf. Callim. fr. 41, 1–2 Pfeiffer, γηράσκει δ' ὁ γέρων κεῖνος ἐλαφρότερον | τὸν κοῦροι φιλέουσι (= Stob. 4.50a.11; Lucian, *Erotes* 48; cf. also §63 below); Xen. *Mem.* 2.1.33 (Choice of Hercules) καὶ οἱ μὲν νέοι τοῖς τῶν πρεσβυτέρων ἐπαίνοις χαίρουσιν, οἱ δὲ γεραίτεροι ταῖς τῶν νέων τιμαῖς ἀγάλλονται ...

sic adulescentes ... gaudent Cf. *Off.* 1.122 *est igitur adulescentis maiores natu vereri, eque eis deligere optimos et praestantissimos, quorum consilio atque auctoritate nitatur; ineuntis enim aetatis inscitia senum constituenda et regenda prudentia est.*

Sed videtis Resuming the main argument: old men can remain active.

ut ... sit *videre* and other verbs of perceiving often take *ut* with either the subjunctive (more common in prose) or the indicative; this is equivalent to an ordinary indirect statement, and it is certainly not the case that *ut* is equivalent to *quomodo*, as often explained. 'See how they run' is not equivalent to 'See in what way they run.' The construction may originally have been an indirect exclamation; cf. H.–Sz. 537–8.

semper agens aliquid et moliens As we say 'always doing something'. The present participle is used as a predicate after *esse* quite often in comedy, but occasionally in prose, especially when co-ordinated with an adjective: cf. *Sest.* 128 *florens fuit*; *Phil.* 14.23; Caes. *BG* 3.19.6; H.–Sz. 388. For the phrase *agere et moliri* cf. *Off.* 3.102 *semper agere aliquid et moliri volunt*; *ND* 1.2; *Mur.* 82. The desirability of remaining active all the time was pointed out by the historical Cato (fr. 141 Peter), *qui tantisper nulli rei sies, dum nihil agas.*

quale cuiusque studium Cf. Ov. *Tristia* 4.8; Lact. *Inst.* 7.12.12.

quid qui ... senex didici? The influence of *quid* extends as far as *didici*: 'What about those who even learn something new, as in the case of Solon ... and as I have done, studying Greek literature in my old age?' There was a strong tradition of disapproval of opsimathy: see Theophr. *Characters*; Cic. *Fam.* 9.20.2 ὀψιμαθεῖς *homines scis quam insolentes sint*; Hor. *Sat.* 1.10.21 *o seri studiorum*; Ar. *Clouds* 129; etc. However, moralists and others were quick to point out that some things can be learnt at any age. In addition to the famous line of Solon referred to here by Cicero, and the musical activities of Socrates, cf. Aesch. fr. 396 N.² καλὸν δὲ καὶ γέροντα μανθάνειν σοφά; [Varro], *Sent.* 158 *nemini quia senex addiscit verecundia est incutienda*; Sen. *Ep.* 76.1–2. Cicero himself in *ND* 1.6 rebuts the idea that he had come late to philosophy.

Solonem versibus gloriantem γηράσκω δ' αἰεὶ πολλὰ διδασκόμενος

158

(fr. 18 Bergk): cf. §50; Plato, *Rep.* 7.536d; *Laches* 188b; 189a; *Erastae* 133c; Plut. *Solon* 31; Val. Max. 8.7 ext. 14 *versibus ... quibus significat se cotidie aliquid addiscentem senescere*; Lucian, *Macr.* 18. Cf. also *Lael.* 104 *quid ego de studiis dicam cognoscendi semper aliquid atque discendi?*; Pliny, *Ep.* 4.23.

addiscentem ... senem fieri The emphatic logically predicative use of the present participle here reflects Solon's Greek: it was not originally a native Latin construction, though Cicero has it a number of times in imitation of Greek style: Laughton, *Participle* 43–4.

et ego Madvig's correction for *ut ego* of the MSS: the first *et* clearly demands a second one. The alternative would be to delete the first *et*, as in some older editions, but that would leave the sentence too disjointed.

litteras Graecas See on §3 above; also §38, and Introd. pp. 19–20. Cicero no doubt exaggerates here; yet *diuturnam sitim* is appropriate for Cato's previous long abstinence from Greek literature. This passage is recalled cynically by Montaigne, *Essais* bk 2, no. 28.

sic This looks forward to *ut*, not to *quasi*; the sentence articulates better that way, and if *sic* and *quasi* had been co-ordinated we should have expected *cuperem* rather than *cupiens* (cf. Lund, *Bidrag* 8n.).

Socratem Cf. Plato, *Euthyd.* 272c ... Κόννῳ τῷ Μητροβίου τῷ κιθαριστῇ, ὃς ἐμὲ διδάσκει ἔτι καὶ νῦν κιθαρίζειν· ὁρῶντες οἱ παῖδες οἱ συμφοιτηταί μου ἐμοῦ τε καταγελῶσι καὶ Κόννον καλοῦσι γεροντοδιδάσκαλον; *Menex.* 235e; *Phaedo* 60e; Philodemus, *De Musica* col. 25, 30ff.; Diog. Laert. 2.32; *Suda* s.v. Σωκράτης; Cic. *Fam.* 9.22.3; Val. Max. 8.7 ext. 8; Sext. Emp. *Adv. math.* 6.13. Varro's Menippean satire called Γεροντοδιδάσκαλος may have had something to do with this, although it is impossible to tell exactly what (cf. P. Lenkeit, diss. Cologne 1966).

in fidibus *fides*, which seems to be an authentic Latin word (related to, though not derived from, the Greek σφίδη: Ernout–Meillet 358), is preferred by Cicero to the Greek borrowings *cithara* and *lyra*, though he does not avoid the latter entirely. For *in* 'in the case of', 'in connection with', see on §22.

vellem equidem etiam illud It is difficult to know whether Cicero in fact believed that Cato would have liked to learn the lyre: Roman convention would have been against it. Perhaps Cicero is not entirely serious.

discebant enim fidibus antiqui As we would say 'they learned the lyre': cf. *docere fidibus* (*Fam.* 9.22.3); *scire fidibus* (Ter. *Eun.* 133). *antiqui* may refer to the Greeks or to the ancient Romans. Some connect this with Cato's statement in the *Origines* concerning the old Roman custom of singing at banquets (fr. 118 Peter, quoted by Cicero in *Tusc.* 1.3; 4.3; *Brut.* 75; cf. Varro, *De vita populi Romani* fr. ap. Non. p. 77 M.; Val. Max. 2.1.9): for a full discussion of this, see A. Momigliano, *JRS* 47 (1957) 104ff., repr. in *Essays in Ancient and Modern Historiography* (Oxford 1977) 231ff. However, the quotations from Cato as we have them do not mention the lyre. Cicero (*Tusc.* 4.3) connects Cato's statement about banquet-songs with Pythagorean music and lyre-playing, and also speaks of the use of the lyre at Roman banquets in *De or.* 3.197 *epularum sollemnium fides ac tibiae* (cf. also *Leg.* 2.38); so he may have known a tradition to that effect, or himself elaborated on Cato's information. In *Tusc.* 1.4, on the other hand, it is of the Greeks that Cicero says *ergo ... musici floruerunt discebantque id omnes*.

27–38 Second complaint: old age lacks physical strength For lack of strength in old age, cf. Hom. *Il.* 4.314; 23.623ff.; *Od.* 11.497; Aesch. *Ag.* 74–5; Soph. *OC* 1236; *Trach.* 1018; Eur. *Andr.* 754; *Heraclid.* 688; Xenophanes fr. 9; Plato, *Rep.* 330e, 366d; *Phaedr.* 267e; *Laws* 9.863d, etc.; Antipho 4.3.2; Pherecr., Kock 1, 248; Plaut. *Men.* 757–8 *vires reliquere*; Lucr. 2.1131; 3.451ff.; Hor. *Sat.* 2.2.85–6; Juv. 10.227; Posidippus, *Anth. Pal.* 9.359; *Epig. Bob.* 25.13–14; Prud. *Symm.* 2.320. The weakness of age is one of the complaints listed by Musonius (cf. above on §15); Juncus p. 1049 W.–H. talks of disease rather than weakness (cf. §35); Plutarch in *An seni* passes over the subject lightly (788c, 789d, 791d; cf. §§17 and 35).

IX 27 Nec nunc quidem *et ... quidem* means 'and indeed' or 'and for that matter'; *nec ... quidem* is the negative equivalent, 'nor indeed'. There has been a great deal of confusion about this phrase, owing no doubt to its similarity with, and constant appearance in MSS instead of, *ne ... quidem*. But the two phrases are quite distinct. *ne ... quidem* would not make good sense here, or at least not as good: 'not even now do I regret not having the strength of a young man' would be more reasonable if a contrast were implied between Cato's activities now and those at an earlier age. Rather than this, the emphasis should be on *vires*, contrasting with the previous discussion of intellectual activity. Other instances of *nec ... quidem* in Cicero are *Fam.* 6.6.2 *nec eis quidem verbis*, 'not indeed in those words'; ibid. 12.1.1 *nec eius quidem rei finem video*, 'nor indeed do I see the end of the matter'; *Att.* 7.5.5 *nec prius quidem*; a particularly clear example showing that *nec ... quidem* is the negative of *et ... quidem* is *Div.* 2.150 *philosophi ... nec ei quidem contemptissimi*. Cf. also *Div.* 1.16; Plaut. *Asin.* 754; Sall. *Jug.* 51.5; Livy 22.60.12; etc. (Other explanations of the phrase *nec ... quidem* have been given, as equivalent to *et ne ... quidem*, or to *et non ... quidem* (i.e. καὶ οὐ ... μέν, looking forward to a following 'but'); but I do not see how either of these might work in the passages quoted.) There are some other passages where *ne ... quidem* is usually read, sometimes with a MS variant *nec*, where it seems that *nec ... quidem* would make equally good or better sense: *Acad. pr.* 2.82; *Div.* 1.16 (*nec* some edd.); *Lael.* 44. If the distinction between the two combinations of particles here outlined holds for Virgil as well as for Cicero, it is difficult not to suppose that *nec ... quidem* should be read in *Georg.* 1.390 and perhaps 1.126 and 3.561. (Cf. Madvig's *De finibus*,

Excursus 3, pp. 809–10; Hand, *Tursellinus* IV, 124ff.; K.–S. II, 45; H.–Sz. 450.)

tauri aut elephanti Cf. Sen. *Ep.* 15.1 *nec vires umquam opimi bovis nec pondus aequabis*; id. *Ep.* 74.15; 124.22; *Benef.* 2.29.1; Philo, *De prov.* 2.14; Galen, *Protrepticus* 21. (On the forms *elephas* and *elephantus*, see *TLL* 5, 2, 354.)

quod est eo decet uti Cf. §33 and note; the idea is authentically Catonian, cf. *orat.* fr. 174 Malcovati (*De sumptu suo*), *si quid est quod utar, utor; si non est, egeo.* Cf. also *Parad.* 6.52 *satis esse putant quod est.*

quidquid agas agere pro viribus 'Whatsoever thy hand findeth to do, do it with thy might' (Ecclesiastes 9.10). The subjunctive *agas* is regular for the generalised second person singular: see Housman, *CQ* 13 (1919) 73ff. = *Papers* III, 987–8 (on this passage, against Reid's change to *agis*); W. Maguinness, *CR* 48 (1934) 212 (comparing *possis* in §72 below); in general, Handford, *Subjunctive* 110. Cf. also §§21 and 47.

vox This word is fairly common in the sense of 'saying' or 'utterance': cf. *Lael.* 87; *Tusc.* 1.111; *Off.* 3.1; etc.

Milonis This anecdote seems to be unknown elsewhere. For Milo as an example of an athlete and a great eater, cf. §33 below and note; *De fato* 30; Arist. *NE* 1106b; fr. 520 Rose; Lucian, *Imag.* 19; *Heracl.* 8; Porph. *Abst.* 1.52; Ov. *Met.* 15.229; Gell. 15.16; *Anth. Pal.* 2.230; P.–W. 15, 2, 1672ff.

athletasque ... videret Contrast Plut. *Gen. Socr.* 593d, ὡς γὰρ ἀθλητὰς καταλύσαντας ἄσκησιν ὑπὸ γήρως οὐ τελέως ἀπολείπει τὸ φιλότιμον καὶ φιλοσώματον, ἀλλὰ ἑτέρους ἀσκοῦντας ὁρῶντες ἥδονται καὶ παρακαλοῦσι.

in curriculo 'on the racecourse' (cf. *TLL* 4, 1506, 10ff.): elsewhere Cicero uses this sense of *curriculum* in metaphorical contexts (*Lael.* 40; *Orat.* 12); cf. [Cic.] *Ad Her.* 4.3.4; Gell. 1.1.2.

nugator A word possibly characteristic of, though certainly not peculiar to, Cato: cf. Gell. 11.8.4, the anecdote concerning Albinus' Greek history (where, however, there is no guarantee that Cato's exact mode of expression is reproduced). For other instances cf. Enn. *scaen.* 423 V.[2], Lucil. ap. Non. p. 35; Plaut. *Capt.* 275; *Trin.* 936; 1138; Cic. *Flacc.* 38; *Att.* 6.1.16; Livy 38.56.6; Pers. 5.127; Gell. 12.2.8; 15.2.2; etc.

ex te I.e. from your moral qualities as opposed to physical ones. Philosophers argued as to whether the body was part of the 'real' person or not: Cicero, in common with most Platonists, inclined to think not (cf. §77 below; *De rep.* 6.26; *Tusc.* 1.52). For a discussion of the history of that doctrine, beginning with the Platonic *Alcibiades I*, see J. Pépin, *REG* 82 (1969) 56–70. The idea here is not explicitly philosophical, though a reader unacquainted with these philosophical views might find it a little strange.

Sextus Aelius S. Aelius Paetus Catus, the jurist: cf. Enn. *Ann.* fr. 331

V. (329 Sk.) *egregie cordatus homo, catus Aelius Sextus* (quoted in *De rep.* 1.30; *De or.* 1.198; *Tusc.* 1.18; Varro, *LL* 7.46); *Brut.* 78; *Fam.* 7.22; *De or.* 1.212; 240; 3.133; P.–W. 1.527; F. Schulz, *History of Roman Legal Science* (Oxford 1946) 35.

Tiberius Coruncanius Also a jurisconsult: cf. on §15.

Publius Crassus P. Licinius Crassus Dives, cos. 205. Cicero refers to his *sapientia* and that of Coruncanius in *De or.* 3.134; cf. §§50 and 61 below; *Brut.* 77; Livy 30.1.4ff.; P.–W. 13, 331ff. It has been thought that he is a bad *exemplum senectutis* because of the anecdote in Plutarch (*Cicero* 25.3), in which M. Crassus says that no member of his family lived to be more than sixty; but it is clear from the context that this was believed neither by Crassus himself nor by anyone else.

usque ad extremum spiritum Cf. the same phrase in §38 below; Sen. *De otio* 4, *usque ad ultimum vitae finem in actu erimus.*

prudentia With particular reference to legal knowledge (*iurisprudentia*): cf. *De or.* 1.256; 3.134; *De rep.* 2.61; *Mur.* 28; etc.

28 orator metuo ne languescat ... oratio This passage, which for some reason has caused much trouble, is best clarified by a translation: 'I fear that an orator may become idle in old age, for his function depends not only on intellect, but also on physical strength and power of lungs. In fact, the resonant quality in the voice actually gains brilliance somehow or other in old age; I myself have not lost it as yet, and you see how old I am. But still, it is a quiet and relaxed style of speech that suits an old man best; and the elegant and gentle speech of an eloquent old man gains itself a hearing on its own account.' *metuo* is not ironical, as some seem to have thought: oratory was strenuous work (cf. *Brutus* 313ff.; C. Knapp, *CR* 14 (1900) 214).

est enim ... virium Cf. Quint. *Inst.* 12.11.2 *neque enim scientia modo constat orator, quae augetur annis, sed voce latere firmitate* (in a similar context, discussing what an orator should do as he gets older).

laterum Cf. §14 *bonis lateribus.*

omnino This both qualifies the previous remark and looks forward to *sed tamen*; it may be translated here 'in fact' or 'indeed'. *omnino* is quite often used in the first of two contrasted statements, like Greek μέν, μὲν οὖν. Cf. below, §45; *Lael.* 69; 98; *Off.* 1.83; etc; Nägelsbach–Müller, *Stilistik*, 778–9. For a somewhat different use cf. §§9 and 76.

canorum illud *Canorus* means 'clear', 'resonant', 'melodious'; the word is of course connected with *canere*, and is used also of musical instruments. Cf. *Brut.* 88 (of Hortensius) *vox suavis et canora*; ibid. 234; 317; *De or.* 3.28 *profluens quiddam habuit Carbo et canorum*; Tac. *Ann.* 4.61.

splendescit Cf. *Brut.* 303 *vox splendida*; ibid. 239, 250. The metaphor is not only acceptable but apt for the 'brightness' of a clear and resonant voice; the objection made by some, that this is incompatible with *languescat* above, is not persuasive, since one may well have a 'bright' and resonant voice without the strength and stamina to make long and heated speeches. (Whether the voice does in fact commonly become 'brighter' in old age is a different question.) (Cf. P. Hennings, *N. Jb. Kl. Phil.* 147 (1893) 781–2; P. O. Barendt, *CR* 13 (1899) 402 and 14 (1900) 356; J. A. Nairn, *CR* 13 (1899) 461; C. Knapp, *Proc. Am. Phil. Assoc.* 29 (1898) v–vii; *CR* 14 (1900) 214; J. F. Paxton, *CR* 14 (1900) 216; A. Kornitzer, *Z. Oest. Gymn.* 48 (1897) 961–4; *Berl. Phil. Woch.* 25 (1905) 510–11; F. G. Moore, *AJP* 23 (1902) 436ff.)

seni This conjecture of Madvig (*Adversaria Critica* (Copenhagen 1873) II, 244), for *senis* of the MSS, seems to me almost certainly right, despite the agreement of the text of Nonius with the MS reading: the corruption is very easy in view of the proximity of the *s* of *sermo. sed tamen est decorus seni | sermo quietus et remissus* is natural and elegant; *sed tamen est decorus | senis sermo quietus et remissus* is unbalanced and unexpected as regards word order (the genitive *senis*, carrying no particular emphasis, should have been after *sermo*); and as regards the meaning, 'A quiet and relaxed style of speaking is suitable for an old man' seems more sensible than 'An old man's quiet and relaxed style of speaking is suitable' (even though *decorus* does not perhaps demand a dative in the same way as 'suitable' does in English).

sermo The word implies a style near to ordinary speech, contrasted with the more energetic types of oratory: cf. *De or.* 1.255, and §31 below on Nestor.

remissus Cf. *Leg.* 1.11 (Atticus talking to Cicero) *sic tu a contentionibus quibus summis uti solebas, cotidie relaxes aliquid . . . quod sustinere cum vel summa senectus posse videatur, nullam tibi a causis vacationem video dari; Brut.* 326. Plut. *An seni* 794c–d has a similar view of the sort of oratory that is suitable for old men; cf. also Isocr. *Panath.* 3.

facitque ... audientiam *Facere audientiam* is a standard phrase, 'to gain a hearing', and *audientia* has no other Ciceronian use: cf. Plaut. *Poen.* 11; [Cic.] *Ad Her.* 4.67; Cic. *Div. in Caec.* 42; *De or.* 2.325; Livy 43.16.8; etc.; *TLL* 2,1260. Often it is the *praeco* who *facit audientiam* for a public speaker, but Cicero does not mean here that the old man does not need a *praeco* to gain attention for him (Wuilleumier's explanation): he simply means that an old man may gain a respectful hearing without the oratorical fireworks that crowds enjoy from younger speakers.

per sepse *pers(a)epe ipsa* αB codd. Nonii: *per se ipsa* λPaSg. It seems from this almost certain that *persaepe ipsa* was in the archetype of the MSS of Cicero, and also in the archetype of Nonius. However, 'very often' has little point in this context (it is surely not very pertinent to mention the fact that old men sometimes do not achieve a hearing), and 'by itself' seems to make much more sense. It would be rash to adopt *per se ipsa* on the authority of λ (and its derivatives) against the combined testimony of the other MSS and Nonius; but I suspect that Cicero wrote *per sepse*, using an archaic form which he also used in *De rep.* 3.12 (cf. Sen. *Ep.* 108, 32, confirming the usage, though Seneca's MSS are corrupt: Housman, *Papers* II, 873–4), *De leg.* 1.34, and probably (as read by Plasberg) in *Tim.* 14. *per sepse* could hardly escape corruption into *persepe* (*persaepe*), while *ipsa* in all MSS would be a gloss inserted at an early stage. The use of a mildly archaic form here would be in keeping with the characterisation of Cato, cf. Introd. p. 22.

compta The MSS both of Cicero and of Nonius vary between *compta* and *cocta*, those of Nonius also presenting a variant *coacta*; this is not very surprising, as *compta* and *cocta* could at one stage have differed only by an m-stroke (*cōta* = comta, *cota* = cocta). The reading of L¹ of Cicero seems to be *octa* or *cota*. There is surely no doubt that *compta* should be accepted. 'Cooked speech' is nonsense. *compta* in rhetorical contexts is amply paralleled, even though it happens to occur only once elsewhere in Cicero (*Part. or.* 19): Sen. *Ep.* 75.6; 100.6; Quint. *Inst.* 10.1.79; Tac. *Hist.* 1.19; *Ann.* 6.15; Suet. *Calig.* 53; and the verb *comere*, Quint *Inst.* 8.3.42; Gell. 1.9.10; *TLL* 3, 1993. Those who favour *cocta* (e.g. Simbeck) attempt to make it mean 'ripe', 'mature', comparing passages in which *coctus* and *mitis* are used together of ripe fruits; but *coctus* in such contexts means specifically and concretely 'ripened by the heat of the sun', and there is no evidence that it can be transferred to other contexts in the general meaning of 'mature'; and in any case it is not clear to me what sense there may be in calling the speech of an old man 'ripe' or 'mature'. (When we talk in English of someone's 'mature style', all we mean is 'the style of his maturity'.) Lahmeyer (*Philol.* 20 (1864) 295) and Reid argue for *composita*, the reading of Q: it is not clear what improvement on *compta* this represents, as it appears to mean almost exactly the same thing, viz. 'polished', 'elegant', 'orderly'.

quam I.e. *orationem* (not *audientiam*). Cf. §38 below, *quae si exsequi nequirem*.

nequeas Subjunctive of the generalised second person singular; cf. §27 above, *quidquid agas*.

29 an ne tales Schiche's conjecture accounts excellently for the reading *annales* of the older MSS (via *ann&ales*); *an ne* has O²RE²ITPb would then be a conjectural correction of the reading of the archetype, as presumably is *an tales* of S¹ (though there is a very slight chance that this percolated through from tradition).

relinquimus The reading of α: β has *relinquemus*. The present and future have equal MS authority and would be equally grammatical (cf.

H.–Sz. 308 and K.–S. II, 519 for the present; H.–Sz. 311 for the future); but the present seems to have the edge logically: 'do we not even leave?' rather than 'shall we not . . .?' The question is about the present course of the argument, not about a future action. (See Madvig, *Opusc.* II, 40–2 and 266.) Nevertheless one might be tempted to prefer *-ī relinquēmus* on rhythmical grounds, though *-ī relinquimus* is perfectly acceptable and common. One must print one of the two, and Madvig's intuition was probably right.

doceat, instituat, . . . instruat Of these three verbs, *docere* is the most intellectual, *instruere* the most moral. Cf. Varro, *Catus de liberis educandis* fr. 5 Riese, *educat nutrix, instituit paedagogus, docet magister.*

omne offici munus The tasks pertaining to one's function in life: cf. §§35 and 72. *TLL* 8, 1663 gives no parallels outside the *Cato* for *munus offici*, though *officium et munus* is common. For the function of old men as educators of the young, particularly in the political sphere, cf. Plut. *An seni* 790e ἀλλ' εἰ διὰ μηδὲν ἄλλο τῷ γέροντι παιδείας ἕνεκα τῶν νέων καὶ διδασκαλίας πολιτευτέον ἐστίν; Sen. *Tranq.* 3.3; Quint. *Inst.* 12. 11.5ff.; cf. §26 above.

Gnaeus et Publius Scipiones For the plural of the *cognomen* or *nomen*, cf. *De or.* 1.9 *Tiberium et Gaium Sempronios; Brut.* 46; etc. This seems to be Cicero's usual practice; the singular is found in other authors, e.g. Sall. *Jug.* 42 (Draeger, *Historische Syntax* I, 1–2). Gnaeus was the uncle, Publius the father of Scipio Africanus the elder. Cf. §§75 and 82 below; *Balb.* 34; *ND* 3.80; *Tusc.* 1.89; etc.; Livy 23.49; 25.32ff.

Lucius Aemilius Scipio Aemilianus' natural grandfather, who died at Cannae: cf. §75 below; *ND* 3.80; *Tusc.* 1.89; *Div.* 2.71.

iuvenum See above on §17.

libidinosa . . . senectuti The converse of this is found below in §34, *potest igitur exercitatio et temperantia etiam in senectute conservare aliquid pristini roboris.* Cf. also Xen. *Mem.* 2.1.31 (Choice of Hercules), τὰ μὲν ἡδέα ἐν τῇ νεότητι διαδραμόντες, τὰ δὲ χαλεπὰ εἰς τὸ γῆρας ἀποθέμενοι, etc.

30 Cyrus Xen. *Cyrop.* 8.7.6 τοὐμὸν γῆρας οὐδεπώποτε ἠσθόμην τῆς ἐμῆς νεότητος ἀσθενέστερον γιγνόμενον. Cicero adapts a later part of the same speech below, §§79–81. Cicero knew the *Cyropaedia* well (*Q. fr.* 1.1.23; *Leg.* 2.56; *Brut.* 112; *Fin.* 2.92; *Tusc.* 5.99); it is not impossible that Cato was acquainted with it, as he seems to have read some of Xenophon at least: cf. below on §59; Introd. p. 19.

cum admodum senex esset *Cyrop.* 8.7.1 μάλα δὴ πρεσβύτης ὤν. For *admodum* cf. §10.

Lucium Metellum Cf. §60; Val. Max. 8.13.2; Pliny, *NH* 7.153; P.–W. 3, 1203. Metellus was cos. I in 251, cos. II in 247, and Pontifex Maximus from 243 until his death in 221.

memini puer An illogical construction found both in Latin and in Greek, e.g. μέμνημαι παῖς ὤν, Plato, *Charm.* 156a; Quint. *Inst.* 8.3.31 *memini iuvenis admodum*. It may perhaps have something to do with the perfect-tense form of *memini* (*vidi puer* would of course be quite logical). Further on, the present infinitive *esse* after *memini* is quite regular for Ciceronian Latin (in colloquial English we would use a participle, 'I remember him being so strong'), though it is treated as past for the sequence of tenses (here *requireret*); cf. *Fin.* 2.55; *Verr. II* 4.32; etc.; K.–S. 1, 703; H.–Sz. 357; *TLL* 8, 651.

requireret For *requirere* 'miss (something one once had)' cf. *Div. in Caec.* 71; *Sest.* 128; Lucr. 3.919; Virg. *Georg.* 3.70; *OLD* s.v. 5.

X 31 videtisne ... praedicet (For this construction cf. §26 above.) This section is virtually a parenthesis, inserted to justify Cato's talking about himself, to which he returns below, *sed redeo ad me*. The real Cato was certainly fond of boasting about his own exploits; he made a speech *de suis virtutibus* (fr. 128 Malcovati, *ORF* p. 51) which, as editors have long pointed out, Cicero may have had in mind when writing this sentence, although the phrase is a very ordinary one. Some might also see self-justification here on Cicero's own part; he had not always resisted the temptation to talk *de suis virtutibus*. The examples of Nestor, Cato and Cicero all occur in Plutarch's essay *De se ipsum citra invidiam laudando* (544d; 544f on Nestor; 544c on Cato; 540f on Cicero).

Nestor In *Il.* 1.260; 7.123–160; 11.668ff.; 23.629ff. Cf. in general *Att.* 14. 17a.2 = *Fam.* 9.14.2 (written 3rd May 44, soon after the *Cato*); *Brut.* 40; *Tusc.* 5.7; Plut. *An seni* 789f; Juncus p. 1064 W.–H.; Lucian, *Macr.* 3; Dio Chrys. 2.21; Themist. 13, p. 211 D.; *Anth. Pal.* 7.144; [Dion. Hal.] *Rhet.* 8.12.306ff.

iam enim tertiam Not *tertiam iam enim*: attachment to P has led editors astray: such a displacement of *enim* would be unparalleled in Cicero, cf. W. S. Watt, *CQ* 30 (1980) 120. The source is *Il.* 1.250 τῷ δ' ἤδη δύο μὲν γενεαὶ μερόπων ἀνθρώπων | ἐφθίαθ', οἳ οἱ πρόσθεν ἅμα τράφεν ἠδ' ἐγένοντο | ἐν Πύλῳ ἠγαθέῃ, μετὰ δὲ τριτάτοισιν ἄνασσεν; cf. van Leeuwen ad loc.; *Od.* 3.425 τρὶς γὰρ δή μίν φασιν ἀνάξασθαι γένε' ἀνδρῶν; R. M. Frazer, *Glotta* 49 (1971) 216–17.

videbat or *vivebat* (PML²D²ς)? The stemma implies the former, which is nearer to the meaning of the Homeric passage: Nestor had lived through and reigned over three generations of men, a generation being reckoned to last about thirty years. However, Homer was sometimes misunderstood (mostly by Latin poets) to mean that Nestor lived three times the normal human lifespan, or three *saecula*: Laevius ap. Gell. 19.7.13 = fr. 9 Morel, Hor. *Od.* 2.9.13 and Nisbet–Hubbard ad loc.; Ov. *Met.* 12.187–8 *vixi | annos bis centum, nunc tertia vivitur aetas*; Courtney on Juv. 10.249. Some have argued that Ovid was directly imitating this passage, and that consequently *vivebat* must be read here: but this is very uncertain indeed. (It is, indeed, just possible that the Ovidian passage caused corruption in the MSS of Cicero: see Introd. p. 37 n. 83.) It seems generally more likely that Cicero should follow the overt meaning of Homer: he had not sufficient taste for the fantastic to predispose him to take the other alternative (and, one might add, his extreme example of human longevity in §69 below is the 120 years of Arganthonius' life); and it may be doubted whether *aetas hominum* (rather than, say, *aetas hominis* – or *saeculum*) is the obvious Ciceronian phrase for 'human lifespan'.

insolens The word does not mean 'insolent', but is near in meaning to *importunus*, doing things out of place. Cf. particularly *De or.* 2.358 *ne in re nota et pervulgata multus et insolens sim*; *Sest.* 119; Gell. 17.10.8; *TLL* 7, 1, 1928ff.

loquax On the loquacity of old men cf. §55 below; Isocr. *Panath.* 88; Dio Chrys. *Euboicus* 1 πρεσβυτικὸν πολυλογία; Maximian 1.204 *o sola fortes garrulitate senes*; id. 6.1.

ex eius lingua *Il.* 1.249 τοῦ καὶ ἀπὸ γλώσσης μέλιτος γλυκίων ῥέεν αὐδή; Cicero does not attempt a verse translation, which would have been inappropriate for Cato. Cf. [Cic.] *Ad Her.* 4.44 *cuius ore sermo melle dulcior profluebat*, quoted anonymously as an example of *superlatio* (or *supralatio*, cf. M. Winterbottom, *BICS* Suppl. 25 (1970) 139); Hes. *Theog.* 83–4 and 97; Cic. *Orat.* 32 (on Xenophon); Sen. *Ep.* 40.2; Pliny, *Ep.* 4.3.3; Lucian, *Imag.* 13; *Parasitus* 44; Jerome, *Ep.* 52.3.

et tamen 'and yet', 'and at the same time': see note on §1.

dux ille ... peritura *Il.* 2.369–74 τὸν δ' ἀπαμειβόμενος προσέφη κρείων Ἀγαμέμνων· | "ἦ μὰν αὖτ' ἀγορῇ νικᾷς, γέρον, υἷας Ἀχαιῶν· | αἲ γὰρ, Ζεῦ τε πάτερ καὶ Ἀθηναίη καὶ Ἄπολλον, | τοιοῦτοι δέκα μοι συμφράδμονες εἶεν Ἀχαιῶν· | τῶ κε τάχ' ἡμύσειε πόλις Πριάμοιο ἄνακτος | χερσὶν ὑφ' ἡμετέρῃσιν ἁλοῦσά τε περθομένη τε."

brevi Emphatic, as shown by its position: 'that the destruction of Troy would come soon'. Note the unemphatic *sit* immediately following the emphatic word: cf. K.–S. II, 602.

32 sed redeo ad me Cf. §30 fin.

quartum ago annum et octogesimum Cato is 83 at the dramatic date of the dialogue: cf. §14 above and Introd. pp. 16–17.

possem The MSS here are in favour of *possem* rather than *posse* (PV²QR²): cf. *Att.* 8.11d.5 where the MSS vary between *fuissem* and *fuisse*. There is no need to object to the succession of similar final syllables *vellem equidem idem possem*: cf. e.g. §6 above, *tamquam longam aliquam viam*; in pronunciation, elision would lessen the effect of repetition. Nor is there any reason to emend to *posse me* (Mähly, *N. Schw. Mus.*, 6 (1866) 243). On the constructions of *volo* see K.–S. I, 713–14; II, 229. One is tempted to wonder whether there is a slight difference of meaning between *vellem possem* and *vellem posse* or *vellem me posse*: the subjunctive seems to be used when the sense is 'I wish I could' (but cannot, in this particular instance), while *vellem* + infinitive (with or without pronoun subject) seems to mean rather 'I would wish to be able' (in general, if it were possible).

Cyrus §30.

sed tamen The construction of this sentence is informal and conversational (cf. Introd. p. 23): note the repetition of *sed tamen*, and the change of construction between the indirect statement *non me quidem eis esse viribus . . . fuerim* and the indicatives *depugnavi* and *non plane me enervavit*.

queo The somewhat old-fashioned *queo* is used a few times by Cicero (the negative *non queo* is used more often; Cicero does not use *nequeo* in the first person, though he has the other persons of *nequire*): cf. *De rep.* 2.6; *Lael.* 71; *Tusc.* 5.108; *De or.* 1.250; Landgraf on *Rosc. Am.* 72; Neue–Wagener III³, 623ff. The choice of the word here may be due to a preference for old-fashioned forms for the characterisation of Cato (cf. Introd. p. 22), or to a purely Ciceronian desire for a smoother rhythm (*hoc queo dicere* forms a double-cretic rhythm of the sort favoured by Cicero) or for avoidance of repetition (as *possem* has already occurred in this sentence).

non me quidem *quidem* qualifies the whole sentence, not just *me*, and looks forward to *sed tamen*. Cato here indulges in a form of reminiscence quite similar to that of Nestor in the *Iliad*, just referred to; but with a different emphasis, in so far as Nestor says 'I wish I were as strong as I was when . . .', whereas Cato says 'I may not be as strong as I was, but I can still carry on an active life to some extent.'

miles bello Punico Cf. §10 above.

consul in Hispania 195 B.C.; cf. Plut. *Cato* 10 (quoting Polybius 19); *Comp. Ar. et Cat.* 2–3; Broughton, *MRR* I, 339; Astin, *Cato* ch. 2.

quadriennio post For the campaign against Antiochus III in 191 B.C., during which Cato was instrumental in winning the battle at Thermopylae, see Plut. *Cato* 12–13 and *Comp. Ar. et Cat.* 3; Livy 36.17–18.

tribunus militaris Cato's official rank on this campaign was military tribune (Plut. *Cato* 12; Front. *Strat.* 2.4.4; App. *Syr.* 18.80; [Victor], *De vir. ill.* 47; Broughton, *MRR* I, 354); but he was also appointed as an envoy, so Livy (36.17.1) calls him *legatus consularis* (cf. Briscoe ad loc.; Broughton ibid.).

Manio Acilio Glabrione Mentioned alone because he was the consul who was actually present on the campaign.

enervavit *enervare* retains at least some of its original sense, 'to take out the sinews': *TLL* 5, 2, 567ff. Cf. the phrase in *Tusc.* 2.27 *nervos omnes virtutis elidunt*.

adflixit 'cast down': *TLL* 1, 1232ff. On Cato's activity in old age, cf. §§18 and 38.

proverbio If it was *vetus laudatumque* in Cicero's time, it is nevertheless unknown to us outside this passage (Otto, *Sprichwörter* 317, no. 2).

monet mature fieri senem For the infinitive of indirect command after *moneo* (used only when the subject of the infinitive clause is general and left unexpressed) see K.–S. 1, 682.

cui fuerim occupatus This is clearly the right reading, though *cui* is only in RQ² and later MSS: the best MSS offer *qui, quominus* or *cum*, of which only the last makes any sense, and that an obviously inferior one. Possibly the corruption derives from the use of the spelling *quoi*. There seems to be no exact parallel to the use of *occupatus* with a dative in this sense, although it seems logical enough, especially in view of the primary meaning of the word, 'engaged in advance'. Editors quote Plaut. *Merc.* 288, *non sum occupatus umquam amico operam dare*, but there *amico* depends on *operam dare*, not on *occupatus*. *TLL* 9, 2, 387 calls *cui* a *dativus incommodi*, but does not quote any parallels. For a similar thought, cf. M. Aur. 1.12.

33   ne vos quidem Not 'not even you', but equivalent to Greek οὐδ' ὑμεῖς ἔχετε: colloquially, 'Well, *you* don't have . . .'.

Titi Ponti centurionis This is no doubt the man mentioned by Lucilius, fr. 89 M. (quoted in *Fin.* 1.9): *Graecum te, Albuci, quam Romanum atque Sabinum,│municipem Ponti, Tritanni, centurionum,│praeclarorum hominum ac primorum signiferumque,│maluisti dici*. Possibly the same Pontius is mentioned in *De fato* fr. 5 (ap. Macrob. *Sat.* 3.16.3) as being part of Scipio Aemilianus' entourage: this would make the present reference especially appropriate. The name is a common Sabine or Oscan one (equivalent to Latin *Quintius*). Centurions in general were types of physical size and strength: Veg. 2.14; Cic. *Phil.* 8.26; Hor. *Sat.* 1.6.72.

moderatio Literally a governing or controlling. 'Provided one keeps control of one's strength . . .'. One should guard against the mistranslation 'a moderate amount of strength'; nor can Wuilleumier's 'faire un usage modéré' be correct, since it contradicts *tantum quantum potest quisque nitatur*. *moderatio* is Cicero's usual word for σωφροσύνη; 'self-control' represents it in English. Cf. note on §1 above; Nauck, *N. Jahrb. Kl. Phil.* Suppl. 12 (1846) 558ff; *TLL* 8, 1205ff.

tantum quantum potest Cf. §27 *agere pro viribus*.

ne ille non magno For this type of phrasing cf. *Tusc.* 3.8 *ne ista gloriosa sapientia non magno aestimanda est*; *Fin.* 3.11; *Fam.* 7.1.3.

Milo Cf. §27. Galen, *Protrepticus* 34 makes the same point as Cicero with this story, contrasting Milo's strength with the wisdom of Themistocles (where Cicero has Pythagoras). The anecdote occurs also in Lucian, *Charon* 8 (a similarly deflating context); Athen. 10.412e, quoting Theodorus of Hierapolis, Alexander of Aetolia, Phylarchus, *Hist.* 3 and an epigram of Dorieus; Quint. *Inst.* 1.9.5. Athenaeus adds also that Milo ate the bull or ox on the spot: even if Cicero knew this part of the story, he probably thought it better to omit it. (The modern record-holder for eating an ox took 42 days over it, according to the *Guinness Book of Records* for 1986, p. 185.)

bovem: utrum igitur This is the text adopted by Manutius and other editors, also supported by Mommsen. *virum* in the β group of MSS seems clearly enough to be a corruption of *utrum*, while *vivum* in α looks like an attempt to turn *virum* into sense (α does this sort of thing on occasion: see Introd. p. 33). In D²H²O²RZBe and other MSS, *utrum* has been restored from tradition or common sense, but *vivum* remains. Some editors prefer to keep *vivum* (e.g. Sommerbrodt, Meissner), but it seems to add little to the point of the story to say that the ox was alive (no doubt in that case it would have been more difficult to carry); and in Galen's version of the story, if the parallel is worth anything, it is made clear that the ox was dead, having just been sacrificed. (In Galen this has a special point: he observes that the soul of the living ox could carry its body better than Milo could.) The other versions of the anecdote do not say at what stage the ox was killed. Rhythmically there is nothing to choose between *sustineret bovem* and *sustineret bovem vivum*.

Pythagorae Cicero uses Pythagoras as a standard example of a philosopher, but there may be a special reason for mentioning him here, insofar as Milo was traditionally connected with the Pythagoreans (Aristoxenus fr. 18 W.; Strab. 6.263; Iambl. *VP* 105ff.; 150; 249; Burkert, *Lore and Science* 180ff.).

isto bono utare dum adsit Cf. §27 *quod est eo decet uti*, and note; Democr. fr. 202 D.–K. ἀνοήμονες τῶν ἀπεόντων ὀρέγονται, τὰ δὲ παρεόντα καὶ παρῳχημένων κερδαλεώτερα ἐόντα ἀμαλδύνουσιν; Teles p. 38 H. βιώσῃ ἀρκούμενος τοῖς παροῦσι, τῶν ἀπόντων οὐκ ἐπιθυμῶν; ibid. p. 10; [Phocyl.] *Sent.* 6; Plut. *Tranq. an.* 465a; Lucr. 3.957 *semper aves quod abest, praesentia temnis*; Sen. *Ep.* 74.12 *praesentibus gaudet, non concupiscit absentia*; ibid. 123.3. Ancient moralists often criticised the fault of μεμψιμοιρία, discontent with one's lot.

adsit ... absit On the subjunctive see K.–S. II, 202,a.

ne requiras This is apparently the only certain example in prose of the Ciceronian age of *ne* + present subjunctive expressing a prohibition. (In *Att.* 9.18.3, read *malim ... actum ne agas* and see Shackleton Bailey ad loc.; cf. also *Att.* 14.1.2; and see C. O. Brink, *PCPS* 15 (1969) 4ff.) The tense here may be explained as old-fashioned and proverbial-sounding; in earlier Latin the present subjunctive tended to be used for general negative prohibitions. See Handford, *Subjunctive* 43ff.; K.–S. I, 188; H.–Sz. 337; Madvig, *Opusc.* II, 105. (With this passage cf. Marbod, *Lib. Dec. Cap.* 5.81ff.)

cursus est certus aetatis On the divisions of life, cf. §4 above, with literature there cited; also §§70 and 76. Here we have the common division into four, *pueritia, adulescentia, aetas media* (or *constans*), *senectus*: cf. E. Eyben, *RhM* 116 (1973) 167. It is a common and obvious idea that each age-group has its own proper character and activities: cf. particularly Horace's discussion of the four ages in *AP* 156ff. (with Brink's commentary ad loc.), which is in the Peripatetic tradition, going back to Arist. *Rhet.* 2.13.1389a ff. L. Alfonsi (*GIF* 24 (1972) 118–19, and in H. Temporini ed., *Aufstieg und Niedergang der römischen Welt* (Berlin and New York) 1, pt 3 (1973) 57–9) tries to make a case for connecting Cicero's discussion here with occurrences of the idea in Pythagorean writings (Aristoxenus fr. 35; Diog. Laert. 8.9–10; Anon. Diod. 10.9.5, see Thesleff, *Pythagorean Texts* 171 and 233; Iambl. *VP* 56, cf. Thesleff op. cit. 183); but the similarity is probably due to a common tradition. In general cf. Sen. *Phaedra* 461; Pliny, *Ep.* 3.1.2; Maximian 1.105–6.

iam constantis aetatis Middle age: cf. §§60 and 76 below; Suet. *Galba* 4; other terms found are *confirmata aetas, Fam.* 10.3.2; *firmata, Cael.* 43; Virg. *Ecl.* 4.37; *corroborata, Cael.* 41; Cels. *Med.* 3.41; *TLL* 1,1129. The Greek is καθεστηκυῖα ἡλικία (Thuc. 2.36; cf. also Plato, *Ep.* 3.316c ἐν ἡλικίᾳ δὲ ὄντος μέσῃ τε καὶ καθεστηκυίᾳ).

percipi Not just 'perceived' but 'enjoyed'; *percipere* in its original and concrete meaning is 'to reap', as in §§24 and 70.

34 audire Present with habitual meaning. (This is the reading of the archetype; *audisse* LD, *audise* A arises from confusion of *r* and *s*: cf. Introd. p. 32 n. 78.)

avitus Cujas' correction for MSS *habitus*. Usually a *hospes avitus* is one whose grandfather was a friend of your grandfather (cf. *Fam.* 13.34; Lucan 9.1028; App. Verg. *Ciris* 112); here it refers to one who was himself a friend of Scipio's (adoptive) grandfather, Scipio Africanus. Cf. *De rep.* 6.9ff. (beginning of *Somn. Scip.*).

Masinissa Cf. Val. Max. 8.13 ext. 1: *Masinissa Numidiae rex hunc modum* [i.e. 90 years] *excessit, regni spatium sexaginta annis emensus, vel ante omnes homines robore senectae admirabilis. Constat eum, quemadmodum Cicero refert libro quem de senectute scripsit, nullo umquam imbri, nullo frigore ut caput suum veste tegeret adduci potuisse.* Various other authors mention Masinissa's living to be 90 or thereabouts (Lucian, *Macr.* 17; Pliny, *NH* 7.156; Plut. *An seni* 791f, quoting Polybius; Frontin. *Strat.* 4.3.11), his endurance in general ([Livy], *Periocha* 50; Val. Max. 5.2. ext. 4 and loc. cit.; Strab. 17.833), his sexual potency in old age (Val. Max. 8.13 ext. 1; Pliny, *NH* 7.61), and – perhaps the most curious feature – his ability to stand still for a number of hours (Polyb. 36.16; Diod. 32.16; Val. Max. loc. cit.), like Socrates in Plato, *Symp.* 220c. See in general P.–W. 14, 2, 2154ff.; 8a, 103–4 on the item in Val. Max.; P. G. Walsh, *JRS* 55 (1965) 149ff.; G. Camps, *Masinissa*

(*Libyca* 8, Algiers 1960). According to Plut. *Cato* 26, Cato himself came into contact with Masinissa when in Africa.

Stories of endurance of weather conditions, long marches etc. were often told concerning generals and other military men: e.g. Xen. *Hell.* 5.1.15; Sall. *Catiline* 5.3; Livy 21.4.6; Suet. *Div. Jul.* 57; etc.; Cf. K. J. Dover, *Greek Popular Morality in the time of Plato and Aristotle* (Oxford 1974) 163.

siccitatem corporis (PRE Nonius read *corporis siccitatem*, which gives a better rhythm; but the archetype of the MSS read *s- c-*, and Nonius may be quoting inaccurately – perhaps under the influence of the following quotation from Varro, which has *c- s-*.) *siccitas*, dryness, i.e. freedom from bodily secretions of all sorts, was considered at least popularly to be a sign of good health. Cf. *Tusc.* 5.99 *adde siccitatem quae consequitur hanc continentiam in victu, adde integritatem valetudinis*; Varro, *Catus de liberis educandis* fr. 27 Riese (quoted by Nonius p. 395 just after this passage of the *Cato*), *Persae propter exercitationes pueriles modicas eam sunt consecuti corporis siccitatem ut neque spuerent neque emungerentur sufflatove corpore essent* (based on Xenophon, *Cyrop.* 1.12.16; cf. R. Müller, *Kl. Phil. Stud.* 12 (Leipzig 1938) 61); Catullus makes fun of the idea in 23.7ff.; cf. also Lucil. fr. 611 *corpus siccassem pila* (i.e. with exercise). (Avoidance of spitting tended to be noticed: Pliny, *NH* 7.22; Petr. *Sat.* 44.9; Amm. Marc. 16.10.10.) Medical opinion on the subject varied. The Hippocratic school favoured a balanced state rather than *summa siccitas*, recognising that the amount of fluid in the body varied with age, physical type and environment, and prescribed measures to restore the balance: see e.g. Περὶ διαίτης ὑγιεινῆς 2: τοὺς δὲ στρυφνούς τε καὶ προσεσταλμένους... τῇ ὑγροτέρῃ διαίτῃ χρῆσθαι τὸ πλεῖον τοῦ χρόνου· τὰ γὰρ σώματα τοιαῦτα ὑπάρχει ξηρὰ ἐόντα... τοῖσι νέοισι τῶν σωμάτων συμφέρει μαλθακωτέροισί τε καὶ ὑγροτέροισι χρῆσθαι τοῖσι διαιτήμασιν· ἡ γὰρ ἡλικίη ξηρή, καὶ τὰ σώματα πέπηγεν. τοὺς δὲ πρεσβυτέρους τῷ ξηροτέρῳ τρόπῳ χρὴ τὸ πλέον τοῦ χρόνου διάγειν· τὰ γὰρ σώματα ἐν ταύτῃ τῇ ἡλικίη ὑγρὰ καὶ μαλθακὰ καὶ ψυχρά. (On the other hand, Galen, *De san. tuend.* 5.3.2–3 and Hippon, A 11 D.–K. (I, 336) say that old men are naturally dry.) Plut. *Qu. conv.* 3. 650d says that dryness is bad for old men. However, there were also those who thought that a dry constitution was the best, particularly for the mental powers: this may have been due to the influence of Heraclitus (frr. 68; 74; 75–6 D.–K.); cf. Galen, *Hipp. praedict.* 1.5; Tert. *De ieiunio* 1.4.

potest ... roboris Cf. §36 on exercise; Sen. *Ep.* 58.32; Lucian, *Macr.* 2; 6–7.

XI Non sunt This seems to be the right reading: it seems to be better to take it as a question, as Wuilleumier does, 'So old age has no strength? But strength is not even required from old men', rather than as a straight objection from an imaginary opponent, which would seem too abrupt. The alternative is to read *ne sint*, which is only in RTQ¹ (though adopted by Halm and Moore from R; cf. *ne desint* φ; see also C. Knapp, *Proc. Am. Phil. Assoc.* 29 (1898) p. vi); this would be improved by the addition of an adversative particle, *sed ne sint* or *at ne sint*, which might possibly help to account for the readings *ne desint* and *non desunt* in the MSS.

legibus et institutis Cf. Sen. *Brev. vit.* 20.4 *lex a quinquagesimo anno militem non legit, a sexagesimo senatorem non citat*; Pliny, *Ep.* 4.23.3 *ut ipsae leges monent, quae maiorem annis otio reddunt*; Varro, *De Vita Pop. Rom.* fr. ap. Non. p. 523 M. For *vacatio militiae* at 50 cf. Livy 40.26.7; 42.31.4; 42.33.4; 43.14.6; those between 46 and 50 were *seniores* (Gell. 10.28) and liable to be called up only in emergencies (cf. Livy 10.21). The age at which attendance at the Senate was no longer required is given by Sen. *Contr.* 1.8.4 as 65; it is thought that the age may have been lowered during the Principate, reflecting the decreased importance of the Senate: Mommsen, *Staatsrecht* III³, 917 n. 2; D. McAlindon, *CR* 7 (1957) 108; also [Quint.] *decl.* 306.

non modo For *non modo non*, οὐχ ὅπως: the second *non* is not inserted when the two parts of the sentence share a common predicate or part of the predicate (here *cogimur*): H.–Sz. 519. In this case in particular the insertion of a second *non* would produce a very harsh effect.

35 offici aut omnino vitae munus For similar phrases, cf. §§29 and 72.

at id quidem ... valetudinis Cf. Plut. *An seni* 791d οἱ δὲ τὰς ἀρρωστίας προβαλλόμενοι καὶ τὰς ἀδυναμίας, νόσου καὶ πηρώσεως μᾶλλον ἢ γήρως κατηγοροῦσι· καὶ γὰρ νέοι πολλοὶ νοσώδεις καὶ ῥωμαλέοι γέροντες; Juncus p. 1028 W.–H. ταῦτα δὴ τὰ παθήματα οὐ μόνον γήρως ἔργα, μυριάκις δὲ ἔκ τινος τύχης ἐπιπαραγίνεται καὶ τοῖς νέοις. The arguments in §§7, 24 and 67–8 may be compared.

Publius Africani filius Cf. *Brutus* 77, *filius quidem eius, is qui hunc minorem Scipionem a Paulo adoptavit, si corpore valuisset, in primis habitus esset disertus; indicant cum oratiunculae tum historia quaedam Graeca scripta dulcissime*; *Off.* 1.121; *ND* 2.14. This P. Scipio was augur from 180, and died about 170 (P.–W. 4, 1437). On the question of whether he is the subject of the epitaph, *CIL* I, 2, no. 10 (=Dessau, *ILS* 4; E. H. Warmington, *Remains of Old Latin* (Loeb) IV, no. 5), see (against) G. V. Sumner, *Orators in Cicero's Brutus* (Toronto 1973) 36; K. M. Moir, *CQ* 36 (1986) 264–6.

quod ni ita fuisset *ni* in Cicero is more or less confined to set phrases along these lines: H.–Sz. 668.

illud ... lumen civitatis The meaning is that Scipio would have come into prominence *as* another luminary of the state; but Cicero assimilates the gender even to a neuter predicative noun, cf. K.–S. I, 34–5. For this metaphorical use of *lumen* cf. e.g. *Off.* 3.66; *TLL* 7, 2, 1821.

magnitudinem animi 'nobility of character'. For a full discussion of this concept, see U. Knoche, *Philol.* Suppl. 27.3 (1935) 1–88 = *Gymnasium* Beiheft 2 (1962) 31–97. *Magnitudo animi* includes the three virtues of *fortitudo, constantia* and *clementia*, and is thus different both from 'our 'magnanimity' (which is *clementia*) and from Aristotle's μεγαλοψυχία.

doctrina uberior Cf. *Brut.* 77, quoted above.

quid mirum ... si infirmi sint The subjunctive is regular after *mirum si ..., quid mirum si ...?* (*TLL* 8, 1074).

cum id ne adulescentes quidem Cf. §67; Cicero would no doubt have been thinking of Tullia; cf. Introd. pp. 2–3.

resistendum 'stand up to' (rather than 'resist').

diligentia Not exactly our 'diligence' (which implies dogged hard work) but 'care', 'attention': see also §59 below. The etymological connection with *diligere* should be kept in mind. Cf. Sen. *Ep.* 58.30 *Plato ipse ad senectutem se diligentia protulit.*

contra morbum Old age and disease of course commonly go together (*subeunt morbi tristisque senectus*, etc.), but there is a *topos* to the effect that old age is itself a disease: Ter. *Phorm.* 575 *senectus ipsast morbus* and Don. ad loc. (quoting a saying of Apollodorus); schol. Pers. 2.41; Sen. *Ep.* 108.28 *senectus insanabilis morbus est*; Democr. fr. 296 D.–K. γῆρας ὁλόκληρός ἐστι πήρωσις; Jerome, *In Psalm.* 89, Migne, *PL* 26, col. 1094.

pugnandum Cf. Pliny, *Ep.* 3.1.8 *hoc quoque exercitationis genere pugnat cum senectute* (cf. below); Sen. *Brev. vit.* 20.4 *cum imbecillitate corporis pugnant, senectutem ipsam nullo alio nomine gravem iudicant quam quod illos seponit.*

36 habenda ratio valetudinis Cf. *Fin.* 2.64 on L. Thorius Balbus of Lanuvium, an epicure – not an Epicurean, as is sometimes said – not otherwise known: *Habebat tamen rationem valetudinis; utebatur eis exercitationibus ut ad cenam et sitiens et esuriens veniret, eo cibo qui et suavissimus esset et idem facillimus ad concoquendum, vino et ad voluptatem et ne noceret.* Much of ancient medicine was concerned with diet, exercise, etc. as means to conserve health, particularly in the Hippocratic school; and cf. Plato, *Timaeus* 89b–c and *Laws* 728e. On Cic.'s views of medicine cf. E. Orth, *Cicero und die Medizin* (Leipzig 1925) (pp. 91–3 on the *Cato*).

exercitationibus modicis Cf. *Fin.* 2.64, quoted above; Sen. *Ep.* 15.4; Plato, *Erastae* 134a; Galen, *Protrepticus* 28; Lucian, *Nigrinus* 26; Pythagorean *Carmen aureum*, 32–5. The sort of exercise envisaged would be walking, playing ball, bathing or declaiming: even being carried in a litter was thought beneficial. For the various sorts of exercise see Plut. *De tuenda sanitate*; *An seni* 793b on light exercise suitable for old men; Pliny, *Ep.* 3.1 describing the daily routine of Vestricius Spurinna at the age of 77; Sen. *Ep.* 15.

tantum cibi ... opprimantur Cf. *Off.* 1.106 *victus cultusque corporis ad valetudinem referatur et ad vires, non ad voluptatem. cibus et potio* is the normal

Latin for 'food and drink': cf. §46 below; *Tusc.* 5.100; *Fin.* 1.37; Varro, *RR* 1.1.5; etc.

menti atque animo The two words are often used together: cf. *Cluent.* 146; Lucr. 1.74; 3.398; Virg. *Aen.* 6.11. On the desirability of exercising the mind, cf. *Off.* 1.123 *senibus autem labores corporis minuendi, exercitationes animi etiam augendae videntur;* §21 above *nisi exerceas;* §38 *exercitationes ingeni;* Sen. *Ep.* 15.5; 80.2–3; Pliny, *Ep.* 3.1.4 *nec minus animum quam corpus exercet;* Plato, *Rep.* 498b προϊούσης δὲ τῆς ἡλικίας, ἐν ᾗ ἡ ψυχὴ τελειοῦσθαι ἄρχεται, ἐπιτείνειν τὰ ἐκείνης γυμνάσια; *Clitopho* 407e; *Timaeus* 88b–c; Diogenes ap. Diog. Laert. 6.70; Plut. *An seni* 788b (see below); Musonius Rufus 6, pp. 24–5 Hense. On exercise in general, cf. Cato's *Carmen de moribus* ap. Gell. 11.2, *nam vita humana prope uti ferrum est: si exerceas, conteritur; si non exerceas, tamen robigo interficit. Item homines exercendo videmus conteri; si nihil exerceas, inertia atque torpedo plus detrimenti facit quam exercitio;* Latro ap. Sen. *Contr.* 2.2.8; Apul. *Flor.* p. 31, 24 Halm.

tamquam lumini oleum instilles This comparison – *lumen* being used in the concrete sense of 'lamp' – seems to be unique in Latin, though the more weakly metaphorical *lumen ingeni*, the light of the mind, is common enough (cf. §41; *TLL* 7, 2, 1816ff.). *exstinguuntur* continues the image. There is a certain similarity with the image of polished brass in Plut. *An seni* 788b, and the context is clearly similar: οὐδὲ γὰρ ἡ τοῦ φρονεῖν ἕξις ὁμοίως παραμένει τοῖς μεθεῖσιν αὐτούς, ἀλλ' ὑπ' ἀργίας ἐξανιεμένη καὶ ἀναλυομένη κατὰ μικρὸν ἀεί τινα ποθεῖ φροντίδος μελέτην ... "λάμπει γὰρ ἐν χρείαισιν ὥσπερ εὐπρεπὴς|χαλκός"; ibid. 792d.

se exercendo *exercitando* φ could be accepted in the passive meaning, 'by being exercised'; but *se exercendo* is preferable, as *se* has a desirable point.

Caecilius See §§24–5 above.

comicos stultos senes A fuller quotation is given in *Lael.* 99: '*ut me hodie ante omnes comicos stultos senes|versaris atque inluseris lautissime*' – *haec enim etiam in fabulis stultissima persona est improvidorum et credulorum senum* (= Caec. incert. fr. 3, p. 243 Ribbeck). (This additional attestation confirms the text *comicos*, which is only in Q² among our MSS.) *Recentiores* of the *Laelius* add, before the quotation, the words *ut in Epiclero*, but these words are not in the earliest MSS. How they got there is uncertain, and they are clearly not sufficient evidence on which to assign the fragment to the *Epiclerus*; but still, it is worth considering the possibility that they derive from tradition or from an informed conjecture, rather than from a completely random guess by a Renaissance editor. *Comicos* means 'in comedy': cf. *Rosc. Am.* 47, *comicum adulescentem;* Horace, *Sat.* 2.5.91; and the similar use of *tragicus*, *Pis.* 47, etc. Cf. also Varro, *Bimarcus* (*Men.* fr. 51 Bücheler) *scena quem senem Latina vidit derisissimum.*

dissolutos 'slack', not here equivalent to our 'dissolute'; *TLL* 5, 1, 1502; Landgraf on *Rosc. Am.* 32.

petulantia Insolence: the word derives from *petere*, cf. Festus p. 226 *petulantes et petulci etiam appellantur qui protervo impetu petunt laedendi alterius gratia*; Cic. *De rep.* 4.6 (Nonius p. 23); Ernout–Meillet 763. For *petulantia* and *libido* together cf. *Phil.* 3.35 *libidinosis, petulantibus, impuris, impudicis, aleatoribus, ebriis*.

non proborum Weaker than *improborum*: cf. *Off.* 3.36; Prop. 2.28.52.

deliratio Cf. *De or.* 2.75 *deliros senes*; *Div.* 2.90; Sen. *Ep.* 49.8; Pliny, *Ep.* 6.15.4; Lucr. 3.452; *TLL* 5, 1, 465. Pliny, *NH* 18.180 and Varro ap. *GLK* VIII, p. 72 explain the derivation from *lira* (cf. Ernout–Meillet 566–7); *lira* is defined there as a ridge made over the seed in the process of *occatio*, harrowing (cf. Varro, *RR* 1.29.2). Columella (2.4.8) says that *lira* is the same as *porca*, the ridge between two furrows made by ploughing; Nonius p. 17, 32 and *Corp. Gloss. Lat.* ed. Goetz, II, p. 494.32 make *lira* mean the furrow itself (cf. *CGL* IV, p. 108, 39). In any case the point is that *delirare* originally means to depart from the straight line in ploughing or harrowing. We have no precisely equivalent metaphor, though 'to go off the rails' is similar. But the translation in this context has to be 'senility'. For the general argument, cf. Diogenes of Oenoanda fr. 63 Chilton [μ]ὴ ἀγνοῶμεν [ὡς οὐ] διὰ τὸ γῆρας ἐγ[ένον]το αἱ παρακο[π]α[ί, διὰ δέ] τινα ἑτέραν [αἰτίαν τ]ῆς φύσεω[ς].

levium *levis* here is the opposite of *gravis* in respect of character: φαῦλος as opposed to σπουδαῖος. Aulus Gellius found the usage noteworthy enough to comment on it (6.11): *veterum hominum qui proprie atque integre locuti sunt, leves dixerunt quos vulgo nunc viles et nullo honore dignos dicimus*, quoting Cicero's *videte levitatem hominis* from *Phil.* 2.77. Actually this meaning is found quite often: cf. *Fin.* 3.38; *Q. fr.* 1.1.37; etc.; *TLL* 7, 2, 1208.

37 Quattuor robustos filios I.e. Ap. Claudius Rufus (cos. 268), P. Claudius Pulcher (cos. 249), the ancestor of the Clodii Pulchri; C. Claudius Cento (cos. 240, cf. §50) and Ti. Claudius Nero, the ancestor of the Claudian emperors. Ap. Claudius Caecus was exceptional in the number of his surviving children (cf. P. A. Brunt, *Italian Manpower* (Oxford 1971) 141); another example of a large family, that of Q. Metellus, is referred to in *Fin.* 5.82. Cf. Val. Max. 8.13.5 … *quattuor filios, quinque filias, plurimas clientelas, rem denique publicam hoc casu gravatus fortissime rexisset*. In §16 above Ap. Claudius appeared as a statesman: here we see him as an ideal *paterfamilias* (cf. T. P. Wiseman, *Clio's Cosmetics* (Leicester 1979) 109).

animum tamquam arcum The comparison of the mind with a bow is not uncommon. Most occurrences of this idea are in exhortations to relax: see Hor. *Od.* 2.10.19 and Nisbet–Hubbard, with passages there cited. The nearest parallel to this passage seems to be Plut. *An seni* 792d τόξον μὲν γὰρ ὥς φασιν ἐπιτεινόμενον ῥήγνυται, ψυχὴ δ' ἀνιεμένη (a Latin translation of this is found in ps.-Seneca, *Monita* 187). *intentum* continues the comparison (*intendere arcum* is to draw a bow, *TLL* 7, 1, 2113), but *intendere* is often used of the mind elsewhere without an explicitly metaphorical significance, e.g. Cic. *Hort.* fr. 6 Grilli; Sen. *Tranq.* 17.4; cf. τόνος used of the soul, Diogenes ap. Epict. fr. 57 Schw. Compare also Aristoxenus' theory of the soul as *ipsius corporis intentio quaedam, Tusc.* 1.20 (and Simmias' doctrine in Plato, *Phaedo* 86b–c).

habebat 'kept' (not just 'had').

succumbebat The word retains to a certain extent its original meaning: Appius did not 'take old age lying down'.

imperium A Roman paterfamilias theoretically had the same powers over his family as a magistrate with *imperium*, and the word is often used of a father's commands to his family and slaves. Cf. *Inv.* 2.140 *imperiis domesticis*; *Pro Caec.* 52; Plaut. *Bacch.* 459 *imperiis patris*; etc.

in illa domo mos patrius et disciplina This is the reading usually adopted by editors, and seems right: the corruption in the earliest MSS seems to arise from haplography, *domos* for *domo mos*; *animus* in the α group looks like a conjecture, making sense of a sort but not eminently good sense; O²RE, as in other places (cf. Introd. p. 39) provide the correct reading. (Cf. G. R. Throop, *CPhil* 6 (1911) 483–4.)

38 si se ipsa defendit Cf. *Acad.* 2.36 *veritas se ipsa defendet*, and §61 below, *miseram esse senectutem quae se oratione defenderet*. Old men must defend their position by their actions.

si nemini emancipata est *emancipata* is supported by the lemma and MS readings of Nonius; not much weight should be attached to the fact that it also appears in the *Cato* MS Sg, which is generally inferior, but it may be that the reading of LAD, *neminēmancipata*, can be taken as supporting it. However this may be, *emancipata* is clearly to be preferred to *mancipata*: *mancipare* is not used in the metaphorical sense needed here, and is not otherwise used at all by Cicero (*TLL* 8, 257–9). For *emancipatus* in the sense of 'surrendered to another's power' cf. Plaut. *Bacch.* 93, Hor. *Epod.* 9.12, Sen. *Ep.* 116.5, *Benef.* 1.3.6, etc; *TLL* 5, 2, 445; A. Fleckeisen, *N. Jb. Kl. Phil.* 95 (1867) 643.

I suspect that there may be an extra point to *emancipata* in this particular context of old age. One of the ancient forms of will recognised in Roman law, the *testamentum per aes et libram*, was originally (and remained in form) a *mancipatio* or conveyance of the testator's estate to the heir, who was entitled for the purpose *familiae emptor*. As in an ordinary sale, the transfer of ownership of the estate took place immediately, and was not delayed until the testator died; hence, although this became merely a formality in the classical period, anyone who made a will of that sort strictly spent the rest of his life deprived of legal rights over his property. In such a case it would be no great exaggeration to speak of such a man as having 'emancipated' himself or his old age, since the effective power of the head of the family passed to the heir.

Apart from this, reminiscences of legal language may be noted throughout this passage: *ius suum* (cf. *sui iuris*), *dominatur* (cf. *dominium*, the legal term for full ownership), *suos* (the legally correct way to refer to those directly under *patria potestas*). This seems to contribute to the plausibility of the above explanation of *emancipata*. On the legal background see Watson, *Roman Private Law* 100ff.; M. Kaser, *Römisches Privatrecht* I² (Munich 1971) 105ff. and 678ff.; II (1959) 341ff.

adulescentem in quo est senile aliquid A young man with something of the wisdom and caution of old age (cf. Aesch. *Septem* 622 γέροντα τον νοῦν, σάρκα δ' ἡβῶσαν φύει).

senem in quo est aliquid adulescentis An old man who has kept his vigour and independence, as Appius Claudius is said above to have done. There is a similar antithesis (though not near enough to show a definite connection) in Epicurus, *Menoec.* 122, recommending philosophy for both the young and the old. There seems to me to be no real connection between this passage and the idea of the prematurely wise and responsible boy (like Ascanius in *Aen.* 9.311), as suggested by K. Büchner, *Gymnasium* 62 (1955) 315ff.: *adulescens* means a man of any age up to his early forties, in whom a moderate (sometimes a large) amount of wisdom and caution may reasonably be expected. Nor is there any real similarity or inconsistency with passages discussing the undesirable reversal of roles and characteristics between old and young, as in Plato, *Rep.* 8.563, Cic. *De rep.* 1.67; [Varro], *Sent.* 74; Sen. *Ep.* 36.4; Incert. *pall.* 95 (Ribbeck, *Com. Frr.* p. 128; cf. Apul. *Apol.* 85). This passage has also been compared with a saying of Cato the Elder, quoted by Pliny, *NH* 7.171, *senilem iuventam praematurae mortis esse signum*; however, there is no contradiction, as that passage is concerned only with physical matters. Different also is *Dicta Catonis* 4.18 *noli ridere senectam, nam cuicumque seni puerilis sensus inhaeret.*

corpore senex esse poterit, animo numquam erit Cf. *Anacreontea* 37 (47) B., the same idea in a different context: φιλῶ γέροντα τερπνόν, | φιλῶ νέον χορευτάν, | ἂν δ' ὁ γέρων χορεύῃ, | τρίχας γέρων μέν ἐστιν, | τὰς δὲ φρένας νεάζει.

septimus ... liber Originum The seventh and last book of the *Origines* dealt with Cato's own time, including the prosecution of Sulpicius Galba in 149. His working on it in old age is mentioned by Nepos, *Cato* 3. The next phrase, *omnia antiquitatis monumenta colligo*, is therefore inappropriate for this work, and may refer to some other writing of Cato's (Meissner,

N. Jb. Kl. Phil. 103 (1871) 57). Cato's historical writings are also referred to below, §§75 and 83.

in manibus Cf. §22.

defendi 'pleaded': *defendere causam* is to plead a case, not necessarily for the defence, and must be distinguished from *defendere aliquem*; cf. *Lael.* 96; *Cluent.* 74; etc.; *TLL* 5, 1, 303.

nunc cum maxime 'now more than ever': the exact explanation of this idiom does not seem to be agreed upon, but it is not an uncommon phrase (cf. Ter. *Ad.* 518; *Andr.* 823; etc.; Cic. *Rosc. Am.* 132; *Cluent.* 12; etc.; *TLL* 8, 74).

conficio orationes Cicero clearly envisaged Cato as 'touching up' some of his speeches for publication quite a long time after they were delivered; this may reflect Cicero's own practice. On Cato's speeches and Cicero's view of them, cf. *Brut.* 63–8; Schanz–Hosius I, 190.

ius augurium pontificium civile For Cato's interest in augural and pontifical law, without any personal connection with the priestly colleges, cf. *orat.* fr. 197 Malcovati. As for civil law, Cato was according to Cicero (*De or.* 1.171) *iuris civilis omnium peritissimus*; cf. also Nep. *Cato* 3.1; Livy 39.40; Quint. *Inst.* 12.11.23; Festus p. 154.

Graecis litteris On Cato's study of Greek literature, cf. note on §3 and Introd. pp. 19–20.

Pythagoreorumque more (The correct spelling is *Pythagoreus*, not -*ius*: Housman, *Papers* II, 887.) At first sight it seems strange that Cicero should attribute this practice to Cato. However, there is no direct evidence to show that Cato could not have done something of the sort, and it is difficult to see why Cicero should have put in the reference unless he believed that Cato did do it. The question is then what his source would have been: the obvious guess is some work of Cato himself, and if one admits the possibility that Cato had Pythagorean connections at all, it is not difficult to suppose that he at least knew about the practice. (See notes on §§39 and 41, and E. Pais in *Mélanges Glotz* (Paris 1932) 681ff.) On the practice itself, see the Pythagorean *Carmen aureum*, 40ff. (= Porph. *VP* 40; Epictetus, *Diss.* 3.10; cf. 4.6.35), μηδ' ὕπνον μαλακοῖσιν ἐπ' ὄμμασι προσδέξασθαι | πρὶν τῶν ἡμερινῶν ἔργων τρὶς ἕκαστον ἐπελθεῖν· | "πῆ παρέβην; τί δ' ἔρεξα; τί μοι δέον οὐκ ἐτελέσθη;" | ἀρξάμενος δ' ἀπὸ πρώτου ἐπέξιθι καὶ μετέπειτα | δειλὰ μὲν ἐκπρήξας ἐπιπλήσσεο, χρηστὰ δὲ τέρπου; Iambl. *VP* 165; 256; Anon. Pyth. ap. Diodor. 10.4.5 (H. Thesleff, *The Pythagorean Texts of the Hellenistic Period* (Åbo 1965) 231); Diog. Laert. 8.22; Sen. *De ira* 3.36 (on Sextius); App. Verg. *De institutione viri boni* 14ff.; Burkert, *Lore and Science* 213; J.–P. Vernant, *Journal de Psychologie* 56 (1959) 1ff., esp. 16; C. Martha, *Études morales sur l'antiquité* (Paris 1896) 191ff.

exercendae memoriae gratia Usually the Pythagorean practice is said to be a form of moral self-examination, as in most of the passages cited above; but sometimes the object of exercising the memory is also there, as in Iambl. *VP* 256 (deriving from Apollonius of Tyana), εἰς δὲ τὴν νύκτα ἀναλογίζεσθαι τί διῳκήκασιν, ἅμα τῷ σκοπεῖσθαι καὶ τὴν μνήμην γυμναζομένους; Diod. 10.4.5. On exercise of the memory, cf. §21: it may be that Cato or Cicero thought this a more practical use of the exercise than examination of conscience. It is surmised that the original point of the memory exercise was not moral at all, but an effort to recall past incarnations: Burkert, op. cit. 213 n. 21; Dodds, *Irrational* 173 n. 107. (For the supposed ability to do this, cf. Emp. fr. 119 and 129 D.–K.; Procl. *In Tim.* 1, p. 124; Porph. *VP* 45.)

commemoro This can mean (though not commonly) merely 'remember', with no connotation of repeating aloud, and probably does so here: cf. *Fam.* 6.21.1; Plaut. *Epid.* 171; Suet. *Aug.* 45; *TLL* 3, 1835. Nonius quotes this passage for the meaning, p. 91, 10 M.

exercitationes ingeni Cf. §36.

curricula Cf. *Orat.* 12 *curricula sermonum; TLL* 4, 1506.

desudans *desudare* is not used elsewhere by Cicero; *TLL* 5, 1, 776.

adsum The word may here have its semi-technical sense of being present as an advocate (Reid); cf. *TLL* 2, 925. In general cf. §32 above, *non curia vires meas desiderat, non rostra, non amici*; and §18 on Cato's senatorial activity.

utroque This, the reading of Vβ, 'to both places' – i.e. to Cato's friends and to the Senate – seems to me preferable to *ultroque* (φ, read by all editors to my knowledge). The latter is explained as referring to unasked-for contributions by Cato in the Senate, and usually connected with the *Carthago delenda est* story (see on §18); but apart from that special case, there seems little point in saying that Cato brings long considered opinions *of his own accord*: presumably he was usually asked for his opinion both privately and publicly, and any senator was entitled to digress within limits. *utroque* also makes for a better balance in the sentence: *adsum amicis, venio in senatum frequens* [note clausula]: *utroque adfero res multum et diu cogitatas*, whereas *ultroque* would naturally connect only with the part about the Senate, leaving the two words *adsum amicis* isolated and the rest of the sentence overweighted. Admittedly Cicero does not elsewhere use *utroque* to refer to persons, but the usage does occur (Livy 45.22.4): for *quo* in a similar context, cf. *Verr. II* 4.38; Plaut. *Asin.* 486; *CIL* 1, 585.24 (an official and legal context); also §12 above on *unde*. Such usages appear to be somewhat formal or old-fashioned, and would suit the context of Cato talking about his official activities as lawyer and senator.

multum et diu Pleonastic: cf. §9.

tueor Cf. §71 *munus offici tueri*.

animi, non corporis viribus Cf. *Off.* 1.79 *omnino illud honestum ...*

animi efficitur, non corporis viribus (followed by the example of Cato's Carthaginian policy).

quae si exsequi nequirem Cf. §28; *quae* refers generally to what precedes (*adesse amicis, venire in senatum*, etc.).

lectulus A bed or couch for any purpose, in this case for reading or study. The similarity of sound between *lectulus* and *oblectaret* is probably accidental, but could be a form of word-play. Cf. Sen. *Ep.* 67.2 *ago gratias senectuti quod me lectulo affixit*; Marbod of Rennes, *Lib. Dec. Cap.* 5.126 *me meus oblectat meditantem talia lectus* (*meus* should be read, not *mens* as in editions). However, Plutarch, *An seni* 788b, observes that ὁ ἐν κλίνῃ διημερεύων ... εὐκαταφρόνητος.

acta vita Cf. §§9, 13 and 62; *Fam.* 4.13.4.

viventi 'for one who lives...' Cf. *Fam.* 9.16.1 *vivas in litteris.*

non intellegitur quando obrepat senectus Cf. §4; Juv. 9.128–9 *dum bibimus ... obrepit non intellecta senectus*, possibly a reminiscence of this passage: if Cicero's words were in the reader's mind, Juvenal's line would have a fine parodistic twist. Ausonius, *Epig.* 13.3, imitates Juvenal.

ita This is sometimes taken (e.g. by Reid) to qualify *sensim*, and the whole sentence to mean 'it is not noticed when old age creeps up on one, so gradually does one's life approach its end', etc. But this seems to unbalance the sentence, and it may be preferable to take *ita* as virtually equivalent to *itaque*, 'in this way'.

sensim This word is said originally to have meant 'perceptibly', then 'just perceptibly', 'gradually' (Ernout–Meillet 924); but by Cicero's time at any rate it would have lost any clear connection with *sensus*, so *sensim sine sensu* would not be felt to be contradictory. The alliteration is rather surprising for Cicero, and one wonders whether there might be a hidden quotation, perhaps from Cato himself or from a poet.

diuturnitate exstinguitur As is seen more clearly in §71 below, *exstingui* in Latin is to go out gradually, not to be put out suddenly (which is *opprimi*). The clausula here is not a common one, and as it occurs at the end of a major section of the work I wonder whether it should not be regularised by changing to *restinguitur* – there would be no difference in the meaning, and no difficulty in explaining the corruption.

39ff. Third complaint: old age lacks pleasures To this third complaint against old age (cf. §§7 and 15) Cicero replies in two different ways: first that old men should be grateful that they are no longer subject to injurious desires and passions (cf. §7 – the argument is Plato's), and secondly that there are in any case some pleasures that old men may still enjoy. There is no logical inconsistency between the two halves of the argument, as different sorts of pleasures are in question.

The idea that pleasure is an evil appears sporadically in the philosophic tradition. The arguments recorded by Aristotle (*NE* 1152b; 1172b fin. – 1173a) as used by the early Academy were designed only to show that pleasure is not the highest aim of action: one of them reappears below (§41). Gellius 9.5 collects examples of philosophical views on pleasure, including that of Critolaus the Peripatetic, *et malum esse voluptatem, et multa alia mala parere ex sese, iniurias desidias obliviones ignavias*, which is similar to one of the arguments used by Cicero (§40). Cf. also Antisthenes ap. Gell. ibid.; Sil. Ital. 15.94–5; Macr. *Sat.* 2.8.10ff.; Iambl. *VP* 85. However, the closest parallel to the present context is a passage of Cicero's own *Hortensius* (fr. 84 Grilli, 77 Ruch, ap. August. *Contra Iul.* 4.14), which is worth quoting at length: *An vero voluptates corporis expetendae, quae vere et graviter a Platone dictae sunt illecebrae esse atque escae malorum?* [cf. §44] *quae enim confectio est valetudinis, quae deformatio coloris et corporis, quod turpe damnum, quod dedecus quod non evocetur atque eliciatur voluptate? cuius motus ut quisque est maximus, ita est inimicissimus philosophiae: congruere enim cum cogitatione magna voluptas corporis non potest. quis enim, cum utatur voluptate ea qua nulla possit maior esse, attendere animum, inire rationes, cogitare omnino quidquam potest? quis autem tantus est gurges, qui dies et noctes sine ulla minimi temporis intermissione velit ita moveri suos sensus, ut moventur in summis voluptatibus? quis autem bona mente praeditus non mallet nullas omnino nobis a natura voluptates datas?* Other Ciceronian examples of the argument occur in *Leg.* 1.47; *Fin.* 1.44 (there used by Torquatus from an Epicurean point of view); *De rep.* 1, fr. 5 ap. Non. p. 424, 31 M.

The first, and more general, part of the argument against pleasure in the *Cato* is presented as a discourse of Archytas of Tarentum, supposed to have been reported to Cato by a Tarentine called Nearchus (§41), who obtained his knowledge of it from local tradition. There has been a considerable amount of scepticism among commentators regarding this scenario, though not always concentrated at the points at which scepticism is most needed.

(a) Those who have decided on other historical grounds that Cato was never at Tarentum naturally have to treat the whole episode as a fiction: in fact there is no good reason to doubt Cato's visit to Tarentum, cf. Appendix 3.

(b) The existence of Nearchus has come under suspicion, for no very good reason. There is, admittedly, no independent proof of his existence, other than Plut. *Cato* 2–3, which represents Cato as visiting him, and hearing from him the same sort of Platonic arguments against pleasure and in favour of temperance as are used by Cicero; it seems highly likely that this passage of Plutarch derives from Cicero, and so cannot be used as independent corroboration (cf. P. Wuilleumier, *Mél. Ernout* (Paris 1940) 383ff; J. J. Hartman, *Mnem.* 34 (1906) 307). However, on the whole

Cicero's practice in dialogues was to use existing historical details with some concern for accuracy, and it would be strange to find him indulging in completely unfounded invention at this point. There are various ways in which one could imagine Cicero acquiring information about Nearchus: his name may have been on record as a 'friend' of Rome (cf. on §41 below), and he may have been mentioned in Cato's writings (cf. E. Rawson, *JRS* 70 (1980) 197). Disbelief in Nearchus' existence has sometimes been based on the eclipse of Pythagoreanism in Italy between the fourth and first centuries B.C.; but the only evidence that Nearchus was a Pythagorean is in Plutarch, and that may only be a guess. In any case, one may suppose that Nearchus had access to a considerable body of Pythagorean lore, whether or not he was a professed Pythagorean. It is known that Ennius had an interest in Pythagoreanism at about the same time: why not Nearchus?

(c) Cato's general opposition to philosophy may be thought to exclude the possibility of his having talked philosophy with Nearchus; but the ideas put forward by Nearchus might well have been thought by Cicero to be appropriate for the young Cato, whatever he may have said against philosophers in later life.

(d) The real reason for scepticism about the Nearchus–Archytas story is not to be found in the person of Nearchus, but in the content of the speech attributed to Archytas. As intimated above, the speech contains little or nothing that is not to be found elsewhere in Cicero, and most of it looks like a simple paraphrase of Cicero's own discussion of pleasure in the *Hortensius*; while the arguments used are virtually all derived either from Plato himself (cf. commentary below) or from his followers in the Academy. There is no doubt a possibility that Archytas may have been recorded as expressing opinions of this sort on some occasion. One particular episode from Aristoxenus' *Life of Archytas* has attracted attention (fr. 50 Wehrli, ap. Athen. 12.545a; cf. D.–K. I, 47 A 9, p. 424): a conversation was narrated between Archytas and the pleasure-loving Polyarchus of Syracuse, in which the latter argued that pleasure was naturally desirable and the chief aim of human action. The reply of Archytas is not preserved; scholars have not unnaturally guessed (though this is indeed no more than a guess) that it was similar to, and indeed the source of, the speech attributed to Archytas here by Cicero. That Aristoxenus should have attributed Platonic arguments to Archytas is not implausible: he was of the persuasion that wished to brand Plato's philosophy as unoriginal and derived from Pythagoreanism (cf. fr. 33 W.). There may, indeed, be some connection here with Cicero's mention of Plato as having been present at the conversation with Archytas: there is no mention of Plato in the surviving fragment of Aristoxenus, but it is possible that Aristoxenus could have timed the conversation on pleasure to coincide with one of Plato's visits to Archytas. However this may be, it should be stressed that the only *known* connection between Cicero and Aristoxenus is that both record a conversation involving Archytas on the subject of pleasure. In Aristoxenus the only other participant mentioned is Polyarchus, while in Cicero the conversation is with C. Pontius the Samnite and Plato (for the chronological difficulties regarding Plato's presence, see Appendix 3; on Pontius, see below on §41). Where, if anywhere, Cicero got the idea of a conversation between these three men must remain unknown. In any case, the device of the Archytas speech was convenient as a means of introducing the extreme case against pleasure into the dialogue, as contrasted with the more moderate views expressed by Cato *in propria persona* in §§44ff. The device whereby a speaker quotes a set speech from another source is standard in dialogue-writing, cf. Plato, *Symp.* 177a, *Tim.* 20d; [Plato], *Axiochus* 371a; Juncus p. 1060 W.–H.; Hor. *Sat.* 2.2.2; G. L. Hendrickson, *AJP* 27 (1906) 185ff.; from the literary point of view it adds a pleasing element of variety.

(e) The transmission of the speech of Archytas via Nearchus to Cato is probably a fiction, though not as implausible a fiction as some have wished to make it. Commentators assume that an oral tradition is implied, and remark how unlikely this is to be authentic (cf. another imagined oral tradition going back to Archytas in *Lael.* 88; also §43 below). Such things seem to have struck Cicero as at least plausible enough to put in a dialogue; but apart from this, there is nothing in Cicero's wording here to imply that Archytas' speech was not envisaged as being transmitted in writing. (E. T. Salmon, *Samnium and the Samnites* (Cambridge 1967) 120–1, envisages an actual work of Nearchus on which he supposes Cicero and Plutarch to have drawn: this is a refreshing change from the excessive scepticism of most commentators, but seems an unnecessary hypothesis.)

Cf. E. Zeller, *Die Philosophie der Griechen* (Leipzig 1923, repr. Hildesheim 1963) III⁵.2, 98; E. Pais, *Mél. Glotz* (Paris 1932) II, 681–98; Wuilleumier, *Tarente* 608; R. E. Smith, *CQ* 34 (1940) 105ff.; L. Alfonsi, *Parola del Passato* 10 (1955) 121ff.; F. della Corte, *Catone Censore* (2nd edn, Turin 1969) 238ff.; Astin, *Cato* 7 and 160 n. 7; W. Burkert, *Philologus* 105 (1961) 236ff.

XII 39   o praeclarum munus Cf. §§42; 44; 46.

accipite enim, optimi adulescentes Cf. *Lael.* 33 *audite vero optimi viri*; Scipio and Laelius were in their mid-thirties, and therefore still counted as *adulescentes* by Roman convention.

Archytae See above. For Archytas cf. *Lael.* 88; *De rep.* 1.16; 59; *Tusc.* 4.78; 5.64; *Fin.* 2.45; 5.87; *De or.* 3.139; Val. Max. 4.1 ext. 1; Varro, *RR* 1.1.8; Hor. *Od.* 1.28; Colum. 1.1.7; Gell. 10.12; Diog. Laert. 8.79–83; D.–K. I, no. 47; Wuilleumier, *Tarente* 67–75; 574–87; P.–W. 2, 600–1.

cum essem adulescens Tarenti 'when I was at Tarentum as a young man': cf. §§ 10–11.

nullam capitaliorem pestem For similar phrases cf. *Lael.* 34; *Off.* 2.9; *Phil.* 4.3 *capitalem et pestiferum.*

cuius voluptatis The repetition of the antecedent ensures clarity (so that *cuius* is not taken to refer to *natura*). For this form of expression, see Landgraf on *Rosc. Am.* 8: there are a number of examples in Cicero (ten in *Inv.*, fewer in later works), and Caesar uses it quite often. Cf. also [Cic.] *Ad Her.* 8.11; 9.13. The word *voluptas* is repeated nine times in various cases in §§39–41; this would presumably be noticed and emphasised in reading aloud.

ecfrenate The MSS seem to support this spelling here; cf. §9 above, *ecferunt.* Cf. *Tusc.* 4.12 *cupiditas effrenata*; *Fin.* 3.36.

ad potiundum Sc. *ea voluptate.* This gerundive is, apparently, usually spelt *-undum* (*OLD* s.v.), though here only V among the MSS so writes it.

incitarentur The meaning is virtually middle here, not passive: cf. for the sense *Tusc.* 4.42 *ipsae se impellunt* (*perturbationes*); C. W. Nauck, *N. Jahrb. Kl. Phil.* Suppl. 12 (1846) 558ff.; E. Claflin, *AJP* 67 (1946) 193–221, discussing middle verbs in the *Cato*, omits this example.

40 hinc ... nasci Cf. *Acad. pr.* 2.27 *quo e vitio et amicitiarum proditiones et rerum publicarum nasci solent;* *Fin.* 1.44 *ex cupiditatibus odia discidia discordiae seditiones bella nascuntur;* *Off.* 3.36 *hinc sicae, hinc venena, hinc falsa testamenta nascuntur;* *Rosc. Am.* 75; Plato, *Phaedo* 66c καὶ γὰρ πολέμους καὶ στάσεις καὶ μάχας οὐδὲν ἄλλο παρέχει ἢ τὸ σῶμα καὶ αἱ τούτου ἐπιθυμίαι; Gell. 9.5.6 (Critolaus, quoted above); Sen. *Ep.* 110.10 *voluptati, cui indulgere initium omnium malorum est;* Lact. *Inst.* 6.9.10 (recalling this passage). Pleasure is 'the root of all evil'.

patriae proditiones Philosophical commonplace rather than referring to any specific instances: cf. *Acad. pr.* 2.27, quoted above; Lucr. 3.85–6 *nam iam saepe homines patriam carosque parentes | prodiderunt ...*

cum hostibus clandestina colloquia Cf. *Phil.* 12.27 *colloquia cum acerrimis hostibus;* for prepositional phrases used as adjective-equivalents, see on §7 above.

cumque ... dedisset Cf. *Parad.* 1.14 *cum tibi sive deus sive mater (ut ita dicam) rerum omnium natura dedit animum, quo nihil est praestantius neque divinius ...*; *Off.* 3.44 *mentem ... qua nihil homini dedit deus ipse divinius;* *Fin.* 5.38; also (for a similar phrase, applied to philosophy), *Acad. post.* 1.7, imitated from Plato, *Timaeus* 47b; Cic. *Timaeus* 52; also *Leg.* 1.58; *Lael.* 47; *Tusc.* 1.64; *Off.* 2.5; *Fam.* 15.4.16.

sive quis deus So most commonly; but *si qui deus* below, §83, *Tusc.* 2.67, etc.; see Löfstedt, *Synt.* II, p. 83–4, n. 2.

41 libidine dominante Cf. *Rep.* 1.59, the converse of this passage, *consilio autem dominante nullum esse libidinibus . . . locum*; *Orator* 219 (quotation from Crassus), *nam ubi libido dominatur, innocentiae leve praesidium est*; Sall. *Cat.* 51.3 (Caesar's speech), *si libido possidet, ea dominatur, animus nihil valet.* The image of pleasure or desire as a tyrannical master is common in Greek philosophy; see note on §47 below (the Sophocles anecdote from Plato's *Republic*); Plato, *Phaedo* 69a; Xen. *Oecon.* 1.18–23; Arist. *NE* 1172a.

consistere Cf. *Fin.* 4.69 *sapientia pedem ubi poneret non haberet.* (This passage is imitated by Marbod of Rennes, *Lib. Dec. Cap.* 7.117ff.)

tanta . . . quanta percipi posset maxima Cf. *Hortensius* fr. 84 Grilli, quoted on §39; Plato, *Philebus* 21a, δέξαι' ἄν . . . σὺ ζῆν τὸν βίον ἅπαντα ἡδόμενος ἡδονὰς τὰς μεγίστας;; Arist. *NE* 1152b 16ff. ἐμπόδιον τῷ φρονεῖν αἱ ἡδοναί, καὶ ὅσῳ μᾶλλον χαίρει, μᾶλλον· οἷον τῇ τῶν ἀφροδισίων· οὐδένα γὰρ ἂν δύνασθαι νοῆσαί τι ἐν αὐτῇ; also Sen. *Vit. Beat.* 5.4.

tamdiu dum Cf. *Catil.* 3.16; *Pis.* 68.

tam detestabile tamque pestiferum quam So MH²O²Q²RSZBeE recc.; this seems to me to be the right reading. The archetype ω of the ninth-century MSS probably read *tam detestabile tamquam* as in V¹β. Editors adopt *tam detestabile quam* from PH¹V²A²D², condemning *tamque pestiferum* as a gloss. However, it is not clear, if the words are a gloss, what they are meant to explain, nor is this hypothesis supported by the presence of *-que*. The reading *tamquam* in V¹β would also be better for being explained. This would be easy if *tam detestabile tamque pestiferum quam* was the original reading, and the writer of ω slipped from *-que* to *quam*, leaving *tam detestabile tamquam*. The correct reading would have been restored in MH²O² etc. from tradition independent of ω, as has been seen to happen in other places (cf. Introd. p. 41). In any case, *tamque pestiferum* is eminently Ciceronian, and adds some desirable weight to the sentence.

longinquior MO²RSZBeE seems definitely preferable for the rhythm, *atque longinquior. maior esset atque longior* seems excessively trochaic, and *atque* should cause suspicion, as Cicero does not generally use it before a consonant except in order to make a good clausula (cf. on §4 above); he could easily have written *maior et longior*, if *longior* had been the correct reading. Again we find a promising reading in M and O²: see preceding note and Introd. p. 41. Usage alone does not decide the issue in this case: though *longinquus* is indeed commoner in the meaning 'long-lasting', *longus* is found in *Sest.* 82, *Phil.* 11.8, *Fin.* 2.88 and – all in the phrase *si longus levis* – ibid. 22; 94; 95. *TLL* 7, 2, 1626 and 1637. Cf. Madvig, *Opusc.* II, 264ff.; G. Lahmeyer, *Philologus* 20 (1864) 298; Krebs–Schmalz, *Antibarbarus* II⁶, 31.

C. Pontio Samnite This C. Pontius, father of C. Pontius the Samnite general at Caudium (321 B.C.), is mentioned again by Cicero in *Off.* 2.75, and by Livy (9.1 and 3) who calls him Herennius Pontius and testifies to his *prudentia*. E. T. Salmon (*Samnium and the Samnites* 120ff.) is sceptical about his Greek learning, but it is not impossible that he had connections with learned Greeks; the Samnites were apparently friendly with Tarentum at this period (Wuilleumier, *Tarente* 89), and Pontius could have known Archytas even if they did not talk philosophy together. (W. Burkert, *Philologus* 105 (1961) 238–9 is uneasy about the chronology, but that is because he confuses Pontius the elder, mentioned here, with his son the victor of Caudium.) Cicero's mention of Pontius here may be linked with his other efforts to prove early Italian connections with Greek philosophers (cf. §78; *Lael.* 13; *Tusc.* 4.2–3).

Nearchus Cf. above, §39.

qui in amicitia populi Romani permanserat Cf. *Verr. II* 5.83 *civitates quae in amicitia fideque populi Romani perpetuo manserant*. This appears to be an official or semi-official phrase: it is clearly the Latin equivalent of the Greek formulation found in the *Senatusconsultum de Oropiis, IG* VII no. 413 (= W. Dittenberger, *Sylloge Inscriptionum Graecarum*, edn 3 (Leipzig 1917) no. 747; C. G. Bruns, *Fontes iuris Romani antiqui*, edn 7 (Tübingen 1909) 180, no. 42), lines 51–2, concerning Hermodorus of Oropus, τοῦ διὰ τέλους ἐν τῇ φιλίᾳ τοῦ δήμου τοῦ Ῥωμαίων μεμενηκότος. Cf. also *S. C. de Thisbensibus, SIG³* no. 646, line 7 (Bruns no. 41); *S. C. de Asclepiade, CIL* I², 2, no. 588, pp. 468–71, lines 19–20 (Greek version) (Bruns no. 37); the phrase could clearly be used either of individuals or of cities. The use of the formula in official contexts seems to have been a recognition of loyalty to the Roman cause, whether or not it also implied that there had been an official conferment of the appellation *amicus populi Romani* or similar (as in the *S. C. de Asclepiade*; cf. Livy 29.19.7 for the pro-Roman party at Locri Epizephyrii; ibid. 44.16 for the Macedonian Onesimus individually enrolled *in formulam sociorum*; etc.). Nearchus will have been a prominent supporter of the Roman cause at Tarentum, who remained loyal when Tarentum seceded; it seems not unlikely that Cicero would have found his name in some official record, together with a recognition of his friendship with Rome. This at any rate seems a more likely hypothesis than the idea that Cicero simply invented Nearchus out of his own imagination. See in general A. J. Marshall, 'Friends of the Roman People', *AJP* 89 (1968) 39–55.

Plato Cf. on §39 above; for the chronology, see Appendix 3. Plato's visits to Italy and Sicily, and his connection with Archytas, were well known, and Cicero refers to them again in *Fin.* 5.87 and *De rep.* 1.16; cf. Riginos, *Platonica* 62ff.

42 Quorsus hoc? A verb of saying in the past must be understood, cf. *ut intellegeretis*: K.–S. II, 179; cf. §§13 and 44.

magnam habendam esse senectuti gratiam Cf. §46; Sen. *Ep.* 67.2;

83.3. On the distinction between *habere gratiam* 'to be grateful' and *agere gratias* 'to thank', cf. E. Wistrand, *Opera Selecta* (Stockholm 1972) 11ff.

impedit enim consilium voluptas Cf. Arist. *NE* 1152b 16 ἐμπόδιον τῷ φρονεῖν αἱ ἡδοναί; cf. above on §41.

mentis ... praestringit oculos Cf. *Fin.* 4.37 *aciem animorum nostrorum ... praestringitis*; *Div.* 1.61; *Div. in Caec.* 46; *Rab. Post.* 43; *Phil.* 12.3; *Ad Brut.* 1.18.4; Varro *Men.* 30; Sen. *Tranq.* 9.1.8. For the idea cf. Plato, *Phaedo* 66d; also Appendix 2, p. 270.

commercium Despite Reid's statement (without examples) that 'the use of *commercium* in the metaphorical sense is common', there seems to be no other instance in which one abstract quality is said to have (or not to have) *commercium* with another. In *Tusc.* 5.66 and Sen. *Ep.* 18.12 human beings are said to have *commercium* with qualities. *TLL* 3, 1875.

invitus feci ut ... (Cf. *Vat.* 21 *invitus facio ut recorder.*) The story of L. Flamininus' crime and degradation is narrated by Livy (39.42.5ff.), Plutarch (*Cato* 17; *Flamininus* 18 – in both places referring to Cicero) and Valerius Maximus (2.9.3). Livy used Cato's own speech on the occasion as a source (cf. Malcovati, frr. 69–71, pp. 32–3). Cf. also Sen. *Contr.* 9.2.25; [Victor], *De vir. ill.* 47.4. There are some differences in the various versions. In the version which Livy reproduces, as he claims, from Cato's own censorial speech, the *scortum* is a male one, a Carthaginian called Philippus; the condemned prisoner is replaced by a noble of the Boii who had come with his family to request protection, and Flamininus kills him spontaneously with his sword, merely offering this as an entertainment to Philippus without having to be persuaded. Plutarch follows this version, expressing surprise that Cicero did not reproduce the version of Cato's speech. Cicero's version, however, is nearer to that of Valerius Antias, also reproduced by Livy (= Val. Ant. fr. 48 Peter, *HRR* 1², 219); in this version the *scortum* is female, a *famosa mulier* (in Cicero there is no indication as to the sex of the *scortum*), and the other details are as in the present passage; this is also the version followed by Valerius Maximus. Probably Cicero's reason for not following the version in Cato's speech was a desire to retain decorum – that version after all is considerably more discreditable to Flamininus and to the Roman name. But he may simply have been quoting from memory, and the version he gives may have been the one that occurred to him first. Cf. P. Fraccaro, *Studi Storici per l'Antichità Classica* 4 (1911) 1–137 = *Opuscula* 1 (Pavia 1956) 417ff.

T. Flaminini Cf. on §1 above. T. Flamininus was censor in 189 (*proximus ante me fuerat*).

septem annis L. Flamininus was consul in 192; seven full years are counted.

notandam The technical word in contexts of censorial degradation.

ut securi feriret For this phrase with the technical meaning 'to execute', cf. *Verr. II* 1.75; *Pis.* 84; Livy 2.5.8; etc. *OLD* s.v. *securis*, 2a.

rei capitalis An uncommon (dactylic) clausula, but the whole phrase is a set technical one and not much could have been done about it (for other dactylic rhythms cf. note on §5).

elapsus est Not surprisingly from the Roman point of view: Q. Fulvius Flaccus, cens. 194, who ejected his brother from the Senate, was regarded as an example of exceptional severity.

Flacco Cato refers by the familiar *cognomen* alone to his colleague in the censorship (and consulship), L. Valerius Flaccus.

neutiquam An old-fashioned, but not strictly speaking archaic word, fitting the mild stylistic characterisation of Cato (cf. Introd. p. 22); it occurs also in Cic. *Tim.* 11; *Att.* 6.9.3; 9.10.6 (quoted from Atticus); *De virtutibus* fr. ap. Char., *GLK* II, p. 186 *illud neutiquam probantes* (W. Ax's Teubner edn of *Off.* with frr. of *De virtutibus*, p. 161); Livy 4.27.10; 7.12.11.

XIII 43   audivi a maioribus natu Cicero seems to use *a(b)* and *e(x)* almost indifferently with *audire* (*TLL* 2, 1275); the MSS are confused here, and the only reason to prefer *a* is consistency with *a senibus* and *a Thessalo Cinea* below (where the MSS are more clearly in its favour, though still not unanimous). Note also *ex eo* a little further on: Cicero seems to prefer *ex* with pronouns, no doubt for added weight. As to the imagined oral tradition, cf. *Lael.* 88 and above, p. 184.

porro 'in their turn': cf. Plaut. *Asin.* 875; Livy 27.51.

C. Fabricium (for Fabricius as an example of Roman virtue, see on §15). Fabricius led an embassy to Pyrrhus in 280/79: cf. *Brut.* 55; *Parad.* 6.48. On the general circumstances and dating see Lévêque, *Pyrrhos* 343, and cf. Appendix 3. This anecdote is reproduced in Plut. *Pyrrhus* 20 and Val. Max. 4.3.6. In both of these versions, however, the saying is attributed to Fabricius himself, not to Curius and Coruncanius as in Cicero.

qui se sapientem profiteretur Cicero makes much of the fact that Epicurus apparently advertised himself as 'wise': *Fin.* 2.7 *qui se unus, quod sciam, sapientem profiteri sit ausus*; *Tusc.* 2.7; cf. Plut. *Non posse suaviter* 1100a.

dedissent I wonder whether *dedidissent* should be read here. *dare se alicui rei* is simply to 'betake oneself' to some activity, to give oneself to it temporarily, while *dedere se* is to give oneself up totally to something, often with the added idea of abandoning some other pursuit (cf. *Off.* 1.71; *Q. fr.* 3.5.4). The latter seems rather more appropriate here; one may add the slight improvement to the clausula ($-\cup-|-\cup--$ instead of $-\cup-\cup--$). Similarly, in *Tusc.* 1.72 *se totos libidinibus dedissent* one might consider reading *dedidissent* (cf. Kühner ad loc.); cf. *De rep.* 2.1 *me totum dedidi*; also *Tusc.* 5.115; *De or.* 1.10. Conversely, in *De rep.* 6.25 I would support Halm's *dederis* for *dedideris*, since the meaning there cannot be 'give up totally'. For *dedere* cf. *De rep.* 6.29 *qui se corporis voluptatibus dediderunt*, and many other places in Cicero. Clearly in a case like this the MSS cannot be trusted too far. Cf. *TLL* 5, 1, 267–8; 5, 1, 1698.

vixerat Manius Curius cum Publio Decio In some sort of *contubernium* presumably: the close associations of the old Roman heroes were very much part of the atmosphere. Curius was somewhat younger than Decius; Decius 'devoted' himself according to the tradition at Sentinum in 295, in the fourth of his consulates (the first was in 312), whereas Curius was consul for the first and only time in 290. Decius' *devotio* – along with that of his father, in the battle of Veseris against the Latins, described by Livy, 8.9 – is mentioned in many places: cf. §75; *Fin.* 2.61; *Tusc.* 1.89; 2.59; *Parad.* 1.12; *Off.* 1.61; 3.16; Livy 10.28.13; Sen. *Ep.* 67.9; *Benef.* 4.27.2; 6.36.2; Frontin. *Strat.* 4.5.15; Diod. 21.6.2; etc.; P.–W. 5, 2279ff.

pulchrum Equivalent to καλόν, though in moral philosophy Cicero often translates that term by *honestum*. This argument against hedonism occurs in a fuller form in *Fin.* 2.61; cf. also *Parad.* 1.12–13 *cogitasse quidquam in vita sibi esse expetendum nisi quod laudabile esset et praeclarum videntur?*

quod sua sponte peteretur For this slightly extended use of *sua sponte*, cf. *Leg.* 1.45 *nam ut vera et falsa, ut consequentia et contraria sua sponte, non aliena iudicantur; Rep.* 3.26 *sapientem sua sponte ac per se bonitas et iustitia delectat; Verr. II* 1.108; *Orat.* 115; *Tusc.* 2.46. The Greek equivalent would be δι' αὐτὸ αἱρετόν (cf. *Fam.* 15.17.3).

44 Quorsus Cf. §§13 and 42.

voluptates nullas magnopere desiderat Cf. on §§7 and 47.

exstructisque 'piled up': cf. *Tusc.* 5.62; *Pis.* 67; Plaut. *Men.* 101; Ov. *Met.* 11.120; Ar. *Eccl.* 838 αἱ τράπεζαί γ' εἰσιν ἐπινενησμέναι; cf. also Hor. *Sat.* 2.6.105.

insomniis Does this mean ἐνυπνίοις (from *insomnium*) or ἀγρυπνίαις (from *insomnia* fem. sing.)? The context leaves the meaning uncertain. Commentators, appealing to their own experience of the bad effects of excessive eating and drinking, divide between those who suffer from bad dreams and those who fail to sleep (or sleep intermittently); there are ancient parallels for both (Macrob. *in Somn. Scip.* 1.3.4–5 characterises the *insomnium* or ἐνύπνιον as resulting from upset digestion, among other causes, while Ecclesiasticus 31.20 speaks of ἀγρυπνία as a consequence of excess; cf. Pliny, *NH* 14.142 *furiales somni et inquies nocturna* – presumably covering both). One supposes, however, that Cicero's readers would know from usage which was meant: it therefore becomes a question of attempting to exclude one or the other on the basis of the usage of Cicero's time. Neither word is used elsewhere by Cicero himself. *insomniae*, pl. of *insomnia*, occurs first in Sallust (with a slightly different meaning from that which would be required here: equivalent to *vigiliae*, staying up deliberately during the night); the singular *insomnia* occurs in Caec. Stat. *com.* fr. 168 R. (in an apparently similar context to the present one) and Ter. *Eun.* 219; Serv. *Aen.* 4.9 calls it *antiqua elocutio* and says that it was used by Ennius and Pacuvius. *insomnia* pl. of *insomnium* occurs first in the well-known passages of Virgil, *Aen.* 4.9 and 6.896 (though in the former *insomnia terret* was also read in antiquity, cf. Serv., and there have been those who interpreted *insomnia* pl. there as meaning sleeplessness rather than dreams; but the parallel with *Aen.* 6, among other arguments, would suggest that dreams were meant, and indeed they seem more likely as the source of Dido's malaise); then in Pliny, *NH* 18.118, etc.; Tac. *Ann.* 11.4. It is generally accepted that *insomnium* is not an original Latin formation but a calque of ἐνύπνιον, though this does not necessarily mean that it was an Augustan invention: a word of this sort might have been used by Cicero (on the etymology see A. Meillet, *Esquisse d'une histoire de la langue latine* (Paris 1966) 219; Ernout–Meillet s.v. *somnus*). The evidence is not at all conclusive, but it does appear marginally more likely that *insomniis* in Cicero would have been taken as coming from *insomnia* f. sing. (Naturally this passage would only refer to sleeplessness as a result of excessive indulgence; it does not exclude the possibility that old men may fail to sleep for other reasons.) Cf. R. J. Getty, *AJP* 54 (1933) 1ff.; *TLL* 7, 1, 1935ff.; C. W. Nauck, *N. Jb. Kl. Phil.* Suppl. 12 (1846) 558ff.; V. Ussani, *Insomnia. Saggio di critica semantica* (Rome 1955), cf. R. D. Williams, *CR* 7 (1957) 165.

sed si aliquid dandum est Cf. *Off.* 1.106 *sin sit quispiam qui aliquid tribuat voluptati, diligenter ei tenendum esse eius fruendae modum.*

blanditiis Cf. *Fin.* 1.33; 3.1; *Leg.* 1.47; *Fam.* 15.16.3.

escam malorum Plato, *Timaeus* 69d ἡδονὴν μέγιστον κακοῦ δέλεαρ. The meaning is that the *mala* use pleasure as a bait to entice men towards them. The phrase is repeated quite frequently: cf. *Hortensius* fr. 84 Grilli (quoted above on §39); Plut. *Cato* 2.4 (quoted in the context of Cato's conversation with Nearchus: cf. §39 above); Epictetus fr. 112 Schw.; Philo, *Vita Moysis* 1.295; Corpus Hermeticum, *Core Cosmou* 46; Themist. *De anima*; Methodius, *Symp.* 4.4.103; Basil, *Reg.* 17.2; Gregory of Nyssa, *Vita Moysis* 2.297; *De virg.* 21; the Latin Fathers copied it from Cicero, see Ambrose, *De Isaac* 7.61; *In Lucam* 7.114; *De bono mortis* 6.24; August. *Solil.* 1.1.3; *Contra Iul.* 4.15.76; 5.8.33. Cf. P. Courcelle in *Hommages L. Herrmann* (Brussels 1960) 244ff.; id., *Connais-toi toi-même* (Paris 1974–5) 429–35; E. Fantham, *Comparative Studies in Republican Latin Imagery* (Toronto 1972) 40.

epulis ... conviviis *convivium modestum est: epulae splendidiores* (C. Langius). Cf. §45 on the etymology of *convivium*.

Duilium The accepted spelling: the MSS here mostly have *Duellium*, but A¹D¹ have *Duillium*, B *Duillum*; the *Fasti Capitolini* have *Duílius* (with apex on the first *i*), and Polybius' Λίβιος (1.22.1; 23.1) is generally thought to be a corruption of 'Bilius', the later form of the name. Cf. also *Orat.* 153; Quint. *Inst.* 1.7.12; P.–W. 5, 1777. Mommsen, *CIL* I¹, p. 39n. (on Columna Rostrata). On Duilius' victory at Mylae (260 B.C.), cf. *De rep.* 1.1; *Planc.* 60; *ND* 2.265; [Livy], *Periocha* 17; Val. Max. 3.6.4; *CIL* VI, 1300 (= *Inscr. Ital.* 13.3.69); Dessau, *ILS* I, 65: a reconstruction of the *columna rostrata*, of Augustan or Claudian date: cf. Mommsen, *CIL* I¹, pp. 37–40 (no. 195); Sil. Ital. 6.665; cf. below.

devicerat The more intensive form is preferable to *vicerat*, and is also better rhythmically.

saepe videbam puer This is not unrealistic: Duilius died at an advanced age around 220 B.C., when Cato was about fourteen.

cereo funali et tibicine *cereo* is clearly correct for *credo* or *crebro* of the older MSS. But is *cereo funali* one thing or two? And if one thing, is *cereo* the noun and *funali* the adjective, or vice versa? The parallel passage in Valerius Maximus (3.6.4), quite possibly copied from Cicero, reads *ad funalem cereum praecinente tibicine*, implying that the single object concerned is a *funalis cereus*. *TLL* (6, 1, 1545) lists this as a solitary instance of *funalis* n. masc. = *funale* (taking Cicero's *funali* to be from *funale*); on the other hand *OLD* takes *cereus* to be the noun, and *funalis* the adjective, the latter (quoted for this sense only in these two passages) being supposed to mean 'made of rope'. Given that both these interpretations involve unparalleled usages, one resorts to common sense: it seems rather more likely that a torch (*funale* or *-is*) should be specified as made of wax (i.e. presumably a rope torch soaked in wax), than that a *cereus*, usually a 'taper' (i.e. a relatively small object), should be turned into a large torch by the addition of the qualification 'made of rope'. On the other hand, *OLD* has in its favour (as regards Cicero) the fact that one would expect an attributive adjective without special emphasis to come after its noun; it is difficult to see why an adjective *cereus* should be particularly emphasised in this context; however, in Val. Max. the two words occur in reverse order. Turning to the wider question of usage, and ignoring Valerius Maximus for a moment, one may observe that in general *cereus*, a taper (*TLL* 3, 862), and *funale*, a rope torch, are two different things, and they are in fact mentioned together as two elements of the privileges of magistrates in the *Lex Coloniae Genetivae Ursonensis* (*CIL* II, 5439 = *ILS* II, 1, 6087), *togam praetextam, funalia, cereos*. One may therefore be tempted to wonder whether the correct reading in Cicero is not *cereo, funali, tibicine* (deleting *et* which appears in the β group of MSS as *e*). On this supposition, one would have to assume further that Valerius Maximus misunderstood the text of Cicero and took *cereo funali* as a single phrase – perhaps not an impossible assumption. (Whether the text of Valerius Maximus is itself sound is another question: for the unreliability of Kempf's Teubner text, cf. P. K. Marshall in *T. & T.* 428, n. 1.)

sumpserat Cicero, Valerius Maximus, Florus (1.18.10) and Ammianus Marcellinus (26.3.5 – also using the phrase *sibi sumere*) imply that Duilius assumed on his own initiative the privilege of being preceded by a torch and *tibicen*; on the other hand *CIL* VI, 31611 (no date given in *CIL*) and [Victor], *De vir. ill.* 38.4 say *permissum est* and *concessum est* respectively, implying some sort of official grant; [Livy], *Periocha* 17 says *perpetuus quoque honos habitus est*, which does not make it clear whether the privilege was officially granted or not. The inscription is probably a product of early imperial antiquarianism, and may not be trustworthy on legal details, while the *De vir. ill.* hardly constitutes independent evidence at all. It seems best, therefore, to take it that Duilius was himself responsible for assuming this privilege – normally confined to magistrates, as the context of Cicero here and the *Lex Ursonensis* (quoted above) makes clear – and that he was not prevented by the authorities. (Florus loc. cit. seems to be wrong in supposing the privilege to be confined to *triumphatores*; and I do not know why Scullard in *OCD* s.v. 'Duilius' calls it a 'Greek honour'.)

tantum licentiae dabat gloria 'such was the privilege his glory gave him', explaining why Duilius was allowed to continue with this practice. It seems a mistake to suppose that any criticism is being levelled here at Duilius. *Licentia* in Cicero simply means 'liberty' or 'privilege', and need not have the disapproving connotations of our 'licence' (cf. *TLL* 7, 2, 1354); *sumere* is often used of taking what is one's due (cf. e.g. Hor. *Od.* 3.30.14); *nullo exemplo* may imply admiration or surprise, but not necessarily disapproval (the innovation was after all many years in the past by Cicero's time, or even by the dramatic date of the dialogue). Criticism of Duilius would be irrelevant in the present context: the example is meant to prove that such things as this may still be a cause of pleasure for old men.

45 alios Sc. *commemoro* or similar.

ad me ipsum Cf. §§32 and 56.

sodalitates A *sodalitas*, like a Greek θίασος, is a society officially constituted, usually with some religious function (unofficial or illegal associations are *sodalicia*). As a Roman institution, *sodalitates* were of great antiquity: this passage certainly does not imply that those set up in 204 B.C. were the first. Macr. *Sat.* 1.16 attributes institutions of this kind to Romulus, and they are mentioned in the Twelve Tables (8, fr. 27). They ranged in importance from national religious organisations (e.g. the *sodales Titii*, cf. Tac. *Ann.* 1.54; Varro, *LL* 5.85) to purely private associations which were little more than mutual benefit societies. Common membership of a *sodalitas* was a bond which could be presumed on in political contexts (Cic. *Brut.* 166; [Q. Cic.] *Pet. cons.* 16). Here the point of mentioning them depends on their convivial functions, which were important. Gell. 2.24.2 mentions dinners held at the *Ludi Megalenses*,

presumably connected with the *sodalitates* mentioned here. In general see
T. Mommsen, *De collegiis et sodaliciis Romanorum* (Kiel 1843); P.–W. s.v.
collegium, 4, 384ff.

autem Perhaps translate 'in fact': so far from disapproving of *sodalitates*,
Cato actually gave his support to them as quaestor (for the quaestorship
cf. §10 above and Appendix 3). However, the support is left for the reader
to deduce, and Cicero may have had no evidence other than the dating.

sacris ... acceptis For the establishment of the rites of the Magna
Mater at Rome in 204 B.C., see Livy 29.10–14; Cic. *Fin.* 5.64; *Har. resp.* 27;
Ov. *Fasti* 4.182ff. and Bömer's note; F. Cumont, *Les Religions orientales dans
le paganisme romain*, edn 4 (Paris 1929) 43ff.; A. Toynbee, *Hannibal's Legacy*
(London 1965) II, 384ff.; H. Graillot, *Le Culte de Cybèle, Mère des Dieux*,
Bibl. Écoles françaises d'Athènes et de Rome, 107 (Paris 1912) 87–91; M.
J. Vermaseren, *Cybele and Attis* (Eng. tr., London 1977) 38ff. The official
Latin title of the goddess was *Mater Deum Magna Idaea*: here *Idaeis* is
transferred to qualify *sacris*, for greater elegance (Cicero avoids more than
one adjective qualifying the same noun).

omnino modice 'modestly indeed, but ...': on this use of *omnino* cf. §28
above.

fervor aetatis *fervor* of course literally means 'boiling' or 'bubbling
over'. Cf. Ter. *Ad.* 152, *defervisse adulescentiam*; Cic. *Cael.* 18 *adulescentiae
cupiditates defervissent*; *Brut.* 316; Hor. *Od.* 1.16.24; *AP* 116; Ov. *Met.* 15.209;
Sen. *Ep.* 68.13. See *TLL* 6, 1, 601.

delectationem Denoting greater approval than *voluptas*.

metiebar This use of *metiri* is a favourite device of Cicero's: cf. *Pis.* 68;
De or. 3.62; *Fin.* 2.56; 5.93; *Off.* 3.12; *Fam.* 7.12.2; etc.

accubitionem epularem A curious phrase, reminiscent of lexico-
graphical style: a similar style is evident in *Fin.* 3.35 *laetitiam ... quasi
gestientis animi elationem voluptariam*. This sort of phrase may derive from the
genus + differentia style of philosophic definition, such as is found most
conveniently in the pseudo-Platonic Ὅροι. Both words, *accubitio* and
epularis, are rare; the former is found only in Cicero (here, *ND* 1.94 and
Off. 1.28; cf. Nonius p. 193 M., quoting this passage) and in late Latin
(*TLL* 1, 338). For *epularis* cf. *De or.* 3.73; Apul. *Met.* 2.19; 3.12; *TLL* 5, 2,
702.

convivium Cf. *Fam.* 9.24.3 (written to Paetus the year after the *Cato*):
*Nec id ad voluptatem refero, sed ad communitatem vitae atque victus, remissionemque
animorum quae maxime sermone efficitur familiari, qui est in conviviis dulcissimus; ut
sapientius nostri quam Graeci: illi συμπόσια aut σύνδειπνα, id est compotationes
aut concenationes, nos convivia, quod tum maxime simul vivitur.* Apart from these
two passages, neither *compotatio* nor *concenatio* occurs elsewhere in classical
Latin: it seems that they were both coined by Cicero as calques of the
Greek words (*TLL* 3, 2143, 57: 4, 19, 42). Note that Cicero uses the Greek

words in an informal letter, but not here: the philosophical works come midway between the letters, in which Greek words are very frequent, and the speeches, in which they are hardly admitted at all: L. Laurand, *Études sur le style des discours de Cicéron* (Paris 1936) 70ff. Cicero also compares Latin etymology with Greek in *Div.* 1.1 *itaque ut alia nos melius multa quam Graeci, sic huic praestantissimae rei* [sc. divination] *nomen nostri a divis, Graeci ut Plato interpretatur a furore duxerunt* (i.e. μαντική, *Phaedrus* 244c.). Cf. also the etymologies of *senatus* (§19), *occatio* (§51), and *viator* (§56).

XIV 46 tempestivis ... conviviis Those which began early so as to last longer: cf. *Att.* 9.1.3; 9.13.6; *Arch.* 13; *Mur.* 13; Curt. 8.1.22; Sen. *De ira* 2.28.6; etc.

nec cum aequalibus solum Cf. Plut. *Cato* 25 (probably recalling this passage, cf. Introd. p. 19 n. 50) οὐ τοῖς καθ᾽ ἡλικίαν μόνοις ἡδὺς ὢν συγγενέσθαι καὶ ποθεινός, ἀλλὰ καὶ τοῖς νέοις; and cf. above, §26.

habeoque senectuti magnam gratiam Cf. §42 and note.

sermonis aviditatem Plato, *Rep.* I, 328d ὡς εὖ ἴσθι ὅτι ἐμοιγε, ὅσον αἱ ἄλλαι αἱ κατὰ τὸ σῶμα ἡδοναὶ ἀπομαραίνονται, τοσοῦτον αὔξονται αἱ περὶ τοὺς λόγους ἐπιθυμίαι τε καὶ ἡδοναί (Cephalus speaking: cf. on §§7–8 above). This Platonic passage is also reproduced by Anaximenes of Lampsacus, fr. 26 Müller = Stob. 4.50c.91; cf. P. Wendland, *Anaximenes von Lampsakos* (Berlin 1905), 13; also Clem. Alex. *Strom.* 3.3.18.4; Theodoret, *Therapeutice* 12.1023, Migne, *PG* 83, 1136. Cf. also Plut. *An seni* 786a; fr. 34, p. 165, 16 Bernardakis.

aviditatem This translates ἐπιθυμίαι: other Latin words for 'desire' tend to be pejorative.

sustulit Cicero misses or decides to omit the exact force of ἀπομαραίνονται, 'wither away'; to say that old age has 'removed' the desire for food and drink seems somewhat of an exaggeration, and does not perhaps fit this context very well.

ne omnino ... videar On these loosely connected final clauses cf. below, §§52, 55, 56, 59; H.–Sz. p. 642.

bellum indixisse Cf. *De or.* 2.155 *philosophiae bellum indixeris*; Hor. *Sat.* 1.5.8.

cuius est fortasse quidam naturalis modus This recalls the Peripatetic doctrine of the mean, though the context is loose and not particularly philosophical; cf. *Acad. pr.* 2.135 *in omni permotione naturalem volebant esse quendam modum* (sc. the Peripatetics and Academics).

magisteria Presidencies at banquets. For *magister* used of the symposiarch, cf. Gell. 15.2.4; Macr. *Sat.* 2.8.5; Apul. *Apol.* 98; Porphyrio on Hor. *Od* 1.4.18 glosses *regna vini* as *magisteria convivarum*; and cf. Plut. *Qu. conv.* 1.4.1, τὴν νενομισμένην ἐπιστασίαν. Reid refers to the appointment of *magistri cenarum* in the *sodalitates* (cf. above, pp. 193–4; Mommsen, *De* *collegiis* 108 and appendix); this official was appointed for a period of time, not for a single occasion like the Greek symposiarch, and his duties were to organise and preside at club dinners. As regards the actual dinner, there would probably be little difference between a *magister cenarum* and a symposiarch; though Reid rightly points out that the former, as a Roman institution, would fit better with the phrase *a maioribus instituta.* Cf. P.–W. 4, 612ff.; 14, 399ff.; A. D. Nock, *Essays on Religion and the Ancient World* (Oxford 1972) 1, 409ff.

a summo Sc. *lecto.* The couches were arranged from left to right (from the point of view of those dining), *summus, medius* and *imus,* on three sides of the table: cf. Blümner, *Privataltertümer* 388; Marquardt–Mau, *Privatleben* 303–6. Wine was handed round from 'top' to 'bottom', i.e. from left to right, ἐπὶ δέξια (the opposite of our custom); when turns were taken to speak this also proceeded from left to right, as in Plato, *Symp.* 213e–214a. Cf. Plaut. *Asin.* 891, *da, puer, a summo; Persa* 771; Lucil. fr. 222 M. The MSS all read *a summo magistro;* the deletion of *magistro* is due to Lambinus, and is clearly correct. *summus magister* would only make sense if there were more than one *magister* at a time; and the *magister* did not necessarily or usually sit on the *summus lectus.* Lambinus adds *cum Turnebus mihi suffragetur, Advers. lib. 13 cap. 6, ubi testatur se in libro antiquissimo hanc vocem 'magistro' non repperisse.* It would be interesting to know more about this MS, but it is unlikely that we ever shall.

in poculo 'over the wine', ἐπὶ τῇ κύλικι (Plato, *Symp.* 214a, etc.); cf. *Phil.* 2.63 *in poculis;* J. Vendryes, *Rev. Phil.,* 3ᵉ série, 15 (1941) 5–10.

sicut in Symposio Xenophontis est Xen. *Symp.* 2.26 ἦν δὲ ἡμῖν οἱ παῖδες μικραῖς κύλιξι πυκνὰ ἐπιψεκάζωσιν. The point of this in the original is that Socrates had just used a comparison with plants that require to be watered gently; ἐπιψεκάζειν is literally 'to sprinkle (water) on'. Cicero however omits the wider context, with the result that the metaphor in *rorantia* becomes rather obscure. No doubt *rorare* was the best available Latin equivalent of Xenophon's word (cf. *CGL* 3, 169, 5 *rorat:* ψεκάζει, δροσίζει; cf. 3, 244, 54; 2, 175, 19). There seems however to be no other instance of *rorare* in the context of watering plants, and the reader would have to recall the passage of Xenophon in order to understand this part of the metaphor. Further, Cicero transfers the idea of 'sprinkling' from the servants to the cups (*pocula rorantia*): this if anything increases the obscurity of the reference. (There seems to me to be no warrant for trying, on the basis of this apparent change on Cicero's part, to identify a precise type of cup, as did H. Herter, *Athena* 73–4 (1972–3) 687ff.; Cicero's *sicut in Symposio Xenophontis est* counteracts any impression that he had something different in mind from Xenophon, who merely says that the cups are too be small; and Athen. 11.784d ἐκ βομβυλιοῦ κατὰ μικρὸν στάζοντος, quoted by Herter and edd. as parallel to *pocula rorantia,* is not quite the same: 'dripping' is not the same as 'sprinkling'.) *rorare* is apparently used of Ganymede pouring wine in Manil. 5.487 *rorantis iuvenis* (though cf. Q. Cic. fr. 1, 13 Morel), while Cicero's phrase is picked up twice by Macrob. *Sat.* 5.17.7 and 7.9.1. On the Xenophon passage, see G. J. Woldinga's commentary (Hilversum 1938) p. 263, and Breitenbach, P.-W. 9A 2, 1877–8. The verb *rorare* is not elsewhere used by Cicero.

refrigeratio aestate Roman country houses were often built with some parts facing towards the sun for winter use, and others positioned to provide shade in summer; dining-rooms were often oriented in this way; see Vitr. 6.4; Varro, *RR* 1.13.7; *LL* 8.29; Hor. *Od.* 2.15.16 with Nisbet–Hubbard; Stat. *Silv.* 1.2.156–7; Colum. 1.6.2; Cic. Q. *fr.* 3.1.2; Pliny, *Ep.* 5.6.15; Juv. 7.183; Blümner, *Privataltertümer* 45; 79; Marquardt, *Privatleben* 249 n. 7. It is possible that Cicero is anachronistic in ascribing these relatively luxurious items of architecture to Cato's generation, though this need not be assumed. Cf. also below, §§57–8. The word *refrigeratio* occurs first in this passage, then (of the weather) in Vitruvius, then Colum. 11.1.16, Pliny the Elder and in late Latin.

etiam Editors interpret this as 'even in the Sabine country' (where such *convivia* would not be expected, as the Sabines were noted for plain living). This may be correct, though part of the point of these *convivia* is their simplicity. It seems more likely that *etiam* simply means 'too', and contrasts with the dinners of the *sodalitates* just mentioned, which presumably took place at Rome. A third possibility is that *etiam* is equivalent to *etiamnunc*, with reference to Cato's age.

in Sabinis This is regular for 'in the Sabine country', there being no separate name for the region itself; cf. *De rep.* 3.40; Nep. *Cato* 1.1; Varro, *RR* 3.1.6; *LL* 5.32; Hor. *Od.* 3.4.21–2; Livy 1.45.3; etc. Sometimes *Tusci, Lucani* etc. are used in the same way, despite the existence of the names *Etruria, Lucania.*

conviviumque vicinorum Cf. Plut. *Cato* 21 ποιούμενος ἑστιάσεις φίλων καὶ συναρχόντων; ibid. 25 ἦν δὲ καὶ τὸ δεῖπνον ἐν ἀγρῷ δαψιλέστερον· ἐκάλει γὰρ ἑκάστοτε τῶν ἀγρογειτόνων καὶ περιχώρων τοὺς συνήθεις καὶ συνδιῆγεν ἱλαρῶς, etc. It is difficult to suppose that Plutarch was not recalling Cicero when he wrote that passage; it is therefore not safe to take Plutarch as independently confirming Cicero's picture of Cato (cf. Introd. p. 19 n. 50). The tradition of Cato's enjoyment of *convivia*, however, also occurs elsewhere: Hor. *Od.* 3.21.11 *narratur et prisci Catonis | saepe mero caluisse virtus*; Sen. *Tranq.* 17.4; Quint. *Inst.* 6.3.105. The Ciceronian picture contrasts somewhat with Cato's own *Carmen de moribus*, p. 83 Jordan: *si quis sese ad convivia applicabat, grassator vocabatur*, although this need not be taken to imply disapproval of *convivia* in all circumstances. Wuilleumier notes that Cato in the *De agricultura* (156) gives a recipe for those who wish to eat and drink freely without ill effects, though the relevance of this to Cato's own habits is perhaps disputable. Nevertheless, we may take it that Cicero was following a traditional, if romanticised, view of Cato, and not merely projecting his own ideas on dining out, though no doubt that was unavoidable to some extent (cf. A. P. McKinlay, *CJ* 22 (1926–7) 525ff.). On *convivia* in the country, cf. also Hor. *Sat.* 2.6.

compleo Though *complere* can take a genitive as well as an ablative (*TLL* 3, 2091ff.), the word order invites the reader to take *vicinorum* more closely with *convivium* than with *compleo*: 'I make up a party of neighbours' rather than 'I fill a party with neighbours'. (It does not, of course, mean that Cato fills the last place in parties given by his neighbours. Cf. Lund, *Bidrag* 11.)

ad multam noctem A common phrase for 'late into the night': *De rep.* 6.10; *Att.* 13.9.1; etc.

quam maxime possumus To be taken with *vario*; the conversation is as varied as possible. It would not fit the tone of the passage so well for Cato to say that he stayed up as late as possible.

47 titillatio This abstract noun occurs in classical Latin only here, in *ND* 1.113, and in Sen. *Ep.* 92.7. The verb *titillare* occurs first in Lucr. 2.429; Cic. *Fin.* 1.39; *ND* 1.113; *Tusc.* 3.47; *Off.* 2.63; Hor. *Sat.* 2.3.179; Sen. *Ep.* 99.27; 113.21; *Vit. beat.* 5.4; then in Christian Latin. Lucretius and Cicero use the words as equivalents of the Greek γαργαλίζειν, γαργαλισμός: the verb occurs in Plato (*Symp.* 189a, *Philebus* 46d and 47a) and Aristotle (*NE* 1150b) but was used particularly by the Epicureans in contexts of physical pleasure (cf. *Fin.* loc. cit. *Epicuri hoc verbum est* and Reid ad loc.; Epicurus frr. 412–14, pp. 89; 280; 356 Usener; for the equivalence cf. *Corp. Gloss. Lat.* 2, 261, 4 and 41; 3, 132, 58; 5, 249, 14–15; 5,158, 8; F. Peters, diss. Münster 1926, p. 12.).

desideratur Not *desideratio* (α): the latter is found nowhere else apart from Vitruvius (*TLL* 5, 1, 697); the contrast between *est* and *desideratur* is quite natural, while *desideratio* would form a strained antithesis with *titillatio*; and rhythmical considerations are clearly in favour of *desideratur*.

nihil autem est molestum Strictly speaking it is not the thing but its absence that is *molestum*: the idiom is sometimes labelled *res pro defectu rei* (cf. W. Rennie on Ar. *Ach.* 615). Cf. §54 below *e filio*.

bene Sophocles For *bene* in anecdotes cf. Arist. *Rhet.* 1380b εὖ Φιλοκράτης εἰπόντος τινός ... ἔφη. The anecdote is from Plato, *Rep.* 1, 329b; Cicero inserts it here, having left it out above (§7) when adapting the rest of that Platonic passage: ... καὶ δὴ καὶ Σοφοκλεῖ ποτὲ τῷ ποιητῇ παρεγενόμην ἐρωτωμένῳ ὑπό τινος, "Πῶς," ἔφη, "ὦ Σοφόκλεις, ἔχεις πρὸς τἀφροδίσια; ἔτι οἷός τε εἶ γυναικὶ συγγίγνεσθαι;" καὶ ὅς, "Εὐφήμει," ἔφη, "ὦ ἄνθρωπε· ἀσμενέστατα μέντοι αὐτὸ ἀπέφυγον, ὥσπερ λυττῶντά τινα καὶ ἄγριον δεσπότην ἀποφυγών." Again we see that Cicero slightly alters Plato's mode of expression, for the sake of decorum: the explicit question ἔτι οἷός τε εἶ...; is left out. The anecdote reappears three times in Plutarch: *An seni* 788e, ὁ γὰρ Σοφοκλῆς ἄσμενος ἔφη τὰ ἀφροδίσια γεγηρακὼς ἀποπεφευγέναι καθάπερ ἄγριον καὶ λυσσῶντα δεσπότην; *Cup. Div.* 525a; *Non posse suaviter* 1094e; cf. also Juncus, pp. 1026–7 W.–H.; Philostr. *Vit. Apoll.* 1.13; Clem. Alex. *Strom.* 3.3.18.5; Theodoret, *Therapeutice* 12.1023, Migne, *PG* 83, 1136; Athen. 12.510b; Val. Max. 4.3 ext. 2; Clem. Alex. *Paed.* 2.10.95.1; and note on §7 above.

On Sophocles in general, and his susceptibility when younger, cf. Cic. *Off.* 1.144; Plut. *Pericles* 8; *Vit. dec. orat.* 838f; Ion of Chios, Ἐπιδημίαι fr. 8 von Blumenthal (=Athen. 13.603e ff.); Schmid–Stählin 1.2, 321. On the decline of sexual desire in old age, cf. Eur. *Aeolus* fr. 23 N.², ἀλλ' ἢ τὸ γῆρας τὴν Κύπριν χαίρειν ἐᾷ, | ἥ τ' Ἀφροδίτη τοῖς γέρουσιν ἄχθεται (Plut. *An seni* 786a; *Qu. Rom.* 285b; *Non posse suav.* 1094f; cf. Plato, *Symp.* 195b); Hor. *Od.* 2.11.6–7; Juv. 10.204ff.; *Anth. Pal.* 11.29–30; 12.240 (contrast Palladas, ibid. 10.56.15); Ptol. *Apotelesmatica* 4.10.12.

adfecto aetate Cf. *De or.* 3.68; *Catil.* 2.20; *adfecta aetas* also occurs, as in *De or.* 1.200; *TLL* 1, 1206, cf. 1208.

libenter vero This reading has the edge stemmatically over *ego vero* (*libenter*), and better represents the Greek ἀσμενέστατα μέντοι.

agresti ἄγριος, 'wild' or 'savage'; *agrestis* in Cicero's time is stronger and more pejorative than *rusticus*, which may often be neutral in tone; cf. *Rosc. Am.* 75 *vita haec rustica quam tu agrestem vocas*. However, *agrestis* is neutral in *Att.* 2.16.4; Lucr. 5.1398; and more frequently later, Virg. *Georg.* 2.493, etc. See *TLL* 1, 1418–19.

profugi The prefix *pro-* imports the notion of success in escaping; ἀποφεύγειν in Greek.

non caret is qui non desiderat This is a philosophical argument used also, more fully, by Cicero in *Tusc.* 1.87–90, esp. 88 *carere igitur hoc significat, egere eo quod habere velis; inest enim velle in carendo, nisi cum sic tamquam in febri dicitur* [sc. when one says that someone *febri caret*], *alia quadam notione verbi; dicitur enim alio modo etiam carere, cum aliquid non habeas et non habere te sentias, etiamsi id facile patiare.* This shows that Cicero was quite clear on the difference between the stronger meaning of *carere* ('lack' or 'miss') and the weaker ('not to have'). *caret* in this sentence therefore means 'to lack' (in the strict sense), and the whole passage should be translated as follows: 'For those who desire such things, perhaps it is annoying and unpleasant to lack them; but for those who have had their fill of them, to lack them is pleasanter than to have them – though of course one who does not miss them cannot be said to lack them; so it is this "not-missing" which I mean to say is more pleasant.' Translators fail to understand the emphasis of the last sentence; all it really means is 'I should have said *non desiderare* rather than *carere.*' Cf. also Sen. *Ep.* 78.11 *Desideria ipsa moriuntur; non est autem acerbum carere eo quod cupere desieris*; Diogenes of Oenoanda fr. 58, II, 7–10 Chilton, and N.F. 121; Lucr. 3.900–1; *contra*, Plato. *Gorg.* 492e. This argument may have some distant relation to Aristotle's discussions of στέρησις, *Categ.* 12a26ff.; *Metaph.* 4.22.1022b22ff.; the argument in *Tusc.* 1 is nearer to Aristotle.

hoc non desiderare This is the reading of the archetype and should be retained; cf. *Fin.* 2.18 *hoc non dolere*; *De or.* 2.24 *hoc ipsum nihil agere*; etc.; Hofmann, *Umgangssprache* 161; Draeger, *Historische Syntax* 1, 305; K.–S. 1, 666. This use of *hoc* with the infinitive is the nearest Latin can get to the Greek article + infinitive.

For the idea that the absence of pleasure, or of the desire for it, may itself be pleasant, cf. Antisthenes ap. Diog. Laert. 6.71 αὐτὴ τῆς ἡδονῆς ἡ καταφρόνησις ἡδυτάτη; Sen. *Ep.* 12.5 *aut hoc ipsum succedit in locum voluptatum, nullis egere*; ibid. 90.34; cf. §§7 and 44.

48 bona aetas Youth: cf. Varro, *RR* 2.6.2; Sen. *Contr.* 2.6.11; Sen. *Ep.* 47.12; 76.1; Nonius p. 2 (quoting this passage); *TLL* 1,1127. Nonius pp. 1–2 quotes also a number of examples of *mala aetas* meaning old age: Accius, *Amphitryo* fr. 85; Turpil. *Philopater* fr. 175; Pacuv. *Periboea* fr. 277; Afranius, *Vopiscus* fr. 378.

ut diximus Slightly puzzling as Cicero has not said exactly this before; the reference is presumably a general one to the last few sections, in which he has certainly implied that the pleasures of youth are not of any great value.

Turpione Ambivio L. Ambivius Turpio was the most famous actor of Cato's time: cf. the prologues of Terence's *Heautontimorumenos* and *Hecyra*, spoken by him; Tac. *Dial.* 20; Symmachus, *Ep.* 1.31.3; 10.2; Schanz–Hosius 1, 106. Again Cicero draws his comparisons from the stage (see note on §5 above); here however there is no more than a simple illustration of a single point, and it is inappropriate to classify this together with the more extensive theatrical imagery of §§5, 64, 70 and 85; there is no striking parallel to this in the Greek popular philosophical tradition, and it is an entirely Roman example.

in prima cavea The phrase is here equivalent to *in prima parte caveae*: the *cavea*, in Cato's time and for some time afterwards, meant the whole auditorium, not a part of it; cf. *Lael.* 24 *qui clamores tota cavea!*; *TLL* 3, 629; Cicero is not here being anachronistic in the use of the word *cavea*, nor does he imply anything about the form of the theatre itself which is anachronistic for Cato's time. At the dramatic date of the dialogue, the theatre would normally have been a temporary wooden stage and enclosure; an attempt to erect a permanent theatre was frustrated officially in 154 B.C. ([Livy], *Per.* 48); cf. P.–W. 5A 2, 1412ff. (Editors for some reason say that

Cicero's wording must refer to the stone theatre of Cicero's own time: I can see no reason to suppose this at all.)

propter Adverbially = 'near': the usage is not uncommon in Cicero (*ND* 2.120; *Inv.* 2.14; *Rosc. Am.* 64; *Leg. Manil.* 13 and 16; *Verr. II* 4.107), but becomes rare after Cicero's time, and may have had a slightly old-fashioned air then (cf. Introd. p. 22); for earlier occurrences cf. Cato, *Agr.* 151; Ter. *Ad.* 576; Lucr. 2.417; etc.

spectans PHD²PaRQ is no doubt correct: *aspectare* means 'to ogle' and is not appropriate here. The theatrical image is still in Cicero's mind: cf. *spectat* above. The corruption was more or less inevitable given the proximity of *eas*.

49 At illi quanti est Previous editions all read *at illa quanti sunt* (following α). *illa* is taken as looking forward to *secum esse secumque ut dicitur vivere*; but the emphatic anticipation is strange. *illi* β seems preferable to *illa* (disregarding *sunt* for a moment); it would refer back to *senectus*, making a desirable connection with the previous paragraph. As for *sunt*, it seems a little surprising in any case to have a plural verb with *secum esse secumque ut dicitur vivere*, which, though formally referring to two things, is most naturally taken as one unit (particularly considering Cicero's general preference for the singular with a compound subject: on this, see on §56). This might have been bearable as long as *illa* was retained, though still strange; but if *illa* is replaced by *illi*, the plural can hardly be tolerated, and the change to *est*, suggested to me by Professor Brink, seems both easy and inevitable.

cupiditatum Cf. Sen. *Ep.* 12.5 *quam dulce est cupiditates fatigasse ac reliquisse!*; Favorinus fr. 15 Barigazzi; Plut. *An seni* 788e.

secum esse Cf. *Tusc.* 1.75 *nam quid aliud agimus, cum a voluptate, id est a corpore, cum a re familiari, quae est ministra et famula corporis, cum a re publica, cum a negotio omni sevocamus animum, quid, inquam, tum agimus nisi animum ad se ipsum advocamus, secum esse cogimus maximeque a corpore abducimus?*; *Tusc.* 1.44; Sen. *Ep.* 58.32 *iucundum est secum esse quam diutissime* (in the context of old age); ibid. 2.1 *secum morari*; cf. 9.13; 104.7; *Tranq.* 14.2; 17.3; *De otio* 1; Pers. 4.52 *tecum habita*; Diog. Laert. 6.6 (on Antisthenes) ἐρωτηθεὶς τί αὐτῷ περιγέγονεν ἐκ φιλοσοφίας, ἔφη τὸ δύνασθαι ἑαυτῷ ὁμιλεῖν; and a remark of Cato's own (only known in Greek), Plut. *Apophth. Rom.* 198f (Cato no. 19), μάλιστα δὲ ἐνόμιζε δεῖν ἕκαστον ἑαυτὸν αἰδεῖσθαι· μηδένα γὰρ ἑαυτοῦ μηδέποτε χωρὶς εἶναι. 'Living with oneself' is no doubt a semi-proverbial expression (hence *ut dicitur*: Otto, *Sprichwörter* 377); *animum* makes the context here somewhat more philosophical in tone than usual. The passage of the *Tusculans* quoted above, which also talks of *animum secum esse*, is at least partly based on Plato, *Phaedo* 65–6, and the phrase may to some extent be supposed to recall Plato's τὴν ψυχὴν αὐτὴν καθ' αὐτὴν γίγνεσθαι, at least in that passage. Here it is not so obvious; it is quite likely that Cicero was echoing (consciously or not) what he had himself recently written in the *Tusculans*, but it is difficult to think that he intended a direct link with Plato. (J. Mähly, *N. Schw. Mus.* 6 (1866) 243ff. suspected *animum*, but the *Tusc.* parallel seems to confirm it despite the difference of context.)

pabulum studi Cf. *Acad. pr.* 2.127; *Tusc.* 5.66; *Att.* 4.10.1. For the recommendation of intellectual pursuits for old age, cf. Prop. 3.5.23ff.; Sen. *Brev. vit.* 19.1.

mori videbamus in studio This, the reading of MRSZ recc., is the only MS reading that makes grammatical sense, and is generally accepted by more recent editors: it is explained by comparison with Hor. *Epist.* 1.7.85 *immoritur studiis et amore senescit habendi*; the phrase *mori in studio* or *immori studio* (neither phrase seems to occur outside these two passages) is taken to mean to work oneself to death in one's enthusiasm, the expression being metaphorical and picturesque (and perhaps colloquial, like its English equivalent); cf. A. Kornitzer, *BPW* 25 (1905) 512. Simbeck, *De Cic. Catone Maiore* 20, compares passages where the circumstances of someone's death are in question, taking *mori* literally, but this can hardly be right: it is no commendation of astronomy as a study of old age, but merely a curiosity, to say that Galus actually died in the course of practising it; and such an interpretation in any case strains the Latin (*mori videbamus* would have to imply a long-drawn-out death, if naturally taken, and *in studio dimetiendi* means 'in enthusiasm for measuring', not 'in the process of measuring'). There have been numerous attempts to emend this passage. The simplest is that of Madvig, Reid and others, who delete *mori* and read *videbamus in studio*; Graevius and Orelli transposed *paene* so as to follow and qualify *mori*; *morari* for *mori* (from the twelfth-century MS Va) is possible; other substitutes for *mori* have been suggested, e.g. *vivere* (I. Müller, Moore), *immori* (Mähly and Havet, deleting *in*, the latter also changing the word order), *exerceri* or *oblectari* or *versari* (Vaucher, the first adopted by Bennett); Anz (Progr. Quedlinburg 1890, pp. 15–16) proposed *vidi amore miro* (deleting *in studio*), and I have wondered about *miro videbamus in studio*; but the text here accepted can be explained so as to give reasonable sense, and any choice of emendation would be somewhat arbitrary, as none of these suggestions seems notably better than any other. However, it only just escapes the obelus. (For *videbamus* in a similar context cf. *De or.* 3.87.)

dimetiendi paene caeli atque terrae *paene* is necessary here, and means more or less the same as *quasi*: astronomers do not literally measure out the sky. Cf. Quint. *Inst.* 12.11.10 *mundum ipsum paene dimetiri*. On *dimetiri* cf. Virg. *Georg.* 1.231; Manil. 2.483; Tac. *Ann.* 6.21; Lact. *Inst.* 2.9.7.

C. Galum C. Sulpicius Galus (on the form of the name, see *Der Kleine Pauly* s.v. Sulpicius, col. 424) was one of the first Romans to study

astronomy scientifically; he predicted the eclipse before the battle of
Pydna in 168 (cf. below, *defectiones solis et lunae*). Cf. *De rep.* 1.21–3; 30; *Brut.*
78; 90; *Lael.* 9; 21; 101; *Off.* 1.19; Livy 44.37; Val. Max. 8.10.1; Pliny, *NH*
2.53.

  defectiones solis et lunae Cf. *ND* 2.153; *Div.* 1.112; Sen. *NQ* 7.3.3.

50 Quid in levioribus studiis Cf. *De or.* 1.212 *ut iam ad leviora artium
studia veniam, si musicus, si grammaticus, si poeta quaeratur*; *Brut.* 3 *in leviorum
artium studio.* Poetry was considered *levior* in comparison with the political
arts, oratory and legal science; also, this passage would suggest, in
comparison with natural science.

  acutis *acuta studia* is an odd and probably unparalleled phrase: a poet
can be *acutus*, and so perhaps can a poem, but it is difficult to see precisely
what is meant by calling the study of poetry itself 'acute' or 'sharp'.
Perhaps 'subtle' will serve as a translation. Cf. *TLL* 1, 465.

  quam gaudebat ... quam Pseudolo? For the form of this sentence,
in which the interrogative *quid* extends its influence over a following
exclamation, cf. §22 above and note; translate 'what about the enjoyment
Naevius had from his *Punic War*?', etc. For Naevius cf. §20 above;
Schanz–Hosius I, 53–4; Cicero mentions the *Bellum Punicum* with approval
in *Brut.* 75. It is not implied here that the *BP* was itself written in Naevius'
old age: W. Beare, *CR* 63 (1949) 48.

  Plautus The dating of Plautus' plays would have been known to Cicero
from the *didascaliae*. The *Pseudolus* has a surviving *didascalia* which dates it
to 191, seven years before Cicero's date (184 B.C., *Brut.* 60) for Plautus'
death; for the *Truculentus*, this passage is our only evidence, and does not
provide a certain date. On Plautus' dates see Beare, *Roman Stage* 37–8;
Schanz–Hosius I, 68 and 73; P. Venini, *Athenaeum* 38 (1960) 98ff., points
out that the traditional date for Plautus' birth, 254, is a round figure based
on nothing more than extrapolation from Cicero's evidence (i.e. 184+70).

  Livium The date of Livius Andronicus' death is placed between 207
and 200 B.C. (cf. Beare, *Roman Stage* 16–17, and *CQ* 34 (1940) 11ff.); Cato
therefore may well have seen him.

  sex annis ... natus sum 240 B.C. This chronology was found by
Cicero *in antiquis commentariis*, and supported by Atticus' chronological
work: see *Brut.* 72–3 and Douglas ad loc.; in that passage he mentions and
rejects the clearly mistaken chronology of Accius. Cf. *Tusc.* 1.3; Livy
36.36.4; Gell. 17.21.42 (who mentions Varro, *De poetis* as an authority: cf.
E. Fantham, *LCM* 6 (1981) 17); Cassiod. *Chron.* 128 M.; Eutropius 3.1–2;
G. Hendrickson, *AJP* 19 (1898) 285; K. Allen, *AJP* 19 (1898) 437;
Wuilleumier, *Tarente* 683ff.; H. B. Mattingly, *CQ* 7 (1957) 159; H. J.
Mette, *Lustrum* 9 (1964) 45; Schanz–Hosius I, 47–8.

  docuisset This translates Greek διδάσκειν: cf. *Att.* 6.1.18 (in a Greek context). More often the purer Latin *fabulam dare* is used. *TLL* 5, 1, 1729.

Centone C. Claudius Ap. f. Cento, son of Ap. Claudius Caecus (cf. §37 above).

Tuditanoque M. Sempronius C. f. Tuditanus. For -*que* joining names of consuls – far less common than *et* – cf. *Fam.* 1.8.9; 13.29.4; *Att.* 5.21.9; 5.21.11; also in Velleius and Tacitus. *TLL* 4, 568–9.

Publi Licini Crassi Cf. §§27 and 61: he was Pontifex Maximus from 212 to 183, and well known for his knowledge of pontifical law (Livy 30.1.5).

huius Publi Scipionis A touch of vivid dialogue technique: P. Scipio Nasica Corculum was indeed made Pontifex Maximus at some time in 150 (cf. *ND* 3.5; *Lael.* 101; *De or.* 3.134; *Brut.* 79; 213; *Tusc.* 1.18; P.–W. 4, 1497ff.). He was a cousin of Scipio Aemilianus; also an opponent of Cato, but that is no reason why Cato should not be made to refer to him in the context of his legal studies (cf. Kienast, *Cato* 130). For *huius* cf. *Off.* 3.66 *huius nostri Catonis*; ibid. 1.121; etc.

atque ... vidimus Cf. *Tusc.* 4.71 *atque horum omnium libidinosos esse amores videmus*, similarly summing up a list of examples. The example of Cethegus then follows as a sort of afterthought, *in dicendo* contrasting with *his studiis*.

studiis flagrantes Cf. *Mur.* 65; *De or.* 1.14; etc.

Marcum ... Cethegum The consul of 204 (cf. §10 above: P.–W. 4, 1279–80). He was well known in his own time for eloquence, though his speeches were not preserved.

Suadae medullam Cf. *Brutus* 57ff., where Cicero quotes Ennius (303–8 V.², Skutsch) at greater length, and explains the metaphor: Πειθώ *quam vocant Graeci, cuius effector est orator, hanc Suadam appellavit Ennius, ut quam deam in Pericli labris scripsit Eupolis sessitavisse, huius hic medullam nostrum oratorem fuisse dixerit.* The quotation appears also in Gell. 12.2.3 (quoting Seneca), Quint. *Inst.* 2.15.4 and Mart. Cap. 9.1.10. The name *Suada* for Πειθώ appears to have been Ennius' invention (this seems to be implied in the *Brutus*): apart from the Ennian passage and other authors' comments on it, the name occurs only in Serv. *Aen.* 1.720 and *CGL* 3,291,50 (perhaps: the MS reads *Suado*). It was presumably formed on the model of such names of deities as *Flora*, cf. Skutsch ad loc.; S. Timpanaro, *Stud. Urb.* 31 (1957) 175–6. It is possible that Ennius used the archaic genitive *Suadai* (anomalously scanned as a spondee), which Skutsch prints; this form may be reflected in the variants of the MSS of Cicero, both here (see apparatus) and in the *Brutus* (*suadat* F¹OGB, *suadai* F²: cf. Douglas's edition). The metaphor in *medulla* is striking and unparalleled in Latin; Skutsch quotes Theocr. 28.18 and Diogenianus 6.51 (Leutsch–Schneidewin 1, 277) as Greek parallels. Cf. further Douglas on the *Brutus* passage; Vahlen, *Ges. Phil. Schr.* II, 237–8; *TLL* 8, 602 s.v. *medulla*.

etiam senem *etiam* should be given its full force, 'even as an old man': Cethegus' enthusiasm for oratory in old age was somewhat more surprising than the other examples mentioned, as oratory required considerable energy (cf. §28).

quae sunt igitur Cf. §64.

scortorum A prosaic and pejorative word, but not in itself vulgar.

atque haec [quidem studia doctrinae quae] quidem ... crescunt This passage is usually printed according to the α text. *Atque haec quidem studia doctrinae* is interpreted as summarising the preceding sentences, as in a passage like *Fin.* 3.5 *atque haec quidem de rerum nominibus.* This text may be objected to on three grounds: (i) the repetition of *quidem* seems very clumsy; (ii) this is not the place for such a summary, which should have the function of dismissing one subject and proceeding to the next one, while in this passage we have not yet reached the end of the section; (iii) the sense of the passage requires that it should be the *pleasures* of intellectual activity that grow continually with age; to say that *studia doctrinae* increase with age is not so appropriate. The problem was seen at least in part by A. Manutius, who omitted *quae quidem*: this disposes of (i) and (ii) but still leaves (iii). Examining the MSS, we find that the β group has *idem* (*idē*) instead of the first *quidem*: this looks suspiciously like a mistake (or not even a mistake) for *id est*. If, therefore, we remove *id est studia doctrinae* as an interpolated gloss on *haec*, and consequentially also remove *quae* (which it would have been necessary to add after the interpolation, in order that the resulting text should make sense), we obtain *atque haec quidem prudentibus et bene institutis pariter cum aetate crescunt*, which makes perfect sense and logic. *haec*, 'these things', would have a general reference to the pleasures of learning just described; while *atque ... quidem* now has its (very common) meaning of 'and indeed', 'and in fact', adding a new point rather than summing up what precedes.

illud Solonis Cf. §26.

XV 51 There follows an extended digression on the pleasures of agriculture; the connection with old age is reverted to a number of times (§§54; 55; 56; 57; 60). It was not unnatural to make Cato the Elder thus speak in praise of an occupation which he clearly held in high esteem (cf. Introd. p. 21; Plut. *Cato* 21; 24–5); but the content and style is Cicero's own. Cato's own praises of agriculture in the *De Agricultura* are either strictly utilitarian, or concerned with the good effects of agriculture on character. Cicero however emphasises the pleasures of being in the country and looking at well-cultivated land, as part of his main argument that there are some pleasures that old men can still enjoy; and he inserts descriptions of the purposive growth of plants that echo the Stoic ideas of the second book of *De natura deorum* (cf. also *Tusc.* 5.37), and have similarities also with

Greek scientific writings such as Theophrastus and the Hippocratic corpus (cf. commentary below). The whole effect is quite unlike Cato, despite the occasional down-to-earth Catonian touch, and reminds the reader far more of Virgil's *Georgics* (which however cannot be shown to be directly influenced by Cicero).

On the literary side, an important influence is that of Xenophon: the *Oeconomicus* is quoted at some length in one place (§59, where see note), and recalled in others, and there is also a possible reminiscence of the *Cyropaedia* (§51). The praise of agriculture as a pleasant as well as praiseworthy occupation seems to occur first in Xenophon (*Oecon.* 5.1ff.; 6.11; cf. P.–W. 9A 2, 1847ff.). The resemblance of Cicero's account of agriculture here to his own *De natura deorum*, and also the apparent similarity with a passage of Posidonius summarised by Seneca, *Ep.* 90.21, has prompted speculation about possible Stoic sources, including Posidonius himself (cf. especially Kröger, *De Cic. in C. M. auctoribus*). However, the Senecan passage proves little: the tone and method of description may be similar, but the point of view is different, as Posidonius is writing primarily in praise of the inventors of agricultural techniques as part of the Stoic exaltation of the 'wise man'; Cicero, however, is concerned with the pleasure to be derived from contemplation of the natural processes of growth and of well-cultivated land. Nevertheless, we need not doubt that praise of agriculture was well established in the philosophical tradition. Cicero himself refers to the topic in *Off.* 1.151 (referring back to the *Cato*), *Rosc. Am.* 48 (echoing Xenophon, *Oecon.* 6.11 and 15.4), *De or.* 2.22–3; 1.249. Later, Musonius Rufus commends agriculture from a Stoic point of view (11 Τίς ὁ φιλοσόφῳ προσήκων πόρος), and praise of country life becomes a standard theme of the rhetoricians (cf. Quint. *Inst.* 2.4.24; Max. Tyr. 24; Themist. 30; Liban. *Progymn.* 10; etc.).

Cicero also draws on what must presumably have been first-hand knowledge of the country and its pursuits: he is precisely correct in his use of agricultural terminology (cf. K. D. White, *Roman Farming* 38; 464 n. 75). His own attitude to country life has been somewhat debated. He was perhaps less of a country gentleman than some of his contemporaries; he was never rich enough to acquire large estates, and he shows little interest in the subject in his letters (cf. E. Rawson, *Cicero* 6). Nevertheless, there seems to be no reason to doubt that he took genuine pleasure in retreating into the country, even if only as a temporary relaxation (e.g. *Att.* 1.5.7); the present passage is certainly a studied piece of rhetorical composition, but the pleasures it describes are – and probably were for Cicero – quite real ones. The passage has tended to be criticised as factitious (Rawson; M. Finley, *G. & R.* 28 (1981) 156ff.), but it is so only in the sense that all rhetorical writing is; and it must be remembered that the *Cato* is a dialogue. Cicero does not in any case recommend a full-time devotion to agriculture; the old Roman heroes whom he mentions were statesmen and generals as well as farmers, and his sentimental evocation of their simple life was surely not meant as a prescription for himself or his contemporaries. Cicero does not explicitly make the assertion that agriculture leads to moral improvement; to have done so would not have fitted the wider context of his argument, though certainly he implies that the character of M.' Curius and others was enhanced by their simple way of life. Nor is it really relevant to point out that the life of a farmer is not as idyllic as Cicero makes it: he was writing for the Roman senatorial class, for whom ownership of country estates was a traditional source of both pleasure and prestige. (On Cicero's attitude to the country, cf. A. Foucher, *Bull. Assoc. Budé*, 4e série (1955) no. 3, pp. 32–49; J. C. Davies, *G. & R.* 18, (1971) 152ff.)

Little can be said for certain about Cicero's influence on later treatments of the theme of agriculture. Syme, *Sallust* 45, has speculated that Sallust's aside in the preface to the *Catiline*, dismissing agriculture and hunting as *servilia officia* and a waste of time, may have been prompted by reaction against Cicero's praise of farming; yet Sallust was not talking about old age, and the remark was made in the specific context of Sallust's choice of occupation after retiring from politics while still in middle life. The praises of agriculture in Varro and the Augustan poets seem to owe little or nothing to Cicero in detail; the most that can be said is that there was some general similarity of attitude, and one may note the susceptibility of this type of writing to parody, as in Hor. *Epod.* 2 or Ov. *Rem. am.* 169ff. (the latter appears to have one or two verbal reminiscences of Cicero). That Columella read Cicero appears from some passages (cf. on §56). The canon of examples of rustic heroes may have gained some impetus from Cicero, though it may have been in the rhetorical tradition before (cf. Introd. pp. 9–10 on *exempla*).

For praise of agriculture in general, cf. H. Kier, *De laudibus vitae rusticae* (diss. Marburg 1933), esp. p. 62 on the connection with old age, though Cicero has little to do with the idealised rustics of Hellenistic poetry, which are the main precedents; R. Vischer, *Das einfache Leben* (Göttingen 1965); André, *L'Otium* 28–33; A. Novara, *Mél. Wuilleumier* (Paris 1980) 261ff. on the *Cato*; Courtney's commentary on Juvenal, p. 24.

ad sapientis vitam The idea that the life of a farmer is near to the perfect 'wise man's' life seems peculiar to Cicero, and would seem paradoxical to most Greek philosophers, though it might be in character for Cato, with his distrust of philosophy, to say something of this sort. Musonius, later on, says that agriculture is a suitable occupation for a philosopher (fr. 11), but only because it leaves one plenty of time for philosophy (cf. Xen. *Oecon.* 6.9). Nearer to Cicero's point of view is Themist. 20.236d (on his father): Γεωργίας μὲν δὴ καὶ σφόδρα ἦν ἐπαινέτης τε καὶ ἐραστής, καὶ τῷ φιλοσόφῳ ῥᾳστώνην ἐπὶ τοῖς πόνοις μόνην πρέπουσαν ἀπέφηνε τὴν γεωργίαν, καὶ μάλιστα γηρῶντι ἤδη καὶ ἐκλυομένῳ ὑπὸ χρόνου τῷ σώματι γυμνασίαν τε ἱκανὴν εἶναι καὶ γέμουσαν τῆς σώφρονος ἡδονῆς (the passage continues with the example of Laertes: cf. §54 below). Posidonius (Sen. *Ep.* 90.21: see above) thought agriculture was developed by *sapientes*, but we do not know that he thought it a way of life particularly suited to the wise man.

habent enim rationem cum terra 'They [the farmers] have an account in earth's bank.' The banking metaphor is continued all through, with a slightly paradoxical point in view of the fact that it is Cato who is speaking, since he disapproved of actual moneylending (*Agr.* preface, and anecdote in Cic. *Off.* 2.89).

impendium Paullus Manutius's conjecture for MSS *imperium*, supported independently by J. Luňák, *Philologus* 52 (1893–4) 347. Even if it could be proved beyond doubt that *imperium* could be used in financial contexts, with the meaning 'order' or 'instructions', it would still give inferior sense (in this context) to *impendium*, 'outlay', which fits well with *quod accepit*: the earth never refuses to accept an investment, nor does it ever give back what it has (thus) received without interest. Other uses of *recusare* with *impendium* (*Att.* 6.1.4, quoted by Luňák) or *impensam* (Livy 44.25.10) admittedly do not quite support this interpretation, as they appear to mean 'to refuse to *make* an investment or outlay'; but *recusare* in general constantly has to have its meaning 'refuse to give' or 'refuse to take' determined by the context, and there would be no trouble in understanding it here. The financial use of *imperium* is apparently supported by Varro, *LL* 5.181; Cic. *Verr.* II 4.111; *TLL* 7, 1, 583; M. Lavarenne, *Latomus* 18 (1959) 612. There are quite a number of passages, all later than Cicero, in which *imperium* and its cognates are used metaphorically in *agricultural* contexts, of the farmer exerting his will over the fields and crops: Virg. *Georg.* 1.99; 2.369–40; Ov. *Fast.* 2.296 (see Bömer ad loc.); Sen. *Tranq.* 17.5; Pliny, *NH* 17.178; Tac. *Germ.* 26; Colum. 3.3.6; etc.; *TLL* 7, 1, 576 and 589. As the financial metaphor is absent from these passages, they seem to have little bearing on the question whether *imperium* is correct here; it is certainly not necessary in order to explain the later passages to suppose that Cicero wrote *imperium*, as the image of the farmer commanding the crops is in any case natural and poetic.

usura Cicero seems to have derived this metaphor from Xenophon, *Cyr.* 8.3.38: μάλα μικρὸν γῄδιον, οὐ μέντοι πονηρόν γε ἀλλὰ πάντων δικαιότατον· ὅ τι γὰρ λάβοι σπέρμα καλῶς καὶ δικαίως ἀπεδίδου αὐτό τε καὶ τόκον οὐδέν τι πολύν· ἤδη δέ ποτε ὑπὸ γενναιότητος καὶ διπλάσια ἀπέδωκεν ὧν ἔλαβεν; cf. Ov. *Rem. am.* 173 + *Obrue versata Cerealia semina terra,| quae tibi cum multo fenore reddat ager*; Tibull. 2.6.22; Manil. 5.273;

Pliny, *Paneg.* 32.3; Ov. *Fast.* 1.694; *Pont.* 1.5.26; Ambrose, *Hex.* 3.8.34; *De excessu fratris* 1.45; 2.56; Quint. *Inst.* 12.10.25 and Austin's note; Men. *Dysc.* 604. In general, for the idea of 'give and take' in agriculture, cf. *Off.* 1.48; Virgil's *iustissima tellus* (*Georg.* 2.460); Tibull. 1.7.31; Colum. 4.3.5; Pliny, *NH* 18.162; Men. fr. 96 K. and com. incert. p. 424 K. (=Stob. 4.15b.25 and 28); Philemon frr. 88 and 105 K.; Xen. *Oecon.* 5.8 and 20.14; Musonius 11, p. 57 H.; Liban. *Progymn.* 10.4.

fenore *fenus* was connected by ancient etymologists with *fetus* and the idea of fertility, cf. τόκος in Greek: Varro, *LL* fr. 57 Goetz–Schoell ap. Gell. 16.12.1; Paul. Fest. p. 86 M; Non. p. 53; 439 M; hence its use in agricultural contexts is particularly appropriate.

vis ac natura For the phrase, cf. *Fin.* 1.50; *Off.* 1.101; also Cato, *Agr.* 157. Xen. *Oecon.* 16.4 talks of the δύναμις and φύσις of various regions of the earth.

quae cum gremio mollito ...vallo aristarum Descriptions of the growth of plants from seed occur in various places. Clearly based on this passage is Ambrose, *Hex.* 3.8.34ff.: *granum ... sparsum cohibet occatio ac velut materno terra gremio fovet et comprimit. Inde cum se granum illud resolverit, herbam germinat grata ipsa iam species herbescentis viriditatis ... paulatimque adolescit ut faenum, culmoque pubescens erigitur et adsurgit. Ast ubi se geniculata iam spica sustulerit, vaginae quaedam futurae frugi parantur ... succedunt quidam ordines spicae mirabili arte formati ... vaginis quibusdam ipse culmus includitur ... tum supra ipsam spicam vallum struitur aristarum, ut quasi quadam in arce praetendat, ne avium minorum morsibus spica laedatur.* An almost equally close paraphrase is found in Ambrose's *De excessu fratris* 2.55. Basil's *Hexahemeron* 5, cols. 100–1 Migne, has a similar though not obviously related description. In earlier Greek writing there is Theophr. *Hist. Plant.* 8: again the thing described is the same, and terms and expressions may be correlated (cf. commentary below), though there is no great similarity in the passage seen as a whole. A nearer parallel is to be found in the Hippocratic Περὶ φύσιος παιδίου, 22, which is in places very reminiscent of Cicero (the context is the comparison of the growth of the seed in the earth with that of the human child in the womb): τό τε γὰρ σπέρμα ὁκόταν καταβληθῇ εἰς τὴν γῆν, ἰκμάδος πίμπλαται ἀπ' αὐτῆς· ἔχει γὰρ ἐν αὐτῇ ἡ γῆ ἰκμάδα παντοίην ὥστε τρέφειν τὰ φυόμενα ... ἰκμάδος δὲ πλησθὲν τὸ σπέρμα φυσᾶται καὶ οἰδέει ... συστραφεῖσα δὲ ἡ δύναμις ὑπὸ τοῦ πνεύματος καὶ τῆς ἰκμάδος, φύλλα γενομένη ῥήγνυσι τὸ σπέρμα, καὶ ἀνατέλλει ἔξω πρῶτον τὰ φύλλα ..., etc. Such descriptions, with their varied applicability to proving philosophical or moral points, may well have existed in more purely philosophical writing in the Hellenistic period, and it is difficult to be certain about Cicero's antecedents: it is not very likely that Theophrastus or the Hippocratic corpus was his immediate source, at any rate.

gremio The phrase *gremium terrae* is very often used, even when there is no further reference to the personification of Mother Earth (see *TLL* 6, 2, 2321–23); for more vivid personification, see Lucr. 1.250–1 and Bailey ad loc.; Virg. *Georg.* 2.325–6: Plato, *Menex.* 238a. Cf. also *ND* 2.83 *terra ... gravidata seminibus omnia pariat et fundat ex sese, stirpes amplexa alat et augeat.*

subacto *subigere* is the normal agricultural term for making the ground suitable for cultivation: cf. §59 *humum subactam*; *Hortens.* fr. 91 Grilli; Cato, *Agr.* 161; Virg. *Georg.* 1.125; 2.50; Lucr. 5.211; Sen. *Ep.* 86.5. Here, however, the conjunction with *gremio* is striking, and suggests a more definite image of the earth as female, and subdued to the farmer's will. Cf. also Plut. *Numa* 14.4 τὴν γῆς ἐξημέρωσιν.

occatio The word means 'harrowing', really derived from *occa* (Ernout–Meillet 695). The derivation from *occaecare*, 'to hide from sight', is of course quite fanciful, as is that from *occidere* which is found in Varro (*RR* 1.31.1) and Verrius ap. Fest. p. 181 M. (Festus also quotes Cicero's etymology). Cicero's etymology is also found in Sept. Ser. fr. 3(2) Morel (ap. Non. p. 61 M.); schol. Pers. 6.26; Isid. *Etym.* 17.2.4; and a fragment of a glossary published by R. Ellis, *ALL* 2 (1885) 321; cf. Ambrose, *De excessu fratris* 2.55. On *occatio* in general, cf. Pliny, *NH* 18.180–1; 17.165; Colum. 11.2.60; 2.4.2; 2.4.5; Pallad. *RR* 6.4; 9.1; Serv. *Georg.* 1.21; *TLL* 9, 2, 342.

vapore *vapor* means 'steam'; it is sometimes rendered as 'heat', as by Bailey on Lucr. 2.150 (cf. D. West, *CQ* 25 (1975) 99), but probably the use of *vapor* in such passages is to be explained by supposing that the Romans imagined steam where we do not. Certainly in the present passage there ought to be no difficulty: steam rises from moist earth on hot days, and it was well recognised by the ancients that both heat and moisture were necessary for the growth and germination of seeds. *vapor* in Cicero occurs only here, in *ND* 2.27 and ibid. 2.118. Cf. Ambrose, *De excessu fratris* 2.55 *semina vapore et compressu terrae soluta.*

compressu This is the only occurrence of the noun *compressus* in Cicero; elsewhere it generally means 'embrace', in human contexts, and something of that sense may be preserved here: the metaphor of *gremio* is still running in the mind. *TLL* 3, 2157.

diffundit *diffundere* is not uncommonly used of the growth of plants, with the sense of 'cause to branch outwards'; it is used with reference to seeds by Sen. *Ep.* 38.2 *vires suas explicat et ex minimo in maximos auctus diffunditur*; here it could be taken to mean 'causes to grow outwards' with reference to the first appearance of the shoot (described in the next part of the sentence) and of the roots. It might be thought that, in an apparently step-by-step description of the germination of the seed, 'growing outwards' is inappropriate for the very first stage, and something like 'causes to swell' would fit better; this however would be an odd sense for *diffundere*. In view of the slight obscurity of *diffundit* I have considered adopting *diffindit*, a conjecture which is to be found in older editions; 'splits' would clearly fit the context well and unambiguously, as Gulielmius comments: *norunt qui in re rustica non plane hospites sunt, granum primo diffindi, tum culmen eicere.* However, even though MS authority counts for very little in this sort of instance, it seems that sense can be extracted from the transmitted reading, and I have left it as it is, though without complete confidence. (Similar confusions occur in the MSS of Colum. 2.9.13 and Ser. Samm. 327. Ambrose's paraphrase of this passage unfortunately does not help much with the textual problem: *cum se granum illud resolverit* and *semina vapore et compressu terrae soluta* may argue for his having found *diffindit* in Cicero, or merely for his having failed to understand *diffundit* and consequently substituted his own conception of what was involved in germination.)

elicit There is a similar problem with this word. *elicit* would mean 'draw out', which gives a reasonable sense: the earth draws out the shoot from the seed. Lambinus suggested *eicit*, however, for which there is something to be said. At first glance it seems odd to say that the earth 'throws out' the shoot from the seed. It is common enough to use *eicere* of the earth itself producing plants etc., and *ex eo* may serve simply to define the origin of the shoot more exactly. There is also a use of *eicere* in contexts of human childbirth, where the midwife *eicit* the baby from the mother (Soranus 17.19 and 25); this appears promising, since it carries on the metaphor of human generation. However, it is not clear whether the use in Soranus reflects earlier Latin usage; and the metaphor would be different from the one that seems implicit in the rest of the passage, where the earth is the mother, not the midwife. Again I follow the MSS, though without total confidence.

(In Colum. 3.10.11 the words *diffudit* and *elicuit* occur close together in a context which, though somewhat different from the present one, could possibly have been influenced by it unconsciously, if, as it seems, Columella knew the *Cato*: *[natura] . . . mox ramis diffudit quasi bracchiis, tum pampinos elicuit velut palmas.* On the other hand, the words are there used in their ordinary and expected senses, and do not help to dispel the apparent obscurity of the present passage, at least as regards the use of *diffundere.* It would be unwise to base any textual argument on this apparent similarity.)

herbescentem ... viriditatem *viriditas* means greenness or freshness, but here clearly the green shoot of the corn, as is shown by the following relative clause. There seems to be no other example in Latin of such a concrete use of the word; the usage seems to be modelled on Greek χλόη, which originally means 'greenness' but is used for the corn-shoot (cf. Theophr. *Hist. Plant.* 8.2.4; also *CGL* 3, 265, 28 *viriditas*: χλόη καὶ φλόη, ibid. 2, 477, 30 χλόη). *herbescens*, growing into green stalks or leaves (the only Ciceronian occurrence of *herbescere*); cf. Aug. *Civ. Dei* 5.7; *TLL* 6, 2–3,

2624. For *herba* used of young corn before the formation of the ear, cf. *Lael.* 68; Virg. *Georg.* 1.134; Ov. *Met.* 5.482; *Fasti* 4.645; *Her.* 17.263.

nixa fibris stirpium Supported by the root fibres: cf. *Tusc.* 3.13 *radicum fibras*; *ND* 2.120.

culmoque erecta geniculato 'raised up on a knotted stalk'. For these various terms, see Varro, *RR* 1.48; Pliny, *NH* 18.14; 18.52ff.; Theophr. *Hist. Plant.* 8.2 and 8.34 for the Greek equivalents, καυλὸς γονατώδης = *culmus geniculatus*, κάλυξ = *vagina*. For *geniculatus* see *TLL* 6, 2–3, 1809.

vaginis includitur This stage is called κύησις in Greek (Theophr. ibid.).

frugem spici ordine exstructam 'grain piled up in the regular formation of the ear'. The flow of the sentence does not encourage a break after *spici*, which is necessary if Reid and Wuilleumier are right in taking it with *frugem* rather than *ordine*; and *spici ordine*, 'the regular formation of (i.e. consisting of) the ear', has more point than 'the grain of the ear', which is virtually tautological. *exstructam* seems better than *structam* for the rhythm; Cicero generally avoids final short vowels before consonant-groups in the clausula, and *ordine structam* seems too much like a heroic clausula for comfort. It might be argued that *structam*, 'built up, arranged', is better than *exstructam*, 'piled up', but the latter word could well be used to emphasise the richness of the growth. Not too much importance should be attached to the MSS in this question: it is difficult to make sense of the distribution of readings in the MSS, which does not correspond with the stemma. It was virtually inevitable that the two words should have been confused, in so far as the preceding word ends with an *-e*: cf. §48 above, *spectans/aspectans*. Regarding the ending of this word, *(ex)structam* is preferable to *(ex)structo*; the sentence is held together better if the participle agrees with *frugem*. (It is possible that Manil. 5.285–6 *et quia dispositis habitatur spica per artem | frugibus, ac structo similis componitur ordo* has some connection with this passage; but it is not close enough to affect the choice of reading.)

contra avium minorum morsus Cf. Ambrose, *Hex.* 3.8.34 (quoted p. 209); Isid. *Etym.* 17.3.17 *Haec* [sc. *arista*] *super spicam vallo instructa munimen praetendit, ne avium minorum morsibus spica suis fructibus exuatur*; Basil, *Hex.* 5, col. 101 Migne ἐν θήκῃ δὲ τὸν κόκκον ἀποθεμένη [sc. ἡ φύσις] ὡς μὴ εὐδιάρπαστον εἶναι τοῖς σπερμολόγοις.

vallo Cf. in addition to Ambrose and Isidore, quoted above, Manil. 5.271.

52 ortus literally 'rising', hence 'growth': this word is not common in botanical contexts but occurs in Lucr. 1.212; 5.211; Pliny, *NH* 22.95; *TLL* 9, 2, 1068.

incrementa The word occurs a number of times in Pliny and the agricultural writers in the sense of 'growth' or 'increase': *TLL* 7, 1, 1045; cf. T. Frank, *CPhil* 11 (1916) 334ff. Presumably *ortus* refers to the earlier stages of growth, *incrementa* to later stages.

meae senectutis *meae* is emphatic, as shown by its position.

requietem Priscian confirms Cicero's use of this form, actually quoting this passage (*GLK* II, p. 242; cf. Charisius, ibid. I, pp. 110 and 142). Among the MSS, PMA²KPaRS¹Z and some later MSS have *requietem*. The form is otherwise transmitted in Cic. *Fin.* 5.54; *Leg.* 2.2; 2.29; the genitive *requietis* in *Att.* 1.18.1; Sall. *Hist.* fr. 41; the ablative *requiete* in Cic. poet. fr. 3.77. The forms with stem in *-t-* do not occur after Cicero, until their use (presumably as an archaising revival) by Tertullian. *Requiem* is transmitted in Cicero, *Arch.* 13; *De or.* 1.224; 1.254; in Lucceius ap. Cic. *Fam.* 5.14.1, the MSS waver between the two forms; from Sallust onwards *requiem* is found consistently. The genitive *requiei* is given as an alternative form by Prisc. *Nom. Pron.* 18, but is not found in classical Latin. *requie* for the abl. occurs in Sall. *Hist.* fr. 142 (quoted by Priscian), App. Verg. *Culex* 92 (?), and in Ovid, Livy, Lucan and later authors. There is no evidence for the usage of these forms before Cicero, but the disappearance of the (etymologically correct) forms with stem in *-t-* after his time suggests that they may have seemed slightly old-fashioned to his contemporaries. Cf. Neue–Wagener I³, 848–9. *requies* should here be translated as 'relaxation' rather than 'rest'.

oblectamentumque Cf. §55; *Verr. II* 4.134; *Parad.* 5.38; *TLL* 9, 2, 80; J. Perrot, *Les Dérivés latins en -men et -mentum* (Paris 1961) 68; 269.

quae generantur e terra There is, as editors point out, no Ciceronian Latin equivalent for 'plants', φυτά, and a periphrasis of this sort is generally used. *stirpes* sometimes approaches the meaning, though it does not cover all varieties of plants; *plantae* means 'saplings', and does not come to mean 'plants' in general until late antiquity. Cf. Madvig on *Fin.* 4.13; Krebs–Schmalz, *Antibarbarus* s.v. *planta*, II, 307.

acini vinaceo *acinus* is the grape, *vinaceus* or *vinaceum* the grape-pip: for the latter as a noun cf. Cato, *Agr.* 7.2; Colum. 3.1.5; 6.3.4; 11.2.69 (*vinaceus* is also an adjective, 'of the vine'). Cf. Ambrose, *Hex.* 3.49 *quis non miretur ex acini vinaceo vitem usque in arboris summum cacumen prorumpere?*; Theophilus of Antioch, *Ad Autolycum* 11.14 τίς γὰρ κατανοήσας οὐ θαυμάσει ἐκ συκῆς κεγχραμίδος γίνεσθαι συκῆν, ἢ τῶν λοιπῶν σπερμάτων ἐλαχίστων φύειν παμμεγέθη δένδρα;

malleoli 'mallet-shoots', vine-cuttings shaped like a hammer at the point of cutting (Pliny, *NH* 17.156; 169; 203; Colum. 3.6ff.; 3.3.12; 3.14.12; Isid. *Etym.* 17.5.5; *TLL* 8, 191).

plantae Cuttings from off the trunk of a tree (Varro, *RR* 1.55; Virg. *Georg.* 2.23).

sarmenta Cuttings from a branch, especially of the vine (cf. below); *De* *or.* 2.88; Cato, *Agr.* 48; Varro, *RR* 1.31.2; Pliny, *NH* 12.118; 22.150; Colum. 3.10.1; 4.24.7; 5.5.16; etc.; *sarmenta* derives from an old verb *sarpere* 'to prune', cf. Paul. Fest. p. 323 M.

viviradices (The obvious correction for MSS *vites radices* or *vitis radices.*) Rooted cuttings: Cato, *Agr.* 33; Varro, *RR* 1.35.1; Pliny, *NH* 17.170, 204; Colum. 3.3.12; many other passages in Colum. and Pliny, *NH*; Festus p. 298 M.; White, *Roman Farming* 244.

propagines Runners (Virg. *Georg.* 2.26; Hor. *Epod.* 2.9; Pliny, *NH* 17.204; 212; Colum. *Arb.* 7.2; Isid. *Etym.* 17.5.33). On the propagation of plants in general, and vines especially, see Cato, *Agr.* 33; Varro, *RR* 1.39; Colum. *RR* 3.

quae natura caduca est Cf. Xen. *Oecon.* 19.18–19: αὐτίκα ἄμπελος ἀναβαίνουσα μὲν ἐπὶ τὰ δένδρα, ὅταν ἔχῃ τι πλησίον δένδρον, διδάσκει ἱστάναι αὐτήν· περιπετανν ύουσα δὲ τὰ οἴναρα, ὅταν ἔτι αὐτῇ ἁπαλοὶ οἱ βότρυες ὦσι, διδάσκει σκιάζειν τὰ ἡλιούμενα ταύτην τὴν ὥραν· ὅταν δὲ καιρὸς ᾖ ὑπὸ τοῦ ἡλίου ἤδη γλυκαίνεσθαι τὰς σταφυλάς, φυλλορροοῦσα διδάσκει ἑαυτὴν ψιλοῦν καὶ πεπαίνειν τὴν ὀπώραν; Cic. *ND* 2.120; Ambrose, *Hex.* 3.49 *quia natura flexibilis et caduca est, quasi bracchiis quibusdam ita claviculis quidquid comprehenderit stringit hisque se erigit et attollit*; Isid. *Etym.* 17.5.2.

claviculis suis quasi manibus Cf. *ND* 2.120 *claviculis adminicula tamquam manibus adprehendunt atque ita se erigunt ut animantes*; Pliny, *NH* 23.5; Colum. 4.6.2; *claviculae,* 'tendrils'.

erratico Used only here by Cicero; the word is used particularly of plants, cf. Cato, *Agr.* 157 (of cabbages); Pliny, *NH* 20.92; etc.; cf. White, *Roman Farming* 237 'The natural habit of the vine, if left to itself, is to grow prolifically in all directions from the stock, running to wood or leaf or both.'

coercet Used as a technical term: Cato, *Agr.* 139; Colum. 3.1.9; 3.21.7; 4.1.5; Quint. *Inst.* 8.3.10; 9.4.5; *TLL* 3, 1434.

ars agricolarum Cf. *Fin.* 5.39 *ars agricolarum quae circumcidat, amputet, erigat, extollat, adminiculet*; *De or.* 2.88. On vine-dressing, cf. Virg. *Georg.* 2.367ff.; 400ff.; Cato, *Agr.* 32–3; Varro, *RR* 1.8.

53   eis I.e. *sarmentis.*

articulos Joints: cf. Pliny, *NH* 16.88; 18.159; Colum. 2.11.9. For the whole passage cf. Ambrose, *Hex.* 3.52 *quae primum veris tepefacta temperie gemmare perhibetur, deinde ex ipsis sarmentorum articulis fructum emittere, de quibus oriens uva formatur paulatimque augescens immaturi partus retinet acerbitatem, nec potest nisi matura iam et cocta dulcescere. Vestitur interea viridantibus pampinis vinea, quibus et adversum frigus omnemque iniuriam non exiguo munitur subsidio, et a solis ardore defenditur. Quid autem eo vel spectaculo gratius vel fructu est dulcius?*; Isid. *Etym.* 17.5.10.

quae gemma dicitur Cicero thought that the original meaning of *gemma*, 'bud', was the metaphorical one: cf. *Orat.* 81; *De or.* 3.155. In fact the meaning 'precious stone', though commoner, is secondary: Ernout–Meillet 413.

defendit ardores *defendere* here = ἀμύνειν, 'keep off'; cf. Cato, *Agr.* 48.2; Cic. *Off.* 3.74; Hor. *Od.* 1.17.3; *Sat.* 1.3.14; Prop. 1.20.11; Stat. *Silv.* 3.1.70; *TLL* 5, 1, 294. Note that Ambrose (quoted above, and *De excessu fratris* 2.55) replaces this with the more usual use of *defendere*, 'to defend'. Cf. also Virg. *Georg.* 1.448 *defendet pampinus uva*; Isid. *Orig.* 17.5.10.

cum fructu laetius, tum aspectu pulchrius For the conjunction of aesthetic pleasure with fruitfulness and utility, cf. *Rosc. Am.* 43 *tot praedia tam pulchra, tam fructuosa*; *De or.* 1.249 *vel fructus causa vel delectationis*; Varro, *RR* 1.2.12; 1.2.10; 1.4.2; in the context of wealth in general, *Off.* 1.25.

ut ante dixi Sc. §51 above, *non fructus modo sed etiam ipsius terrae vis ac natura delectat*. We would have to place the parenthesis differently in English: 'not only its usefulness but, as I said before, its cultivation and nature itself'.

capitum iugatio Vines were, and still are in Italy, grown on frames with a cross-piece (*iugum*) at the top: the process of making this is *iugatio*. See Varro, *RR* 1.82; Colum. 4.17; *TLL* 7, 2, 626; White, *Roman Farming* 232ff., where the various methods of growing vines are illustrated. Cf. Ambrose, *Hex.* 51 *quid ego adminiculorum ordines iugationisque describam gratiam?*

religatio *religare* is used of the tying up of plants, Pliny, *NH* 19.131; Colum. 2.18.5. The noun *religatio* apparently occurs only here in classical Latin.

quam dixi In §52 above.

aliorum amputatio Cf. Ambrose, ibid. *reciduntur alia sarmenta, alia propagantur*.

immissio This means 'allowing to grow freely', 'letting loose': the abstract noun occurs only here in classical Latin (*TLL* 7, 1, 466). Cf. the use of *immittere* in Varro, *RR* 1.31.1; Pliny, *NH* 16.141; Virg. *Georg.* 2.364. *immittere* in connection with plants can also have the quite different meaning 'to implant' (Virg. *Georg.* 2.80; Colum. *Arb.* 7).

irrigationes Cf. *Off.* 2.14; *ND* 2.152; Cato, *Agr.* 151; Varro, *RR* 1.35; White, *Roman Farming* 146ff.

repastinationes *repastinatio* is the digging over of a field or (especially) vineyard to increase fertility; the *pastinum*, from which it is named, was a two-pronged fork (Colum. 3.18). The abstract noun occurs only here and in Colum. 2.2.13, *Arb.* 1.5; 2.1, and in the glossaries; the verb however is common enough, cf. Cato, *orat.* fr. 128 Malcovati; Varro, *RR* 1.18; 1.37; Pliny, *NH* 13.84, etc.; Colum. 2.13, etc.; Fest. p. 281 M.; Isid. *Etym.*

20.14.8; K. D. White, *Agricultural Implements of the Roman World* (Cambridge 1967) 109ff.; Blümner, *Privataltertümer* 554.

54 stercorandi Cato mentions manure of various sorts frequently in the *De agricultura* (29; 36–7; 151; etc.; cf. next sentence); he seems to have been considered an authority on the subject, since Pliny (*NH* 18.174) quotes him on it. Cf. Xen. *Oecon.* 20.3; Theophr. *Hist. Plant.* 8.7.7; Varro, *RR* 1.2.21; 1.38; Pliny, *NH* 18.192; 17.50; Colum. 2.14; 4.8.3; Mart. Cap. 3.305; White, *Roman Farming* 125ff.; 238; P.–W. 5, 1756ff. and Blümner, *Privataltertümer* 556.

doctus Hesiodus Hesiod is *doctus* both as a poet and as a didactic writer; however, it is difficult not to think that the epithet is intended a little ironically here; Cato is surprised at his omission. For *doctus* as a common epithet of didactic writers, see *TLL* 5, 1, 1756–7; poets are also often *docti* (cf. *Tusc.* 4.71; Lucr. 2.600; Tibull. 1.4.61; Catull. 35.17; Hor. *Epist.* 2.1.56; etc.) both individually and generally; in a Roman, to be *doctus* implies Greek learning, while Greeks are called *docti* when in their own language they would be called σοφοί. Cf. Dio, *Eub.* 110 Ἡσίοδος σοφὸς ὤν.

Homerus There was controversy in Cicero's time regarding the date of Homer. Cicero here affirms the usual view, against both Varro (who thought that Homer and Hesiod were roughly contemporary) and Accius (who put forward arguments for the priority of Hesiod: see Gell. 3.11); cf. also Sen. *Ep.* 88.6. K. Allen, *AJP* 19 (1898) 437ff., compares this passage with the refutation of Accian chronology in §50 above, and sees in it no more than a piece of mild antiquarian polemic; but it does add something to the argument: Hesiod could have been defended for omitting all reference to manuring by theorising that manuring techniques were not developed in his time; but Cicero claims to have found a reference to them in Homer, which disproves the idea (cf. below, however).

saeclis The word must be so spelt, or at least pronounced, for the rhythm, *ante saeclīs fuī*.

Laertam This form of the accusative of *Laertes* occurs nowhere else, but it seems to be right for Cicero. The nominative *Laerta* appears in Sen. *Tro.* 709 and Hyg. *Fab.* 169; Ovid however has the accusative *Laerten* (*Her.* 1.113). Greek names of the first declension in -*es*, when used in Latin, are either kept as they are, with the Greek accusative in -*en*, or (in Cicero's time and earlier almost invariably, and sporadically later) turned into Latin first-decl. names in -*a*, which decline, naturally, like other nouns of that class. (Patronymics in -*ides* are usually retained unchanged; note however *Heraclidam*, Cic. *Flacc.* 45.) Cf. *Aeetam*, *Tusc.* 3.39; *Philoctetam*, *Q. fr.* 2.10.4; *Fin.* 5.32; *Tusc.* 2.19; 2.33; Neue–Wagener I³, 58–60. Housman, *Papers* II, 833, states that the -*a*, -*am* declension is only used for 'servile or barbarous' names; this only applies to the Augustan poets, and certainly not to Cicero or the earlier poets. It is possible that the older Latinised forms were kept more regularly for the names of epic heroes, under the influence of early Latin epic and tragedy.

The Homeric passage is *Od.* 24.226ff.: τὸν δ' οἶον πατέρ' εὗρεν ἐϋκτιμένῃ ἐν ἀλωῇ, | λιστρεύοντα φυτόν ... πένθος ἀέξων, etc.

lenientem desiderium The phrase corresponds to nothing in our text of Homer, and may simply be inference on Cicero's part; but one is tempted to wonder whether Cicero read πένθος ἀλέξων instead of the puzzling ἀέξων of our text. (The difficulties of the passage have not escaped commentators on Homer: cf. D. Page, *The Homeric Odyssey* (Oxford 1955) 109.)

During his retirement due to Caesar's dictatorship, Cicero saw himself as living a Λαέρτου βίον, according to a lost letter quoted by Plutarch, *Cic.* 40.3. The example of Laertes occurs also in Pliny, *NH* 17.50; Plut. *An seni* 788b; Themist. 20. 237a; also, in a rather different context, in Teles pp. 34 and 52 H. and Aristo of Chios, fr. 350 von Arnim, cf. Appendix 2: this tells us nothing about the sources of the *Cato*.

stercorantem (*eum* refers to *agrum*.) Homer says λιστρεύοντα, which means digging round the plant with the λίστρον (= *rastrum*; cf. schol. vet. Odyss. ad loc., λιστρεύοντα· περιξύοντα καὶ περισκάπτοντα). However, the process of digging round the roots of vines (*ablaqueatio* in Latin) involved the addition of manure to fertilise the soil (cf. Cato, *Agr.* 5.8, etc.), and Cicero clearly thought that this was what Laertes was doing. Still, the reference to Homer does not help his argument very much, as there is no explicit reference to manure in the original (though Homer does mention it in *Od.* 17.296). See S. Boscherini, *Quad. Urb. Cult. Class.* 1969, no. 7, 36ff.; Helm, P.–W. 22, 145. (Pliny, *NH* 17.50, also says that Laertes was using fertiliser of some sort, *laetificans*: this may derive from Cicero.)

facit Cf. §3.

nec vero segetibus solum ... florum omnium varietate The arrangement of the different parts of agriculture in this sentence has been compared by E. de St-Denis, *REL* 16 (1938) 308ff. (followed by Wuilleumier in his edition) with the plan of the *Georgics*; compare also Varro's *De re rustica*, Quint. *Inst.* 1.12.7 *cur non idem suademus agricolis ne arva simul et vineta et oleas et arbustum colant, ne pratis et pecoribus et hortis et alvearibus avibusque accommodent curam?*, and the prayer to Mars in Cato, *Agr.* 141, *utique tu fruges frumenta vineta virgultaque grandire beneque evenire siris; pastores pecuaque salva servassis* ... The order is obviously ancient and natural: cf. also Genesis 1.11–12; 24–5; 29. I find it difficult to agree with de St-Denis that the plan of the *Georgics* was due to the influence of this sentence of Cicero.

217

laetae 'fruitful' or 'fertile': this meaning is apparently the original one (Ernout–Meillet 518; Palmer, *Latin Language* 69–70).

pecudum pastu Cf. Xen. *Oecon.* 5.3. A. Foucher, cited above on §51, comments that the perfunctory mention of pasturage in Cicero is more appropriate for Cicero's own time than for Cato's; Cato himself regarded pasturage as better than arable farming (*Off.* 2.89). But I doubt whether Cicero was thinking about that aspect of the matter; having described the cultivation of corn and vines at length, he could hardly write another section on pasturage without unbalancing the work; and the attractions of pasturage for the gentleman farmer of mature years are less obvious.

consitiones *consitio* occurs only here and in Colum. 3.16.3; 4.3.5 and several other passages of Columella, all with reference to the planting out of vines (cf. §52 above on modes of propagation): *TLL* 4, 473, 41ff.

insitiones Grafting (again, no doubt, with reference to vines): cf. Cato, *Agr.* 40; Virg. *Georg.* 2.73ff.; Hor. *Epod.* 2.14; Pliny, *NH* 15.14; Varro, *RR* 1.40.5; Colum. 3.9.6; *Arb.* 8.2; Ov. *Rem. am.* 195.

XVI 55 Possum Translate 'I could': cf. above, §24.

ignoscetis The future of polite request; the tense may be kept in translation, 'you will forgive me'.

provectus sum 'I have been carried away' or 'made to go on longer' by enthusiasm for farming; cf. *Fin.* 3.74 *sentio me esse longius provectum quam proposita ratio postularet.*

senectus est natura loquacior Cf. note on §31 above. This is a piece of self-conscious urbanity which suits a Ciceronian conversation and gives it an extra touch of realism – though one may doubt whether the real Cato would have apologised in this way (cf. Introd. pp. 20; 24).

ergo Resuming, like Greek οὖν, μὲν οὖν: 'so then'.

Manius Curius A favourite example of *continentia*: cf. §§15 and 43. It is a good guess that this anecdote came from Cato's own writings: this seems to be suggested by *De rep.* 3.40 (fr. ap. Non. pp. 66 and 522); Laelius is speaking: . . . *cuius etiam focum Cato ille noster, cum venerat ad se in Sabinos, ut ex ipso audiebamus, visere solebat; apud quem sedens ille Samnitium, quondam hostium, tum iam clientium suorum, dona repudiaverat.* (This shows that the Samnites were not bringing the gold as a bribe, but simply as a tribute to their *patronus*: the refusal of such a gift is an outstanding example of *continentia*, whereas that of a bribe would merely have been common morality.) Cf. Val. Max. 4.3.5 (ibid. 4.3.6 has a similar anecdote about Fabricius; cf. Gell. 1.14. quoting Hyginus, and Frontinus, *Strat.* 4.3.2); Pliny, *NH* 19.87; schol. Juv. 11.78f. (quoting this passage of Cicero); Plut. *Cato* 2.2 (possibly depending on Cicero: cf. Introd. p. 19 n. 50); *Apophth. Rom.* Curius 2; Athenaeus 10.419a (= Megacles, *FHG* 4, 443); Flor. 1.13.22; [Victor] *De vir. ill.* 33.7. Plutarch, Pliny and the *De vir. ill.* include the detail that

Curius was cooking himself a dinner of turnips when the Samnites arrived; Megacles ap. Athen. absurdly says that he never ate anything else. On Curius in general cf. *De rep.* 3.6, quoting the line of Ennius *quem nemo ferro potuit superare nec auro* ; *Parad.* 1.12, etc.; *Leg.* 2.3; *Mur.* 31; Hor. *Od.* 1.12.41; etc.; P.–W. 4, 1841ff.

triumphavisset Over the Sabines and Samnites in 290 and Pyrrhus in 275, according to the usual account.

56   tantus animus I.e. *ea magnitudo animi*, 'such a noble character': cf. above on §35. Note also that the Aristotelian μεγαλόψυχος, in *NE* 1124b, εὐεργετούμενος αἰσχύνεται. The argument here is the familiar one, already seen above in §7, etc., that it is one's character that determines the quality of one's old age.

senatores, id est senes See on §19.

Lucio Quinctio Cincinnato Traditionally dictator in 458 and 439; the anecdote about his being called from the plough is usually linked with the first dictatorship, while the sedition of Maelius was supposed to be the occasion of the second; Cicero's compression of the two may reflect variant traditions, and historians are sceptical about the second dictatorship in any case; see Livy 3.26.6–8 and 4.12, with Ogilvie's commentary; Cic. *Fin.* 2.12; *De rep.* 2.49; *Phil.* 2.114; *Mil.* 72; *Lael.* 28; 36; *Catil.* 1.3; Val. Max. 2.7.7; 4.4.7; etc.; Pers. 1.73–5; Colum. 1, praef. 13; Pliny, *NH* 18.20; Flor. 1.5.12; Dio Cass. fr. 23.1–2; Dion. Hal. 12.2.5; etc.; P.–W. 24, 1020ff. According to the traditional dating Cincinnatus would have been 61 and 458 and 80 in 439.

cuius dictatoris 'of whom as dictator' rather than 'of which dictator', so that the repetition of *dictatorem/dictatoris* is not otiose; contrast *cuius voluptatis* in §39.

regnum [appetentem] occupantem Editors here follow the α group of MSS, which reads *regnum appetentem occupatum*, and interpret 'caught him in the act of desiring to establish a tyranny and killed him', as if it had been *regnum appetentem occupavit atque interemit.* But the juxtaposition of the two participles is very awkward and un-Ciceronian, and *occupatum* does not make a great deal of sense. (Laughton, *Participle* 132 has difficulty with the passage, though he does not question the received text; he quotes various parallels for the two juxtaposed participles – all easier than this passage.) Now the pedigree Latin phrase for 'to establish a tyranny' is *regnum occupare* (*Lael.* 41; *De rep.* 2.49; *Off.* 3.90; cf. *Tusc.* 5.57; Cass. Hem. *Hist.* fr. 22; Val. Max. 3.24 *occupare imperium*). I have little doubt that β preserves the correct reading, *occupantem*, and that *appetentem* should be ejected as an interpolated gloss on that word. *regnum occupantem interemit* gives excellent sense, 'killed him as he was [in the process of] establishing a tyranny'.

219

arcessebantur The reading of β: α has *arcessebatur*. On Cicero's use of singular or plural verbs with compound subjects, see C. O. Brink, *PCPS* 28, 1982, 32; Lebreton, *Études* 1–24, esp. 17ff.; H. Anz, Progr. Quedlinburg 1884, 1–18 esp. 15–17. This is a rather special instance: in order to be exactly parallel, a passage would have to be one in which (a) the predicate precedes the subject; (b) the two parts of the subject are joined by *et . . . et*, not a single conjunction; (c) the second element of the subject is a plural noun; (d) the first element is a proper name; (e) both subjects are logically third person. In general, it is clear enough that Cicero has a preference for making the verb agree with the nearest element of the subject, viz. when the nearest element is singular, the verb is generally singular. Yet the plural appears to be commoner with a following subject than with a preceding one; with *et . . . et* than with simple *et*; when one element of the subject is plural than when both are singular; and when one or more elements of the subject are proper names. There are no exact parallels, as defined above, quoted by Lebreton or Anz from anywhere in Cicero; but the coincidence of all these factors, though none of them individually would argue for the plural, inclines me to think that the plural is at any rate more likely to be right here than in almost any other instance where there is doubt. Even so, the singular would be equally permissible; the choice of reading in this case is bound to be a somewhat subjective one; but an editor has to come down on one side or the other. (There is little good in arguing about the merits of MSS in a case of this sort, where the difference is of one letter between equally intelligible and grammatical forms.) The use of the plural in Colum. 1, praef. 18, which recalls this passage (cf. below) cannot be probative, since Colum. recasts the passage, though it could be thought to support the plural here.

viatores The official name for the messengers of Roman magistrates, as contrasted with the lictors who attended them personally. Cf. *Vat.* 22; Varro ap. Gell. 13.12.6; Livy 2.56.3; 3.56.5; etc.; Pliny, *NH* 18.21; Colum. 1, praef. 18 *a villis arcessebantur in senatum; ex quo qui eos evocabant, viatores nominati sunt*; Festus p. 508. It appears that the word is being derived here and in Columella from *villa*: quite implausibly (G. Schneider, *Z.f.d.Gymn.* 36 (1882) 432ff.; but cf. P. Schwenke, *Bursian* 35 (1883) 104). Cf. the etymologies of *senatus* (§20), *convivium* (§45) and *occatio* (§51). For the summoning of senators from the fields, cf. also on Atilius Serranus (*Rosc. Am.* 50; Virg. *Aen.* 6.844; Val. Max. 4.4.5; Pliny, *NH* 18.20); and Plut. *An seni* 788c αἱ πόλεις . . . πολλάκις ἐξ ἀγροῦ κατάγουσαι γέροντα μὴ δεόμενον μηδὲ βουλόμενον ἠνάγκασαν . . . εἰς ἀσφαλὲς καταστῆσαι τὰ πράγματα; Plutarch does not give the standard examples, but no doubt he was thinking of Cincinnatus and Serranus.

miserabilis Here, as usually, *miserabilis* preserves its full meaning 'capable of being pitied'; for a clear illustration of this see Ov. *Ibis* 115 *sisque miser semper nec sis miserabilis ulli.*

agri cultione *agri cultio* occurs only here and in *Verr. II* 3.226, then in late Latin: *TLL* 4,1317, cf. 1, 1426.

haud scio an nulla Not *ulla*; cf. Hand, *Tursellinus* 1, 314ff.; G. Lahmeyer, *Philologus* 20 (1864) 298ff.; K.–S. II, 521.

qua dixi This ablative is regular, cf. (in Cicero) *Acad. Pr.* 2.4; *Att.* 10.8.7; *Inv.* 2.152; Madvig on *Fin.* 1.29; (elsewhere) Plaut. *Cas.* 932; Ter. *Heaut.* 87; [Cic.] *Ad Her.* 1.11; *Bell. Afr.* 41; 69; Varro, *RR* 2.2.5; Hor. *Sat.* 1.6.15; etc. The misnamed 'attraction' of the relative is most plausibly traced back to an ellipse of the rest of the relative clause: e.g. in *Acad. pr.* 2.4 *qui esset ea memoria qua ante dixi*, we supply *eum esse* with *ante dixi*. Here it is a little more difficult to supply the rest of the sentence, but it can still be done: *qua dixi (nullam senectutem beatiorem esse posse).* But it does seem that this sort of construction became regular even outside those passages in which the rest of the relative clause can be easily supplied. Cf. H.–Sz. 566–7; R. Förster, *N. Jahrb. Kl. Phil.* Suppl. 27 (1900) 170ff.

saturitate The only occurrence of this word in Cicero; it occurs in Plaut. *Capt.* 109; 771; 865; 877; *Rud.* 758; then Sen. *Ep.* 18.10; 19.7; 119.14; Colum. 4.4; Pliny, *NH* 9.138, etc.; [Quint.] *Decl.* 252, p. 32, 5 Ritter; Suet. fr. 3 Reiff.; Apul. *Flor.* p. 82; and in Tertullian. Charisius (p. 106, 21 K.) volunteers the information *saturitas in cibo tantum dicitur, in ceteris vero satietas*, but that is not very appropriate to the present passage. One wonders whether Cicero preferred it to the commoner *satietas* (a) because it is less often pejorative: 'sufficiency' or 'abundance', rather than 'satiety', and (b) for a certain old-fashioned effect, judging from its occurrence in Plautus (cf. Introd. p. 22). But neither of these explanations is certain.

ad victum hominum, ad cultum etiam deorum Cf. Xen. *Oecon.* 5.2; 5.10; 15.4; Musonius p. 58 H.

cella vinaria Cf. Cato, *Agr.* 3.2 *patrem familiae villam rusticam bene aedificatam habere expedit, cellam oleariam, vinariam . . . et rei et virtuti et gloriae erit*; Varro, *RR* 1.13.7; Plaut. *Mil.* 857; Vitr. 1.4; Pliny, *NH* 14.89.

olearia Cf. Cato and Varro ibid.

penaria Cf. *penus, Penates*; Cato ap. Cic. *Verr. II* 2.5 (Sicily the *cella penaria* of Rome); Varro, *LL* 5.162.

porco haedo . . . The singular is used of the commodity rather than the animal itself: Löfstedt, *Synt.* I², 13; K.–S. I, 68; Nisbet–Hubbard on Hor. *Od.* 1.19.12.

iam For this connective use ('And then . . .' vel sim.: not Eng. 'now') see Hand, *Tursellinus* III, 145ff.

succidiam alteram *succidia* is a flitch (Isid. *Etym.* 20.2.24 *succidia, carnes in usum repositae, a succidendo dictae*; Varro, *LL* 5.110 *ab suibus caedendis*;

Ernout–Meillet 1008 support Varro's etymology). The word occurs in classical Latin only here, in Cato (*orat.* fr. 59 Malcovati[2], ap. Gell. 13.25.12, a metaphorical context, and *Orig.* fr. 39 ap. Varr. *RR* 2.4.11) and in Varro, *RR* 2.4.3. It was clearly a genuine rustic word, and may have carried some Catonian atmosphere for Cicero and his readers (cf. Introd. pp. 21–2). The apparently proverbial *succidia altera* is not attested elsewhere (Otto, *Sprichwörter* 334). M. E. Hirst, *CR* 24 (1910) 50, attempts to explain it with reference to App. Verg. *Moretum* 56ff., *non illi suspensa focum carnaria iuxta . . . ergo aliam molitur opem . . . hortus erat iunctus casulae*, etc. The most that one can say is that there may be some connection.

condītiora Cf. §10.

supervacaneis 'spare-time activities'; for *supervacaneus* = 'spare' cf. Cato, *Agr.* 12.

57　plura dicamus The reading of β: there is little to choose between this and *plura dicam* (α). *dicamus* gives some variety, and involves the audience attractively. The proximity of *praecidam* may be thought to argue for *dicam*, but it may merely explain why *dicamus* was corrupted.

retardat For *retardare ad faciendum aliquid* cf. *Sull.* 49; Caes. *BG* 7.26.2.

invitat atque allectat Cf. *Lael.* 99 *allectant et invitant*.

ubi enim potest . . . salubrius? Based on Xen. *Oecon.* 5.9 χειμάσαι δὲ πυρὶ ἀφθόνῳ καὶ θερμοῖς λουτροῖς ποῦ πλείων εὐμάρεια ἢ ἐν χώρῳ τῳ; ποῦ δὲ ἥδιον θερίσαι ὕδασί τε καὶ πνεύμασι καὶ σκιαῖς ἢ κατ' ἀγρόν; Cf. also §46 above and note; Hor. *Epist.* 1.15; Virg. *Georg.* 2.469ff. Cicero refers elsewhere to the relaxation the country provides, *De or.* 2.22–3; *Q. fr.* 3.1.3.

apricatione Cf. Pers. 5.179 *aprici . . . senes*; Juv. 11.203.

58　sibi habeant 'Let them keep': the subject is indefinite. For *sibi habere* in general cf. *Lael.* 18; *Att.* 7.11.1; for the long list with anaphora of *sibi*, *Flacc.* 104, *Sull.* 26; G. Monaco (in *Studi Classici in onore di Q. Cataudella* (Catania 1972) III, 21ff.) regards those two passages and the present one as directly imitating Plaut. *Curc.* 178 *sibi sua habeant regna reges, sibi divitias divites, sibi honores, sibi virtutes, sibi pugnas, sibi proelia*, but this is not certain. See further Munro on Lucr. 3.135; Duff on Juv. 3.188; Fordyce on Catull. 1.8; G. Landgraf, *ALL* 8 (1893) 45; *TLL* 6, 2399, 47; 2429, 21.

clavam A wooden club or stick, used for practice instead of a sword: cf. Veg. *Mil.* 1.11, 14; Juv. 6.247; *TLL* 3, 1297.

pilam Cf. *De or.* 3.58 *ad pilam se aut ad talos aut ad tesseras conferunt*; Ov. *Trist.* 2.485. In contrast to this passage, Pliny, *Ep.* 3.1.8 recommends the *pila* as an exercise for old men, and Trimalchio's ball-playing is well known (Petr. *Sat.* 27.2), though it is not altogether clear what view the reader is meant to take of it.

venationes The reading of DT: *aenationes* in BL[1]A[1] must be a corruption of *venationes* (*a* and *u* are often confused in this group of MSS); *nationes* P¹H could have arisen by corruption either from *natationes* or from *venationes*. The stemma does not compel a choice; but it seems more likely that the line of corruption was *venationes–aenationes–nationes–natationes* than *natationes–nationes–venationes–aenationes*; the latter would presuppose that a moderately ingenious conjecture (*venationes* for *nationes* – much less obvious than *natationes*) was made at a very early stage, and then re-corrupted into *aenationes*. Another marginal argument in favour of *venationes* is that *natatio* is not otherwise used by Cicero. From the point of view of the context, it may seem a little odd to dismiss hunting in this way so soon after having mentioned it (§56) with approval as part of the farmer's way of life; but Cicero is here talking specifically about old men, as he was not in §56, and there is no real inconsistency. Both hunting and swimming were standard activities of young men; for hunting, cf. *Tusc.* 2.34; *Lael.* 74; *Fin.* 1.69; *Off.* 1.104; Hor. *AP* 162 and Brink's note; Ter. *Andr.* 56–7; *Phorm.* 6–7; Blümner, *Privataltertümer* 512ff.; J. Aymard, *Essai sur les chasses romaines* (Paris 1951).

talos ... et tesseras Cf. Juv. 14.4 *senem iuvat alea*; Suet. *Aug.* 71, *lusimus* γεροντικῶς; *Claud.* 33; Sen. *Apocol.* 12.3. *tali* are knuckle-bones, ἀστράγαλοι; *tesserae* are the equivalent of our dice: cf. *De or.* 3.58, quoted above, and Ov. *Trist.* 2.471ff. Plato similarly recommends draughts-playing for old men, *Laws* 7.820c; cf. *Phaedr.* 274c–d, *Polit.* 299e, *Gorg.* 450d; Stein, *Platons Charakteristik* 69. Plut. *An seni* 795f regards dice-playing as a waste of time for old men. Sidonius, *Ep.* 1.8, talks of a reversal of roles between old and young: *student pilae senes, aleae iuvenes*.

utrum libebit 'whichever they like' (i.e. whether they leave old men their dice or not); *faciant* is understood. For *utrum* = *utrumcumque* (not uncommon, though it has caused editors much trouble here), cf. *Sest.* 92; *Verr. II* 2.150; 3.106; *Fin.* 5.86; *Div.* 2.141; *Tull.* 28; *ND* 3.4 *utrum voles faciam*; Livy 21.18.13 *daret utrum vellet*. Here *libebit* makes it even easier, since *utrumlibet* is quite regular.

XVII 59 Xenophontis libri It does not seem that Cicero is being unrealistic in making Cato recommend the works of Xenophon, as he may well have been acquainted with them: it has been pointed out that a fragment of the *Origines* (fr. 1 Peter: cf. on §80 below) appears to recall the beginning of Xenophon's *Symposium*, and there may be influence from Xenophon's *Oeconomicus* in the *De agricultura*. There is in any case no reason to doubt that Xenophon was read at Rome in the second century B.C.; Scipio (Aemilianus, presumably) is said by Cicero to have been very fond of the *Cyropaedia* (*Q. fr.* 1.1.23; cf. *Tusc.* 2.62). Cf. K. Münscher, *Philologus* Suppl. 13.2 (1920) 70ff; see also Introd. p. 6; 19. It may be noted that Cato's commendation *perutiles* is characteristically practical: he does not dwell on Xenophon's literary qualities. For other references to Xenophon in this work see §§30; 46; 79.

legite ... ut facitis Cf. *De or.* 1.34 *pergite ut facitis, adulescentes, atque in id studium in quo estis incumbite. ut facitis* presumably alludes to Scipio's fondness for Xenophon.

eo libro qui est de tuenda re familiari This exemplifies the formally correct way of describing the subject of a book, (*is*) *liber qui est de ...* rather than merely *liber de ...* Here there is an extra reason for avoiding *in libro de tuenda re familiari*, viz. that this latter expression would imply that *De tuenda re familiari* was the title. In more informal contexts, however, Cicero does use the shorter form of expression: cf. e.g. *Att.* 9.9.2 *Demetri librum de concordia*; and it is also regular when the number of the book is given: *ND* 1.41; 1.123; *Tusc.* 1.53. Cf. K.–S. I, 215.

regale Cf. *De rep.* 5.3 (*nihil esse tam*) *regale quam explanationem aequitatis*; the meaning is 'worthy of a king', in a good sense, despite the Roman distrust of monarchs.

loquitur Reid says that *loqui* with accusative and infinitive is collo-quial, but there does not seem to be much evidence for this: the construction is quite common in oratory (*TLL* 7, 2, 1670; see e.g. *Verr. II* 3.145; 149). Perhaps the idea ('talking of how ...' as opposed to 'saying that ...') is more likely to occur in colloquial speech than elsewhere.

Cicero here adapts, with considerable freedom, Xen. *Oecon.* 4.20ff. Cicero clearly knew this work well; he had at some time written a Latin translation, or (more probably) adaptation of it (cf. C. Virck, *Cicero qua ratione Xenophontis Oeconomicum Latine verterit*, diss. Berlin 1914), but there is no reason to suppose that he quotes literally from his own translation here (cf. D. M. Jones, *BICS* 6 (1959) 25). On the whole the rendering here has not much wrong with it, though one whole section is omitted, and there seems to be a definite mistake at the end of the section (see below on *virtuti tuae fortuna coniuncta est*); minor variations are noted below. Cf. F. de Caria, *RCCM* 16 (1974) 321ff.; also notes on the other translations from Plato and Xenophon in this work, §§6–8 and 79ff.

Οὗτος τοίνυν ὁ Κῦρος λέγεται	Cyrum *minorem, Persarum regem praestantem ingenio atque imperi gloria,*
Λυσάνδρῳ, ὅτε ἦλθεν ἄγων αὐτῷ τὰ παρὰ τῶν συμμάχων δῶρα,	cum Lysander *Lacedaemonius, vir summae virtutis,* venisset ad eum Sardis eique dona a sociis attulisset,
ἄλλα τε φιλοφρονεῖσθαι,	et ceteris in rebus comem erga Lysandrum atque humanum fuisse,

ὡς αὐτὸς ἔφη ὁ Λύσανδρος ξένῳ
ποτέ τινι ἐν Μεγάροις
διηγούμενος,
καὶ τὸν ἐν Σάρδεσι παράδεισον   et ei quendam consaeptum agrum
ἐπιδεικνύναι αὐτὸν ἔφη.   *diligenter consitum* ostendisse.
ἐπεὶ δὲ ἐθαύμαζεν αὐτὸν ὁ   Cum autem admiraretur Lysander
Λύσανδρος ὡς καλὰ μὲν τὰ δένδρα   et proceritates arborum et
εἴη, δι' ἴσου δὲ πεφυτευμένα, ὀρθοὶ   derectos in quincuncem ordines
δὲ οἱ στίχοι τῶν δένδρων, εὐγώνια
δὲ πάντα καλῶς εἴη,   *et humum subactam atque puram*
ὀσμαὶ δὲ πολλαὶ καὶ ἡδεῖαι   et suavitatem odorum qui
συμπαρομαρτοῖεν αὐτοῖς   adflarentur e floribus,
περιπατοῦσι,
καὶ ταῦτα θαυμάζων εἶπεν· "ἀλλ'   tum eum dixisse mirari se *non modo*
ἐγώ τοι, ὦ Κῦρε, πάντα μὲν ταῦτα   *diligentiam sed etiam sollertiam* eius a
θαυμάζω ἐπὶ τῷ κάλλει, πολὺ δὲ   quo essent illa dimensa atque
μᾶλλον ἄγαμαι τοῦ   descripta;
καταμετρήσαντός σοι καὶ
διατάξαντος ἕκαστα τούτων."
ἀκούσαντα δὲ ταῦτα τὸν Κῦρον   et Cyrum respondisse, 'atqui ego
ἡσθῆναί τε καὶ εἰπεῖν, "ταῦτα   ista sum omnia dimensus; mei sunt
τοίνυν, ὦ Λύσανδρε, ἐγὼ πάντα καὶ   ordines, mea descriptio, multae
διεμέτρησα καὶ διέταξα· ἔστι δ'   etiam istarum arborum mea manu
αὐτῶν," φάναι, "ἃ καὶ ἐφύτευσα   sunt satae';
αὐτός."
καὶ ὁ Λύσανδρος ἔφη, ἀποβλέψας   tum Lysandrum, intuentem
εἰς αὐτὸν καὶ ἰδὼν τῶν τε ἱματίων   purpuram eius et nitorem corporis
τὸ κάλλος ὧν εἶχε καὶ τῆς ὀσμῆς   ornatumque Persicum multo auro
αἰσθόμενος καὶ τῶν στρεπτῶν καὶ   multisque gemmis, dixisse,
τῶν ψελίων καὶ τοῦ ἄλλου κόσμου
οὗ εἶχεν, εἰπεῖν, "τί λέγεις,"
φάναι, "ὦ Κῦρε; ἦ γὰρ σύ ταῖς
σαῖς χερσὶ τούτων τι ἐφύτευσας;"
καὶ τὸν Κῦρον ἀποκρίνασθαι,
"θαυμάζεις τοῦτο," φάναι, "ὦ
Λύσανδρε; ὄμνυμί σοι τὸν Μίθρην,
ὅτανπερ ὑγιαίνω, μηπώποτε
δειπνῆσαι πρὶν ἱδρῶσαι ἢ τῶν
πολεμικῶν τι ἢ τῶν γεωργικῶν
ἔργων μελετῶν ἢ ἀεὶ ἕν γέ τι
φιλοτιμούμενος." καὶ αὐτὸς μέντοι
ἔφη ὁ Λύσανδρος ἀκούσας ταῦτα
δεξιώσασθαί τε καὶ εἰπεῖν·

"δικαίως μοι δοκεῖς, ὦ Κῦρε,   'rite vero te, Cyre, beatum ferunt,
εὐδαίμων εἶναι· ἀγαθὸς γὰρ ὢν   quoniam virtuti tuae fortuna
ἀνὴρ εὐδαιμονεῖς."   coniuncta est'.

Cyrum minorem The meeting of Cyrus and Lysander is mentioned, but without the present anecdote, in Xen. *Hell.* 1.6.1 and Plut. *Lysander* 9.

regem Cf. Xen. *Oecon.* 4.16, just before the passage reproduced here, εὐδοκιμώτατος δὴ βασιλεύς. The word is used loosely; Cyrus the younger was never actually king of Persia. Translate 'prince'.

praestantem ... gloria The phrase should go closely with *regem*, and there should not be a comma separating them, as in editions; it partly represents Xenophon's εὐδοκιμώτατος, which closely qualifies βασιλεύς; and in general, Cicero does not tend to use adjectives or participles in loose apposition without a noun for them to depend on; see K.–S. I, 226. (There is a similar point in *De rep.* 6.9 (*Som. Scip.* 1) *quam ut Masinissam convenirem, regem familiae nostrae iustis de causis amicissimum.* The sentence has often been printed with a comma after *regem*, but both the flow of the sentence and the rhythm $\overline{conven}\overline{\iota}r\overline{e}m$ indicate that the break should be before *regem*.)

Lysander Cf. below, §63; *Div.* 1.75; 96; 2.68; *Off.* 1.76; 109.

vir summae virtutis Not in Xenophon, but inserted by Cicero to reinforce the atmosphere: the greatness of the great men of the past must be made explicit. It is rather different from the judgement of Lysander in *Off.* 1.109 *versutissimum et patientissimum*, 'very crafty and would do anything to get his own way'.

ad eum Sardis (*Sardīs*=Σάρδεις.) Latin joins the accusative of the place with the person + *ad*; we say 'came to see him *at* Sardis' or 'came to Sardis to see him'. Cf. *Rosc. Am.* 20, *res ad Chrysogonum in castra Luci Sullae Volaterras defertur* – a threefold example. By putting *Sardis* here instead of where Xenophon puts it (τὸν ἐν Σάρδεσι παράδεισον below), Cicero avoids the difficulty of translating the Greek article + prepositional phrase, but misses the implication that Cyrus had estates elsewhere than at Sardis.

comem ... atque humanum φιλοφρονεῖσθαι; cf. *Fin.* 2.80 *comem et humanum*, and Madvig ad loc. The α group of MSS reads *communem*: though *communis* can mean virtually the same as *comis*, that sense is not very common, and *comem* is preferable here.

consaeptum agrum Precisely right for παράδεισος, which is from an Old Persian word corresponding to Avestic *pairidaēza*, derived from words meaning 'around' (cf. περί) and 'wall' (cf. τεῖχος): P. Chantraine, *Dict. étym. de la langue grecque* 857. Cf. Xen. *Hell.* 4.1.15 περιειργμένοις παραδείσοις. *paradisus* is not used as a common noun in Latin until the ecclesiastical writers; it is still a foreign word for Aulus Gellius (2.20.4) who gives *vivarium* as the Latin equivalent. A παράδεισος did not always contain animals (Cyrus' does not seem to have done), but it often did, and was used as a hunting park by the Persians.

proceritates arborum A more grandiose expression than Xenophon's simple ὡς καλὰ μὲν τὰ δένδρα εἴη. Cf. the well-known passage of *ND*, 2.98, *fontium gelidas perennitates, liquores perlucidos amnium, riparum vestitus viridissimos, speluncarum concavas altitudines, saxorum asperitates* ...; Plato, *Laws* 625b κυπαρίττων τε ἐν τοῖς ἄλσεσιν ὕψη καὶ κάλλη θαυμάσια.

derectos in quincuncem ordines Cicero, by the use of a handy Roman term, compresses Xenophon's δι᾽ ἴσου δὲ πεφυτευμένα, ὀρθοὶ δὲ οἱ στίχοι τῶν δένδρων, εὐγώνια δὲ πάντα καλῶς εἴη.

derectos Some have tried, from Isidore onwards, to draw a distinction between *derigere* and *dirigere*, but none is observable in classical usage; inscriptions etc. from antiquity itself consistently write *derigere* until the time of Diocletian, and usually thereafter, although *dirigere* is now the normal spelling. Certainly *de-* is etymologically correct; there is no word *disrigere*. Here the spelling *derectos* is preserved by B and Nonius, and I therefore retain it. Cf. *TLL* 5, 1, 1232, cf. 1251; for this agricultural use of the word, ibid. 5, 1, 1236, 53ff.

quincuncem The *quincunx* was the common Roman arrangement for trees: Virg. *Georg.* 2.278ff.; Varro, *RR* 1.7.2; Colum. 3.13.4; 3.15.1; etc.; Quint. *Inst.* 8.3.9; Pliny, *NH* 17.78. The name derives from the resemblance of the pattern to a repetition of the mark on a five-*uncia* weight or coin (as in Fig. 2a or 2b), also used, then as now, for the five on dice (but in that context called not *quincunx* but *quinio*: Isid. 18.65; H. Chantraine, P.-W. 24, 1112). The quincuncial arrangement may be thought of as a series of diagonal lines; cf. Caes. *BG* 7.73 *obliquis ordinibus in quincuncem dispositis* (Fig. 3). Cicero has been accused of forgetting that Cyrus was a Persian, and giving him a Roman tree-plantation; but no

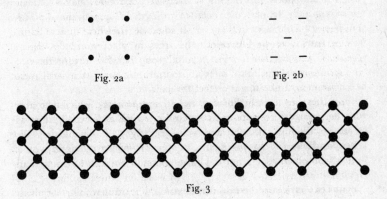

Fig. 2a   Fig. 2b

Fig. 3

doubt his regular arrangement of trees, as described in Xenophon, approximated to the *quincunx*, and Cicero is merely following the common Roman habit of using Roman terms for equivalent objects or institutions in other places (like *senatus* for the councils at Athens or Carthage). Cf. Blümner, *Privataltertümer* 403. This passage is taken by Sir Thomas Browne as the starting-point for his *Garden of Cyrus*.

et humum subactam atque puram An addition of Cicero's, unless (which is quite unlikely) something has dropped out of the text of Xenophon. Cf. above, §51 *terrae ... gremio mollito ac subacto*, and note. *puram*, free from stones, roots or weeds.

non modo diligentiam sed etiam sollertiam This is slightly different from the original. Xenophon's Lysander says 'Indeed I wonder at the beauty of all this; but I am much more amazed at the skill of the man who laid it out for you'; the point seems to be that Cyrus was displaying the garden as his own, and Lysander gently reminded him that the credit must go to the gardener, not knowing that Cyrus himself had planted the trees. This more or less disappears in Cicero's version; Romans of his time would naturally assume that aristocrats did not plant their own trees. Instead of the slightly pointed phrase τοῦ καταμετρήσαντός σοι καὶ διατάξαντος..., Cicero's Lysander merely says 'Not only has your gardener spent a great deal of care on these trees, he is also very clever and professional.'

dimensa Used in passive sense: cf. Caes. *BG* 2.19.5; 4.17.3; Quint. *Inst.* 9.4.27; Virg. *Georg.* 1.231; 2.284; Cic. *Att.* 1.6.1; etc.

descripta This, the reading of the archetype, should probably be kept. Manuscripts often vary between *describere* and *discribere*, and it is not always easy to see which should be read; but it is generally taken that *discribere*, when properly used, contains a notion of division or distribution of a whole into parts, which is not in place here. *Describere* in these contexts means originally 'to mark out', then 'to arrange'. Cf. *descriptio* below; *TLL* 5, 1, 657, 22 and 664, 71. However, it could be argued that 'arranging' here is equivalent to 'disposing' the trees in different places; cf. *in quincuncem disposita*, Caes. *BG* 7.73; and that therefore the prefix *dis-*, corresponding to Greek δια-, is the appropriate one. Also, we have already had *dimensa*, and one might expect the pair of words to have the same prefix rather than slightly different ones; though *demensa* could also be read with no change in meaning. The question should not be regarded as certainly settled. Cf. also above on §5.

respondisse Cicero leaves out Xenophon's ἡσθῆναι, 'he said with a flush of satisfaction'; Cicero's Cyrus is less self-congratulatory than Xenophon's.

atqui ego ista sum omnia dimensus 'But it was I who laid them all out': note the emphatic position of *ego*.

multae Xenophon only says ἔστι δ᾽ αὐτῶν ἅ...; but *multae* need not imply a great many (that would be *plurimae* or *permultae*), and *aliquae* would have been weaker in effect.

mea manu Cf. ταῖς σαῖς χερσί below in Xenophon (in the part omitted by Cicero).

purpuram Not in Xenophon, but Cicero no doubt assumed that Cyrus was wearing purple as a member of the royal family; cf. Xen. *Cyrop.* 2.4.6, πορφυρίδα ἐνδὺς καὶ ψέλια λαβὼν καὶ στρεπτὸν περιθέμενος.

nitorem corporis ornatumque Persicum Compressed somewhat from the original, ἀποβλέψας εἰς αὐτὸν καὶ ἰδὼν τῶν τε ἱματίων τὸ κάλλος ὧν εἶχε καὶ τῆς ὀσμῆς αἰσθόμενος ... καὶ τοῦ ἄλλου κόσμου οὗ εἶχεν. The perfumes are left out; Cicero no doubt regarded them as too much of a sign of luxury, particularly for men, though they add more point to Lysander's surprise in the original. For *nitor*, cf. Ter. *Eun.* 242; Hor. *Od.* 1.19.5; Juv. 9.13; Stat. *Silv.* 5.2.73; this too is not universally approved of: see Cic. *Cael.* 77 *si offendit ... nitor*. Cicero himself, in common no doubt with many Romans of the old school, thought that one could be too well-groomed (cf. *Off.* 1.129–30). *ornatum*, κόσμος: like our word 'costume', this often refers to unusual or luxurious dress.

Here Cicero leaves out a considerable section of the Greek: in the original, Lysander's surprise is emphasised, and Cyrus swears by Mithras that he never lets a day pass without some honourable deed in war, farming or elsewhere.

rite vero te ... est Cicero mistranslates Xenophon here. The Greek reads δικαίως μοι δοκεῖς, ὦ Κῦρε, εὐδαίμων εἶναι, ἀγαθὸς γὰρ ὢν ἀνὴρ εὐδαιμονεῖς. The exact construction of the last five words cannot be preserved in Latin any more than in English; but their meaning is clearly not the same as that of Cicero's *virtuti tuae fortuna coniuncta est*. In the Greek, the emphasis is on the participial clause, i.e. on the statement that Cyrus is an ἀγαθὸς ἀνήρ; εὐδαιμονεῖς merely picks up the preceding εὐδαίμων εἶναι. Cicero would have been nearer the mark if he had written *fortunae tuae virtus coniuncta est*. In mistaking the emphasis of the Greek, Cicero had in fact made nonsense of the first part of the sentence as well: 'You are deservedly happy since, being virtuous, you are happy' could not stand; this explains why Cicero also changed Xenophon's δικαίως μοι δοκεῖς ... εὐδαίμων εἶναι (where μοι δοκεῖς means merely 'you seem to me', and δικαίως goes with εὐδαίμων εἶναι) to *rite vero te ... beatum ferunt*. It makes sense of a sort – though not as good nor as simple as Xenophon's – for Lysander to say 'You are deservedly said to be happy, for you are both virtuous and fortunate as well.' (Cf. Schröter, *De Cic. C. M.* 27; H. Herter, *Athena* 73–4 (1972–3) 687ff.; F. de Caria, cited above, fails to defend Cicero's translation convincingly.)

Cicero's alteration of the original meaning was doubtless unintentional, but he may have been unconsciously influenced by ideas familiar to him elsewhere. A similar sentiment to that of Cicero's version here occurs in *Arch.* 24 *noster hic Magnus qui cum virtute fortunam adaequavit* (and cf. the discussion of Pompey's *fortuna* in the *Pro Lege Manilia*). As to the first part of the sentence, Cicero may well (as de Caria, art. cit., notes) have had in mind the philosophical debate as to whether virtue was sufficient for happiness, discussed by him in *Tusc.* 5: Cicero's Lysander apparently takes the (Peripatetic) view that one must have a certain degree of external good fortune in order to be called properly εὐδαίμων. The wider context of this passage may also have influenced him to some extent: the point of the whole argument so far has been to show that agriculture is a source of pleasure, and this is certainly supported better by Cicero's erroneous translation than by Xenophon's original. The word *fortuna* is picked up in the following sentence (cf. Schröter, ibid.).

60 fortuna Cf. above.

senibus This appears to have a certain emphasis; Cyrus was not an old man, and it has to be pointed out explicitly that the *fortuna* he enjoyed could still be enjoyed in old age. *aetas* also is emphatic: *age* (at least) does not prevent us from enjoying these things (though other things possibly may).

Marcum ... Valerium Corvinum P.–W. 7A2, 2413ff. (s.v. 'Valerius' 137). Cf. Val. Max. 8.13.1 (apparently copied from this passage of Cicero) *M. Valerius Corvinus centesimum annum complevit; cuius inter primum et sextum consulatum XL et VI anni intercesserunt, suffecitque integris viribus corporis non solum speciosissimis publicis ministeriis, sed etiam exactissimae agrorum suorum culturae;* ibid. 8.15.5. Pliny, *NH* 7.157 gives the same statistic about Valerius' age and consulates, adding his record of 21 curule magistracies; in general, see also Livy 7ff.; App. *Gall.* 10; *B. civ.* 3.88; Gell. 9.11; [Victor] *De vir. ill.* 29; etc. Like Cincinnatus (§56 above), Valerius Corvinus (or Corvus) is the subject of a number of traditions of a heroic sort, about which later Romans were sceptical: it is to be noted that Cicero here says *accepimus*, and does not vouch for the truth of the statement about his living to his hundredth year.

centesimum annum According to traditional dating, Valerius lived from 371 to 271.

perduxisse Sc. *agri colendi studia*; the ellipse does not really present any problem, and there is no need to invoke an alleged intransitive meaning of *perducere*. The only parallel that is quoted for such a meaning is *Lael.* 33 *quod summi puerorum amores saepe una cum praetexta toga ponerentur; sin autem ad adulescentiam perduxissent ...*, where it is almost as easy to supply *amores* as to supply *studia* here, though not quite, since *amores* is nominative in the preceding part of the sentence. (Cf. P. Fedeli, *RhM* 115 (1972) 165.)

inter primum et sextum consulatum The interval of 46 years is mentioned also by Pliny and Valerius Maximus; Plut. *Marius* 28.6 says forty-five; but the traditional dates for Valerius' first and last consulates are 348 and 299, which are separated by an interval of 48 years. His second consulate was in 346, which gives the required interval of forty-six; Cicero or his source may have confused the two, or (more probably) reckoned the interval inexactly. It is unlikely that Cicero deliberately altered the chronology to make the point (as Wuilleumier suggests). A. Klotz (cited Introd. p. 10 n. 27) thinks Cicero omitted four years of dictatorship when there were no consuls, but this would be odd, and would in any case give 44 years, not 46.

maiores ... esse voluerunt That *senectus* began at 46, the age of military discharge during the Republic, was an old idea that no longer obtained; in Cicero's own time *senectus* was reckoned to begin around sixty (cf. Introd. p. 2 n. 8, and note on §34 above); it is not clear whether the older view persisted until the time of Cato. The appeal to the *maiores* is characteristically Catonian, and the phrase *maiores nostri esse voluerunt* occurs in Cato fr. 235 Malcovati, = *orat. incert.* 4 Jordan (quoted in Cic. *Off.* 3.104).

apex The only instance of this metaphor in classical Latin, discounting imitations of this passage in Amm. Marc. 27.7.2 and August. *Civ. Dei* 10.32. The Roman *apex* was originally an olive-twig tied round with wool, placed in the cap of the *flamines* (cf. Virg. *Aen.* 8.664; Serv. *Aen.* 2.683; 10.271; etc.; P.–W. 1, 2699; Tarquinius Priscus has an *apex* in Cic. *Leg.* 1.4). The word is used elsewhere with the generalised meaning 'crown': Hor. *Od.* 3.21.20; 1.34.14; etc. Though the context is otherwise thoroughly Roman, it is possible to imagine that the metaphor may have derived from a Greek reference to a διάδημα or στέφανος: cf. Plut. *An seni* 789e καὶ καθάπερ ὁ νόμος τὸ διάδημα καὶ τὸν στέφανον, οὕτω τὴν πολιὰν ἡ φύσις ἔντιμον ἡγεμονικοῦ σύμβολον ἀξιώματος ἐπιτίθησι; Antisthenes ap. Stob. 2.31.33 ἐρωτηθεὶς ὑπό τινος ποῖος στέφανος κάλλιστός ἐστιν, εἶπεν "ὁ ἀπὸ παιδείας"; Proverbs 16.31 'The hoary head is a crown of glory'; Ecclesiasticus 25.6 στέφανος γερόντων πολυπειρία.

61 **Lucio Caecilio Metello** Cf. §30.

Aulo Atilio Calatino The restoration of the *praenomen* seems necessary (Fleckeisen, *Kritische Miscellen* (Leipzig 1864) 55). Calatinus is another of Cicero's favourite Roman heroes: cf. *Fin.* 2.116; *Tusc.* 1.13; 1.110; *ND* 2.165; *De rep.* 1.1; *Pis.* 14; *Leg. agr.* 2.64; *Planc.* 60 (together with Fabricius and Curius); P.–W. 2, 2079ff.

elogium 'epitaph': it seems generally agreed that the word derives from the Greek ἐλεγεῖον, with a slight change of meaning: Ernout–Meillet 298; *TLL* 5, 2, 405; for a use closer to the original Greek cf. §73 below.

hunc unum The MSS read *unicum* here, and in the same epitaph quoted in *Fin.* 2.116, the MSS vary between *uno cum* and *uno cui*; Madvig restored *hunc unum* on the analogy of the still existing epitaph of L. Scipio Barbati f., *CIL* I², 2, 9; *ILS* 3, *Honc oino ploirume consentiont R[omai] | duonoro optumo fuise viro* . . . (cf. Ernout, *Recueil de textes latins archaiques* (Paris 1957) no. 14, pp. 14ff.); cf. T. Bergk, *Comment. de Reliquiis Comoed. Att. Ant. Libri II* (Leipzig 1838) 23; Madvig on *Fin.* loc. cit. The tomb of Calatinus was near those of the Scipiones, outside the Porta Capena (cf. *Fin.* loc. cit. and *Tusc.* 1.13). Cicero reproduces the first two lines of what was presumably a somewhat longer inscription (*totum carmen*); the epitaphs of the Scipiones run to six or seven Saturnian lines, and this one was probably similar.

notum est enim totum My correction: it seems to be necessary to account for the nonsensical reading *notum est itiotum* of P¹BLAD; otherwise the commonly accepted *notum est totum* would have been satisfactory. Mommsen suggested *notum est id totum* (cf. A. Kornitzer, *Berl. Phil. Woch.* 25 (1905) 512; Mähly, *N. Schw. Mus.* 6 (1866) 243ff.; Fleckeisen, *Krit. Miscellen*, cited above). But *iti* of the MSS is probably a corruption of the (originally insular) abbreviation for *enim*, viz. ⫫, which itself occurs occasionally in our MSS. *notum est enim totum* would be paralleled by other passages in which Cicero breaks off a quotation and proceeds with *enim*, cf. §1 above *licet enim mihi* . . . , §§16 and 20; *Div.* 2.115. (Reid had previously suggested replacing *totum* by *enim*, but very tentatively; cf. also Vahlen, *Ges. Phil. Schr.* 1, 572.)

Publium Crassum Cf. §§27 and 50. *nuper* does not imply the very recent past; Crassus was Pont. Max. from 213 to 183. Reid compares *Lael.* 13 and Pliny, *Ep.* 1.2.2.

Marcum Lepidum Pont. Max. 180–152, succeeded in 150 by P. Scipio Nasica Corculum (cf. §50); P.–W. 1, 552–3 (s.v. 'Aemilius' 68).

Paulo Cf. §§15; 49; 77; 82–3.

Africano Cf. §§19; 29; 82.

aut ut iam ante The older MSS all read *aut iam ante*, except that S² adds *ut* above the line: unfortunately it spoils the effect by also adding *dixi* after *ante*, suggesting that the additions are merely a gloss, of a type in which S² abounds. Baiter–Halm's apparatus attributes *ut* to I (s. xii–xiii), but this must be a mistake; I have myself examined this MS, and it reads *aut iam ante* with no sign of *ut*. Nevertheless, there seems to be little doubt that *ut* should be inserted. Vahlen (cited above) and O. Plasberg, *RhM* 53 (1898) 85, tried to defend the transmitted reading; neither appears to see the problem, comparing passages in which the verb is past; here the difficulty is that *loquar* refers clearly to a contemplated future action, while *ante de Maximo* refers equally definitely to an action already completed in the past (i.e. in §§10–13 above).

nutu Cf. *De or.* 1.38 *non accurata orationis copia sed nutu atque verbo*. Note the official and senatorial connotations of the words used in this passage, *auctoritas, sententia, honorata* ('honoured with public office', cf. *cursus honorum*); Wuilleumier notes also a use of *nutus* in senatorial contexts, comparing Livy 7.30.20.

ut ea plus sit quam omnes adulescentiae voluptates Cf. Pericles' funeral speech, Thuc. 2.44, τὸ γὰρ φιλότιμον ἀγήρων μόνον, καὶ οὐκ ἐν τῷ ἀχρείῳ τῆς ἡλικίας τὸ κερδαίνειν ὥσπερ τινές φασι μᾶλλον τέρπει, ἀλλὰ τὸ τιμᾶσθαι; also Juncus pp. 1029–30 W.–H.

XVIII 62 fundamentis adulescentiae Cf. §9 and note. The importance of education and a well-spent life in general is emphasised by philosophers; Musonius 17, p. 91 H. (Τί ἄριστον γήρως ἐφόδιον) says εἰ μὲν οὖν τις τύχοι πρότερον ἔτι νέος ὢν παιδείας ὀρθῆς ἐπιμέλειαν πεποιημένος ... οὗτος ἂν ἐν γήρᾳ ... ζώη κατὰ φύσιν, etc.; Aristotle ap. Diog. Laert. 5.21 apparently said that παιδεία was the best viaticum for old age (see on §9, where other similar sayings are quoted); Varro, *Catus de liberis educandis* fr. 9 quotes one 'Ariston' on the importance of a good start in education (cf. Appendix 2); cf. also Lact. *Inst.* 7.12.12 *senectus non minuit sapientiam, sed auget, si tamen iuvenilis aetas virtute decursa est*; Evagrius of Pontus, Πνευματικαὶ γνῶμαι 19–20, Migne, *PG* 40, 1270 (quoted in Maximus Confessor, *Loci communes* 41, Migne, *PG* 91, 917), τὸ ἔντιμον ἐν γήρᾳ εἶναι, ἀπόδειξις τοῦ φιλόπονον πρὸ γήρως γεγονέναι· τὸ σπουδαῖον ἐν νέῳ ἐχέγγυον τοῦ ἔντιμον ἐν γήρᾳ ἔσεσθαι. The metaphor of 'foundations' occurs also in Plut. *De lib. educ.* 8c καλοῦ γὰρ γήρως θεμέλιος ἐν παισὶν ἡ τῶν σωμάτων εὐεξία.

miseram esse senectutem ... defenderet Cato, *dict.* 71, p. 109 Jordan: this saying is not elsewhere attested, and its context and occasion are quite obscure. It means, presumably, that old men should not need to defend themselves with speeches, since their past life should make them respected. Cf. on §38 above.

non cani nec rugae ... adripere possunt (For *cani* alone = 'grey hair', see *TLL* 3, 297, 8off.: this is the only instance of the usage in Cicero. Some commentators say that it is poetic, but it is not exclusively so.) Cf. Sen. *Brev. vit.* 7.10 *non est itaque quod quemquam propter canos aut rugas putes diu vixisse: non ille diu vixit, sed diu fuit; Const. sap.* 12.1; Varro, *Men.* fr. 5 B. *nec canitudini comes virtus*; Men. fr. 553 Koerte = 639 Kock, οὐχ αἱ τρίχες ποιοῦσιν αἱ λευκαὶ φρονεῖν; Cleanthes ap. Diog. Laert. 7.171, fr. 602 von Arnim; Democr. fr. 183 D.–K.; Philo, *Anth. Pal.* 11.419–20; Basil ap. Simeon Metaphr. *Sermo* 24.3 (Migne, *PG* 32, 1380); John Chrysostom *De sacerdotio* 3.8 (Migne 48, 640); *In Epist. ad Hebr.* 4, *Homil.* 7 (Migne 63, 65–6); [John Chrysostom], *In Psalm. L* (Migne 55, 568); cf. Maximus Confessor, *Loci Communes* 41 (Migne 91, 617); Hense, *Teletis Reliquiae*, introd. p. cxx; E. Curtius, *European Literature and the Latin Middle Ages*, Eng.

233

edn. p. 99. Contrast Plut. *An seni* 789e, οἷς ἡ γελωμένη πολιὰ καὶ ῥυτὶς ἐμπειρίας μάρτυς ἐπιφαίνεται καὶ πειθοῦς συνεργὸν αὐτῷ καὶ δόξαν ἤθους προστίθησι.

honeste acta Cf. §§9, 38, 69, and notes; Epicurus, in *Gnom. vat.* 17 οὐ νέος μακαριστὸς ἀλλὰ γέρων βεβιωκὼς καλῶς.

fructus See on §9 above; cf. §71; Plut. *An seni* 789f τὴν φρόνησιν ἧς καθάπερ ὀψικάρπου φυτοῦ τὸ οἰκεῖον ἀγαθὸν ... ἡ φύσις ἀποδίδωσι.

63　honorabilia This word occurs only here before Tertullian: *TLL* 6, 3, 2931.

appeti To be sought after: *TLL* 2, 284, 16ff.

decedi To have others give way: cf. Plaut. *Amphitr.* 984; *Trin.* 481; Suet. *Nero* 4.

assurgi According to Hdt. 2.80 the custom of rising at the approach of an older man was observed by the Egyptians and, alone of the Greeks, by the Spartans; on the Spartan custom, cf. also Plut. *Apophth. Lac.* 232b and 232f. Clearly it was also a Roman custom: cf. Cic. *Inv.* 1.48, *commune est ut maioribus natu assurgatur*; Sen. *De ira* 2.21; Juv. 13.54 *si iuvenis vetulo non assurrexerit*, and Mayor's note ad loc.; according to Socrates in Xen. *Mem.* 2.3.16 this and other ways of showing respect to the old πανταχοῦ νομίζεται; cf. *Cyrop.* 8.7.10; and it is envisaged as part of traditional Athenian good manners in Ar. *Clouds* 994. Cf. also Leviticus 19.32, 'Rise up before the hoary head'; [Phocyl.] *Sent.* 220; C. H. Petzsch, *De honore senibus assurgendi* (Progr. Meissen 1742).

deduci To be escorted from home to the forum or Senate (though it can also mean the same as *reduci*, to be escorted home). Cf. Val. Max. 2.1.9, *iuvenes senatus die utique aliquem ex patribus conscriptis ad curiam deducebant, affixique valvis exspectabant donec reducendi etiam officio fungerentur*. This was a common custom in Rome; Aulus Gellius (2.15) mentions a supposed Spartan connection: *a conviviis quoque, ut scriptum in antiquitatibus est, seniores a iunioribus domum deducebantur, eumque morem accepisse Romanos a Lacedaemoniis traditum est, apud quos Lycurgi legibus maior omnium rerum honos aetati maiori habebatur*. Cf. also Callimachus fr. 41 (see §26 above) γηράσκει δ' ὁ γέρων κεῖνος ἐλαφρότερον | τὸν κοῦροι φιλέουσι, νέοι δέ μιν οἷα τοκῆα | χειρὸς ἐπ' οἰκείην ἄχρις ἄγουσι θύρην; Tibull. 1.4.80; Shakespeare, *Macbeth* 5.3.24. These modes of expressing respect for old age show clearly the greater accessibility of public figures in ancient times than nowadays: it was not an annoyance but an honour to be followed round by a crowd of young men.

honestissimum domicilium senectutis Cf. Plut. *An seni* 795f πρὸς τί βλέψας ὁ Λύσανδρος εἶπεν, ὡς ἐν Λακεδαίμονι κάλλιστα γηρῶσιν;; id. *Apophth. Lac.* 235f (a similar saying, not attributed to Lysander).

memoriae proditum est Cf. *Inv.* 2.3; *Verr. II* 4.103; *Phil.* 2.54; etc.; *TLL* 8, 675–7.

Athenis ludis The locative of the place is juxtaposed with the locative-ablative *ludis*: cf. *ND* 2.6 *ludis Olympiae*, where the parallel with the present passage invites one to take *Olympiae* as locative rather than genitive; other instances of either case do not seem to be forthcoming. *TLL* s.v. *ludus* is no help; Pease ad loc. quotes a Greek use of the locative but omits the *Cato* passage.

quidam in theatrum grandis natu venisset This anecdote is found also in Val. Max. 4.5, ext. 2 (probably copied from this passage), and in two different versions in Plut. *Apophth. Lac.* 235c; of these latter, one places the incident at Olympia, the other agrees with Cicero that it took place at Athens, identifying the festival concerned as the Panathenaea.

legati Ambassadors had special seats reserved at the front of the theatre (προεδρία).

64 ex eis quendam I.e. one of the Spartans.

scire quae recta essent ... nolle Cf. *Lael.* 24 *cum homines quod facere ipsi non possent, id recte fieri in altero iudicarent*; Ov. *Met.* 7.20 *video meliora proboque,│deteriora sequor* and Bömer ad loc.; Sen. *Ep.* 108. 8–9; Demosth. *Olynth.* 3.3; Eur. *Hipp.* 380–1; *Chrysippus* fr. 841 N.²; Plato, *Prot.* 352d.

vestro Scipio and Laelius were augurs (as was Cicero himself): Cato was not (cf. on §38). The reading *nostro* in SBe and some earlier editions is wrong.

ut quisque aetate antecedit Cicero refers to a similar custom of the Syracusan council in *Verr. II* 4.142; cf. also Plut. *An seni* 784c.

honore ... cum imperio *honore* denotes present or past magistracies; *cum imperio* only present consuls or praetors (or dictators), who took precedence on all normal occasions.

splendide Cf. *Tusc.* 3.61 *acta aetas honeste et splendide*.

fabulam aetatis For the comparison of life with a stage performance, see on §5 above; cf. §§48, 70 and 85. In §5 it was said that Nature was not likely to have botched the last act of the play, in her capacity as poet: here the stress is on men as actors in the drama of life. Cicero uses the comparison also in *Q. fr.* 1.1.46 with reference to Quintus' governorship of Asia, adding the idea that the end of the play should be the best part; cf. also Suet. *Aug.* 99, *admissos amicos percontatus, ecquid eis videretur mimum vitae commode transegisse*; Teles p. 16 H. (cf. Hense's introduction pp. cxiv ff.) ὥσπερ ὁ ἀγαθὸς ὑποκριτής ... οὕτω καὶ ὁ ἀγαθὸς ἀνὴρ εὖ καὶ τὰ πρῶτα τοῦ βίου, εὖ καὶ τὰ μέσα, εὖ καὶ τὴν τελευτήν; App. Vat. 369 τοῦ βίου καθάπερ δράματος τὰ τελευταῖα κάλλιστα δεῖ εἶναι.

65 At sunt morosi ... senes This conventional characterisation of old men as bad-tempered, etc., is indirectly an objection to what goes before, since bad temper, anxiety and meanness could well detract from the capacity of old men to 'use the prizes of authority gloriously'. There is no reason to suppose that this objection derives specifically from Aristotle's characterisation of old men in the *Rhetoric* (1389b ff.); it simply represents the common unphilosophical view, which Aristotle also uses as the basis for his characterisation, and this accounts amply for any similarity. The case is rather different with Horace, *AP* 169ff., where direct Peripatetic influence seems likely (see Brink ad loc.).

morosi Cf. Eur. *Bacch.* 1251–2; *Androm.* 727–8; Men. fr. 874 K.; Isocr. *Panath.* 234c; [Arist.] *Probl.* 30.1.29ff.; John Chrysostom, *In Epist. ad Titum* II, Homil. 4, Migne, *PG* 62, 681. See also above on §7 *difficiles*.

anxii Arist. *Rhet.* 1389b δειλοὶ καὶ πάντα προφοβητικοί; Hor. *AP* 172 (with Bentley's correction) ⟨*p*⟩*avidusque futuri*.

iracundi Arist. *Rhet.* loc. cit. καὶ οἱ θυμοὶ ὀξεῖς μέν εἰσιν, ἀσθενεῖς δέ; Hor. *AP* loc. cit. 173–4; Sen. *De ira* 1.13.5; 3.9.4.

si quaerimus 'in fact' or 'if the truth be told'; cf. *Off.* 3.80; *Fam.* 12.8.1; etc.

avari *avaritia* in Latin covers two vices distinguished by the Greeks, ἀνελευθερία (meanness or lack of generosity) and αἰσχροκερδεία (our 'avarice', desire for illiberal gain); cf. Arist. *NE* 4.1121b ff.; Theophrastus in the *Characters* adds μικρολογία ('penny-pinching') as a species of ἀνελευθερία. It is ἀνελευθερία which is specifically linked with old age; cf. Arist. *NE* 1121b13, δοκεῖ γὰρ τὸ γῆρας καὶ πᾶσα ἀδυναμία ἀνελευθέρους ποιεῖν; *Rhet.* loc. cit. καὶ ἀνελεύθεροι· ἓν γὰρ τῶν ἀναγκαίων ἡ οὐσία, ἅμα δὲ καὶ διὰ τὴν ἐμπειρίαν ἴσασιν ὡς χαλεπὸν τὸ κτήσασαι καὶ ῥᾴδιον τὸ ἀποβαλεῖν. Cf. also Plut. *An seni* 786b; Ter. *Ad.* 833–4.

morum vitia Cf. §7 and note.

ac ... tamen 'and anyway': see above on §16.

habent aliquid excusationis Cf. *Leg. agr.* 3.5; *Att.* 8.12.2; Sen. *De ira* 2.10.3.

non illius quidem iustae For this use of *ille* (*quidem*) see K.–S. I, 623–4 (Anm. 8).

probari In a rather weak sense: something may 'seem to admit of approval' without being 'just': we should probably say 'not altogether legitimate, but understandable'.

contemni ... despici Cf. §7 above; *contemnere* and *despicere* are constant companions in Cicero, and one should not perhaps be too insistent on finding a distinction between them in such contexts as this. Nevertheless, there is a distinction in usage when the words are used separately; one can say *mortem contemnere* for 'to treat death as of no account' but hardly *mortem despicere*; Cicero could say *contempsi Catilinae gladios*, but *despexi* would imply that he himself had better swords. Nonius p. 436 M. says that *despicere* is stronger than *contemnere*, while schol. Cic. *Verr. I* 9 gives the difference as *despicimus inferiores, contemnimus aequales*; the true difference seems to be that *despicere* keeps its concrete meaning of 'look down on' to some extent, and hence implies a judgement of one's own superiority in the matter under consideration, while *contemnere* is simply a refusal to be cowed by something, or to respect it.

illudi Cf. *Lael.* 99 *quid autem turpius quam illudi?*

offensio In a predominantly physical sense: for other instances see *TLL* 9, 2, 498.

quae Surely not referring back to *morum vitia* (it is nonsense to say that bad character is made more pleasant by good character), but to the external disadvantages of old age, *contemni* etc.

artibus In the old-fashioned sense of 'qualities of character'.

Adelphis It is quite plausible to make Cato refer to the *Adelphi*, which he could have seen at its first production in 160 at the funeral games of L. Aemilius Paulus.

duritas The reading of ML²H²PaRS²ZQI, probably to be preferred to *diritas*, despite the latter's superior MS attestation and Nonius' two quotations (one of which is included to illustrate this word): the difference is so small that Nonius could easily have had the inferior reading in his text of Cicero. For *duritas* cf. Terence's own descriptions of Demea's character, *Ad.* 45 *duriter se habere*; 64 *nimis ipse est durus*; 859 *duram vitam*; also Cic. *Cael.* 36 *durus senex*, and *durus pater* in Ter. *Heaut.* 204, 439; Cic. *Cael.* 37; Hor. *Sat.* 1.2.17; Ov. *Met.* 14.587; *TLL* 5, 1, 2307, 42ff. *diritas* really means 'cruelty' and is not appropriate to Demea's character. *duritas* is used once elsewhere by Cicero (*Orat.* 53) in the context of rhetorical style; *TLL* 5, 1, 2289, 55ff.

sic se res habet: ut enim 'That is how things are' (i.e. in real life, as well as in the play): 'for just as not every wine, so too not every human character grows sour with age'. This interpretation (not favoured by translators) has the merit of giving some meaning to *enim*, which translators and commentators mostly ignore, or explain away as a singular and archaic usage (cf. Hand, *Tursellinus* II, 379); *sic* is mostly taken as referring forwards, '*This* is how things are', but there is nothing to prevent it from referring back to what has just been said.

non omne vinum The parallel of the human character with wine occurs in a number of places, mostly in Greek comedy: Antiphanes fr. 240b K. σφόδρ' ἐστιν ἡμῶν ὁ βίος οἴνῳ προσφερής· | ὅταν ᾖ τὸ λοιπὸν μικρόν, ὄξος γίγνεται; Alexis fr. 45 K. (ap. Athen. 2.36e and Stob. 4.50a.5); id. fr. 278 (Athen. 2.36f); Eubulus frr. 124–5 K. (Athen. 1.25f); also anon. *Anth. Pal.* 9.127. A fragment of an unidentified Aristo quoted in Sen. *Ep.* 36.3 has the same comparison, though not quite in the same connection (see Appendix 2). Cf. also *Lael.* 67 *veterrima quaeque, ut ea vina* *quae vetustatem ferunt, esse debent suavissima*; Sen. *Ep.* 108.26; Ecclesiasticus 9.10; Mishnah *Aboth* 4.26.

coacescit For this metaphorical use cf. *Scaur.* 43; *TLL* 3, 1368, 27ff.

66 quid sibi velit For *sibi velle* cf. *Verr. II* 3.118; G. Landgraf, *ALL* 8 (1893) 45.

viae ... viatici Cf. Sen. *Ep.* 77.3 *quantulumcumque haberem, tamen plus iam mihi superesset viatici quam viae* (probably derived from Cicero); [Sen.] *De moribus* 18 *Monstro similis est avaritia senilis. quid enim stultius est, quod dici solet, quam via deficiente augere viaticum?*; Marbod, *Lib. dec. cap.* 5.46–7. This is a neat piece of rhetorical moralising, not notably consistent either with Cicero's argument in §24 (on providing for future generations) or with Cato's character as depicted by sources outside Cicero: on Cato's tendency to meanness, see Livy 39.40; Plut. *Cato* 4–6; 21.

66ff. Fourth complaint: old age is near to death The placing of a section on the fear of death at the end of this work has clear rhetorical advantages, enabling Cicero to produce a fine peroration on the immortality of the soul. This complaint is not in fact one of the more prominent ones in other ancient treatments of old age. It occurs in Anacreon (fr. 44), and Cephalus in Plato's *Republic* (330d) admits to fear of punishment after death; otherwise it is found as an object of refutation in the moralistic writers, Sen. *Ep.* 12.5–6; Musonius p. 92 H.; Juncus p. 1030 W.–H.; it may have occurred also in the Περὶ γήρως of Favorinus, since immortality is mentioned in a fragment of that work (12B Barigazzi: B.'s note takes it to refer to the pleasures of old age, but the mention of Plato and Pythagoras points to immortality as the topic under consideration). The immortality of the soul is a familiar Ciceronian topic, and his discussion of it here bears a resemblance to those in *Tusculans* I, the *Somnium Scipionis*, and fragments of the *Hortensius* and *Consolatio* (see commentary below). The *Cato* passage presents the Platonic arguments for immortality in an abbreviated form, and aims throughout at rhetorical effect rather than logical conviction. There are parallels also with the semi-philosophical tradition of consolatory writing (cf. Introd. pp. 10–11 nn. 30, 31). Somewhat different is the topic found in Lucretius' third book, where old men are chided for unwillingness to die: old men are traditionally φιλόζωοι (see note on §72 below).

To make Cato discourse on immortality in Platonic terms was doubtless Cicero's greatest departure from historical realism and character-portrayal in this dialogue; yet the overall effect is mitigated by the attribution of some of the ideas to the Pythagoreans, of whose doctrine Cato might have learnt something through his connections with Ennius and with southern Italy (see above on §§38 and 39), and by the use of a passage of Xenophon, an author with whose works Cato was almost certainly acquainted.

On the Platonic ideas themselves, and Cicero's use of them in general, see Boyancé, *Songe de Scipion*; id., *Assoc. G. Budé, Congrès de Tours et Poitiers: Actes du congrès* (Paris 1953) 195–221 = *Études sur l'humanisme cicéronien*, Coll. Latomus 121 (Brussels 1970) 222–47; id., *REG* 65 (1952) 337ff.; P. Festugière, *La Révélation d'Hermès Trismégiste* II (Paris 1949) and III (Paris 1953); F. Cumont, *Afterlife in Roman Paganism* (Yale 1922) 91ff.; L. Alfonsi, *Convivium* 22 (1954) 385ff.; R. M. Jones, *CPhil* 18 (1923) 202ff., esp. 214ff., against Posidonian source-criticism.

XIX Quarta restat causa See §15.

quae maxime angere ... videtur Cf. Musonius p. 92 H. τὸν τοῦ θανάτου φόβον ἐξαιρεθείη ἄν, ὃς μάλιστα θορυβεῖ τε καὶ πιέζει τοὺς γέροντας, ὥσπερ ἐπιλελησμένους ὅτι παντὶ θνητῷ θάνατος ὀφείλεται. καὶ τό γε ἀθλιώτατον ποιοῦν τὸν βίον τοῖς γέρουσιν αὐτὸ τοῦτό ἐστιν, ὁ τοῦ θανάτου φόβος ...

atque sollicitam habere This *atque* is unusual for Cicero, since it does not seem to be used for any obvious rhythmical reason (cf. above, §4); it could be Catonian, as Cato used *atque* notoriously often.

non potest esse longe Cf. *Tusc.* 1.91 *mors quae propter incertos casus cotidie imminet, propter brevitatem vitae numquam potest longe abesse*; Sen. *Ep.* 12.5; Fronto, *Ad amicos* 2.7. For *esse longe* cf. *Q. fr.* 3.8.2 *quam longe sint nescio*.

quae aut plane neglegenda est ... aut etiam optanda This is the standard dilemma on death, which goes back to Plato's *Apology* (40c): δυοῖν γὰρ θάτερόν ἐστιν τὸ τεθνάναι · ἢ γὰρ οἷον μηδὲν εἶναι μηδὲ αἴσθησιν μηδεμίαν μηδενὸς ἔχειν τὸν τεθνεῶτα, ἢ κατὰ τὰ λεγόμενα μεταβολή τις τυγχάνει οὖσα καὶ μετοίκησις τῇ ψυχῇ τοῦ τόπου τοῦ ἐνθένδε εἰς ἄλλον τόπον, etc.; it reappears in many places, cf. §81 below (from Xenophon); 74; 85; *Tusc.* 1.25–6; 82; 117–18; *Lael.* 14; *Sest.* 47; *Fam.* 5.16.4; Sen. *Polyb.* 9.2 and 23; *Marc.* 19.4–6; *Prov.* 6.6; *Ep.* 24.18; 57.8; 65.24; 71.16; 93.10; [Plato], *Axiochus* 365d ff.; Hyperides 6.43; M. Aur. 3.3.2; 5.33.5; 8.25; 8.58; 9.3; *Dicta Catonis* 3.22; Ambrose, *De bono mortis* 4.13 (from Cicero).

tertium certe nihil inveniri protest Cf. *Tusc.* 1.82 *quoniam nihil tertium est.* No attempt is made to show that eternal life is necessarily pleasant.

67   aut non miser ... aut beatus Cf. *Tusc.* 1.25 *aut beatos nos efficiet animis manentibus, aut non miseros sensu carentes.*

cui sit exploratum ... victurum Cf. *Fin.* 2.92 *an id exploratum cuiquam potest esse, quomodo se hoc habiturum sit corpus, non dico ad annum, sed ad vesperum?*; §74 and note; Simonides fr. 6.1 Diehl (16 Page); Eur. *Alc.* 783–4; Philodemus, *De morte* 37.23ff. (Gigante, *Ricerche filodemee*[2] 181, 193); Pap. Herc. 1251, col. 16.1 (W. Schmid, *Studia Herculanensia* fasc. 1, Leipzig 1939).

facilius in morbos incidunt For *incidere in morbum* cf. *Fam.* 13.29.3;

Cluent. 175; etc.; Greek ἐμπίπτειν. For the idea cf. [Hippocrates], *Aphorisms* 2.39 οἱ πρεσβῦται τῶν νέων τὰ μὲν πολλὰ νοσέουσιν ἧσσον. This is probably true of infectious illnesses, owing to the progressive build-up of immunity to them; and before the development of modern medicine, to survive to old age at all implied an originally strong constitution.

tristius curantur Cf. *Off.* 1.83 [*medici*] *leviter aegrotantes leniter curant, gravioribus autem morbis periculosas curationes et ancipites adhibere coguntur.*

mens ... et ratio et consilium Cf. §§17 and 19.

istud Wesenberg's conjecture (proposed on *Sest.* 9); the oldest MSS have *istius*, which is nonsense (though Simbeck printed it), while O²GRE recc. have *illud* (cf. Introd. p. 39: there is a chance that this may be right, and in any case it may well derive from tradition rather than conjecture). *istud* accounts satisfactorily for both of these readings; there is little to choose on grounds of sense between *istud* and *illud*.

cum adulescentia esse commune Cf. Sen. *Ep.* 12.6 *ista* [sc. *mors*] *tam seni ante oculos debet esse quam iuveni; non enim citamur ex censu;* id. *Rem. fort.* 4.1; [Plut.] *Cons. ad Apoll.* 113b ff.; Juncus p. 1030 W.–H. ἀλλὰ μὴν τὸ κοινὸν τοῦ θανάτου τέλος, καὶ ὅτι οὐδεὶς ἐπ' αὐτῷ νόμος ἢ χρόνος ὑπὸ τῶν θεῶν γέγραπται, ἴσον οἶμαι ποιεῖ τὸ πρᾶγμα τοῖς τε νέοις καὶ τοῖς γέρουσιν; cf. also §35 above.

68   filio M. Cato, the son of the Censor, died as praetor designate in or around 152, that is, two years before the dramatic date of this dialogue; cf. on §§15 and 84; *Lael.* 9; *Tusc.* 3.70; *Fam.* 4.6.1; Plut. *Cato* 24; [Livy], *Periocha* 48. Cicero in writing this was no doubt thinking of his own recent loss of Tullia: see also on §§12 and 35.

exspectatis ad *ad* is only in MH²O²Pa²Gς; it is necessary for the sense, but the usage is almost unparalleled; the nearest approach to a parallel is *De domo* 57 *ad meam pristinam dignitatem exspectatum atque revocatum,* where *revocatum* makes it considerably easier; cf. *TLL* 5, 2, 1901.

fratribus Apart from Scipio Aemilianus and Q. Fabius Maximus Aemilianus, Aemilius Paulus had two other sons, of whom one died five days before, the other three days after their father's triumph in 168, at the ages of fourteen and twelve (according to Plutarch: the other way round according to Livy). See *Fam.* 4.6.1; *Lael.* 9; Livy 45.40–1; Plut. *Aemil.* 35; Sen. *Marc.* 11.3; *Polyb.* 14.5.

diu se esse victurum This should be read, both for word-order (*se* in second place) and for rhythm (*essĕ vī̆|ctŭrŭm*).

idem This appears usually to be taken as neuter agreeing with *quod,* although it seems better to take it as masculine – 'the same man when he is old'.

ne quod speret quidem habet Cf. Sen. *Ep.* 30.4 *nil habet quod speret quem senectus ducit ad mortem.*

eo meliore ... cum *eo* + comparative ... *cum* + indic. is a regular phrase for 'so much the (better) in that': cf. *De or.* 2.154; *Att.* 3.23.4; *Quinct.* 63; *Fam.* 7.28.1; Ter. *Ad.* 897; H.–Sz. 619; Hale, *The Cum Constructions* 243; Draeger, *Hist. Syntax* II, 679.

69   o di boni! The *o* perhaps makes this slightly less colloquial: 'great heavens' rather than 'good gracious'. *di boni* is usually followed by either a question or an exclamation: Hofmann, *Umgangssprache* 30; Fraenkel, *Horace* 441; *TLL* 5, 1, 892, 34ff.

   quid est in hominis natura diu? Cf. *Tusc.* 1.94 *quae vero aetas longa est, aut quid omnino homini longum?*; Iambl. *Protrepticus* p. 47, 21 (generally taken to derive from Aristotle's *Protrepticus*, for which see W. Jaeger, *Aristotle* 60ff.: this reference = fr. 10a Walzer) τί δ' ἐστὶ μακρὸν ἢ τί πολυχρόνιον τῶν ἀνθρωπίνων;; also Virg. *Aen.* 10.861 *diu, res siqua diu mortalibus ulla est,* | *viximus.*

   ut scriptum video We should not, perhaps, take this to imply that Cicero thought Cato read Herodotus, though Plutarch credits him with knowledge of the Greek historians (*Cato* 12), and he certainly knew about the battle of Thermopylae (*Orig.* fr. 83 Peter; Plutarch ibid.).

   Arganthonius Cf. Hdt. 1.163; Anacreon fr. 8 Diehl; Pliny, *NH* 7.154; Val. Max. 8.13, ext. 4; Lucian, *Macr.* 10; Strab. 3.2.14 (quoting Anacreon); Cens. 17.3; Phlegon of Tralles, Περὶ μακροβίων, fr. 29.4 Jacoby (= Westermann, *Paradoxographi Graeci* 201); App. *Hisp.* 63; Sil. Ital. 3.396ff.; Themist. *or.* 2.38a. This man was proverbial for the length of his life and reign, though little else is known about him; in Herodotus he is the king who welcomes the Phocaean colonists, *c.* 600 B.C. (Regarding his name, it has been thought that it is cognate with *argentum*: it may be Celtic, since Irish *airgead*, Welsh *arian* (formerly *ariant*) and Breton *arc'hant* (formerly *argant*) imply a root *argant*-; however, the suffix causes problems. The region of Gades was inhabited by Celts in Strabo's time, but it is not clear of what race the original inhabitants were.) The tradition varies as to the length of his life. Anacreon, if taken literally (... ἔτεα | πεντήκοντά τε κἀκατὸν | Ταρτησσοῦ βασιλεῦσαι) implies 150 years as the length of his reign; but Pliny, Appian, Phlegon and Lucian took him to mean that Arganthonius lived 150 years. Phlegon, Lucian and Censorinus clearly omitted to look at Herodotus, since they report him as giving the same figure as Anacreon; Censorinus and Lucian both regard the figure of 150 as mythical. Herodotus, here followed by Cicero, gives 120 years for the life and 80 for the reign; Valerius Maximus gives this pair of figures, and also quotes Asinius Pollio for a figure of 130 for the life; Pliny, after quoting Anacreon's figure as mythical, reproduces those of Herodotus as *confessa*. Cicero's phrasing here perhaps implies that he knew the mythical version, while himself keeping to the Herodotean account, and substituting the well-known Gades for the doubtfully located Tartessus. See P.–W. 2, 686; 7, 439ff. on Tartessus; O. Gruppe, *Hermes* 10 (1876) 51ff.

regnaverit ... vixerit The subjunctive is due to 'virtual indirect speech'. *regnaverit* should be pronounced *regnarit* for the rhythm (double trochee rather than *clausula heroica*); it appears thus in a few MSS, and this no doubt explains the reading *regnavit* in V¹βR.

ne diuturnum quidem ... aliquid extremum Cf. Cic. *Pro Marc.* 27 *Quid enim est omnino hoc ipsum diu, in quo est aliquid extremum? quod cum venit, omnis voluptas praeterita pro nihilo est*; Sen. *Ep.* 77.20; 99.7; *Ad Marc.* 21.1; Metrodorus fr. 52 K., = Stob. 4.50b.77; August. *In Ev. Ioh.* 32.9 *quid est enim longum quod aliquando finitur?*

tantum remanet ... consecutus sis This sentiment seems authentically Catonian: see Cato *or.* fr. 17 Malcovati (speech at Numantia) *si quid vos per laborem recte feceritis, labor ille a vobis cito recedet, bene factum a vobis dum vivitis non abscedet.* Cf. also on §9; M. Aur. 6.30 εἰς καρπὸς τῆς ἐπιγείου ζωῆς, διάθεσις ὁσία καὶ πράξεις κοινωνικαί (cf. also §71).

horae quidem cedunt Cf. *Tusc.* 1.76 *volat aetas*; Ov. *Ars am.* 3.64; Virg. *Georg.* 3.284; Sen. *Ep.* 123.10; Marbod, *Lib. dec. cap.* 9.75ff.

quod cuique temporis ... contentus That one should be content with one's allotted lifespan is a common moralistic theme, and appears often in consolatory literature. Cf. the next section; *Tusc.* 1.109 *nemo parum diu vivit qui virtutis perfectae perfecto functus est munere*; *Phil.* 2.119; Lucr. 3.931–77 (this is a standard Epicurean theme: see Epicurus, *Ep.* 3.126; Cic. *Fin.* 1.63); Sen. *Ep.* 93.4; 101.15; *Marc.* 24.1; *Benef.* 5.17.6; M. Aur. 2.14; 4.50; 12.35 (see below); [Plut.] *Cons. ad Apoll.* 111a (see below); Milton, *Paradise Lost* 11.553 (cf. also Sen. *Ep.* 24.24, quoted on §72).

70 neque enim histrioni ... peragenda fabula est (On dramatic similes in general, see on §5). This comparison occurs in very similar forms in a number of places: Sen. *Ep.* 77.20 *quomodo fabula, sic vita; non quam diu sed quam bene acta sit refert*; M. Aur. 3.8 (the opposite idea: actors *must* finish the play, but there is no such thing as an incomplete life); 12.35–6 οἷον εἰ κωμῳδὸν ἀπολύοι τῆς σκηνῆς ὁ παραλαβὼν στρατηγός. "ἀλλ' οὐκ εἶπον τὰ πέντε μέρη, ἀλλὰ τὰ τρία." καλῶς εἶπας· ἐν μέντοι τῷ βίῳ τὰ τρία ὅλον τὸ δρᾶμά ἐστιν; Epictetus, *Ench.* 17; also [Plut.] *Cons. ad Apoll.* 17.111a οὐχ ὁ μακρότατος βίος ἄριστος ἀλλ' ὁ σπουδαιότατος· οὐδὲ γὰρ ὁ πλεῖστα κιθαρῳδήσας ἢ ῥητορεύσας ἢ κυβερνήσας, ἀλλ' ὁ καλῶς ἐπαινεῖται. Presumably what is being envisaged in Cicero's image is something like what happened to Turpio Ambivius at the first performance of Terence's *Hecyra*, as narrated by himself in the prologue: *primo actu placeo; cum interea rumor venit | datum iri gladiatores, populus convolat, | tumultuantur, clamant, pugnant de loco: | ego interea meum non potui tutari locum.* Marcus Aurelius envisages the actor as dismissed by the presiding officer; in Seneca and Epictetus, the performance is simply a short one.

'plaudite' The 'final curtain': cf. Hor. *AP* 155; Quint. *Inst.* 6.1.52; Suet. *Aug.* 99.

breve enim tempus aetatis ... vivendum Cf. above, §69; *Tusc.* 1.109; Sen. *Ep.* 101.15 *quam bene vivas referre, non quam diu*; ibid. 49.10; 13.13; 92.24ff; *Benef.* 5.17.6. Cicero is not being dogmatically philosophical here, but one may mention by way of background the debate between Stoics and Peripatetics as to whether length of time affected εὐδαιμονία: the latter thought that a complete life was necessary before one could be said to be happy (Arist. *NE* 1.1098a18ff.), where the Stoics maintained that the quality of εὐδαιμονία was not increased by possessing it for longer (Cic. *Fin.* 3.46=*SVF* III, 524; Plut. *Comm. Not.* 1061f; Sen. *Ep.* 70.5; etc.). Cf. also Wisdom of Solomon 4.7 γῆρας γὰρ τίμιον οὐ τὸ πολυχρόνιον; Reid quotes Jonson, *Underwood* 88, 'In short measures, life may perfect be'.

ver enim ... accommodata sunt The comparison of the four ages of man with the four seasons is not uncommon. There is a tradition that links it with Pythagoreanism; it occurs in the speech of Pythagoras in Ov. *Met.* 15.199ff., esp. 209ff. *excipit autumnus, posito fervore iuventae | maturus mitisque inter iuvenemque senemque | temperie medius, sparsus quoque tempora canis: | inde senilis hiems tremulo venit horrida passu, | aut spoliata suos, aut quos habet, alba capillos*; the idea is also attributed to Pythagoras in Diog. Laert. 8.9–10 (see also on §33; A. Rostagni, *Il verbo di Pitagora* (Turin 1924) 92). Elsewhere see Favorinus fr. 10 Barigazzi = Eratosthenes ap. Stob. 4.50b.78 (cf. Introd. p. 28 for Favorinus) τῆς ἡλικίας ἔφη τὸ μὲν ἀκμάζον ἔαρ εἶναι, τὸ δὲ μετὰ τὴν ἀκμὴν θέρος καὶ μετόπωρον, χειμῶνα δὲ τὸ γῆρας; Metrocles ap. Stob. ibid. 84 τὸ γῆρας τοῦ βίου ἔλεγε χειμῶνα; Galen, *Protr.* 8; Plut. *Quaest. conv.* 8.10.736a; Pericles ap. Arist. *Rhet.* 1.7.34.1365a; Pöschl, *Bibl. Bildersprache* 499. In modern times the best-known example is perhaps Keats, 'Sonnet: The Human Seasons'. In the majority of examples, old age corresponds to winter, and is regarded pessimistically; here, in keeping with the rest of the argument, Cicero makes old age equivalent to autumn.

ostenditque For this sense of *ostendere* in connection with future events, cf. *Fam.* 9.8.1; *ND* 2.7; etc. (*OLD* s.v. ostendere 13).

fructus Cf. §§9 and 62 above; *Cael.* 77 *in adulescentia vero tamquam in herbis significant* [sc. *studia*] *quae virtutis maturitas et quantae fruges industriae sint futurae.*

accommodata *accommodatus*+dative of the gerundive apparently occurs only here in Cicero: H.–Sz. 377.

71 Omnia autem ... in bonis Cf. *Fin.* 5.89–91, esp. 89 *bonum appello quidquid secundum naturam est*; *Leg.* 1.54 *antiqui omne quod secundum naturam esset* *quo iuvaremur in vita, bonum esse decreverint; hic* [i.e. *Zeno*] *nihil nisi quod honestum esset putavit bonum*. This formulation is not Stoic; it belongs strictly to Antiochus' version of Academic philosophy, and was attributed by him to Plato and Aristotle (cf. *Fin.* 4.72); but here it is merely a piece of semi-philosophical moralising, and not intended to be dogmatic. The Stoics would reject the idea that anything external in nature (whether *secundum naturam* or not) could be called 'good'.

On the naturalness of death, cf. Eur. *Hypsipyle* 95–6 (757 N.) τί ταῦτα δεῖ | στένειν, ἅπερ δεῖ κατὰ φύσιν διεκπερᾶν; (quoted in a number of places: see [Plut.] *Cons. ad Apoll.* 110e; Cic. *Tusc.* 3.59 – his own verse translation; M. Aur. 7.40; Clem. Alex. *Strom.* 4.7.53); M. Aur. 9.3; 9.21; 12.35.

flammae vis opprimitur ... consumptus ignis exstinguitur Note the difference between *exstinguere* and *opprimere*: our 'extinguish' corresponds to *opprimere*, whereas *exstinguere* implies a gradual burning out. Cf. §38; *Lael.* 78 *exstinctae potius amicitiae quam oppressae esse videantur*. Aristotle, *De sen. et iuv.* 5, compares the death of young men and old men in similar terms: ἀλλὰ μὴν πυρός γε δύο ὁρῶμεν φθοράς, μάρανσίν τε καὶ σβέσιν. καλοῦμεν δὲ τὴν μὲν ὑφ' αὑτοῦ μάρανσιν, τὴν δ' ὑπὸ τῶν ἐναντίων σβέσιν· τὴν μὲν γήρᾳ, τὴν δὲ βίαιον; ibid. 24 ὁ μὲν ἐν γήρᾳ θάνατος μάρανσις τοῦ μορίου δι' ἀδυναμίαν τοῦ καταψύχειν ὑπὸ γήρως; cf. also on §72 below. A. Wünsche, *Z. f. d. alttestamentliche Wissenschaft* 3 (1883) 126–8, notes that the metaphors of fire and of ripening fruit occur together, in an exactly similar context to this one, in the Midrash on Ecclesiastes 5.11: the parallel is striking, but it is not clear whether any direct connection can be established. For other Jewish parallels see on §§21; 24; 65. L. Alfonsi (in *Das neue Cicerobild*) quotes Petrarch, *Trionfo della Morte* 5,160ff.: Petrarch was well acquainted with the *Cato*, as his *Senilium rerum libri* show.

quasi Equivalent to *sicut*, a not too common use, which disappears after Cicero's time and may have been old-fashioned then: cf. Cato *orat.* fr. 201 Malcovati[2]; Plaut. *Merc.* 695; *Stich.* 539; Lucr. 3.492; Cic. *Fam.* 9.16.2. Cf. H.–Sz. 674; *OLD* s.v. *quasi* 4; Introd. p. 22.

poma ex arboribus Cf. the very similar comparison in an epitaph, *CIL* 12,533 = Bücheler, *CLE* 465, 19–21 (from Aquae Sextiae, end of second century A.D.) *ut* [*citrea*] *poma* | [*quae*] *matura cadunt* [*aut*] *immatura* [*leguntur*]; cf. Bücheler 1490; 1542–3; Lattimore, *Epitaphs* 255. See also Philodemus, *De morte* col. 9, 12ff. (Gigante, *Ricerche filodemee* 124 and 160); M. Aur. 4.48; Milton, *Paradise Lost* 11.535ff; and the article of A. Wünsche cited above.

vitam ... maturitas Quoted by Montaigne, *Essais* 3, 13. *maturitas*: cf. §§5 and 85; Varro, *Tithonus* (cf. Introd. pp. 26–7) fr. 547 B. *sic invitata matura anima corporeum corticem facile relinquit*.

in portum A common image; cf. *Att.* 14.19.1 (written in May 44) *ille* [i.e. *Brutus*] *exsilium meditari: nos autem alium portum propiorem huic aetati videbamus; Tusc.* 1.118 *portum potius paratum nobis et perfugium putemus*; ibid. 107; Sen. *Ep.* 70.3; *Polyb.* 9.6–7; Pliny, *NH* 25.24; Epict. *Diss.* 4.10; M. Aur. 3.3.2; Plut. *Tranq. an.* 476a; Juncus p. 1031 W.-H. (of an old man's death in particular: cf. also Themist. *De anima*); Ael. *VH* 4.7; Sotades ap. Stob. 4.52b.31; *Anth. Pal.* 9.49 and 9.172, cf. Bücheler, *CLE* 1498; C. Bonner, 'Desired Haven', *Harvard Theological Review* 34 (1941) 49ff. On the image of the voyage of life in general, see Pöschl, *Bibl. Bildersprache* 547, Nisbet–Hubbard on Hor. *Od.* 2.10.1; L. Alfonsi in Büchner, *Cicerobild* 225.

XX 72   munus offici Cf. above, §§29 and 35.

tueri Cf. *Tusc.* 5.113; *Fam.* 10.11.1.

possis et tamen mortem contemnere This is fairly clearly the correct reading; some edd. read *possit* with PH[1] etc., but it is difficult to extract a subject for *possit* from the impersonal *vivitur*, whereas the generalised second person *possis* gives a much smoother transition; the subjunctive is regular in the generalised second person, whereas it would not be so in the third person (W. Maguinness, *CR* 48 (1934) 211). *tamen* means 'at the same time': i.e. one should keep on with the occupations of one's life, and at the same time one should not be so attached to them that one is afraid to let them go in the event of death.

animosior ... et fortior For the combination of adjectives see *Mil.* 92; Hor. *Od.* 2.10.21; *TLL* 2, 88, 41ff. For the idea, cf. Sen. *Ep.* 104.2 *me fortiorem senectus ad multa reddiderit*; ibid. 4 *senectutem ... cuius maximus fructus est securior sui tutela et vitae usus animosior.* Contrast the usual (and Aristotelian) idea of the old man as *iners pavidusque futuri* (Hor. *AP* 172): see on §65 above.

hoc illud est This sentence is more or less parenthetic; the next sentence resumes the main argument. *hoc illud est* = Greek τοῦτ' ἐκεῖνο; cf. *Div.* 1.122. This anecdote is found in Plut. *An seni* 794f τοῦ Πεισιστράτου ... πυνθανομένου τίνι πεποιθὼς ταῦτα πράττει, "τῷ γήρᾳ" εἶπεν; id. *Solon* 31. For Solon's resistance to Pisistratus cf. also [Arist.] *Ath. pol.* 14.2.

audaciter This is in all MSS except V²RBe¹, and it is probable that Cicero used this spelling: Priscian quotes *Rosc. Am.* 104 for *audaciter*, and it occurs also in the MSS of *Font.* 11; *Dom.* 28; [Cic.] *Ad Her.* 4.28; see *TLL* 2, 1428, 64ff.; Neue–Wagener ii³, 685. Quintilian (*Inst.* 1.6.17) regards the form as pedantic, and it may have had a certain old-fashioned effect in Cicero's time.

It is possible that in Cicero's time the word was pronounced *audacter* even when written with the -*i*-; that pronunciation would give a commoner clausula here.

integra mente Referring to sanity, not morality: cf. Hor. *Od.* 1.31.18

and Nisbet–Hubbard ad loc.; *TLL* 7, 1, 2075; Sen. *Ep.* 58.33 *si modo mens sine iniuria est et integri sensus animum iuvant*; *Acad. pr.* 2.19 *integris incorruptisque sensibus.*

eadem quae coagmentavit natura According to Diog. Laert. 4.64, Carneades, just before he died, kept saying ἡ συστήσασα φύσις καὶ διαλύσει; cf. also Sen. *Ep.* 30.11 (*coagmentatio* = σύστατον σῶμα in Cic. *Tim.* 17 = Plat. *Timaeus* 33a).

dissolvit Cf. *Tusc.* 1.71; Sen. *Ep.* 26.4 *Ecquis exitus est melior quam in finem suum natura solvente dilabi?*; [Plato], *Axiochus* 365e; Epictetus, *Diss.* 4.7; M. Aur. 9.3; 9.21; 2.17.2; cf. §80.

navem ... aedificium Cf. Sen. *Ep.* 30.2; 58.35; 102.6; *De ira* 2.28.4; *NQ* 6.10.1–2; also the anecdote concerning Gorgias in Stob. 4.51.28.

iam 'and then': cf. §56 above.

conglutinatio The word occurs here and in *Orat.* 78, *conglutinatio verborum*, then in late Latin: *TLL* 4, 284, 24.

recens aegre, inveterata facile *inveteratus*, like 'inveterate' in English, can often have the connotation of being hardened and toughened by age, but it does not have it here; the image of old ships and houses is still in the mind. For the idea that death comes easily in old age, as a sort of dissolution, see Plato, *Timaeus* 81d–e μεθιᾶσι τοὺς τῆς ψυχῆς δεσμούς, ἡ δὲ λυθεῖσα κατὰ φύσιν μεθ' ἡδονῆς ἐξέπτατο ... καὶ θάνατος δὴ ... ὁ μετὰ γῆρας ἰὼν ἐπὶ τέλος κατὰ φύσιν ἀπονώτατος τῶν θανάτων καὶ μᾶλλον μεθ' ἡδονῆς γιγνόμενος ἢ λύπης; Arist. *sen. et iuv.* 23.

illud breve vitae reliquum Editors quote Bion, fr. 64 Kindstrand (*Gnom. vat.* 163) τὸ γῆρας ἔφη εἶναι λείψανον τοῦ βίου (cf. Sen. *Ep.* 102.2; Palladas, *Anth. Pal.* 11.54); but there is no real parallel here. Cicero is not saying that old age is a 'leftover' of life; that would have been *reliquiae*, not *reliquum* (cf. Introd. p. 14 n. 36, and Appendix 2). It would be more to the point to refer to Plaut. *Merc.* 547–8 *breve iam relicuum vitae spatiumst: quin ego | voluptate vino et amore delectavero* (following the reading of A: that of P in l. 547 is even nearer, *decurso spatio breve quod vitae relicuumst ...*). Whether Cicero was really alluding to this passage cannot, of course, be certain; but such an allusion would have some point; Demipho in Plautus is saying, if not that he 'avidly desires' to live longer, at least that he is determined to enjoy whatever life is left to him; thus in a sense he is attached to life (φιλόζωος). One may also wonder whether *illud* in Cicero implies that the following words are a quotation or allusion; perhaps one might even go so far as to print *illud 'breve vitae relicuum' nec avide appetendum* ... But the phrase is not distinctive enough to make this more than a hypothesis.

nec avide appetendum ... deserundum sit cf. Sen. *Ep.* 58.32 *quam* [i.e. *senectutem*] *ut non puto concupiscendam, ita ne recusandam quidem*; ibid. 24.24 *ne nimis amemus vitam et ne nimis oderimus*. On φιλόζωοι γέροντες, those who cling desperately on to life, see Soph. fr. 63 N.²; Eur. *Alc.* 669–72; *Suppl.*

1108ff.; Aristo of Chios fr. 399 von Arnim (cf. Appendix 2); Philodemus, *De morte* col. 39, 6 (Gigante² p. 224); Sen *Brev. vit.* 11.1; *Ep.* 101.10–15 (quoting Maecenas fr. 4 Morel); Lucian, *Dial. mort.* 6.2; 27; Menecr. or Lucil. *Anth. Pal.* 9.55.

73 vetatque Pythagoras ... decedere This sentence expands on *sine causa deserundum*. *sine causa* looks like a concession to the Stoics, who believed that suicide was permissible if there was a good reason for it; but Cicero now refers to the Platonic and Pythagorean prohibition of suicide, as he had done previously in *De rep.* 6.15 (*Somn. Scip.* 7) *nisi enim deus is cuius hoc templum est omne quod conspicis, istis te corporis custodiis liberarit, huc tibi aditus patere non potest; quare et tibi, Publi, et piis omnibus, retinendus animus est in custodia corporis, nec iniussu eius a quo ille est vobis datus ex hominum vita migrandum est, ne munus humanum assignatum a deo defugisse videamini; Tusc.* 1.74 *vetat enim dominans ille in nobis deus iniussu hinc nos suo demigrare;* cf. 1.118; *Scaur.* 5 *Pythagoram aut Platonem ... qui tamen mortem ita laudant ut fugere vitam vetent atque id contra foedus fieri dicant legemque naturae.* The immediate source of the ideas expressed in these passages is, without doubt, the passage of Plato's *Phaedo* (61d ff.) where the prohibition of suicide is discussed; one of the authorities there quoted by Plato's Socrates is Philolaus the Pythagorean, and there is no reason to doubt that Cicero here is right in claiming the doctrine as Pythagorean (cf. also above, p. 238). The prohibition of suicide also occurs in another Pythagorean source, Euxitheus quoted by Clearchus of Soli fr. 38 Wehrli (ap. Athen. 4.157c; D.–K. 44B14); this has sometimes been supposed to have been derived from the *Phaedo*, Euxitheus being an invented character, but certainly *prima facie* it is further evidence for the existence of the doctrine among Pythagoreans; cf. Wehrli ad loc., p. 59; Burkert, *Lore and Science* 124 n. 21; P.–W. 6, 1539; Burnet on *Phaedo* loc. cit. However, it is doubtful whether Cicero would have known the doctrine from any source other than Plato.

The reason given by Cicero here for the prohibition is quite clear: human life is envisaged as a sort of guard-duty under the command of a god, and to commit suicide is to desert one's post. There is a similar thought behind §77 below *ut essent qui terras tuerentur*; and the idea of life as a military campaign is common enough, at any rate in later times (cf. Epictetus, *Diss.* 1.9.10–10; 3.24.31–2 and 95ff.; M. Aur. 3.5.1; [Plut.] *Cons. ad Apoll.* 111d; Sen. *Ep.* 96.5; Otto, *Sprichwörter* 377; Pöschl, *Bibl. Bildersprache* 524; W. R. Halliday, *The Pagan Background of Early Christianity* (Liverpool 1925) 302). It is possible that the use of the military image owes something to Plato, *Apol.* 28d, in which Socrates compares his own philosophical activity to military service under divine command, though that passage makes no mention of suicide. It is worth noting that Epictetus, who clearly recalls this passage of Plato, does make the explicit connection with suicide; this could reflect post-Platonic interpretation.

It is difficult not to think, however, that Cicero here reflects the 'secret doctrine' of *Phaedo* 62b ὡς ἔν τινι φρουρᾷ ἐσμὲν οἱ ἄνθρωποι καὶ οὐ δεῖ δὴ ἑαυτὸν ἐκ ταύτης λύειν οὐδ' ἀποδιδράσκειν. In that passage, the phrase ἔν τινι φρουρᾷ can be taken to mean either 'on guard' or 'under guard' (i.e. in prison).[1] Considering this passage alone, it is easy enough to suppose that Cicero is here alluding to the 'on guard' interpretation. However, in the *Somnium Scipionis* (quoted above) and in *Tusc.* 1.74, he seems clearly to interpret φρουρά as 'prison'. The word *custodia*, which he uses in the *Somnium*, is an exact equivalent of φρουρά, and shares its ambiguity, but the context makes it plain that 'prison' is meant. Yet a few lines later in that passage, Cicero brings in the idea of guard-duty, *ne munus humanum assignatum a deo defugisse videamini*. Boyancé's solution was to suppose that the *Cato* passage is not meant to reflect the *Phaedo* at all (*Songe de Scipion* 121ff.). It seems to me more likely that Cicero was aware of both interpretations, and used one or other of them as his context demanded, incorporating both in the *Somnium* passage.

Solonis Fr. 21 Bergk: M. L. West, *Iambi et Elegi Graeci* II, 133; quoted in Stob. 4.54.3; Plut. *Solon et Publ.* 1 μηδέ μοι ἄκλαυτος θάνατος μόλοι, ἀλλὰ φίλοισι|καλλείποιμι θανὼν ἄλγεα καὶ στοναχάς. Cicero refers to the couplet also in *Tusc.* 1.117, quoting his own Latin version (which would clearly have been inappropriate here, since Cato is speaking), and making exactly the same comparison with Ennius. The couplet of Solon's, as we learn from Plutarch, belonged to a poem addressed to Mimnermus, in which he said that he would rather die at eighty than at sixty (as Mimnermus had written, fr. 6: cf. Introd. p. 25 n. 62). *elogium* here simply means an elegiac poem or extract, not an epitaph as above in §61.

vult, credo, se esse carum suis Not, as some take it, = *vult dicere se esse carum*, but = *vult esse carum*; for *velle se esse* = *velle esse*, cf. *Off.* 1.113; *Tusc.* 2.64; 3.64; and often in comedy; K.–S. 1, 714.

nemo me lacrimis ... faxit Ennius, *varia* fr. 17 V.[2]: see also *Tusc.*

[1] On this vexed question see the commentators on *Phaedo* loc. cit.; Courcelle, *Connais-toi toi-même* (cited p. 191) 345ff., esp. 246 n. 110 and bibliography; Boyancé, *Rev. Phil.* 37 (1963) 7ff. Plato may have been deliberately ambiguous, but if a choice has to be made it seems that the 'prison' interpretation is more likely: the idea of human life as a prison is common throughout the later tradition, and it is specifically connected with the prohibition of suicide in the Euxitheus fragment referred to above; apart from the *Somnium Scipionis*, discussed above, later references to the *Phaedo* passage seem fairly unambiguously in favour of 'prison', cf. [Plato], *Axiochus* 365e, Dio Chrys. *Or.* 30.10, Macr. *In somn. Scip.* 1.13.5ff. Contemporary usage of φρουρά does not help very much, as there are no strictly parallel instances: in *Gorgias* 525a, the only other occurrence of the word in Plato, it means 'guarded place' or 'prison', but the context is quite different, and otherwise ἐν φρουρᾷ seems to be most naturally used to mean 'on guard' (cf. Burnet on the *Phaedo*). For *custodia* in both senses see *TLL* 4,1555ff.

1.34; 117 for quotations of this epigram. On the epigram itself see Schanz–Hosius I, 97–8; M. Lausberg, *Das Einzeldistichon: Studien zum antiken Epigramm* (Munich 1982) 276–7; W. Suerbaum, *Unters. zur Selbstdarstellung älterer römischer Dichter* (Hildesheim 1968) 168ff.; S. Lundström, *Hermes* 104 (1976) 186–7, comparing Thgn. 240.

lacrimis Bergk (*Philol.* 15 (1859) 187) proposed to read *dacrumis*, an archaic form which would alliterate with *decoret*. We know that Livius Andronicus used *dacruma* (Paul. Fest. p. 60, 5), but have no information on Ennius: Reid takes this absence of any positive statement in the grammarians as evidence that Ennius did not use the form, though it may possibly have been modernised in the texts of Ennius to which the grammarians had access. The form may be plausibly restored in the text of Plautus once at least, in *Pseud.* 100–1, where there seems to be a pun on *drachumae/dacrumae*. If Ennius used the form, it may have been as a conscious archaism or Graecism, and/or in order to help the alliteration. There is no evidence on the date of the *d–l* change in other words, and no satisfactory explanation has been advanced for its happening in some words but not in others; see Sommer, *Laut- u. Formenlehre* p. 193; Leumann, *Laut- u. Formenlehre* pp. 155–6. (On this passage cf. also A. Fleckeisen, *N. Jb. Kl. Phil.* 87 (1863) 192; G. Lahmeyer, *Philol.* 20 (1864) 286.)

immortalitas There is no mention of literal immortality in Ennius' epigram, which makes it clear that it was his verses that were to be immortal. In *Tusc.* 1.31ff., Cicero argues that the desire for glory after death, as manifested by Ennius here, implies that the soul survives to enjoy it (cf. a similar argument in §82 below). But here the argument is left out, and the impression is given that Cicero has confused poetic immortality with the immortality of the soul.

74 **sensus moriendi** Cf. *Lael.* 12 *moriendi autem sensum celeritas abstulit*; *Tusc.* 1.82; Sen. *Ep.* 30; Arist. *sen. et iuv.* 23.

optandus aut nullus See §66.

meditatum For the idea that one must practise not fearing death, cf. Sen. *Ep.* 26.8–10 (quoting Epicurus fr. 205 Usener) *meditare mortem*; 30.18; 36.7ff.; 69.6; etc.; *Brev. vit.* 7 *tota vita discendum est mori*; Epictetus, *Diss.* 3.10.6; *Ench.* 21; Plut. *Tranq. an.* 465b; 476d–e; [Plut.] *Cons. ad Apoll.* 104a; Musonius p. 92 H.; Porph. *De abst.* 1.51. It is not clear whether Cicero was thinking here of Plato's μελέτη θανάτου (*Phaedo* 67e, cf. *Tusc.* 1.74ff.), which is somewhat different.

moriendum enim certe est Cf. *Tusc.* 1.14 *quae enim potest in vita esse iucunditas, cum dies et noctes cogitandum sit iam iamque esse moriendum?*; 1.91 *mors quae propter incertos casus cotidie imminet*; 5.15 *quis enim potest mortem aut dolorem metuens, quorum alterum saepe adest, alterum semper impendet, esse non miser?*; *Fin.* 1.60; Sen. *Ep.* 26.7; 30.17; etc. (see A. L. Motto, *Guide to the Thought of L.*

Annaeus Seneca (Amsterdam 1970) 60); Demetr. *Form. epist.* 5 (given as a standard theme for consolations). Cf. also Macrob. *In somn. Scip.* 1.10.16 (with the story of the Sword of Damocles) *sic semper mortem nobis imminentem videmus. aestima, quando esse felix poterit, qui timere non desinit?*

qui poterit If *qui* (adverbial) is right here, an indefinite subject must be understood from *nemo* above, though this is rather difficult. More difficult still is the proposal of K.–S. 1, 224 to take *timens* as substantival: there are no Ciceronian parallels for this in the nominative singular (Laughton, *Participle* 72–3). Certainly *qui* adverbial is very common before parts of *posse* (cf. above on §4); but it may be better to adopt *quis* (VM, etc.) or to take *qui* as equivalent to *quis*.

75 qua Sc. *morte*.

Lucium Brutum ... duos Decios ... Marcum Atilium ... duos Scipiones ... Lucium Paulum ... Marcum Marcellum There are a number of Ciceronian passages where a whole series of Roman heroes is referred to. In *Tusc.* 1.89 the argument is the same as here, and so virtually are the examples, except that three Decii are mentioned, Regulus is omitted (as the list there only includes those who died in battle), Cn. Servilius Geminus is added as a second casualty of Cannae, and two later examples are added at the end. Cf. also ibid. 1.110; *De rep.* 1.1; *Off.* 1.61; *Parad.* 1.12; *ND* 3.80. (See also Appendix 1, p. 267.) On Brutus see Livy 2.2–6: he was traditionally said to have been killed fighting Arruns Tarquinius.

duos Decios See on §43.

Marcum Atilium Regulus: P.–W. 2, 2086ff. (Atilius 51). Cf. *Off.* 1.39; 3.99; *ND* 3.80; *Fin.* 2.65; *Sest.* 127; Sen. *Helv.* 12.5–7; *Tranq.* 16.4; *Prov.* 3.4; *Benef.* 5.3.2; *Ep.* 67.7–12; 98.12; Hor. *Od.* 3.5; etc.

Scipiones Gnaeus and Publius: cf. §§29 and 82; *Parad.* 1.12 *Carthaginiensium adventum corporibus suis intercludendum putaverunt*; *ND* 3.80 (see Pease ad loc.); *Tusc.* 1.89; *Off.* 1.61; *De rep.* 1.1; *Balb.* 34.

Paulum Cf. §§29 and 82; *Tusc.* 1.89; *ND* 3.80; *Div.* 2.71.

collegae C. Terentius Varro, the surviving, and later much blamed, commander of the Roman army at Cannae: see Polyb. 3.107–18 and Walbank's note; Livy 22, 43–9; P.–W. 1, 581; 3, 1483–4.

Marcellum Killed by the Carthaginians near Venusia in 208; the tradition is that Hannibal sent his ashes back to Rome. Cf. *Tusc.* 1.89; 1.110; *ND* 2.165; 3.80; *Off.* 1.61; *Div.* 2.77; Livy 27.26; Plut. *Marc.* 30; Virg. *Aen.* 6.856ff.

crudelissimus Hannibal was traditionally *crudelis* or *dirus*: cf. *Lael.* 28; *Off.* 1.38; Livy 21.4; Hor. *Od.* 2.12.2; 3.6.36; etc.

honore sepulturae It was customary among the ancients to perform funeral rites for fallen enemies, or to allow them to be performed: for the Greeks, cf. Eur. *Suppl.* 524; Isocr. *Plat.* 416.

legiones ... arbitrarentur = *Orig.* 4, fr. 8 Jordan, fr. 83 Peter (linked by both edd., for no very compelling reason, with the story of the tribune Caedicius); cf. *Tusc.* 1.101 *legiones scribit Cato saepe alacres in eum locum profectas unde redituras se non arbitrarentur.* Cf. also Sen. *Ep.* 82.22, quoting an unnamed Roman general, *ire illo necesse est, unde redire non est necesse*; the anonymous form of this item may reflect a Catonian origin, since he excluded names of generals from at least part of his history. Cicero also invokes the courage of whole Roman armies in *Tusc.* 1.89 and *Off.* 1.61.

quod igitur adulescentes ... extimescent? Cf. *Tusc.* 2.39, *ergo haec veteranus miles facere poterit, doctus vir sapiensque non poterit?*; ibid. 41.

76 satietas Cf. §85 below; *Tusc.* 1.109; *Marc.* 27 (to Caesar, recalling his own remark *satis diu vixi vel naturae vel gloriae*).

pueritiae ... adulescentiae ... aetas quae media dicitur ... senectutis For the fourfold division of human life, see §33; also on §§4 and 70.

tempus maturum Cf. §§5; 33; 71–2; 85.

XXI 77 Non enim video Probably to be preferred to *equidem non video*; though *enim* refers back to nothing more definite than the mention of death in the last sentence, it seems desirable as a connection.

eo cernere ... melius from Plato, *Rep.* 330e καὶ αὐτὸς ἤτοι ὑπὸ τῆς τοῦ γήρως ἀσθενείας ἢ καὶ ὥσπερ ἤδη ἐγγυτέρω ὢν τῶν ἐκεῖ μᾶλλόν τι καθορᾷ αὐτά.

Publi Scipio tuque Gai Laeli Cf. *Lael.* 100 *C. Fanni et tu Q. Muci*: the fuller nomenclature gives a solemn effect in this climactic passage. The MSS, except VMO²Gς, have *tu* instead of *P(ubli)*; but if we have one *praenomen* we must have both, and the isolated vocative *tu* does not connect well with the context. (There is however no problem with *tuque*: having addressed Scipio, Cato now turns to Laelius.)

numeranda So MR²Q only: but I have little hesitation in adopting this reading (wherever it comes from in those MSS). There is perhaps little to choose between *numeranda* and *nominanda* as regards the sense, though it seems to me (maybe subjectively) that *numeranda* has the edge: 'that life which alone should be counted as life' puts the emphasis where it should be, on substance rather than names. The main improvement is in the rhythm: *sola vita nominanda* is a surprisingly trochaic clausula, especially at this climactic point in the text, while *vita numeranda* could not be improved on. For this use of *numerare*, common enough in Cicero, cf. *Brut.* 221; *Att.* 7.1.3; *ND* 1.33; etc.; *OLD* s.v. 8.

The doctrine that life after death is the only true life reappears in §82 below; Cicero had previously made use of it in *De rep.* 6.14 (*Somn. Scip.*) *immo vero hi vivunt qui e corporum vinculis tamquam e carcere evolaverunt, vestra vero quae dicitur vita mors est*; *Scaur.* 4; *Tusc.* 1.75 (context largely derived from Plato's *Phaedo*). Cicero seems convinced that the idea is Platonic (he attributes it to Socrates' last conversation in *Scaur.* loc. cit.), but Plato nowhere claims it as his own, nor does Socrates in Plato: it is attributed to οἱ σοφοί (*not* to the Orphics: cf. Dodds, *Irrational* 169, n. 87) in *Gorg.* 492d, quoting Eur. *Polyidus* fr. 639 N.; cf. *Crat.* 400c. The striking *vita mors est* seems to have become popularly associated with the idea of Platonic immortality; but the expression of the idea is rather toned down in the present passage, perhaps in order to conform with the character of Cato.

inclusi Cf. Lucr. 3.774 *conclusa manere in corpore* (making fun of the idea); 1.414 *vitai claustra*; see note on §81 *corporum vinculis*.

munere … necessitatis Cf. Plato, *Timaeus* 42a σώμασιν ἐμφυτευθεῖεν ἐξ ἀνάγκης; Plotinus, *Enn.* 2.9.18. However, the idea that human life is a *munus* and *grave opus* is more Ciceronian than Platonic: cf. the next sentence, §73 and note; *De rep.* 6.15 *munus humanum adsignatum a deo*.

est enim animus caelestis Cf. *De rep.* 6.15 *eisque* [sc. *hominibus*] *animus datus est ex illis sempiternis ignibus, quae sidera et stellas vocatis*; *Hortensius* fr. 115 Grilli (August. *Trin.* 14.19.26); *Tusc.* 1.51; *Consolatio* fr. ap. Cic. *Tusc.* 1.66; *Leg.* 1.26; Virg. *Aen.* 6.730 *igneus est ollis vigor et caelestis origo*; Quint. *Inst.* 1.1.1; Josephus, *BJ* 2.8.11 (Essenes).

The idea of the descent of the soul from an original heavenly state derives from *Timaeus* 41d–e, and was much elaborated in later Platonism: cf. P. Festugière, *La Révélation d'Hermès Trismégiste* III, 63ff.; Boyancé, *Songe de Scipion* 129–33.

locum divinae naturae aeternitatique contrarium Cf. *De rep.* 6.17 *infra autem iam nihil est nisi mortale et caducum, praeter animos …, supra lunam sunt aeterna omnia.* There is no exact Platonic authority for this idea, as G. Schneider, *Z. f. d. Gymn.* 33 (1879) 689ff., points out; it derives naturally enough from Plato's view of the visible world as transitory and inferior to the intelligible world, though the contrast is here with a heaven presumably located somewhere in space – doubtless a popularised version of the idea.

sparsisse animos Cf. *Timaeus* 42d ἔσπειρε; 42a ἐμφυτευθεῖεν; Cic. *Leg.* 1.24; Plut. *De facie* 945c; cf. P. Boyancé, *CRAI* 1960, 253–88 = *Romanitas* 3.3–4 (1961) 111–17 = *Études sur l'humanisme cicéronien*, Coll. Latomus 121 (Brussels 1970) 294–300.

tuerentur 'watch over' or 'guard' (not 'contemplate': Schneider, art. cit.). Cf. *De rep.* 6.15 *homines enim sunt hac lege generati, qui tuerentur illum globum*; *ND* 2.99 *quasi cultores terrae constituti*; above, §73. Note also the similar doctrines in the Latin *Asclepius* (Corpus Hermeticum) 11 on the purpose of human life: *mirari atque adorare caelestia, . . . incolere atque gubernare terrena* (p. 306); *munde mundum servando* (p. 310).

caelestium ordinem contemplantes, imitarentur eum Cf. *ND* 2.37 *ipse autem homo ortus est ad mundum contemplandum et imitandum, nullo modo perfectus, sed est quaedam particula perfecti*; ibid. 140; *Tusc.* 1.43; 69; 72; *Leg.* 1.26; *Fin.* 4.11. This is again derived from the *Timaeus*, 47c: ἵνα τὰς ἐν οὐρανῷ κατιδόντες τοῦ νοῦ περιόδους . . . ἐκμαθόντες δὲ καὶ λογισμῶν κατὰ φύσιν ὀρθότητος μετασχόντες, μιμούμενοι τὰς τοῦ θεοῦ πάντως ἀπλανεῖς οὔσας τὰς ἐν ἡμῖν πεπλανημένας καταστησαίμεθα (cf. Plut. *De sera numinis vindicta* 550d; Procl. *De prov.* col. 130, 26ff.; also Plato, *Timaeus* 90a–d; *Theaet.* 176a–c; H. Tarrant, *CQ* 33 (1983) 187–7). The idea that contemplation of the heavenly order is either the whole end of human existence or an important part of it recurs frequently. Perhaps the earliest instance is Anaxagoras ap. Arist. *Eth. Eud.* 1216a (cf. Diog. Laert. 1.3.10) ἀποκρίνασθαι πρός τινα . . . διερωτῶντα τίνος ἕνεκ' ἂν τις ἕλοιτο γενέσθαι μᾶλλον ἢ μὴ γενέσθαι, "τοῦ," φάναι, "θεωρῆσαι τὸν οὐρανὸν καὶ τὴν περὶ τὸν ὅλον κόσμον τάξιν"; similar to this is Posidonius, fr. 186 Edelstein–Kidd (ap. Clem. Alex. *Strom.* 2.21.129) who defined the τέλος as ζῆν θεωροῦντα τὴν τῶν ὅλων ἀλήθειαν καὶ τάξιν. Cf. also Arist. Περὶ φιλοσοφίας, fr. 10 Rose; Sen. *Ep.* 65.16; *NQ* praef. 11–12; *Ad Marc.* 18; M. Aur. 11.27 and 7.47 (attributing the idea to the Pythagoreans); Plut. *Tranq.* 20; Dio Chrys. *Olymp.* 12 (the world compared to a temple of the mysteries: cf. *De rep.* 6.15, the world a *templum*); Iambl. *Protrepticus* 51; Juncus p. 1027 W.–H.; Euryphamus the Pythagorean ap. Stob. 4.39.27, p. 915 on 'imitation', ἐμιμάσατο δὲ καὶ τὰν τῶ παντὸς διακόσμασιν, δίκαις τε καὶ νόμοις κοινωνίαν πολίων συναρμοξάμενος. Even the Epicureans retained the belief in the gods as an example of order and happiness (Philodemus, Περὶ εὐσεβείας 28, etc.).

vitae modo In the regularity or order of their lives.

summorum philosophorum Sc. Plato and Pythagoras. Cf. *Hortensius* fr. 114 Grilli *consulares philosophos*; ibid. fr. 115 *si ut antiquis philosophis eisque maximis longeque clarissimis placuit, aeternos animos ac divinos habemus*; *Tusc.* 1.39; 1.49; Favorinus fr. 12 Barigazzi (cf. Introd. p. 28 n. 70 and p. 238 above).

78 audiebam Pythagoram Pythagoreosque On the Pythagoreans, cf. §§38; 39ff.; 73. *audiebam* is very vague (especially compared with the details in §41 etc.), and is simply a way of including this piece of philosophical doctrine in the dialogue; Cato may have had some acquaintance with Pythagoreanism, but is unlikely to have been familiar with this sort of idea (Introd. p. 21).

incolas paene nostros Cf. *Lael.* 13 *vel eorum qui in hac terra fuerunt, magnamque Graeciam (quae nunc quidem deleta est, tum florebat) institutis et* *praeceptis suis erudierunt*; *Tusc.* 4.2; the attempt to claim the Pythagoreans as Italians, and to find Roman connections with them, was a characteristic product of the antiquarianism of Cicero's time.

Italici philosophi The Pythagoreans are Ἰταλικοί in Arist. *Metaph.* 1.6.987a; 1.7.988a, etc.; *Meteor.* 342b; *Cael.* 293a; cf. W. Burkert, *Philol.* 105 (1961) 238.

ex universa mente divina delibatos animos Cf. *ND* 1.27 *nam Pythagoras, qui censuit animum esse per naturam rerum omnem intentum et commeantem, ex quo nostri animi carperentur* ... (cf. Min. Fel. *Oct.* 19.6); *Tusc.* 5.38 *humanus autem animus decerptus ex mente divina*; *Div.* 1.110 *naturam deorum a qua ... haustos animos et libatos haberemus*; 2.26; Cratippus ap. Cic. *Div.* 1.70; *Leg.* 1.24; *De rep.* 6.16; 26; *Tim.* 4; the doctrine is also attributed to the Pythagoreans by Diog. Laert. 8.28 εἶναι δὲ τὴν ψυχὴν ἀπόσπασμα αἰθέρος ... καὶ τὸ ἀφ' οὗ ἀπέσπασται ἀθάνατόν ἐστι; it appealed particularly to Stoics, cf. Posidonius fr. 99a Edelstein–Kidd (Diog. Laert. 7.142–3) ζῷον ἄρα ὁ κόσμος· ἔμψυχον δέ, ὡς δῆλον ἐκ τῆς ἡμετέρας ψυχῆς ἐκεῖθεν οὔσης ἀποσπάσματος; Epictetus, *Diss.* 1.14.6; 2.8.11; Hor. *Sat.* 2.2.79 *divinae particulam aurae*; Manil. 2.116; 4.910; M. Aur. 2.1; 5.27.1; 12.26; Sen. *NQ* 7.25; *Helv.* 6; *Ep.* 66.12; cf. also Arist. *De anima* 411a18; Diogenes of Apollonia, fr. A19 D.–K.; Sen. *Suas.* 6.6; Pliny, *NH* 2.95 (quoting Hipparchus); Firm. Matern. *Astrol.* 1.5.12; Philo, *Opif. mundi* 146; *Leg. alleg.* 3.161; *Det. pot. insid.* 90.

delibatos Probably reflecting Greek ἀπόρροια or ἀπόσπασμα, cf. *carperentur* (*ND* 1.27), *decerptus* (*Tusc.* 5.38), *haustos et libatos* (*Div.* 1.110). *delibare* presumably originally meant 'pour off', 'draw off', in contexts of liquids (cf. Lucr. 6.621; Paul. Fest. p. 73 M.); but it is used of other things in contexts where such an image would seem strange to us, e.g. plucking flowers (Enn. *Ann.* 303–8 V.^{2}, cf. §50 above; Cic. *Sest.* 119 – both metaphorical contexts), trees (Colum. 2.2.26), fruits (Hyg. *Fab.* 130), and it has a range of metaphorical uses (*TLL* 5, 1, 441f.) The best translation here is perhaps 'emanating'.

Socrates ... disseruisset Cicero does not imply that all the arguments which follow are from the *Phaedo*; in fact only the last two are.

omnium sapientissimus Plato, *Apol.* 21a; schol. Ar. *Clouds* 144; Cic. *Lael.* 7 and 13.

sic persuasi mihi The more regular order would be *sic mihi persuasi*, read by H^{2}O^{2}GRQ recc. and Nonius, with the pronoun in second place (Wackernagel's Law); but the reading of the majority of the MSS may be retained, as conferring emphasis on *persuasi* and giving a better Ciceronian rhythm. *sic* refers forwards, to the Platonic arguments for the immortality of the soul which Cicero here summarises. The first argument, from the swiftness and capacities of the mind, does not actually occur in precisely this form in Plato's writings, but seems to have been part of popularised

Platonism: Cicero had already presented it at length in *Tusc.* 1.58–66 and referred to it in the *Somnium Scipionis* (*De rep.* 6.26); some related arguments in *Tusc.* 1.22 are attributed by Cicero to Aristotle (concerning the immaterial nature of the soul); it also occurs in the pseudo-Platonic *Axiochus* (370b) and in Philo, *Det. pot. insid.* 87ff.

celeritas animorum Cf. *Tusc.* 1.43 *nulla est celeritas quae possit cum animi celeritate contendere*; ibid. 1.63; Lucr. 3.184; Xen. *Mem.* 4.3.13; Hom. *Od.* 7.36; *Il.* 15.80.

tantae scientiae There is no reason to doubt that this is an instance of the plural of *scientia*: cf. *De or.* 1.61 *physica ista ipsa et mathematica . . . scientiae sunt eorum qui illa profitentur*; Vitr. 1.17; 3 praef. 1 and 3; then in Christian Latin, Tert. *Anim.* 19; Arnob. 2.18; Chalc. *comm.* 252; Aug. *Civ. Dei* 17.4. Some have insisted that *scientiae* both here and in the *De or.* passage should be taken as genitive, on the purely *a priori* ground that Cicero ought not to use the plural; but in both passages, and especially here, the nominative plural fits the context much better than a genitive would. Cicero would surely have found another way of saying 'belong to the knowledge of those who profess those things', or 'so many arts requiring such great knowledge', if those had been the intended meanings. Here the anaphora *tot . . . tantae . . . tot* clearly argues for the nominative plural; if it is asked by way of objection why Cicero wrote *tantae* instead of *tot* in second place, one may reply (a) to avoid monotony, (b) that Cicero himself may have felt slight uneasiness about the plural, and chose in consequence to stress the extent of the individual 'knowledges' rather than their number. The use of the plural is no doubt a Graecism (= ἐπιστῆμαι); cf. Cicero's use of the plural *sapientiae* in *Tusc.* 3.42, in a passage directly translated from Epicurus. Cf. Neue–Wagener 1³, 639; Nägelsbach–Müller, *Stilistik*⁹ 199ff.

cumque semper agitetur ... relicturus Plato, *Phaedrus* 245c–d ψυχὴ πᾶσα ἀθάνατος· τὸ γὰρ ἀεικίνητον ἀθάνατον· τὸ δ᾽ ἄλλο κινοῦν καὶ ὑπ᾽ ἄλλου κινούμενον, παῦλαν ἔχον κινήσεως, παῦλαν ἔχει ζωῆς· μόνον δὴ τὸ αὐτὸ κινοῦν, ἅτε οὐκ ἀπολεῖπον ἑαυτό, οὔποτε λήγει κινούμενον, ἀλλὰ καὶ τοῖς ἄλλοις ὅσα κινεῖται τοῦτο πηγὴ καὶ ἀρχὴ κινήσεως, etc., translated by Cicero in *De rep.* 6.27 (= *Tusc.* 1.53–4); the version in the present passage is abbreviated. Cf. also *ND* 2.32; Apul. *Plat.* 1.9; [Albinus], *Did.* 25; Themist. *De anima* 90b; Sext. Emp. *Adv. math.* 9.76; Lact. *Inst.* 7.8.4; Serv. *Aen.* 6.727; Macrob. *Somn. Scip.* 2.13.1ff.

cum simplex animi natura esset ... dividi This argument comes from *Phaedo* 78ff., again heavily abbreviated: cf. *Tusc.* 1.71 *dubitare non possumus . . . quin nihil sit animis admixtum . . . quod cum ita sit, certe nec secerni nec dividi nec discerpi nec distrahi potest; ne interire quidem igitur.* This passage of Cicero is recalled by Lact. *Inst.* 7.22.9 (cf. R. M. Ogilvie, *The Library of Lactantius* 78 and 80), and by Ambrose, *De excessu fratris* 2.126.

esset The change of tense from present to imperfect may be due to the fact that Cicero is now resuming the actual arguments used by Socrates on the occasion referred to above, i.e. in the *Phaedo*. Lebreton, *Études* 273ff. quotes a large number of examples of this sort of change of sequence.

magnoque esse argumento ... recordari This sentence means 'the fact that children learn ... is an important proof for the idea that men know things before they are born'; the further step from pre-existence to immortality is not made explicit. The argument from recollection, which Cicero only alludes to here, comes from *Phaedo* 72e ff. and *Meno* 83ff.; it is treated by Cicero at greater length, and with less than absolute conviction, at *Tusc.* 1.57–8.

XXII 79 Apud Xenophontem *Cyrop.* 8.7.17–22; cf. §30. The two passages follow in parallel:

"οὐ γὰρ δήπου τοῦτό γε σαφῶς δοκεῖτε εἰδέναι, ὡς οὐδὲν ἔτι ἐγὼ ἔσομαι, ἐπειδὰν τοῦ ἀνθρωπίνου βίου τελευτήσω.

Nolite arbitrari, *o mihi carissimi filii*, me cum a vobis discessero nusquam aut nullum fore.

οὐδὲ γὰρ νῦν τοι τήν γ' ἐμὴν ψυχὴν ἑωρᾶτε, ἀλλ' οἷς διεπράττετο, τούτοις αὐτὴν ὡς οὖσαν κατεφωρᾶτε.

nec enim dum eram vobiscum animum meum videbatis, sed eum esse in hoc corpore ex eis rebus quas gerebam intellegebatis; *eundem igitur esse creditote, etiamsi nullum videbitis.*

τὰς δὲ τῶν ἄδικα παθόντων ψυχὰς οὔπω κατενοήσατε οἵους μὲν φόβους τοῖς μιαιφόνοις ἐμβάλλουσιν, οἵους δὲ παλαμναίους τοῖς ἀνοσίοις ἐπιπέμπουσιν; τοῖς δὲ φθιμένοις τὰς τιμὰς διαμένειν ἔτι ἂν δοκεῖτε εἰ μηδενὸς αὐτῶν αἱ ψυχαὶ κύριαι ἦσαν;

nec vero clarorum virorum post mortem honores permanerent, si nihil eorum ipsorum animi efficerent quo diutius memoriam sui teneremus.

οὗτοι ἔγωγε, ὦ παῖδες, οὐδὲ τοῦτο πώποτε ἐπείσθην, ὡς ἡ ψυχή, ἕως μὲν ἂν ἐν θνητῷ σώματι ᾖ, ζῇ, ὅταν δὲ τούτου ἀπαλλαγῇ, τέθνηκεν· ὁρῶ γὰρ ὅτι καὶ τὰ θνητὰ σώματα ὅσον ἂν ἐν αὑτοῖς χρόνον ᾖ ἡ ψυχή, ζῶντα παρέχεται·

mihi quidem numquam persuaderi potuit, animos dum in corporibus essent mortalibus vivere, cum excessissent ex eis emori;

οὐδέ γε ὅπως ἄφρων ἔσται ἡ ψυχή, ἐπειδὰν τοῦ ἄφρονος σώματος δίχα γένηται, οὐδὲ τοῦτο

nec vero tunc animum esse insipientem, cum ex insipienti corpore evasisset, sed cum omni

πέπεισμαι, ἀλλ᾽ ὅταν ἄκρατος καὶ
καθαρὸς ὁ νοῦς ἐκκριθῇ, τότε καὶ
φρονιμώτατον αὐτὸν εἰκὸς εἶναι.
διαλυομένου δὲ ἀνθρώπου, δῆλά
ἐστιν ἕκαστα ἀπιόντα πρὸς τὸ
ὁμόφυλον, πλὴν τῆς ψυχῆς· αὕτη
δὲ μόνη οὔτε παροῦσα οὔτε
ἀπιοῦσα ὁρᾶται.

ἐννοήσατε δ᾽", ἔφη, "ὅτι
ἐγγύτερον μὲν τῶν ἀνθρωπίνων
θανάτῳ οὐδέν ἐστιν ὕπνου· ἡ δὲ
τοῦ ἀνθρώπου ψυχὴ τότε δήπου
θειοτάτη καταφαίνεται καὶ τότε τι
τῶν μελλόντων προορᾷ· τότε γὰρ
ὡς ἔοικε μάλιστα ἐλευθεροῦται.

εἰ μὲν οὖν οὕτως ἔχει ταῦτα ὥσπερ
ἐγὼ οἴομαι καὶ ἡ ψυχὴ καταλείπει
τὸ σῶμα, καὶ τὴν ἐμὴν ψυχὴν
καταιδούμενοι ποιεῖτε ἃ ἐγὼ
δέομαι· εἰ δὲ μὴ οὕτως, ἀλλὰ
μένουσα ἡ ψυχὴ ἐν τῷ σώματι
συναποθνῄσκει, ἀλλὰ θεούς γε τοὺς
ἀεὶ ὄντας καὶ πάντ᾽ ἐφορῶντας καὶ
πάντα δυναμένους, οἳ καὶ τήνδε
τὴν τῶν ὅλων τάξιν συνέχουσιν
ἀτριβῆ καὶ ἀγήρατον καὶ
ἀναμάρτητον καὶ ὑπὸ κάλλους καὶ
μεγέθους ἀδιήγητον, τούτους
φοβούμενοι μήποτ᾽ ἀσεβὲς μηδέν
μηδὲ ἀνόσιον μήτε ποιήσητε μήτε
βουλεύσητε."

admixtione corporis liberatus,
purus et integer esse coepisset, tum
esse sapientem.
atque etiam cum hominis natura
morte dissolvitur, ceterarum
rerum perspicuum est quo
quaeque discedat; abeunt enim
illuc omnia unde orta sunt;
animus autem solus nec cum adest
nec cum discessit apparet.
iam vero videtis nihil esse morti
tam simile quam somnum;
atqui dormientium animi maxime
declarant divinitatem suam, multa
enim cum remissi et liberi sunt
futura prospiciunt; *ex quo
intellegitur quales futuri sint cum se
plane corporum vinculis relaxaverint.*
quare si haec ita sunt, sic me
colitote', inquit, '*ut deum;*

sin una est interiturus animus cum
corpore,
vos tamen deos verentes, qui hanc
omnem pulchritudinem tuentur et
regunt,

memoriam nostri pie inviolateque
servabitis.'

It must be admitted that the effect of the passage is considerably changed
by Cicero, as he takes it out of its original context, and makes it serve the
purposes of his own argument. In Xenophon, the point of Cyrus' speech is
to persuade his sons Cambyses and Tanaoxares to behave well after his
death, his argument being that they cannot be certain that his soul will not
survive to keep them in order. The arguments for immortality are
introduced only to support this idea, and immortality is presented
throughout only as a possibility. Cicero makes the speech more dogmatic

in tone, and though he retains the alternative argument that even if the soul is not immortal, the gods still exist, he entirely alters its point (see below). He also leaves out one sentence that was essential to the original argument, but not so desirable in Cicero's context (τὰς δὲ τῶν ἄδικα παθόντων ψυχάς ... ἐπιπέμπουσιν;): the idea of the unjust being haunted by the ghosts of their dead victims would have inserted a jarring note into the general optimism of Cicero's account of the state of souls after death. Otherwise, Cicero keeps reasonably closely to the original, though he expands the argument in some places (italicised above) and obscures it in one or two others by abbreviation; the expansions seem to incorporate ideas derived from other sources (see notes below). On the whole this passage leaves a certain amount to be desired, if judged purely as a translation; but even though Cicero explicitly acknowledges the source (contrast the adaptation from Plato in §§6–8), it must be accepted that the purposes of the immediate argument here weigh against the desire for exact reproduction of the original; Cicero should not be criticised for failing to produce a wholly accurate translation when he was not intending to do so. (Cf. J. Sommerbrodt, *RhM* 21 (1866) 285–90; F. de Caria, *RCCM* 16 (1974) 321ff.; and especially D. Krömer, *Würzburger Jahrbücher* NF 3 (1977) 93ff. I am grateful to Dr Krömer for drawing my attention to this article.)

Nolite arbitrari Cyrus said only 'You cannot be sure that I will not exist': Cicero is here much more dogmatic (Krömer, cited above, p. 95).

o mihi carissimi filii The affection implied by the interjection *o* and the superlative *carissimi* is entirely absent from the original.

cum a vobis discessero Cicero's addition of *a vobis* again makes the speech more emotional and personal than it is in the original; Xenophon's Cyrus merely says ἐπειδὰν τοῦ ἀνθρωπίνου βίου τελευτήσω.

nec enim ... animum meum videbatis Cf. *Tusc.* 1.70 *sic mentem hominis, quamvis eam non videas, ut deum non vides, tamen ut deum agnoscis ex operibus eius*; Xen. *Mem.* 1.4.9 οὐδὲ γὰρ τὴν σαυτοῦ σύ γε ψυχὴν ὁρᾷς, ἡ τοῦ σώματος κυρία ἐστίν; M. Aur. 12.28; Min. Fel. *Oct.* 32.6; [Arist.] *De mundo* 6; Theophilus of Antioch, *Ad Autol.* 1.2 and 5.

intellegebatis Distinctly weak for κατεφωρᾶτε; however, the Greek participial phrase ὡς οὖσαν ... was intractable, and none of the Latin words for 'tracking down' can take an accusative and infinitive.

eundem ... videbitis Added by Cicero, again with the effect of making the argument much more dogmatic; such an exhortation to faith would have been out of place in Xenophon's original (cf. above; p. 96 of Krömer's article, cited above).

80 clarorum virorum *clarorum* is added by Cicero; the original merely says τοῖς δὲ φθιμένοις. *clarorum virorum* could almost be described as a

Catonian motto, being the opening words (or at any rate near the beginning) of the *Origines*, fr. 1 Peter (=fr. 2 Jordan) ap. Cic. *Planc.* 66; cf. Tacitus' echo of this at the beginning of the *Agricola* (see Ogilvie and Richmond ad loc.); also Cato ap. Cic. *Brut.* 75. If it seems far-fetched to suppose deliberate Catonian reminiscence in these two very ordinary words, in a context otherwise translated from Xenophon (though *Orig.* fr. 1 is also adapted from Xenophon!), the reader may consider the parallel case of the English words 'famous men', which many people would doubtless link almost automatically with Ecclesiasticus 44.

post mortem These words are 'sandwiched' between *clarorum virorum* and *honores*, making it clear that the honours referred to are posthumous ones: *c- v- honores post mortem permanerent* would set us thinking of the honours paid to them during life, and wondering how those were supposed to survive after death. For this function of 'sandwiching' word order, cf. K.–S. II, 620, Anm. 1.

mihi quidem numquam ... emori The argument that since the soul is the vital principle in the body, it would be strange if it were itself to die when separated from the body, is used in Plato, *Phaedo* 105c–d; Xenophon could have borrowed it from there, but the two authors could equally well be independently reproducing a genuine Socratic argument. Cf. also [Albinus], *Didasc.* 25. Cicero here abbreviates the original somewhat, leaving out the sentence ὁρῶ ... ζῶντα παρέχεται which is essential for the reasoning; again, this has the effect of making the idea a matter of faith rather than logic.

insipienti corpore τοῦ ἄφρονος σώματος. ἄφρων has a double meaning, 'senseless' (cf. Xen. *Mem.* 1.4.4) or 'stupid'; Cicero's *insipiens* more or less reproduces the deliberate ambiguity. Cf. Plato, *Phaedo* 67a σώματος ἀφροσύνη; *Timaeus* 44b. The argument is virtually the same as that in *Phaedo* 66–7.

dissolvitur Cf. §72 *natura dissolvit* and note.

perspicuum est quo quaeque discedat Cf. Eur. *Suppl.* 532ff. ὅθεν δ' ἕκαστον ἐς τὸ φῶς ἀφίκετο, | ἐνταῦθ' ἀπελθεῖν, πνεῦμα μὲν πρὸς αἰθέρα, | τὸ σῶμα δ' ἐς γῆν; id. *Hypsipyle* 93ff.; id. fr. 836 N. (quoted by M. Aur. 7.50); Epicharmus fr. 9 D.–K. (1⁷, 200) συνεκρίθη καὶ διεκρίθη κἀπῆλθεν ὅθεν ἦλθεν πάλιν, | γᾶ μὲν εἰς γᾶν, πνεῦμα δ' ἄνω· τί τῶνδε χαλεπόν; οὐδὲ ἕν; [Plato], *Axiochus* 365e; [Phocylides] *Sent.* 107–8; Enn. *Ann.* 13–14 V.² = 6–7 Sk. (Homer's speech), cf. Varro, *LL* 5.60 and Pacuvius fr. 93 Ribbeck, also quoted there by Varro; Lucr. 2.999ff. *cedit item retro, de terra quod fuit ante, | in terras, et quod missum est ex aetheris oris, | id rursum caeli rellatum templa receptant*; Epictetus, *Diss.* 3.13; Menander Rhetor 2, p. 414, 21 Sp. (in a list of consolation themes); Plut. *Romulus* 28.8 quoting Pind. fr. 131b Sn.; Genesis 3.19; Ecclesiastes 12.7; Ecclesiasticus 40.11; Lattimore, *Epitaphs* 304ff.

The unspoken conclusion of this argument, in Cicero as in Xenophon, is that there is no reason why the soul should not also be thought to go πρὸς τὸ ὁμόφυλον / *unde ortus est*, that is, to heaven (according to Platonic and other views of the origin of the soul); but this naturally begs the question of the soul's nature and origin, which is not discussed here either in the original or by Cicero. (Cf. p. 101 of Krömer's article cited above).

nihil esse morti tam simile quam somnum Cf. *Tusc.* 1.92 *somnum imaginem mortis*; ibid. 97; 117; Hom. *Il.* 14.231 Ὕπνῳ ... κασιγνήτῳ Θανάτοιο; *Od.* 13.80; Hes. *Theog.* 212; 756; Plato, *Apol.* 40c–41b; Mnesimachus fr. 11 Kock; Sen. *Herc. Fur.* 1065ff.; Virg. *Aen.* 6.278; 522; Ov. *Am.* 2.9.41; [Plut.] *Cons. ad Apoll.* 107d ff.; Anaxagoras ap. Stob. 4.52.39, p. 1084 W.–H.; Ael. *Var. Hist.* 2.35 = Stob. 4.51.22; *Dicta Catonis* monost. 19; Ambrose, *De excessu fratris* 2.126.

81   maxime declarant divinitatem suam Dreams were more or less universally thought to be (at least potentially) prophetic in the ancient world; cf. Pind. fr. 131, 3–5 B.; Aesch. *Eum.* 104 εὕδουσα γὰρ φρὴν ὄμμασιν λαμπρύνεται, etc. For philosophical reference to this, see Plato, *Rep.* 571d ff.; *Timaeus* 71e; Arist. fr. 12a Walzer = 10 Rose (Περὶ φιλοσοφίας) ὅταν ... ἐν τῷ ὑπνοῦν καθ᾽ ἑαυτὴν γένηται ἡ ψυχή, τότε τὴν ἰδίαν ἀπολαβοῦσα φύσιν προμαντεύεταί τε καὶ προαγορεύει τὰ μέλλοντα· τοιαύτη δέ ἐστι καὶ ἐν τῷ κατὰ τὸν θάνατον χωρίζεσθαι τῶν σωμάτων; Hippocr. Περὶ διαίτης 4.86; Anon. Vit. Pyth. ap. Phot. cod. 249 (Thesleff, *Pythagorean Texts* 238) εἰ γὰρ κατὰ ποσόν τι ἡ ψυχὴ τοῦ σώματος ἐν τῷ ζῆν τὸ ζῷον χωριζομένη βελτίων γίνεται ἑαυτῆς, ἔν τε τοῖς ὕπνοις κατὰ τοὺς ὀνείρους ... πολλῷ μᾶλλον βελτιοῦται ὅταν τέλεον χωρισθῇ ἀπὸ τοῦ σώματος; Cic. *Div.* 1.62–4, esp. 63 *cum ergo est somno sevocatus animus a societate et a contagione corporis, tum meminit praeteritorum, praesentia cernit, futura praevidet*; ibid. 110; 115; 129; Posidonius fr. 108 Edelstein–Kidd; Dodds, *Irrational* 135ff.

ex quo ... relaxaverint Added by Cicero, and nearer to the quotation from Aristotle referred to above; although there is nothing here that is not implied by Xenophon.

corporum vinculis This is a common image throughout Platonism: *vincula* may just mean 'bonds' joining the soul to the body, the δεσμοί of Plato, *Timaeus* 42e; 44b; 81d; but there is often the further implication that the body is a prison for the soul, and this may have been in Cicero's mind here: cf. esp. *De rep.* 6.14 *e corporum vinculis tamquam e carcere*; also *Tusc.* 1.75 *compedibus corporis*; *Div.* 1.110; *Lael.* 14; *Scaur.* 4; Sen. *Suas.* 6.6; Sen. *Ep.* 65.16. For Platonic antecedents cf. *Crat.* 400c, *Phaedo* 67d, 82e, *Phaedr.* 250c, *Gorg.* 492d; [Plato], *Axiochus* 365e; possibly the cave simile in *Rep.* 515c (cf. Pohlenz on *Tusc.* 1.75); also Macrob. *In somn. Scip.* 1.11.3 on the etymological play on δέμας/δεῖσθαι.

colitote Cf. *creditote* above: the more solemn *-tote* form of the imperative is clearly appropriate here; if the traditional account of these forms as 'future imperative' has any truth in it, that would also be well exemplified in this passage since Cyrus is referring to the time after his own death; cf. K.–S. I, 198.

ut deum These two words do not correspond to anything explicit in the original, but they do not change the meaning greatly; if Cyrus's soul is to survive after death in a sufficiently active form to have an effect on his sons' lives, their reverence for it would be hardly different in quality from that due to a god; *colitote* on its own would not have conveyed the required meaning, since *colere* is often used with personal objects in the sense of 'pay court to' or 'cultivate the friendship of'. Nevertheless, it may be that Cicero was here influenced in his interpretation of Xenophon by Platonic and Aristotelian ideas of the divinity of the soul, which he often expresses elsewhere (*De rep.* 6.26; *Leg.* 2.55; *Tusc.* 1.52; 1.65; *Fin.* 2.114; *ND* 1.31; *Off.* 3.44; cf. C. Josserand, *Ant. Class.* 4 (1935) 141ff.). The idea would also in any case come easily to a Roman, for whom the dead were *Di Manes, Di Parentes*, and the recipients of prayers and sacrifices, although this did not usually encompass the idea of divinity of individual souls. The attraction Cicero felt towards this idea is sufficiently shown by his plan (never put into practice) of erecting a shrine to Tullia: see Shackleton Bailey, *Cicero's Letters to Atticus* v, 404ff.; P. Boyancé, *REA* 46 (1944) 179ff. (J. Mähly, *RhM* 20 (1865) 146, speculates quite implausibly that Cicero used a different text of Xenophon from ours; cf. J. Sommerbrodt, ibid. 21 (1866) 285.)

memoriam nostri pie inviolateque servabitis Completely altered from the original thought, which was 'Even if my soul is not there to keep you in order, then at any rate the gods will be'; this point is thoroughly obscured by Cicero's omission of ποιεῖτε ἃ ἐγὼ δέομαι and of τοὺς ἀεὶ ὄντας . . . δυναμένους.

XXIII 82 **nostra** Not only Roman but family matters.

Africani patrem aut patruum I.e. Gnaeus and Publius Scipio, mentioned above in §§29 and 75.

tanta esse conatos ... nisi ... cernerent Strictly speaking this construction is anacoluthic, a mixture of *tanta esse conatos cum non cernerent* and *tanta conaturos fuisse nisi cernerent*; but Cicero's anacoluthon is more elegant than either of the correct constructions. Cf. H.–Sz. 665; K.–S. II, 406–7; H. Nutting, *AJP* 44 (1923) 164–7. Comparable, though not entirely parallel, constructions may be found in *Att.* 2.24.2; *Lael.* 11; Livy 3.50.6. The argument is a standard Ciceronian one: cf. *Tusc.* 1.32f.; *Rab. perd.* 19; *Arch.* 29; *Planc.* 90; cf. also on §73 above.

ad se ipsos pertinere This is Opitz's conjecture for *ad se posse pertinere* of most MSS, *ad se pertinere* O²GRE: *posse* is fairly clearly not wanted for the sense, and gives an undesirably trochaic clausula, while *ad se* seems in itself rather weak for this emphatic position, nor would it explain the presence of *posse* in the other MSS (T. Opitz, *N. Jb. Kl. Phil.* 107 (1873) 609). If it were not for the rhythmical consideration, I should be inclined to read *ad sepse pertinere*: this gives the requisite emphatic form of *se* while explaining the corruption even better; on *sepse*, a slightly archaic form, see above on §28, where I have introduced it into the text. For the idea, cf. *Tusc.* 1.31 and 91.

more senum On this self-depreciating reference to the habits of old men, cf. §§30–31 and 55 above; Introd. p. 24. *me* is emphatic, as is shown by its position: 'do you think that *I* would have undertaken . . .?'

diurnos nocturnosque domi militiaeque Two successive 'polar' expressions: see on §13.

eisdem finibus . . . terminaturus Cf. *Tusc.* 1.32 *eisdemne ut finibus nomen suum quibus vita terminaretur?*; *Arch.* 29; *Rab. perd.* 29; *Phil.* 14.32.

otiosam aetatem et quietam Cf. *De rep.* 1.1 *Marco vero Catoni . . . certe licuit Tusculi se in otio delectare*, etc.; *Tusc.* 1.33. Cf. also Pind. *Ol.* 1.83, who uses the inevitability of death as an argument for trying to gain as much glory as one can: θανεῖν δ' οἷσιν ἀνάγκα, τί κέ τις ἀνώνυμον | γῆρας ἐν σκότῳ καθήμενος ἕψοι μάταν, | ἁπάντων καλῶν ἄμμορος; No doubt Cicero had in mind here the Epicurean champions of the quiet life. Cf. also §13.

tum denique victurus esset Cf. §77 and note; *Tusc.* 1.75 *tum denique vivemus.*

83 quid quod sapientissimus quisque . . . iniquissimo Cf. [Plato], *Epist.* 2.311c–d, ὃ δὴ καὶ ἐγὼ τεκμήριον ποιοῦμαι ὅτι ἔστι τις αἴσθησις τοῖς τεθνεῶσι τῶν ἐνθάδε· αἱ γὰρ βέλτισται ψυχαὶ μαντεύονται ταῦτα οὕτως ἔχειν, αἱ δὲ μοχθηρόταται οὔ φασι, κυριώτερα δὲ τὰ τῶν θείων ἀνδρῶν μαντεύματα ἢ τὰ τῶν μή; also perhaps *Tusc.* 1.109.

Equidem efferor . . . videndi The eagerness to meet the dead in the afterlife attributed here to Cato is no doubt akin to that of Socrates in Plato, *Apol.* 41a (cf. Cic. *Tusc.* 1.98), though the setting for the reunion is a heaven on the lines of the *Somnium Scipionis* rather than the mythical Hades; cf. below, *illud divinum animorum concilium.* Cf. also Nisbet–Hubbard on Hor. *Od.* 2.13.

conscripsi In the *Origines*; cf. §§38 and 75.

nec tamquam Peliam recoxerit According to the well-known version of the myth, Pelias was killed under the pretext of a magical rejuvenation, after the process had first been demonstrated to work on Aeson (Ov. *Met.* 7.159–349; see Bömer ad loc. for earlier accounts of the rejuvenation of Aeson) or on a sheep (Diod. 4.51ff.; Apollod. *Bibl.* 1.9.27; Hyg. *Fab.* 24). One would think that Cicero was just referring loosely to

the story here (perhaps with an ironical implication that such a rejuvenation would not work anyway), if it were not for Plaut. *Pseud.* 869ff. *item ut
Medea Peliam concoxit senem,| quem medicamento et suis venenis dicitur| fecisse
rursus ex sene adulescentulum*, where it is implied that the rejuvenation of
Pelias was successful. It is unlikely that Cicero and Plautus both made the
same mistake independently, and it may be that the Plautine passage
reflects, or was responsible for, a current mistaken version of the legend.
(Varro, *Men.* 285 B. speaks only of Pelias wishing to be rejuvenated.) It
seems quite implausible that Cicero and Plautus reflect an earlier Greek
tradition in which Pelias was successfully rejuvenated, as argued by C.
Dugas, *REA* 46 (1944) 5ff.; there is no good evidence for such a version
having existed in Greek literature.

si qui deus ... valde recusem (On *si qui* | *si quis* cf. §40.) Cf. Arist.
Eth. Eud. 1215b ὁ βίος ὃν ζῶσιν ἔτι παῖδες ὄντες· καὶ γὰρ ἐπὶ τοῦτον
ἀνακάμψαι πάλιν οὐδεὶς ἂν ὑπομείνειεν εὖ φρονῶν; [Plato], *Epinomis* 974a;
Hor. *Sat.* 1.6.93 *si natura iuberet| a certis annis aevum remeare peractum* ...;
August. *Civ. Dei.* 21.14; Browne, *Religio Medici* i, 42 '. . . yet for my own
part, I would not live over my hours past, or begin again the thread of my
days; not upon Cicero's ground, because I have lived them well, but for
fear I should live them worse' (cf. §84 below).

repuerascam Cf. Plaut. *Merc.* 296; Cic. *De or.* 2.22; Varro, *Men.* 44
Bücheler.

decurso spatio Cf. Plaut. *Stich.* 81 *decurso aetatis spatio*; Ter. *Ad.* 860;
Lucr. 2.78; 4.1196; *Tusc.* 1.15; *Lael.* 101; *Fam.* 8.13.1; *Quinct.* 99; Varro,
Men. 288 and 544 B. (the latter from the *Tithonus*: see Introd. p. 26); Hor.
Sat. 1.1.114; *AP* 412; Sen. *Ep.* 30.13; Prop. 2.15.4; Ov. *Tristia* 3.4.33; *TLL*
5, 1, 229 (for the literal meaning) and 232 (for metaphorical uses). *calx* is
the finishing-line, marked with chalk (later *creta*, Sen. *Ep.* 108.32); *spatium*
is the course or a lap of the course (see on §14 above); *decurrere* is the *vox
propria* for running a course.

84 quid habet enim vita commodi? This is a consolation theme, and
appears to derive from Crantor's Περὶ πένθους: Crantor is quoted in
[Plut.] *Cons. ad Apoll.* 104c as saying τό γε πολλαχῇ εἶναι ἐργῶδη καὶ
δύσκολον τὸν βίον ἄγαν ἀληθές; cf. also ibid. 115b πολλοῖς γὰρ καὶ σοφοῖς
ἀνδράσιν οὐ νῦν ἀλλὰ πάλαι κέκλαυσται τἀνθρώπινα (cf. just below,
deplorare vitam quod multi et ei docti saepe fecerunt); 115c (quoting Arist.
Eudemus, fr. 44 Rose); the theme was prominent in Cicero's own *Consolatio*,
as we may see from *Tusc.* 1.75–6 and 83; but in the *Tusculans*, as here, he
rejects the negative attitude that seems to have prevailed in Crantor and
the *Consolatio*: (1.83) *quid ego nunc lugeam vitam hominum? vere et iure possum;
sed quid necesse est ... vitam efficere deplorando miseriorem?* Cicero refers in the
Tusculans to the Cyrenaic Hegesias, who lamented the human condition so

effectively that many of his audience committed suicide (1.83), and to Alcidamas, who wrote an encomium of death *quae constat ex enumeratione humanorum malorum* (1.116). For the general theme of the misery of human life, cf. Soph. *OC* 1225ff. τίς οὐ καμάτων ἔνι; ; [Plato], *Epinomis* 973d–974a; [Plato], *Axiochus* 366d (which claims to quote Prodicus) τί μέρος τῆς ἡλικίας ἄμοιρον τῶν ἀνιαρῶν; ; Sen. *Marc.* 11.1 *tota flebilis vita est*; ibid. 21.2–4; Pliny, *NH* 7 praef. and 168; Teles p. 49 H.; Menander Rhetor 2, p. 414 S.; Ambrose, *De bono mortis* 2.4 *Quid enim boni est homini in hac vita?*; August. *Civ. Dei.* 19.4.22; cf. P. Courcelle, *Connais-toi toi-même* II, 295–323.

multi et ei docti Probably the right reading, 'many men, and learned men at that'; cf. K.–S. I, 619; I do not know whether *multi et docti*, read by the older MSS, is acceptable Latin for πολλοὶ καὶ σοφοί.

neque me vixisse paenitet On the meaning of *paenitet*, cf. §19 above: 'nor am I dissatisfied that I have lived'. Cf. Gell. 1.3.2 on Chilon, *'Dicta'*, inquit, *'mea factaque in aetate longa pleraque omnia fuisse non paenitenda . . .'*

tamquam ex hospitio Cf. Sen. *Ep.* 120. 14 *nec domum esse hoc corpus sed hospitium, et quidem breve hospitium*; ibid. 31.11; 102.24; Apul. *Apol.* 24 *animo hominis extrinsecus in hospitium corporis immigranti*; Manil. 4.890; Hadrian fr. 3 (Morel, *FPL*) *animula . . . hospes comesque corporis*; also [Plut.] *Cons. ad Apoll.* 117f, life is an ἐπιδημία; ibid. 120b; [Plato], *Axiochus* 365b; M. Aur. 2.17; Epictetus, *Diss.* 2.23. For different versions of the image, cf. *Tusc.* 1.51; 1.118; *Hortensius* fr. 115 Grilli *ex hac in aliam haud paulo meliorem domum . . . demigrare*; *De rep.* 6.25; 29; Sen. *Ep.* 70.16; 65.21; 66.3; Nepos, *Att.* 22.1; Plato, *Phaedo* 117 τὴν μετοίκησιν τὴν ἐνθένδε ἐκεῖσε; *Apol.* 40c; Bion fr. 68 K. (quite unreasonably picked on as the source of Cicero's idea here: see Introd. p. 14 n. 36 and Appendix 2); Favorinus fr. 16 Barigazzi (cf. Introd. p. 28); there is also a similarity with the image of life as a banquet, for which see Brink, *Horace on Poetry* III, Appendix 20, pp. 444–6.

divinum animorum concilium Cicero probably thought here of the *Somnium Scipionis*, in which the habitation of departed souls is said to be the Milky Way (*De rep.* 6.16); cf. Heraclides Ponticus fr. 97 Wehrli; Gottschalk, *Heraclides of Pontus* 98ff. and Appendix 1; Manil. 1.758ff.; other passages in later authors cited by Boyancé, *Songe de Scipion* 134 n. 1. Cf. also §83 above; *Tusc.* 1.72 *concilio deorum*; Sen. *Marc.* 25 *excepit illum coetus sacer, Scipiones Catonesque* (presumably influenced by Cicero); also perhaps Plato, *Phaedo* 81a μετὰ θεῶν διάγουσα.

colluvione The idea of the material world as impure seems to be a popularised version of Platonic doctrine; cf. also Plut. *Gen. Socr.* 591f.; Themist. *De anima* ap. Stob. 4.52b.49. The idea adapts itself very smoothly to a Christian context, and Ambrose seems to recall this passage clearly in *De bono mortis* 12.52 and *De excessu fratris* 132.

Catonem So Cicero refers to (and addresses) his son as 'Cicero', *Fam.* 14 passim; *Off.* 1.3; 3.5. On Cato's son, see also on §68.

cuius a me corpus est crematum Cato became one of the standard examples of fathers who had borne the death of their sons bravely (cf. below, *fortiter ferre visus sum*); for others, see note on §12. In general, cf. Hdt. 1.87; Juv. 10.240f. (one of the evils of old age); Polyb. 12.26.7; Demetrius of Phalerum, Περὶ γήρως (the only surviving fragment; see Introd. p. 26). Cicero was no doubt again thinking of his own loss of Tullia: cf. §§12, 35 and 68.

quod contra This phrase, which occurs in *Lael.* 90, *Quinct.* 87, *Off.* 1.49, Varro, *LL* 6.77 and Lucr. 1.82 in addition to this passage, clearly means 'whereas on the contrary', but opinion is divided as to whether it is an anastrophised version of *contra quod* 'in contrast to which', or a combination of *quod* as a conjunction (cf. *quod si*) and the adverb *contra*. The latter explanation is encouraged by comparison with phrases like *quod contra est* (Sall. *Jug.* 85.21) where *contra* must be the adverb: cf. Cic. *Div.* 1.105 *quod longe secus est*; in these two cases it is difficult to find an antecedent for *quod* as a relative pronoun, and it seems much easier to take it as a conjunction. See *TLL* 4, 742; Hand, *Tursellinus* II, 121ff.; K.–S. II, 322, Anm. 2.

decuit ab illo meum Cf. the epitaph *quod decuit natam patri praestare sepulto,| hoc contra natae praestitit ipse pater* (Bücheler, *CLE* 1486); the same theme occurs a number of times in epitaphs; cf. *CLE* 169; 1888–9 (also beginning *quod decuit*): also 164–8; 170–5; 1478–85; *CIL* 6, 8054; Lattimore, *Epitaphs* 187–91; also E. Engström, *Carmina Latina Epigraphica* (Göteborg 1911) nos. 31–4; 295; 308; 376–7.

non me deserens sed respectans Cf. Sen. *Polyb.* 9.9 *non reliquit ille nos sed antecessit*; *Ep.* 64.16; *Rem. fort.* 13.4; 'Not lost, but gone before'.

non longinquum ... discessum fore Imitated by Ambrose, *De excessu fratris* 135.

85 libenter erro Cf. *Tusc.* 1.39 *errare mehercule malo cum Platone ... quam cum istis vera sentire*; 1.24 *etiamsi non sit, mihi persuaderi tamen velim*; *Orat.* 42; Ambrose, *De excessu fratris* 134; Chrysippus, *SVF* 2, 126 von Arnim (= Plut. *Stoic. Rep.* 1046a). Cicero the rhetorician here triumphs over Cicero the philosopher.

extorqueri Cf. *Fin.* 2.16.

minuti philosophi Without doubt referring principally to Epicureans, though there were others also who denied immortality (e.g. Carneades); cf. *Div.* 1.62 *hos minutos philosophos*; *Tusc.* 1.55; *Brut.* 256. *Minuti* means 'insignificant', not 'over-subtle' (a meaning which occurs in later Latin): cf. Pease on the *Div.* passage.

peractio This word occurs only here in classical Latin; it may possibly be an actor's technical term, as *peroratio* is an orator's; the verb *peragere* in this sense is not uncommon, cf. §§64 and 70. Paul. Fest. p. 74 M. casts little

265

light on the word by using it to gloss the otherwise unexampled *deactio*. Otherwise *peractio* is found only in Christian writers.

tamquam fabulae On theatrical comparisons see on §5.

satietate Cf. §§76 and 84.

Haec habui Cf. the end of the *Laelius* (104) *haec habui de amicitia quae dicerem*; *ND* 2.168; Becker, *Technik und Szenerie* 30.

ad quam utinam perveniatis An unfulfilled wish in Scipio's case; Laelius lived until his late sixties.

APPENDIX 1   THE DATE OF COMPOSITION

The *Cato* was certainly completed at some time before 11 May 44 B.C. (*Att.* 14.21.3). A *terminus post quem* is not so immediately apparent, but one assumes that the reference to the work in *Div.* 2.3 *interiectus est etiam nuper liber is quem ad nostrum Atticum de senectute misimus* implies that it was written not much before the *De divinatione* itself: *nuper* would naturally be taken in this context to mean recently in comparison with the other philosophical works mentioned, of which the last was the *De natura deorum* (autumn of 45 B.C.).

The *De divinatione* itself was completed after the Ides of March 44, as references to the death of Caesar make clear (1.119; 2.23; 36–7; 99); *Div.* 2.4 and 7 imply that Cicero's philosophical writing had been interrupted by his return to public life after the Ides, and therefore that this latest in the series of philosophical works (apart from the *De fato* which is there mentioned as projected) was completed not long after that date. However, it is not possible to establish a more precise date for the completion of the *De div.*; R. Durand's argument (*Mél. Boissier* (Paris 1903) 173ff.) from the silence of the letters to Atticus to a completion date before 7 April, when the letters resume, is not convincing (cf. W. Falconer, *CPhil* 18 (1923) 310ff.), and the work could have been finished some time later than that.

M. Ruch (*Préambule* 173–4) has argued that the phrasing of the *De div.* passage implies that the *Cato* was completed before the Ides of March, since the list in which it occurs appears superficially to be of works completed before that date. However, closer inspection shows that this need not be the case, as the list includes both the *De div.* itself and the as yet unfinished *De fato*. All that can be deduced from this passage is that the *Cato* was written before the *De div.* was finished.

External evidence, therefore, gives no reason for a more precise dating of the composition of the *Cato* between *c.* the beginning of 44 and 11 May of that year. Apart from this, argument has centred on the question of whether it is more probable that Cicero would have written this work before or after the Ides of March. Attempts have been made to find covert references to the death of Caesar in the allusions to L. Brutus (§75) and Maelius (§56), but this is quite implausible; the two examples were simply part of his normal repertoire of Roman heroes, and could have occurred to him as easily before as after the assassination of Caesar; the example of Brutus actually occurs also in the *Tusculans*, written in 45 (*Tusc.* 1.89).

The arguments from probability rest on (a) the time Cicero had available for writing, (b) his general mood and other preoccupations at the various relevant times, and (c), in particular, the possibility that he might have been inspired to write the section on old men in public life (§§15ff.) by the prospect of his own return to politics. This last view is argued by E. Stettner (*Z. Oest. Gymn.* 61 (1910) 684ff. and 865ff.); but the *Cato* as a whole, and that passage in particular, can equally well (perhaps more plausibly) be read as expressing nostalgia for Cicero's lost position, rather than advertisement of his presence; if the latter had been his intention there would have been other, more effective, ways to carry it out.

In view of Cicero's known speed of writing, it is not impossible that the *Cato* was completed between the Ides of March and 11 May, in the intervals of other occupations. Nevertheless it seems more plausible to suppose that at least the greater part of the composition was done before the Ides; otherwise one would have to explain the apparent slowing down of his literary production in Jan.–March 44, when he was otherwise working only on the *De divinatione*.

It seems in general more likely that Cicero should have conceived the idea of writing a reflective work on old age before the Ides, than after his return to public life. In the preface to the *Cato*, Cicero refers very vaguely to matters which are worrying both himself and Atticus, to alleviate which would be a large task needing to be postponed to another time. This doubtless refers to the political situation; Cicero is too reticent about it to permit any very definite conclusions, and the reticence itself has been taken to point both ways. On the whole it seems more probable that it refers to the circumstances of Caesar's dictatorship, rather than uneasiness about the way events would turn after the Ides, but either is possible.

It should be added that *Att.* 16.3.1, which has sometimes been taken to refer to a second, revised version of the *Cato*, does not in fact seem to refer to the *Cato* at all, but rather to the *De gloria*. Parallels of subject-matter between passages of the *Cato* and the letters (*Cato* 31 and *Fam.* 9.14.2; 45 and *Fam.* 9.24.3; 34 and *Att.* 14.19.1) prove nothing about the dating of the *Cato*, as it is impossible in each case to establish the priority of either member of the pair.

On balance, therefore, it looks as if it is more likely that the *Cato* was written at some time between January and March 44.

(See Schanz–Hosius 1, 513 and 515; T. Maurer, *N. Jb. Kl. Phil.* 129 (1884) 385ff.; Schwenke, *Bursian* 47 (1887) 291ff.; K. Allen, *AJP* 28 (1907) 297ff.; C. Thiaucourt, *Essai sur les traités philosophiques de Cicéron* (Paris 1885) 174; Pease on *Div.*, introd. pp. 13–14; and editions.)

APPENDIX 2   ARISTO CHIUS OR ARISTO CEUS? (*Cato* 3)

οὐ Χῖος ἀλλὰ Κεῖος (Aristophanes, *Frogs* 970).

(a) Evidence outside the *Cato*

(i) Other references in Cicero. Cicero mentions both the Chian and the Cean elsewhere; the frequency of mentions of the Chian (*c.* 20 in the philosophical works) is no argument for supposing that the Chian is meant here. The single mention of the Cean elsewhere (*Fin.* 5.13) bears a certain similarity to *Cato* 3: *ea quae desideratur a magno philosopho gravitas in eo non fuit: scripta sane et multa et polita, sed nescioquo pacto auctoritatem oratio non habet*; cf. in the *Cato: parum enim esset auctoritatis in fabula … quo maiorem auctoritatem haberet oratio*. The criticism in *Fin.* 5 is general, that in the *Cato* relates only to the use of mythology in philosophical writings; but it is essentially the same point that is made in both passages. Clearly this is evidence for the Cean.

(ii) Plutarch, *De aud. poet.* 1.14e, refers to the *Abaris* of Heraclides and the *Lycon* of Aristo as containing 'doctrines concerning the soul, mixed with mythology'. The Aristo mentioned by Plutarch is fairly certainly the Cean; Lycon was his predecessor as head of the Lyceum. It appears, therefore, that this Aristo used mythology in philosophical writings, and that may render it more likely that the work criticised by Cicero was also by him. However, this argument is very far from conclusive; myths of various sorts were a common ingredient of philosophical literature.

(iii) Peripatetic interest in old age is certified by the existence of works on the subject by Aristotle, Theophrastus and Demetrius of Phalerum (see Introd. pp. 25–6). No comparable essay by an early Stoic is known – unless this of Aristo's was one; hence, again, it seems more likely that we are dealing with the Peripatetic Aristo.

(iv) Seneca, *Ep.* 94, tells us that Aristo the Stoic attached little importance to particular ethical precepts, since he thought that ethics should deal with the whole man (Aristo of Chios frr. 356–9 von Arnim). Wehrli considers this to exclude the possibility of the Chian having written about old age; others have not been so certain, but again it is clearly evidence for the Cean.

(v) A catalogue of works survives, under the heading of Aristo of Chios, in Diogenes Laertius 7.163. Diog. Laert. reports that Panaetius and

Sosicrates attributed all the listed works except some letters to the Cean. There is no entry for any work on old age; it has been thought that the entry Διάλογοι might have included a dialogue on old age. Even if this were so, it would not tell us which Aristo was the true author, since the attribution of the catalogue is doubtful.

(vi) Nor can any enlightenment be derived from Varro, who wrote a Menippean satire entitled *Tithonus* ἢ περὶ γήρως, and who quotes a not certainly identified Aristo in the *logistoricus* entitled *Catus de liberis educandis*. Nothing whatsoever can be said about the sources of the Menippean satire, apart from the vague possibility that it recalled the same Aristo as Cicero mentions (because of the parallel reference to Tithonus – though that would in any case be an obvious enough example in contexts of old age). The *Catus* fragment (fr. 9 Riese) concerns education, and has been thought to be parallel with *Cato* 62, but is not notably similar. Even the speculation that the Aristo quoted by Varro is the same as Cicero's seems risky on the basis of such a tenuous parallel; certainly it tells us nothing about Cicero's Aristo. (Wehrli attributes it to the Cean, fr. 27, with reservation; Gottschalk, *Mnem.* 4, 33 (1980) 359, argues for the Chian, but without mentioning the *Cato*.)

(b) Evidence involving passages of the *Cato* itself

(i) Parallels or alleged parallels with fragments of Aristo of Ceos. These do not amount to much. The only real one is the image of dazzling the mind's eye in *Cato* 42; but it is a common idea, occurring a number of times in Cicero himself as well as in Plato, and it would be far-fetched to link it specifically with the quite different context of Aristo, Περὶ τοῦ κουφίζειν ὑπερηφανίας col. 12, 15ff.; in fact one may also compare Aristo of *Chios* in Sen. *Ep.* 94.5. Otherwise, scholars have referred to the mention of Seriphos (*Cato* 8; Aristo ibid. col. 14, 24), of Lysander (*Cato* 59 and 63; col. 15 = fr. 13, 5 Wehrli) and of Themistocles and Aristides (*Cato* 21; frr. 19 and 20 Wehrli); but there is absolutely no similarity in the contexts, and the sources of the first two references in Cicero are clearly identified as Plato and Xenophon respectively. This sort of searching for 'parallels' is worse than useless.

(ii) Parallels with Aristo of Chios. These constitute the only evidence of any cogency in favour of the Chian, but on closer examination they do not seem to prove anything much. The only genuine one is *Cato* 4 *eis nihil malum potest videri quod naturae necessitas adferat* with Aristo of Chios ap. Sen. *Ep.* 94.7 *omnia fortiter excipienda quae nobis mundi necessitas imperat*. This is however a commonplace sentiment in both its forms, and the verbal echo between one Latin author and another is of dubious significance in the search for Greek sources (one does not know how closely Seneca reproduces Aristo). Other parts of this Senecan letter have been used on behalf of the Chian, e.g. 94.3 on exercise, but I can see no other real parallels. It should also be remembered that this is the same letter of Seneca's as was used above (a, iv) *against* the Chian as Cicero's source.

Certain stock comparisons are common to Cicero and Aristo of Chios, e.g. that of the actor (see on *Cato* 5; Aristo of Chios fr. 351 von Arnim), the helmsman (*Cato* 17 and fr. 396, from Aristo's ὁμοιώματα), and wine (*Cato* 65 and fr. 397); but the contexts are quite different, and the shared images show only that the two writers drew on a similar tradition. In all cases there are closer parallels with Cicero's thought elsewhere. A ὁμοίωμα of Aristo of Chios is preserved (fr. 399) which concerns, in part, old age, and may be used as evidence that the Chian did concern himself with such subjects (against points iii and iv above), but it is not remotely similar to anything in Cicero.

(iii) Parallels with fragments attributed to an 'Aristo' not further identified. These clearly cannot be of any help in resolving the question of the identity of Cicero's Aristo, so I restrict myself to listing them: apart from the Varronian quotation in (vi) above, *Cato* 65 and Sen. *Ep.* 36.3 (comparison with wine, and commendation of seriousness in young men: cf., perhaps, *Cato* 38); Aristo ap. Plut. *De san. tuend.* 133c (Aristo of Chios fr. 389 von Arnim), disparaging athletes, is linked by A. M. Ioppolo with *Cato* 27 and 33, but there is no real resemblance; similarly the recommendation of physical exercise by Aristo ὁ φιλόσοφος (probably the Chian) in *Gnom. vat.* 123, with *Cato* 35–6.

(iv) The parallels between the *Cato* and Bion of Borysthenes (see Introd. p. 14 n. 36) have been adduced in the present argument: they constitute evidence for the Cean if Strabo (10, p. 486) is right in characterising the Cean Aristo as ὁ τοῦ Βορυσθενίτου Βίωνος ζηλωτής. It would in that case be possible to theorise (as Hense does, *Teletis Reliquiae*, introd. pp. cxviii ff.) that Aristo of Ceos was the intermediary who transmitted Bion's thoughts to Cicero. Yet this does not entirely convince: the parallels with Bion are not as impressive as has sometimes been thought (see Introd.), and it is by no means proved that the passages of Cicero in question were influenced by him either directly or indirectly. In addition, Strabo's information has been doubted, not always for reasons connected with the *Cato* (e.g. Kindstrand, *Bion of Borysthenes* 79ff.); it seems to me that Strabo's evidence is the least suspect part of the argument (cf. M. Lancia, *Elenchos* 1 (1980) 276ff.).

(v) Parallels with Plutarch's *An seni* have been invoked in this argument, but he does not mention Aristo there, and there is nothing in the work on which to base any conclusions; in general, see Introd. p. 28.

(vi) As pointed out above, Introd. p. 16, the general philosophical character of the *Cato* is not sectarian enough to prove anything about sources: the odd piece of watered-down Stoicism (e.g. *Cato* 4) could easily have come from Cicero himself, and certainly does not prove that he used a Stoic model. Clearly the occurrence, real or alleged, of material from other Stoics or Peripatetics does not affect the Aristo question.

Conclusion. Virtually all the arguments here outlined are inconclusive in themselves, and some prove nothing either way. The balance of evidence, however, seems to me to be fairly clearly in favour of the Cean, and accordingly I read *Aristo Ceus* in *Cato* 3. For the evidence of the MSS, see note ad loc.

(See for the Cean F. Ritschl, *RhM* 1 (1842) 193ff. = *Opuscula* (Leipzig 1886) 1, 551ff.; Hirzel, *Dialog* 331; F. Wehrli, *Die Schule des Aristoteles* VI, *Lykon und Ariston von Keos* (Basle 1952) 32 and 52; A. Gercke, *Arch. Gesch. Phil.* 5 (1892) 198ff.; id., P.–W. 2, 955; 10, 953; K. Mras, *Wien. Stud.* 39 (1955) 88ff.; L. Alfonsi, *P. del P.* 10 (1955) 121ff.; id., *Aevum* 31 (1957) 366ff.; O. Hense, *Teletis Reliquiae*, edn. 2, pref. pp. cxvi ff.; W. Knögel, *Der Peripatetiker Ariston bei Philodem* (Leipzig 1933) 80. For the Chian, Schröter, *De Cic. C. M.* and Kröger, *De Cic. in C. M. auctoribus*, both criticised by A. Lörcher, *Bursian* 204 (1925) 103ff.; A. Giesecke, *N. Jb. Kl. Phil.* 145 (1892) 206ff.; A. Oltramare, *Les Origines de la diatribe romaine* (Geneva 1926) 120; A. M. Ioppolo, *Aristone di Chio e lo stoicismo antico* (Naples 1980) 292ff., reviewed by me in *CR* 32 (1982) 101–2. Most recent editors seem to be in favour of the Cean.)

APPENDIX 3   THE *CATO* AS A
HISTORICAL SOURCE

A number of passages of the *Cato* raise problems concerning history and chronology, and it is convenient that these should be discussed together here. Before dealing with the individual points, it should be noted in general that historians have tended to be excessively sceptical of the value of the *Cato* as a historical source (see esp. Fraccaro, cited below). Certainly, the *Cato* is a philosophical dialogue, not a work of historical narration; the historical details mentioned in it have the function of filling out the background and setting of the dialogue, or else they are inserted into the argument as rhetorical illustrations. Yet this does not mean that they are automatically to be distrusted. Even Cicero's literary purposes would have been better served by the introduction of genuine facts than by simple invention; Cicero seems to have been well aware of the limits to which fiction could reasonably be taken in a Roman dialogue, and he was clearly concerned and careful about getting his facts right, as may be seen from e.g. *Att.* 12.23.2 and 13.30.2. When Cicero makes Cato the Elder talk Platonic philosophy, we may smile at the incongruity; when he makes Cato recall the early events of his career, we expect them to be more or less factually correct, and nothing would have been gained by distorting them. In all, we must presume that the *Cato* is to be treated as a historical source like any other, and reject the information it contains only when there is a balance of evidence against it.

Much of the historical information in the *Cato* doubtless came from Cicero's general knowledge, compounded of his reading of diverse sources throughout his lifetime, and his recollection and judgement may of course have been faulty. It is however possible that he did a certain amount of *ad hoc* chronological research: this seems to be indicated by the use of the word *reperio* in §41 (though it must of course be remembered that it is Cato, not Cicero, who is speaking, and there is difficulty in accepting the dating there given: see (f) below). Some of the information on Cato's career and activities may have come from Cato's own writings, though it is to be noted that Cicero does not follow Cato's version of the L. Flamininus incident (a fact that is pointed out with surprise by Plut. *Cato* 17: cf. on §42).

Otherwise there is no indication of the sources used by Cicero for the historical background of this dialogue. In particular, there is no positive evidence that Cicero used the *Liber annalis* of Atticus; that is merely a theory of Münzer (*Hermes* 40 (1905) 50ff.), whose arguments that the chronology in the *Cato* reflects use of tendentiously distorted sources by Atticus are entirely speculative. It is not unlikely that Atticus helped Cicero with his chronology, here as elsewhere, but it is hazardous to assume this in any particular case in the absence of other evidence.

(a) The early career of Cato (§10)

Much has been made of the differences between Cicero's account of Cato's early career and the version of Nepos' abbreviated life of Cato, which Münzer took to represent an alternative uncorrupted account. In fact the discrepancies are hardly disturbing. Both accounts are incomplete, and it is not at all difficult to construct an account of Cato's movements that includes all the events mentioned by both. Cicero professes only to list those occasions on which Cato was associated with Fabius Maximus, or events that could be correlated with major points in Fabius' life; there is no reason whatever to suppose that any of the items mentioned were distorted or invented in order to argue for a closer connection with Fabius than actually obtained.

The first event mentioned by Cicero is the expedition to Capua in 214: *cumque eo quartum consule adulescentulus miles ad Capuam profectus sum.* Nepos says that Cato campaigned in Sicily in that year as military tribune (presumably under the other consul, M. Claudius Marcellus). The rank of tribune is certainly not excluded by Cato's modestly depreciative phrase *adulescentulus miles,* and Cato could well have spent some time on both campaigns. Since Fabius stayed at Capua, it is quite natural that Cato should say *ad Capuam profectus sum* even if he then immediately went on to Sicily; the two armies may have marched together for the first part of the journey. It is certainly not stated that Cato stayed for the whole of the siege of Capua.

The account of Nepos then continues *inde ut rediit, castra secutus est C. Claudii Neronis, magnique opera eius existimata est in proelio apud Senam.* This has been thought to exclude Cato's having been present at the recapture of Tarentum in 209, as Cicero says. But there is a period of seven years between 214, when Cato was in Sicily according to Nepos, and the Metaurus campaign in 207 when he served under Claudius Nero; Cato cannot have stayed in Sicily for seven years without a break. *Inde ut rediit* is probably nothing more than a formula of transition in this highly epitomated version of Cato's life, and should not be taken to imply that nothing happened in between the two events mentioned. This provides no reason to disbelieve information that Cato was at Tarentum with Fabius Maximus. Consequently there is no need to think of reasons (such as a desire to establish Pythagorean influence on Cato) why Cicero might have wished to invent a visit to Tarentum: there is no evidence that he did invent it. (See further note on §§39ff.)

It has been alleged that the accounts of Cicero and Nepos differ on the date of Cato's quaestorship; but there is no reason to suppose, as Münzer does, that Nepos represents a different tradition from Cicero, Livy and Plutarch, all of whom place the quaestorship in 204 B.C.; Cicero actually specifies the consuls, Tuditanus and Cethegus. Nepos' account reads *quaestor obtigit P. Africano consuli*. Scipio Africanus' consulate was indeed in 205; but Cato was Scipio's quaestor in Africa in 204, and *consuli* may well be used loosely there to refer to Scipio's proconsulship; besides, it would have been during Scipio's actual consulate that the election of the quaestors and the apportionment of their duties took place. Again Nepos provides no reason to question Cicero's evidence. Nor is there any reason to suppose that the textual confusion in the MSS of this passage has anything to do with doubt about the chronology, as on any showing the consular date for Cato's quaestorship is a certain reading, and such confusion doubtless arose at a time when chronological matters of this sort had long ceased to cause concern; cf. note ad loc.

(See P. Fraccaro, *Atti Accad. Virgiliana* NS 3 (1910) 99–135 = *Opuscula* I (Pavia 1956) 139ff., with Exc. II, *Opusc.* I, 171ff.; E. Pais, 'Questioni Catoniane: Il filosofo pitagorico Nearco' in *Historia, Studi storici per l'antichità classica,* Milan, 6 (1932) 367ff. = *Mélanges Glotz* (Paris 1932) II, 681ff.; F. Cassola, *I Gruppi Politici Romani nel III secolo a. C.* (Trieste 1962) Appendix IX, pp. 347–8, with bibliography; H. Scullard, *Roman Politics 220–150 B.C.*, edn. 2 (Oxford 1973) 111 n. 2; R. E. Smith, *CQ* 34 (1940) 104ff.; E. V. Marmorale, *Cato Maior* (Catania 1944); F. della Corte, *Catone Censore*[2] 238ff.; Astin, *Cato* 7ff.)

(b) The dates of Fabius Maximus' birth and death (ibid.)

There is no inconsistency here between Cicero's information and that provided by other sources, but it is not clear whether reliable chronology is produced by combining it with them; traditions may have been unclear, and Cicero's references to Fabius' age at various times may have been deliberately vague, and merely deduced from the dates of his magistracies. The relevant fixed dates are Fabius' first consulate in 233, mentioned by Cicero as the year after Cato's birth, and the date of his death, 203, given by Livy 30.26.7. The sources there quoted by Livy say that Fabius had been augur for 62 years, as does Valerius Maximus 8.13.3, cf. Pliny *NH* 7.156; but Livy says *si quidem verum est* with a nuance of scepticism, and the tradition may well be exaggerated.

Cicero makes Fabius *admodum senex* in 204, but *non admodum grandis natu, sed tamen iam aetate provectum* when Cato first knew him, hardly earlier than 218 (if Cato assumed the *toga virilis* at the normal age). If the sixty-two-year augurate is authentic, Fabius became augur in 265 and was therefore born *c.* 285, if it is assumed that he became augur around twenty years of age; he would then have been just over fifty at the time of his first consulate, around 67 when Cato made his acquaintance, and 82 at the time of his death. This all makes reasonable sense of Cicero's phraseology, but if the information on the augurate is exaggerated, it is quite possible and consistent with Cicero's evidence to suppose that Fabius was born a few years later.

(c) Fabius Maximus' opposition to the Flaminian land law (§11)

qui consul iterum, Spurio Carvilio collega quiescente, C. Flaminio tribuno plebis quoad potuit restitit, agrum Picentem et Gallicum contra senatus auctoritatem dividenti: the phrase *consul iterum* places this event in 228 (Broughton, *MRR* 228). The law itself was passed by Flaminius as tribune in 232 (Polybius 2.21.7–8, cf. Walbank ad loc.). Some have seen a contradiction here; but there is not necessarily any difficulty in accommodating both Cicero and Polybius. Cicero says that Fabius opposed Flaminius as he was dividing the land: the natural implication of this is that the law had already been passed, and that Flaminius was himself putting the provisions of his law into effect (no doubt as a member of a commission like those set up by the Gracchi). It is difficult to make the Latin mean anything else, though some scholars, convinced that Cicero is wrong in his dating and actually meant to refer to the passing of the law, have tried to do so: *dividenti* can hardly mean 'passing a law directing the land to be divided', without further qualification, and a future or conative meaning ('about to divide' or 'attempting to divide'), such as some envisage, would be hard to parallel in Cicero (H.–Sz. p. 387; Laughton, *Participle* p. 40f.). Nevertheless, some minor difficulties remain. Flaminius is referred to as tribune in the context of activities taking place some years after his tribunate; but a looseness of this sort need not cause much trouble. A more serious question is raised by the implication that the division of the land was still going on and was being opposed by Fabius four years after the law was passed, especially since Polybius (2.23.1) refers to events of 225 as occurring in the eighth year after the division of the land (μετὰ τὴν τῆς χώρας διάδοσιν). There is, however, nothing prima facie improbable in the four-year delay before the carrying out of the law's provisions, particularly in view of the senatorial opposition; and at a stretch Polybius could be taken to be loosely identifying the 'division of the land' with the passing of the law.

There have been various attempts to amend Cicero's information. Niccolini, followed by Broughton, thought that Cicero confused Fabius' two consulates. Certainly, the last three months or so of Fabius' first consulate would have overlapped with Flaminius' tribunate, on the assumption that Flaminius entered office in December 233 while Fabius did not relinquish the consulate until March 232; and if Flaminius passed the law in the winter of 233–2, Fabius could have opposed it as consul. However, there is no need for this dismissal of Cicero's evidence if it is remembered that Cicero does not refer to the passing of the law, but to the actual division of the land. Cicero refers explicitly to Fabius' colleague of 228, Sp. Carvilius, as well as specifying *consul iterum*. Broughton thinks the reference to Carvilius was introduced to explain away his non-involvement after the chronological mistake had been made; but it surely makes good sense, in this laudatory passage, to say that Fabius opposed the land-division even in the absence of support from his colleague.

There are other features of the passage that make better sense if it is assumed that Cicero's information is right, or at least that he had an accurate idea of what he thought had happened. *quoad potuit* implies that Fabius' opposition may not have been very effective: this would suit a time at which the law had already been passed and was about to be put into effect. One of the principal modes of obstruction left available to Fabius would have been by means of the auspices, and this provides a context for the remark quoted by Cicero immediately afterwards in this passage. Fabius' remark about the auspices would make excellent sense if he was contending that the law had been passed *contra auspicia* (*ferri* there would naturally refer to the passing of a law). If a defect in the auspices had been alleged, and the matter referred to the College of Augurs, such a pronouncement by Fabius as augur in this context would be particularly surprising and noteworthy.

All in all, Cicero cannot here be convicted of inconsistency or implausibility, and there is no reason to suppose that he did not obtain his information from a reputable source – by far the best guess being Cato, who was interested in Fabius, in land-division, and in auspices, their use and misuse.

(See F. Cassola, *I Gruppi Politici Romani nel III secolo a.C.* 243; 260–1; Broughton, *MRR* I, 225; Münzer, P.–W. s.v. 'Flaminius' col. 2497; L. Lange, *Römische Altertümer* II, edn. 2 (Berlin 1867) 139; J. Bleicken, *Das Volkstribunat der klassischen Republik* (Munich 1955) 28–9; G. Niccolini, *I Fasti dei tribuni della plebe* (Milan 1934) 87–9, with bibliography; C. F. Hermann, *RhM* 2 (1843) 573ff.; I. Müller-Seidel, *RhM* 96 (1953) 269 n. 119; H. François, *Anales de Filología Clásica* 5 (1950-52) 145ff.; Z. Yavetz, *Athenaeum* NS 40 (1962) 325ff. esp. 330 n. 23.)

(d) Appius Claudius' intervention in the Senate
against peace with Pyrrhus (§16)

Cicero places this famous incident 'in the seventeenth year after Appius' second consulate'; the second consulate was in 296, hence Cicero implies a date during the consular year 279 (viz., given that consuls took office in March at this period, March 279–March 278). Appius' intervention traditionally took place on the occasion of the embassy of Cineas to Rome; this embassy, together with that of Fabricius to Pyrrhus, is placed by all sources except the much-epitomated Justin–Trogus between the battle of Heraclea (in the campaigning season of 280) and that of Ausculum (in that of 279). Justin–Trogus places it after Ausculum, later in 279. There is disagreement among the other sources as to the order of the two embassies: the Livian tradition places that of Fabricius first, while Plutarch and Appian place it after that of Cineas. It has been thought that the evidence of Cicero here supports Justin–Trogus against the other sources, and the Justinian dating has acquired considerable popularity as a result; but there is no need to assume this. Cicero could perfectly well have had in mind a dating of Cineas' embassy in the *spring* of 279, before Ausculum but after the beginning of the consular year. In this case, the information of Cicero would agree with the Livian tradition, which makes the embassy of Cineas the second of the two, rather than with Plutarch and Appian, since it would be difficult to place both embassies in the spring of 279. Whether Cicero's dating is right is another matter, to be decided on grounds of historical probability; the point that needs to be made here is that it does not conflict, as has been thought, with the most reliable of the other sources.

(See Lévêque, *Pyrrhos* 362–3; A. Garzetti, *Athenaeum* 25 (1947) 175–224, esp. 219–22 and n. 1 on p. 219; B. Niese, *Hermes* 31 (1896) 481; A. Passerini, *Athenaeum* 21 (1943) 92–112.)

(e) The date of Scipio Africanus' death (§19)

This is a case of inconsistency within Cicero's account, unless our MSS are wrong. The death of Scipio is placed by Cicero (i) in the 33rd year before the dramatic date of the *Cato*; the dramatic date is the consular year 150, the thirty-third year before that is 183; (ii) in the year before Cato's censorship, which is also nine years after Cato's consulate; this means 185. (The nine years are reckoned in full from the end of Cato's consulate in 195/4, and extend to the beginning of the consular year 185; it is most misleading to assume that 'inclusive reckoning' is used.) This discrepancy in Cicero's own dating can hardly be resolved other than by correcting the text (to *quintus* or *sextus* from *tertius*: either could be acceptable), or by assuming that Cicero merely made a mistake.

In fact the other sources also differ as to the date of Scipio's death. Polybius and Rutilius quoted in Livy 39.52 gave 183, Valerius Antias gave 187; Livy himself places it in 184, arguing that he must have died before the censorship of Cato and Flaccus (when a new *princeps senatus* was chosen to replace him), but that a speech against him by a tribune, Naevius, showed that he must have lived well into the tribunician year 184 (viz. Dec. 185–Dec. 184). Cicero's *anno ante me censorem* may have been based on a similar train of reasoning to that of Livy. However, it is doubtful whether the confusion in Cicero has much to do with these differing traditions.

(f) The date of Plato's visit to Tarentum mentioned in §41

cum quidem ei sermoni interfuisset Plato Atheniensis, quem Tarentum venisse L. Camillo Ap. Claudio consulibus reperio. The consuls are those of 349, two years before Plato's death in 347. This visit of Plato to the West cannot be identified with any of the three which are mentioned in the *Seventh Letter*, and which are usually reckoned to be the only ones he made: these were in 389–8, 367 and 361–0, the last synchronised by Plutarch with the eclipse of 361 (*Dion* 19). There is no reason why the visit referred to by Cicero should not have been a fourth one distinct from these, except for the general improbability of his undertaking another such journey at the age of 79. The situation is complicated by the fact that Aulus Gellius (17.21.28f.), depending apparently on Roman sources, records a visit of Plato to Italy between A.U.C. 400 (354 B.C.) and the battle of Chaeronea (338); this could refer to the same tradition as appears in Cicero (on this chapter of Gellius see E. Fantham, *LCM* 6 (1981) 7–17).

As explained in the note on §§39ff., it is not easy to see how much factual truth there is, or is meant to be, behind Cicero's statement that Archytas of Tarentum, Plato and C. Pontius the Samnite had a conversation on pleasure at Tarentum on this occasion, nor where Cicero obtained the idea that they may have done. The mention of Plato's visit may be nothing more than 'artistic verisimilitude', designed to support Cicero's idealised picture of the contacts between Italians and Greek philosophers in past ages. Nevertheless, the word *reperio* implies some sort of chronological record, and it is probable that the dating of Plato's visit to around 349 goes back at least to whatever sources were used by Cicero and Gellius, whether it is true or not. (For attempts to explain the mistake, if it is a mistake, see E. Pais, art. cit., and A. Gudeman, *BPW* 33 (1913) 1343.)

BIBLIOGRAPHY

1. Works cited by short title

André, J. M. *L'Otium dans la vie morale et intellectuelle romaine des origines à l'époque augustéenne*, Paris 1966. (André, *L'Otium*)

Archiv für lateinische Lexikographie und Grammatik, ed. E. Wölfflin, Leipzig 1884–1909 (*ALL*)

Astin, A. E. *Cato the Censor*, Oxford 1978 (Astin, *Cato*)

Axelson, B. *Unpoetische Wörter, ein Beitrag zur Kenntnis der lateinischen Dichtersprache*, Lund 1945 (Axelson, *Unpoetische Wörter*)

Beare, W. *The Roman Stage*, London 1950 (Beare, *Roman Stage*)

Becker, E. *Technik und Szenerie des ciceronischen Dialogs*, diss. Münster, Osnabrück 1938 (Becker, *Technik und Szenerie*)

Blümner, H. *Römische Privataltertümer*, Munich 1911 (Blümner, *Privataltertümer*)

Boyancé, P. *Études sur le Songe de Scipion*, Paris 1936 (Boyancé, *Songe de Scipion*)

Broughton, T. R. S. *The Magistrates of the Roman Republic*, New York, 1951–60 (Broughton, *MRR*)

Bücheler, F. *Carmina Latina Epigraphica*, Leipzig 1895–1926 = *Anthologia Latina*, ed. Bücheler and Riese, part II (Bücheler, *CLE*)

Büchner, K., ed. *Das neue Cicerobild*, Darmstadt 1971 (Büchner, *Cicerobild*)

Burkert, W. *Lore and Science in Ancient Pythagoreanism*, tr. E. L. Minar, Harvard 1972 (Burkert, *Lore and Science*)

Corpus Inscriptionum Latinarum, Berlin 1963– (*CIL*)

Diels, H. and Kranz, W. *Die Fragmente der Vorsokratiker*, edn 6, Berlin 1951 (D.–K.)

Dodds, E. R. *The Greeks and the Irrational*, Berkeley 1951 (Dodds, *Irrational*)

Draeger, A. *Historische Syntax der lateinischen Sprache*, edn 2, Leipzig 1878 (Draeger, *Historische Syntax*)

Ernout, A. and Meillet, A. *Dictionnaire étymologique de la langue latine, histoire des mots*, edn 4 (augm. and corr. J. André), Paris 1979 (Ernout–Meillet)

Gigante, M. *Ricerche filodemee*, edn 2, Naples 1983 (Gigante, *Ricerche filodemee*)

Grammatici Latini, ed. H. Keil, Leipzig 1857, etc. (*GLK*)

Hale, W. G. *The Cum Constructions*, Ithaca 1887 (Hale, *The Cum Constructions*)

Hand, F. *Tursellinus seu de particulis Latinis commentarii*, Leipzig 1829–45, repr. Amsterdam 1969 (Hand, *Tursellinus*)

Handford, S. A. *The Latin Subjunctive: Its usage and development from Plautus to Tacitus*, London 1947 (Handford, *Subjunctive*)

Hirzel, R. *Der Dialog: ein literarhistorischer Versuch*, Leipzig, 1895, repr. Hildesheim, 1963 (Hirzel, *Dialog*)

Hofmann, J. B. *Lateinische Umgangssprache*, 3. Aufl. Heidelberg 1951 (Hofmann, *Umgangssprache*)

Hofmann, J. B. and Szantyr, A. *Lateinische Syntax und Stilistik*, Munich 1965 (H.–Sz.)

The Classical Papers of A. E. Housman, ed. J. Diggle and F. R. D. Goodyear, Cambridge 1972 (Housman, *Papers*)

Inscriptiones Latinae selectae, ed. H. Dessau, Berlin 1892–1916 (*ILS*)

Kammer, U. *Untersuchungen zu Ciceros Bild von Cato Censorius*, Frankfurt 1964 (Kammer, *Untersuchungen*)

Kienast, D. *Cato der Zensor*, Heidelberg 1954 (Kienast, *Cato*)

Krebs, J. P. and Schmalz, J. H. *Antibarbarus der lateinischen Sprache*, edn 7, Basel 1905 (Krebs–Schmalz, *Antibarbarus*)

Kühner, R. and Stegmann, C. *Ausführliche Grammatik der lateinischen Sprache: Satzlehre*, edn 3, revised A. Thierfelder, Darmstadt 1955 (K.–S.)

Lattimore, R. *Themes in Greek and Latin Epitaphs* (= Illinois Studies in Language and Literature 28, 1942, 1–2) Urbana 1962 (Lattimore, *Epitaphs*)

Laughton, E. *The Participle in Cicero* (Oxford Classical and Philosophical Monographs), Oxford 1964 (Laughton, *Participle*)

Lebreton, J. *Études sur la langue et la grammaire de Cicéron*, Paris 1901 (Lebreton, *Études*)

Leumann, M. *Lateinische Laut- und Formenlehre* (Leumann–Hofmann–Szantyr, *Lateinische Grammatik*, 1), Munich, 1977 (Leumann, *Laut- u. Formenlehre*)

von Leutsch, E. L. and Schneidewin, F. G. *Corpus Paroemiographorum Graecorum*, Göttingen 1839 (Leutsch–Schneidewin, *Paroem.*)

Lévêque, P. *Pyrrhos* (Bibl. Écoles Françaises d'Athènes et de Rome, 185), Paris 1957 (Lévêque, *Pyrrhos*)

Lindsay, W. M. *Early Latin Verse*, Oxford 1922 (Lindsay, *ELV*)

Löfstedt, E. *Syntactica: Studien und Beiträge zur historischen Syntax des Lateins*, Lund, vol. I edn 2, 1956; vol. II, 1933 (Löfstedt, *Synt.*)

Malcovati, H. *Oratorum Romanorum fragmenta liberae rei publicae*, edn 2, Turin, 1955 (Malcovati, *ORF*)

Marquardt, J. and Mau, A. *Das Privatleben der Römer*, edn 2, Leipzig 1886 (Marquardt, *Privatleben*)

BIBLIOGRAPHY

Merguet, H. *Lexikon zu den Schriften Ciceros, 2. Lexikon zu den philosophischen Schriften.* Jena, 1887 (Merguet, *Lexikon*)

Mommsen, T. *Römisches Staatsrecht,* edn. 3, Leipzig 1887–8 (Mommsen, *Staatsrecht*)

von Nägelsbach, K. F. and Müller, I. *Lateinische Stilistik,* edn. 9, Nuremberg 1905 (Nägelsbach–Müller, *Stilistik*)

Munk Olsen, B. *L'Étude des auteurs classiques latins aux XIe et XIIe siècles: I. Catalogue des manuscrits classiques latins copiés du IXe au XIIe siècle: Apicius–Juvenal.* Paris 1982. (Munk Olsen)

Neue, F. and Wagener, C. *Formenlehre der lateinischen Sprache,* edn. 3, Berlin 1892–1905 (Neue–Wagener)

Otto, A. *Die Sprichwörter und sprichwörtlichen Redensarten der Römer,* Leipzig 1890, repr. Hildesheim 1962 (Otto, *Sprichwörter*)

The Oxford Classical Dictionary, ed. N. G. L. Hammond and H. H. Scullard, edn. 2, Oxford 1970 (*OCD*)

Oxford Latin Dictionary, ed. P. G. W. Glare, Oxford 1982 (*OLD*)

Palmer, L. R. *The Latin Language,* London 1954 (Palmer, *Latin Language*)

Pauly–Wissowa, *Realencyclopädie der classischen Altertumswissenschaft,* Stuttgart, 1893–   (P.–W.)

Pöschl, V., Gärtner, H. and Heyke, W. *Bibliographie zur antiken Bildersprache,* Heidelberg 1964 (Pöschl, *Bibl. Bildersprache*)

Ribbeck, O. *Scaenicae Romanorum Poesis Fragmenta,* edn. 2, Leipzig 1871–3, repr. Hildesheim 1962. I. *Tragicorum Fragmenta;* II. *Comicorum Fragmenta* (Ribbeck. *Trag. Frr.; Com. Frr.*)

Riginos, A. *Platonica* (Columbia Studies in the Classical Tradition 3), 1976 (Riginos, *Platonica*)

Ruch, M. *Le Préambule dans les œuvres philosophiques de Cicéron: Essai sur la genèse et l'art du dialogue* (Publications de la Faculté des lettres de l'Université de Strasbourg, 136), Paris 1958 (Ruch, *Préambule*)

Schanz, M. and Hosius, C. *Geschichte der römischen Literatur* I, edn. 4, Munich 1927 (Schanz–Hosius)

Schmid, W. and Stählin, O. *Geschichte der griechischen Literatur,* Munich 1929, etc. (Schmid–Stählin)

Shackleton Bailey, D. R. *Cicero's Letters to Atticus,* Cambridge 1965 (Shackleton Bailey, *Cicero's Letters to Atticus*)

Skutsch, O. *The Annals of Quintus Ennius,* Oxford 1985 (Skutsch, *Ennius*)

Sommer, F. *Handbuch der lateinischen Laut- und Formenlehre,* edn. 3, Heidelberg 1914 (Sommer, *Laut- u. Formenlehre*)

Stein, A. *Platons Charakteristik der menschlichen Altersstufen,* Bonn 1966 (Stein, *Platons Charakteristik*)

Texts and Transmission: A Survey of the Latin Classics, ed. L. D. Reynolds, Oxford 1983 (*T. & T.*)

Thesaurus Linguae Latinae, Leipzig 1900– (*TLL*)

Thesleff, H. *The Pythagorean Texts of the Hellenistic Period,* Åbo 1965 (Thesleff, *Pythagorean Texts*)

Vahlen, J. *Gesammelte Philologische Schriften,* Leipzig and Berlin, I, 1911; II, 1923 (Vahlen, *Ges. Phil. Schr.*)

Volkmann, R. *Die Rhetorik der Griechen und Römer in systematischer Übersicht,* edn. 2, Leipzig, 1885, repr. Hildesheim, 1963 (Volkmann, *Rhetorik*)

Watson, W. A. J. *Roman Private Law around 200 B.C.,* Edinburgh 1971 (Watson, *Roman Private Law*)

White, K. D. *Roman Farming,* London, 1970 (White, *Roman Farming*)

Wuilleumier, P. *Tarente des origines à la conquête romaine* (Bibl. des Écoles françaises d'Athènes et de Rome, 148), 1939 (Wuilleumier, *Tarente*)

2. Bibliographical surveys and lists

Deiter, H. *Bursian* 84 (1895) 69ff.

Engelmann, W. *Bibliotheca Scriptorum Classicorum* (Leipzig 1882) II, 153–5 (editions), 185–227 (articles etc.)

Heine, O. *Philol.* 24 (1867) 474ff. esp. 529ff.

Klussmann, R. *Bibliotheca Scriptorum Classicorum 1878–1896* (Leipzig 1909) II.1, 259ff.

Lörcher, A. *Bursian* 162 (1913) 167–71; 204 (1925) 103ff.

Orelli, J. C. and Baiter, J. G., eds. *Onomasticon Tullianum* (Zürich 1836) I, 315–19

Schweiger, F. L. A. *Bibliographisches Lexicon der Römer* (Leipzig 1834) repr. Amsterdam 1962

Schwenke, P. *Bursian* 35 (1883) 102ff.; 47 (1887) 291ff.; 76 (1893) 233ff.

3. Select list of editions since 1800 (in chronological order)

(For older editions cf. Introd. p. 49; full lists in Otto's edition (1830) pp. xxx–xl, and in Orelli–Baiter, *Onomasticon Tullianum,* for which cf. above.)

Gernhard, A. G., Leipzig 1819

Otto, F. W., Leipzig 1830

Klotz, R., Leipzig 1831

Madvig, J. N., Copenhagen 1835

Tischer, G., Halle 1847

Sommerbrodt J. (edn. 1), Berlin 1851

Nauck, C. W., Berlin 1855

Lahmeyer, G., Leipzig 1857

Orelli, J. C., Baiter, J. G. and Halm, C., vol. IV, Zürich 1861

Baiter, J. G. and Kayser, C. L., vol. VII, Leipzig 1864

Meissner, K., Leipzig 1870, revised G. Landgraf, 1907

Müller, C. F. W., vol. IV, Leipzig 1878

Reid, J. S., Cambridge 1879 (edn. 2, 1886)

Schiche, T., Leipzig 1884

Kornitzer, A., Vienna 1888

Anz, H., Gotha 1889

Weissenfels, O. and Wessner, P., Leipzig 1891

Moore, F. G., New York 1904

Simbeck, K., Leipzig 1912–1917

Wuilleumier, P., Paris (Budé) 1940–1955–1961

Venini, P., Turin (Corpus Paravianum) 1959

4. Articles, etc., on text, manuscripts and interpretation

From the following list are omitted:

(a) articles dealing with single passages, cited in the commentary;
(b) bibliography on manuscripts cited in my article in *Texts and Transmission* (see p. 30, n. 75), or in the Introduction to this edition;
(c) reviews of editions.

Anz, H. *Kritische Bemerkungen zu Ciceros Cato Maior, Paradoxa, Somnium*, in *Festschrift zur Feier des 350jährigen Bestehens des Königlichen Gymnasiums zu Quedlinburg*, 1890

Baehrens, E. *N. Jb. Kl. Phil.* 125 (1882) 402

Baiter, J. G. *Philol.* 21 (1864) 535ff., 675ff.

Brieger, A. *Beiträge zur Kritik einiger philosophischen Schriften des Cicero*, in *Festgabe des Lehrerkollegiums des Königlichen Friedrich-Wilhelms-Gymnasiums zur 300jährigen Feier des Kön. Marien-Gymnasiums*, Posen 1873 (cf. I. Müller, *Bursian* 3 (1874–5) 697–8)

Calvo, A. G. *Emerita* 21 (1953) 38

Claflin, E. F. *AJP* 67 (1946) 193ff.

Contarini, V. *Variarum lectionum liber*, Venice 1606, pp. 101ff.

Cornelissen, J. J. *Mnem.* NS 6 (1878) 308

Cremaschi, G. *Aevum* 28 (1954) 76–7

Dahl, B. *Zur Handschriftenkunde und Kritik des ciceronischen Cato Maior*, I. *Codices Leidenses*, II. *Codices Parisini*, Christiania, 1886 (Dahl, *Handschriftenkunde*)

Earle, M. L. *Rev. Phil.* 28 (1904) 123–4

Fleckeisen, A. *N. Jb. Kl. Phil.* 87 (1863) 192

   N. Jb. Kl. Phil. 95 (1867) 643–4

Gercke, A. *N. Jb. Kl. Phil.* Suppl. 22 (1896) 50ff.

Havet, L. *Journ. Sav.* 1902, 370ff.; 401ff.

   ALL 12 (1902) 124.

   In *Album Gratulatorium H. van Herwerden*, Utrecht 1902, pp. 85ff.

   Manuel de critique verbale, Paris 1910, pp. 371ff. (cf. P. Wuilleumier, *Rev. Phil.* 1931, 108ff.)

Kleine, O. F. *Adnotationes in Ciceronis Catonem Maiorem et Laelium* (Progr. Wetzlar), 1854 (cf. Hölscher, *Z. f. d. Gymnasialwesen* 14 (1860) 620)

Kraffert, H. *Beiträge zur Kritik und Erklärung lateinischer Autoren* iii, Aurich, 1883 (cf. P. Schwenke, *Bursian* 35 (1883) 83; 102; 104)

Lahmeyer, G. *Philol.* 23 (1866) 473ff.

   Philol. 20 (1864) 284ff.

Langius, C. *In Ciceronem Adnotationes*, 1615

Ley, J. *N. Jb. Kl. Phil.* 127 (1883) 734

Lincke, K. *Hermes* 19 (1884) 465

Lund, G. F. W. *Bidrag til Fortolkningen af nogle Steder i Ciceros Cato Major og Laelius*, Nyköbing, 1851 (Lund, *Bidrag*)

Lütjohann, C. *RhM* 37 (1882) 496–505

Madvig, J. N. *Opuscula Academica*, edn. 2, pp. 615–626 (Madvig, *Opuscula*)

Mähly, J. *Neues Schweizerisches Museum* 6 (1866) 243ff.

Meissner, K. *N. Jb. Kl. Phil.* 103 (1871) 57ff.

   N. Jb. Kl. Phil. 131 (1885) 209ff.

Müller, O. M. *Annotationes ad M. T. Ciceronis librum de senectute*, Coeslin 1823

Nassau, H. J. *Adnotationum nonnullarum in librum Ciceronis De senectute, quas conscripsit H. J. N., fasc.* i, Groningen 1829

Nauck, C. W., *N. Jb. Kl. Phil.* Suppl. 8 (1842) 552ff.

   N. Jb. Kl. Phil. Suppl. 12 (1846) 558ff.

Nutting, H. C. *CQ* 19 (1925) 106

   CJ 21 (1925–6) 42

Otto, A. *Die Interpolationen in Ciceros Cato Maior* (Philologische Abhandlungen Hertz), Berlin 1888, pp. 94ff.

Polle, F. *N. Jb. Kl. Phil.* 131 (1885) 807

   N. Jb. Kl. Phil. 143 (1891) 707

di Prima, A. *Paideia* 12 (1958) 247ff.

Rüdiger, C. A. *Z. f. d. Gymnasialwesen* 18 (1864) 798–9

Salanitro, G. *RIL* 109 (1975) 284ff.

   GIF 20 (1967) 291ff.

   Sic. Gymn. 21 (1968) 76ff.

   Helikon 9–10 (1969–70) 622ff., 698ff. (cf. P. Venini, *Athenaeum* NS 49 (1971) 426ff.)

Schaeffer, I. *Z. f. d. Gymnasialwesen* 17 (1863) 80

Seyffert, M. *Z. f. d. Gymnasialwesen* 15 (1861) 67–9
 Z. f. d. Gymnasialwesen 15 (1861) 699

Simbeck, K. *De Ciceronis Catone Maiore* (progr. Kempten 1911/12), Leipzig 1912

Sommerbrodt, J. *N. Jb. Kl. Phil.* 123 (1881) 139ff.

Stangl, T. Progr. Munich 1888, p. 9 (cf. P. Schwenke, *Bursian* 76 (1893) 233ff.)

Steuding, H. *N. Jb. Kl. Phil.* 137 (1888) 862

Throop, G. R. *CPhil* 6 (1911) 483–4

Tomanetz, K. *Über den Wert und das Verhältnis der Handschriften von Ciceros Cato Maior*, Progr. Oberrealschule Josephstadt Wien, 1883

Tophoff, T. *Aliquot locos ex illo Ciceronis libro qui inscriptus est Cato Major, est interpretatus Dr. T. T.*, Paderborn 1847 (cf. G. Tischer, *N. Jb. Kl. Phil.* 53 (1848) 400–1)

Vaucher, L. *In M. Tulli Ciceronis libros philosophicos curae criticae*, fasc. II, Lausanne 1864, pp. 116ff.

Wagner, G. *Z. f. d. Gymnasialwesen* 15 (1861) 148

Weidner, A. Progr. Dortmund 1885 (cf. P. Schwenke, *Bursian* 47 (1887) 291ff.)

Wölfflin, E. *Philologus* 11 (1856) 192 (cf. G. Lahmeyer, ibid. pp. 592–3; R. Rauchenstein, ibid. p. 593)

Wuilleumier, P. *Rev. Phil.* 55 (= 3ᵉ série, 3) (1929) 43ff.

Wunder, E. *Variae lectiones librorum aliquot M. Tulli Ciceronis ex codice Erfurtensi enotatae*, Leipzig 1827, pp. 111–21

5. General discussions of the Cato

(See also Introd. p. 4 n. 14.)

Alexandre, F. D. A. *Appréciations médicales sur le Traité de la vieillesse de Cicéron*, Amiens 1868

Alfonsi, L. *Sic. Gymn.* 8 (1955) 429ff.
 Parola del Passato 10 (1955) 121ff.
 In *Studi E. Santini* (Palermo 1956) 1–16, repr. (in German) in Büchner, *Cicerobild*, 208ff.
 Ciceroniana 3 (1961) 3ff.

Blaiklock, E. M. *Cicero on Old Age*, Univ. of Auckland Bulletin 73, Classics Series 7, 1966

Büchner, K. 'Cicero, Grundzüge seines Wesens', *Gymnasium* 62 (1955), 299ff., repr. in *Cicerobild* 417ff. and in *Studien zur römischen Literatur*, II. *Cicero*, Wiesbaden 1962, 1ff.

Couch, H. N. *Cicero on the Art of Growing Old*, Providence, RI 1959

Knapp, C. 'An analysis of Cicero's Cato Maior', *CW* 8 (1915) 177f., 185–6

Kröger, H. *De Ciceronis in Catone Maiore auctoribus*, diss. Rostock 1912 (Kröger, *De Cic. in C. M. auctoribus*)

Manfredini, M. *RFIC* 98 (1970) 278ff.

Orsi, G. G. *Ragionamento ad un amico sopra il dialogo di Cicerone intitolato Cato Maior vel de Senectute*, Padua 1724

Pacitti, G. 'Sul significato ultimo del Cato Maior', *GIF* 18 (1965) 236ff.

Philippson, R. in P.–W. 7A1, 1163ff.

Rudd, N. 'Cicero's *De Senectute* and *The Vanity of Human Wishes*', *Notes and Queries* (March 1986) 59

Schröder, R. A. 'Nachwort' to his translation (1934) reprinted in Büchner, *Cicerobild* 1–9

Schröter, J. *De Ciceronis Catone Maiore*, diss. Weiden 1911 (Schröter, *De Cic. C. M.*)

Süss, W. *Cicero: eine Einführung in seine philosophischen Schriften*, Mainz 1966, pp. 134ff. (Süss, *Cicero*)

Svoboda, K. *Listy Filologicke* 46 (1919) 257ff. (cf. Lörcher, *Bursian* 204 (1925) 193ff.)

Thiaucourt, C. *Essai sur les traités philosophiques de Cicéron et leurs sources grecques*, Paris 1885

van der Ton, P. J. *Annales academiae Lovaniensis* 3 (1822) 1ff.

Tornos, A. M. 'La historia en el dialogo De senectute', *Humanidades* (Santander) 5 (1953) 272–80 (cf. *L'Année Philologique* 28 (1957) 57)

Tosi, T. *Civiltà Moderna* 1 (1929) 264ff.

Sul Cato Maior de Cicerone, in *Scritti di filologia e di archeologia*, ed. N. Terzaghi, Florence 1957, 186ff.

Venini, P. 'La vecchiaia nel *De senectute* di Cicerone', *Athenaeum* 38 (1960) 98ff.

INDEX

INDEX

INDEX

periphrastic future, *see* participle.
Persius, 120, 201, 219, 222
Petrarch, 244
Petronius, 172, 222
petulantia, 176
Philemon, 116, 209
Philip V of Macedon, 95
Philo of Alexandria, 161, 191, 254, 255
Philodemus, 155, 159, 239, 244, 247, 253
Philolaus, 247
philosophical language, 23, 204–5
Philostratus, 131
φιλόζωοι γέροντες, 238, 246–7
Phlegon of Tralles, 10n., 241
[Phocylides], *Sent.*, 170, 234, 259
Phylarchus, 169
Pindar, 121, 126, 144, 147, 259, 260, 262
Pisistratus, 16n., 28, 85, 245
planting trees for posterity, 155
plants, absence of word for, 213
Plato, 5–6, 9, 12, 15, 16, 17n., 21, 23, 24, 28, 60, 72, 73, 88, 94, 105, 107, 110–20, 130–1, 140, 147, 153, 159, 160, 161, 171, 174, 175, 177, 178, 181, 183–4, 185, 186, 187, 188, 191, 195, 198–9, 200, 201–2, 210, 223, 224, 227, 235, 238, 239, 244, 246, 247–8, 249, 251, 252, 253, 254, 255, 256, 258, 259, 260, 262, 264, 270, 279
[Plato], *Axiochus*, 10–11, 25n., 106, 157, 184, 239, 246, 248n., 255, 259, 260, 264; *Epinomis*, 263, 264; *Epist.* 2, 262
Plautus, 76, 97, 98, 110, 125, 145, 155, 157, 160, 169, 196, 203, 221, 222, 234, 246, 249, 263
pleasure, harmfulness of, 181–2, 185
pleonasm, 101, 121, 180
Pliny the Elder, 10n., 25n., 103, 126, 131, 148, 165, 172, 176, 178, 190, 208, 210, 212, 213, 214, 215, 216, 217, 218, 219, 220, 221, 227, 230, 231, 241, 245, 254, 264, 275
Pliny the Younger, 148, 159, 167, 171, 173, 174, 175, 197, 209, 222
Plotinus, 252
plural, first person, used by single speaker, 101, 107

Plutarch, 11, 16n., 18, 19n., 20, 27, 28, 93, 95, 103, 107, 116, 119, 120, 122, 126–7, 128, 131, 134, 135, 136, 138, 140–1, 143, 144, 148, 150, 152, 159, 160, 161, 163, 165, 166, 168, 170, 172, 173, 174, 175, 177, 181, 182–3, 188, 189, 191, 195, 197, 199, 201, 210, 217, 218, 220, 223, 226, 231, 233, 234, 235, 236, 238, 240, 241, 243, 245, 248, 252, 253, 259, 264, 269, 271, 273, 275, 278, 279
[Plutarch], *Cons. ad Apoll.*, 240, 242, 244, 247, 249, 260, 263, 264
'polar' expressions, 129–30, 262
polite formulae in conversation, 24, 110, 113–14, 134
Pollio, Asinius, 146, 241
Polyarchus of Syracuse, 183–4
Polybius, 95, 126, 168, 191, 250, 265, 276, 279
Pompey, 230
pontifical law, 179, 204
Pontius, C., victor of Caudium, 72; his father, 72, 184, 186–7, 279
Pontius, T., centurion, 68, 169
Porta Capena, 232
Posidonius, 206, 208, 239, 253, 254, 260
poverty in old age, 119–20
praenomen, use of, 95–6, 104, 251
prepositional phrases used adjectivally, 117, 185
Priscian, 44, 48, 93, 213, 245
prison, image of, 248, 260
probe, 132
Proclus, 253
proper names in plural, 129, 165
propter, adverbial, 22, 201
prose rhythm, 24, 50, 106, 108, 116, 118, 132, 133, 140, 157, 165, 168, 170, 180, 181, 186, 189, 192, 216, 226, 239, 240, 245, 251, 262
provenire, 146
proverbs, 114, 149, 169, 222
Publilia, 3
Publilius Syrus, 156
punctuation, 50–1, 122, 141, 226
pure, in moral sense, 130
Pydna, battle of, 135, 203
Pyrrhus, 61–2, 73, 78, 136, 138, 148, 189, 219, 278
Pythagoras, 64, 68, 85, 87, 108, 153, 169–70, 238, 243, 247, 253

295

Pythagoreans, Pythagoreanism, 21, 70, 87, 160, 170, 171, 174, 179–80, 183, 238, 243, 247, 253–4, 260, 274

quasi, 22, 129, 159, 244
-que added to short final vowel, 138, 152; double, 97–8
queo, 168
qui adverbial, 106–7, 250
quid . . .?, 149, 158, 203
quid est aliud . . .?, 109–10
quies, quiescere, in political sense, 127
quiet life, vs. active life, 130, 262
quincunx, 227–8
Quintilian, 20, 97, 103, 115, 131, 142, 148, 162, 164, 165, 169, 179, 197, 202, 204, 206, 209, 214, 217, 227, 243, 252
quod contra, 265
quorsus, -um, 129

regnum occupare, 219
repastinatio, 215
requires, 22, 213
requirere, 166
Res Gestae Divi Augusti, 142
restituere rem publicam, 144
reversal of roles between old and young, 178, 223
rising at approach of old man, custom of, 234
Romulus and Remus, 146
rorare, 196–7

Sabines, *ager Sabinus*, 64, 74, 78, 197, 219
saepenumero, 104
Saint-Victor, 40n.
Salinator, C. Livius, 57, 59, 116, 126–7
Sallust, 131, 147, 186, 190, 207
Saltus, 143
salutare, 148
Samnites, 73, 78, 187, 218, 219
sapiens, sapientia, 104, 107, 120, 207–8
Sardinia, 125
Sardis, 80, 226
saturitas, 22, 221
Satyrus, 150–1
scientia, in plural, 255
Scipio, Gnaeus and Publius, 10n., 67, 86, 89, 165, 250, 261
Scipio, L. Cornelius Barbati filius, 232

Scipio, L. Cornelius, 148
Scipio, P. Cornelius, Africanus Maior, 20, 67, 81, 89, 129, 165, 171, 232, 275, 278–9
Scipio, P. Cornelius, Aemilianus (Africanus Minor), 5, 17, 56ff., 102, 135, 143, 165, 169, 171, 184, 204, 223, 235, 240, 266
Scipio, P. Africani filius, adoptive father of the above, 69, 173
Scipio, P. Cornelius, Nasica Corculum, 76, 204, 232
seasons, comparison of human life with, 243; *see also* divisions of human life
Second Sophistic, 29
senate, 63, 141, 143, 173, 234
Senatusconsultum de Asclepiade, 187; *de Oropiis, de Thisbensibus*, 187
Seneca the Elder, 128, 147, 173, 188, 254, 260
Seneca the Younger, 11, 27, 105, 109, 117, 128, 130, 131, 154, 155, 158, 161, 162, 165, 167, 170, 171, 172, 173, 174, 179, 181, 185, 187, 197, 200, 201, 204, 206, 208, 223, 233, 234, 235, 236, 237, 238, 239, 240, 242, 243, 245, 246, 247, 249, 250, 251, 253, 254, 260, 263, 264, 265, 270–1
senecta, 157
senility, 151, 176
senium, 132
sensim, 181
sepse, 163–4, 262
Seriphos, Seriphian, 58, 119, 270
Servilius Ahala, C., 79
Servilius Geminus, Cn., 250
Shakespeare, 234
ship, comparison of state with, 139–40
sibi habere, 222
Sibyl, 10n.
Sicily, 274
Sidonius Apollinaris, 223
Silius Italicus, 182, 241
Simmias, 177
Simonides, 64, 116, 152, 239
sleep, like death, 260
Socrates, 12, 24, 25, 29, 66, 80, 87, 110ff., 120, 153, 158–9, 171, 234, 247, 254, 259, 262
sodalitates, 193–4, 197